Superst

Trails East

Hikes, Horse Rides, and History

Jack Carlson
Elizabeth Stewart

First Edition

SUPERSTITION WILDERNESS TRAILS EAST
HIKES, HORSE RIDES, AND HISTORY

BY JACK CARLSON AND ELIZABETH STEWART

Clear Creek Publishing
P.O. Box 24666, Tempe, Arizona 85285 U.S.A.

All rights reserved. No part of this book may be reproduced or transmitted in any form or by any means, electronic or mechanical, including photocopying, recording, or by any information storage and retrieval system without written permission from the authors, except for the inclusion of brief quotations in a review.

Copyright © 2010 by Jack Carlson and Elizabeth Stewart
Printed and bound in the United States of America.

Cover and book design by Ron Short, Santa Fe, New Mexico, (www.ronshortstudios.com).

Cover photograph of Rogers Canyon cliff dwelling by the authors. Inset photo of Salado pottery by Dave Leach.

Back cover photographs, left to right: Elisha Reavis by H. Beuhman, circa 1890s, courtesy Arizona Historical Foundation (N-2617); Angel Basin in Rogers Canyon; Rogers Canyon cliff dwellings; Tony Ranch cabin in Haunted Canyon.

Images of the boots, book and pen, spur, and horseshoe are courtesy of the Grand Canyon National Park Museum.

Photographs not otherwise credited were taken by the authors.

Publishers Cataloging-in-Publication Data
Carlson, Jack C.
Superstition Wilderness trails east : hikes, horse rides, and history/ by Jack Carlson and Elizabeth Stewart.
1st ed.
352 p. : ill., maps ; 22 cm.
Bibliography: p. 334-335
Includes index.
1. Hiking—Arizona—Superstition Wilderness—Guidebooks. 2. Superstition Wilderness (Ariz.)—Guidebooks. 3. Frontier and pioneer life—Arizona—Superstition Wilderness. I. Stewart, Elizabeth (Elizabeth J.) II. Title.

917.9175 dc22   Library of Congress Control Number: 2008910940
978-1-884224-08-9

10 9 8 7 6 5 4 3 2 1

Two roads diverge in a wood, and I—

I took the one less traveled by,

And that has made all the difference.

Robert Frost, 1874–1963

Acknowledgments

Many people contributed to this guidebook. We thank everyone. We are indebted to the other authors who have documented their Superstition Mountain travels and experiences. We acknowledge their books, photographs, and contributions throughout *Superstition Wilderness Trails East*.

The newspaper and historical records of Greg Davis and *The Chronological History of the Superstition Wilderness Area* by Tom Kollenborn were essential for our research. John Fritz, Dave Cameron, Todd Gartman, Joe Bartels, Irv Kanode, Wally Farak, Mike Stivers, Kent Struble, and the all folks who wrote comments on www.hikearizona.com and www.arizonahikers.com provided us with trail updates. Discussions of current research on the www.thelostdutchman.net site were useful and helped us with sources for our own research. Howard Horinek taught Jack how to ride a horse and wrangle a packhorse, which gave us a better appreciation of the hazards facing stockmen. Exploratory hikes and discussions of historical events with Jack San Felice, Greg Davis, and Dick Walp anchored the dialogue to the physical locations in the mountains.

The ranching history was revealed to us by Ken and Nancy McCollough; Bill, Helen, and George Martin; the late Jim Herron, Phyllis and Frank Herron; Chuck and Judy Backus; Howard Horinek; the late George Cox and Hazel Cox; Ed and Earl Bacon; Dwight Cooper; Leroy and Velma Tucker; Peter Busnack; Betty Porter Gilbert; Marion Williams; Fred McCauley; Harry Smith; the late Gladys Walker; the late John Olson; Earline Horrell Tidwell; Cindy Tidwell Shelton; the late John Schulze and the late Helen Schulze; Linda Haught; Dutch Ortega; Mick Holder; Denise Cortelyou; Susan Clardy; Manny Ruiz; Tom and Jane Hale; Royce Johnson; and Louis Ruiz.

For their advice and assistance, we thank Bob and the late Helen Corbin; Kraig Roberts; Tom Glover; Clay Worst; George Johnston; Larry Hedrick; Ron, Jayne, Jesse, and Josh Feldman; Ken Nelssen; Scotty McBride; Greg Hansen; Russ Orr; Don Van Driel; Connie Lane; the late Pete Weinel; Michael Sullivan; Steve Germick; Scott Wood; Martin McAllister; Brad Orr; Stew Herkenhoff; Anthony Miller; Gwen Henson; Helen Thompson; Hazel Clark; the late Bill Sewrey; the late Tom Clary; John Wilburn; Ray and Louis Ruiz; Dave Hughes; Rick Gwynne; Joe Ribaudo: Chris Coleman; Rosemary and Larry Shearer; Anne Coe; Don Wells; Tony Backus; Merlin Yeager; Mike and Amy Doyle; Beth Roth; Susan and Joe Yarina; Bill Smith; George Harbin; Ted Tenney; Bob and Lou Ann Schoose; Shelly Dudley; Ileen Snoddy; Bob and Kay Stewart; Kathy Winston; Barbara Stewart, Robert Stewart; Bill and Gini McKenzie; John Stanley; Deborah Shelton; Melanie Sturgeon; Nancy Sawyer; Wendi Goen; Don Langlois; Julie Hoff; Tony Smith; the late K. C. Nash; Margaret Baker; Bill and Lynn Haak; Donna Anderson; Chris Reid; John Tanner; John Langellier; Charlie Gann; Susan Lintelmann; Neal Berg; Robert Mason; Dave Leach; Cindy Hayostek; Bob Pugh; Clay Workman; Art Christiansen; and Paul Blanc.

The organizations that helped us are Superstition Mountain Historical Society; Tonto National Forest—Phoenix Office, Mesa District, Tonto Basin District, and Globe District; BLM Phoenix Office; Reevis Mountain School; Salt River Project Research Archives; Arizona Book Publishing Association; Tempe Library; Arizona Department of Library and Archives; Arizona Historical Society; Arizona Historical Foundation; Gila County Historical Society; Gila County Recorder and Treasurer; Pinal County Historical Society; Pinal County Recorder and Treasurer; Superior Historical Society; Northern Arizona Genealogical Society; Rim Country Historical Society; Superstition Area Land Trust; University of Arizona Library and Special Collections; Arizona State University Library and Special Collections; Grand Canyon National Park Museum; Sharlot Hall Museum and Archives; Arizona Game and Fish Department; Arizona State Land Department; Mesa Library; Mesa Family History Center; Impression Makers; Costco Photo, Tempe; Image Craft; Thomson-Shore, Inc.; United States Military Academy Library; National Archives, Washington, DC; National Archives, College Park, MD; National Geodetic Survey, Silver Spring, MD; USGS, Denver; Arizona Geological Survey, Tucson; New Mexico Genealogical Society; New Mexico State Archives; Silver City Museum; Grant County Recorder, NM; Arizona Department of Mines and Mineral Resources; and University of Nevada, Reno—Mackay School of Mines and Getchell Library.

We wish to give a special thanks to three people that helped a great deal on the project: book and cover designer Ron Short of Ron Short Studios, editor Gwen Henson of Sagebrush Publications, and editor Kathy Winston of Robstown, Texas.

Warning and Disclaimer

Hiking, climbing, horse riding, and all outdoor activities are inherently dangerous.

Trail and route conditions continually change due to flash floods, erosion, and other natural or man-made events. Although every effort has been made to check the accuracy of the information in this book, errors and omissions may still occur. You must decide whether the trail and weather conditions are safe and satisfactory for you to initiate or continue your trip.

In addition, you must determine whether your own skill, knowledge, and physical conditioning is commensurate with the requirements of a particular trip. You are on your own, and your decisions are entirely your responsibility.

The authors, publisher, and those associated with this publication, directly or indirectly, assume no responsibility for any accident, injury, damage, or loss that may result from participating in any of the activities described in this book.

Table of Contents

Acknowledgments 4

Warning and Disclaimer 6

Preface 11

Trip Summary Chart 12
Introduction 14
How To Use This Book 14
How to Get There 21
Superstition Wilderness 22
Wilderness Ethics 23
Safety and Dangers 26
Ranch Roads and Trails 29
Homesteaders and Ranchers 31
Miners and Prospectors 35
Mining and Treasure Hunting 35
Water 37
Easy Trips 38
Equipment and Clothing 39
Trailheads 40

Reavis Trailhead 46
    Trip 1. Reavis Ranch from Reavis Trailhead 48
    Trip 2. Reavis Falls 59
    Trip 3. Reavis Falls from Reavis Ranch 64

Pine Creek Trailhead 69
    Trip 4. Lower Pine Creek 73
    Trip 5. Yellow Jacket Spring 80
    Trip 6. Pine Creek to Reavis Falls 82
    Trip 7. Middle Pine Creek 84

Roosevelt Lake Area 90

Roosevelt Cemetery Trailhead 98
    Trip 8. Roosevelt Cemetery Trail 100
    Trip 9. Thompson Trail 102

Frazier Trailhead 104
    Trip 10. Cottonwood Trail to Roosevelt Lake Bridge 107
    Trip 11. Cottonwood Trail to FR83 112

Tule Trailhead 117
    Trip 12. Tule Trail to Two Bar Ridge 122

Campaign Trailhead 128
    Trip 13. Campaign Trail to Fire Line Trail 135
    Trip 14. Mountain Spring and Horrell Creek 143
    Trip 15. Campaign Trail to West Fork Pinto Creek 147
    Trip 16. Campaign Trail to Circlestone 151
    Trip 17. Campaign Trail to Reavis Ranch Loop 154
    Trip 18. Reavis Gap Trail to Reavis Ranch 160
    Trip 19. Upper Pine Creek 164
    Trip 20. Two Bar Ridge Trail 169

Pinto Creek Trailhead 175
    Trip 21. Tony Ranch from Pinto Creek 181

Haunted Canyon Trailhead 188
    Trip 22. Tony Ranch from FR287A 193
    Trip 23. Paradise Trail Loop 199

Miles Trailhead 202
    Trip 24. West Pinto Trail to Oak Flat 209
    Trip 25. Bull Basin Loop 213
    Trip 26. Rock Creek from Bull Basin Trail 217
    Trip 27. Spencer Spring Creek 223
    Trip 28. Cuff Button Trail 227
    Trip 29. Campaign Trail to Pinto Divide 232
    Trip 30. Paradise Trail 236
    Trip 31. West Pinto Trail to Rogers Trough 238
    Trip 32. Wildcat Canyon to Cuff Button Spring 243

Rogers Trough Trailhead 247
    Trip 33. Rogers Canyon Cliff Dwellings 250
    Trip 34. Rogers Trough to Reavis Ranch 257
    Trip 35. Rogers Trough to Reavis Ranch Loop 265
    Trip 36. Rogers Ridge 272
    Trip 37. Iron Mountain 277
    Trip 38. Silver Spur Cabin Site 280
    Trip 39. West Pinto Trail 284

Montana Mountain Trailhead 289
    Trip 40. Reavis Canyon Trail 293
    Trip 41. Spencer Spring Trail 299
    Trip 42. 1891 Road Survey Route 301
    Trip 43. Rock Creek from FR650 305

Woodbury Trailhead 309

Peralta Trailhead 310

Dons Camp Trailhead 311

Carney Springs Trailhead 312

Hieroglyphic Trailhead 313

Broadway Trailhead 314

Lost Dutchman State Park Trailheads 315

Crosscut Trailhead 316

Massacre Grounds Trailhead 317

First Water Trailhead 318

Canyon Overlook Trailhead 319

Canyon Lake Trailhead 320

Tortilla Flat Trailhead 321

Tortilla Trailhead 322

Trans-Wilderness Trips 323
    Trip 44. Reavis Trailhead to Peralta Trailhead 323
    Trip 45. Reavis Trailhead to First Water Trailhead 323
    Trip 46. Miles Trailhead to First Water Trailhead 323
    Trip 47. Arizona Trail. Rogers Trough to Frazier Trailhead 324
    Trip 48. Tule Trailhead to Frazier Trailhead 324
    Trip 49. Campaign Trailhead to Reavis Trailhead 324
    Trip 50. Peralta Trailhead to First Water Trailhead 324
    Trip 51. Peralta Trailhead to Canyon Lake Trailhead 324
    Trip 52. Peralta Trailhead to Tortilla Trailhead 325
    Trip 53. Carney Springs Trailhead to Lost Dutchman State Park . . 325
    Trip 54. First Water Trailhead to Canyon Lake Trailhead 325
    Trip 55. Tortilla Trailhead to Woodbury Trailhead 325
    Trip 56. Woodbury Trailhead to Rogers Trough Trailhead 325

Reference Notes 326

Selected Bibliography 334

Useful Addresses 336

Index 338

About the Authors 351

Trailheads and Trails Map 352

Superstition Wilderness boundary sign on the Reavis Ranch Trail (109) near the Rogers Trough Trailhead. Photo was taken in December 2008.

Preface

When we published *Hiker's Guide to the Superstition Wilderness* in 1995, we left out several interesting trips to keep the book at a reasonable size. That book covered the western part of the Superstition Wilderness in much greater detail than the eastern portion. Since that book was published, we have explored more trails in the eastern region and discovered new trails in the western part of the Wilderness. We decided that there are so many interesting hikes and rides in the Superstition Wilderness that it deserves two volumes.

We selected the Reavis Ranch, Rogers Canyon, and Frog Tanks Trails as the dividing line between the east and west halves of the Wilderness. *Superstition Wilderness Trails East* covers Reavis Ranch, Rogers Canyon, Pine Creek, and the Roosevelt Lake area. Our companion book, *Superstition Wilderness Trails West*, covers the JF Trail and all the country going west to the Lost Dutchman State Park. That title closely follows the information in *Hiker's Guide to the Superstition Wilderness* with the addition of new trails and more detailed history. Each book describes all trailheads in the Superstition Wilderness with a brief explanation of the trails from each trailhead.

New for this book is a more in-depth look at the primary source material behind the events and stories of the late 1800s and early 1900s. City, county, state, and federal documents provided dates, names, and sometimes reflections of the times. We tried to wrap the individual events into a larger story to show that the Superstition Mountains and the surrounding communities were closely connected.

After observing more horse riders on the trail and participating in horse pack trips ourselves, we decided to include additional information for stockmen. The trail descriptions, therefore, provide information about potential hazards for horses and riders and other details that may be useful to stockmen. We talked with outfitters and other riders to supplement our knowledge of riding and packing. We hope our comments are helpful.

Recognizing the widespread use of the Global Positioning System (GPS), we included GPS coordinates for trailheads and some points of interest that would make travel in the mountains more precise. We did not give the exact locations for petroglyphs and other sensitive sites, but those with a persistent desire will be able to locate them with a little thought and research.

We hope you have many fine trips in the Superstition Wilderness. See you on the trails.

Trip Summary Chart

Trip Number and Name	Historic Areas	Prehistoric Areas	Scenic Trip	Easy Trip	Challenging Trip	Day Trip	Multi-day Trip	Hike Difficulty Rating	Ride Difficulty Rating
1 Reavis Ranch from Reavis Trailhead	•							2	2
2 Reavis Falls		•	•		•	•	•	3	3
3 Reavis Falls from Reavis Ranch	•		•		•			4	4
4 Lower Pine Creek						•		3	X
5 Yellow Jacket Spring						•		3	X
6 Pine Creek to Reavis Falls					•	•	•	3	X
7 Middle Pine Creek					•		•	3	X
8 Roosevelt Cemetery Trail	•			•				1	X
9 Thompson Trail			•	•		•		1	2
10 Cottonwood Trail to Roosevelt Lake Bridge			•	•		•		2	2
11 Cottonwood Trail to FR83		•				•		2	2
12 Tule Trail to Two Bar Ridge	•		•					2	3
13 Campaign Trail to Fire Line Trail				•		•	•	1	2
14 Mountain Spring and Horrell Creek				•		•		1	2
15 Campaign Trail to West Fork Pinto Creek			•				•	3	3
16 Campaign Trail to Circlestone		•			•		•	3	3
17 Campaign Trail to Reavis Ranch Loop	•	•			•		•	3	3
18 Reavis Gap Trail to Reavis Ranch	•				•		•	3	4
19 Upper Pine Creek	•						•	3	4
20 Two Bar Ridge Trail	•		•			•		3	4
21 Tony Ranch from Pinto Creek			•					2	3
22 Tony Ranch from FR287A	•		•					2	2

Trip Summary Chart

Trip Number and Name	Historic Areas	Prehistoric Areas	Scenic Trip	Easy Trip	Challenging Trip	Day Trip	Multi-day Trip	Hike Difficulty Rating	Ride Difficulty Rating
23 Paradise Trail Loop	•					•		2	3
24 West Pinto Trail to Oak Flat	•		•			•		2	2
25 Bull Basin Loop	•	•	•			•		2	3
26 Rock Creek from Bull Basin Trail	•		•			•		2	X
27 Spencer Spring Creek	•		•			•		2	3
28 Cuff Button Trail	•		•		•	•		3	3
29 Campaign Trail to Pinto Divide	•		•			•		3	3
30 Paradise Trail	•		•			•		2	3
31 West Pinto Trail to Rogers Trough	•		•		•	•		3	3
32 Wildcat Canyon to Cuff Button Spring							•	3	4
33 Rogers Canyon Cliff Dwellings		•	•					2	X
34 Rogers Trough to Reavis Ranch	•	•	•			•		2	3
35 Rogers Trough to Reavis Ranch Loop	•		•		•		•	3	X
36 Rogers Ridge	•		•		•	•		2	3
37 Iron Mountain							•	3	X
38 Silver Spur Cabin Site	•					•		2	3
39 West Pinto Trail	•					•	•	2	3
40 Reavis Canyon Trail	•	•				•		2	3
41 Spencer Spring Trail	•				•		•	2	3
42 1891 Road Survey Route	•					•		4	X
43 Rock Creek from FR650	•					•		2	X

Introduction

This book, *Superstition Wilderness Trails East*, describes the trails in the eastern half of the Superstition Wilderness. The Reavis Ranch, Rogers Canyon, and Frog Tanks Trails form the approximate dividing line between this book and our companion volume, *Superstition Wilderness Trails West*. The map on the last page of this book shows the area contained in each book. GPS coordinates for trailheads, important trail junctions such as the Reavis Falls turnoff along Reavis Ranch Trail, and many points of interest are provided.

On the far eastern end of the Superstition Wilderness, we write about the Arizona Trail as the trail enters the Wilderness near Roosevelt Lake. We describe the Roosevelt Lake Visitors Center and several Forest Service campgrounds that provide excellent facilities for both stockmen and hikers at Roosevelt Lake.

On the southeastern edge of the Wilderness, we added the little known Miles Trailhead on West Fork Pinto Creek and the popular Haunted Canyon Creek area. The Arizona Trail passes through Rogers Trough Trailhead at the edge of the Wilderness, so it seemed appropriate to include its extension with the neighboring Reavis Canyon Trail on Montana Mountain.

Trans-wilderness trips between trailheads are becoming more popular, so we included all the trailheads surrounding the Superstition Wilderness. In the section on trans-wilderness trips, we provide the trail mileage, shuttle mileage, and a brief trip outline.

How To Use This Book

Trailheads

Trailhead defines a point normally accessed by vehicle. Trips are organized in the Table of Contents according to the nearest *Trailhead*. This arrangement will help you quickly find all the trips available for each starting point.

Itinerary

This section gives a summary of the trip noting the main trails used. Alternate routes and trails to or from the destination may be listed.

Difficulty

The *hiker's boot* symbol, for hikers, and the *horseshoe* symbol, for stockmen, are printed on the first page of each trip for a quick reference to the trip's difficulty. The trips are rated *easy, moderate, difficult,* and *very difficult.*

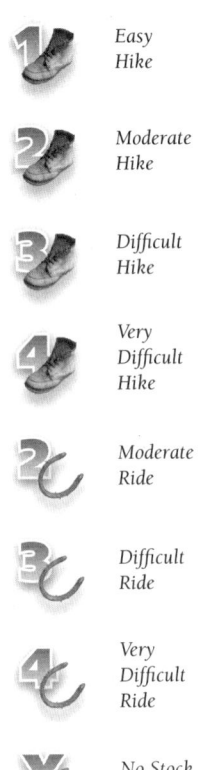

Easy Hike

Moderate Hike

Difficult Hike

Very Difficult Hike

Moderate Ride

Difficult Ride

Very Difficult Ride

No Stock Animals

Hiker ratings are established on the premise that a hiker can complete the hike in the time suggested under the Length and Time heading. The rating considers both physical and mental abilities needed to complete the hike. Hikes covering a short distance with a long hiking time indicate extremely rough terrain or a large elevation gain.

Stockman ratings only reflect the trail conditions and hazards since we have not attached mileage criteria to those ratings. Some trips display an X *horseshoe* symbol because that trip may not be appropriate for horses or only part of the trip can be ridden. We sometimes provide a turnaround point for riders so they can at least travel on part of that trek. Each trip has a description of the unusual hazards so riders can decide for themselves if the trip is suitable for their horse. Experienced riders and horses are required on all trips. Beginning riders joining an outfitter company or supervised by experienced friends should be able to ride the moderate trails.

Bouldering is a term used in the text to describe a type of climbing familiar to most hikers who explore canyons blocked by large rocks. The highest point of this climbing is usually within jumping distance to the ground; therefore, this technique requires no climbing equipment. The hiker should be skilled in balance and have a knowledge of foot and handhold techniques. Do not try any of the trips requiring *bouldering* unless you have the necessary skills. Join a climbing club, or take a class to learn how to boulder.

Hikers and riders need not complete the entire trip to have an enjoyable outing, but may enjoy the first part of a more difficult trip by selecting a turnaround point such as a stream crossing, pass, ridge line, or a trail intersection as their destination. Having fun and traveling at a comfortable pace is more important than completing the entire trip.

Easy Trip

An *easy* hike usually follows established trails with trip length less than 5 miles and a time less than 3 hours. A few *easy* trips follow the creek bed through a canyon. Some beginning hikers may find the elevation gain or length of the hike more strenuous than they expected.

For riders, none of the Superstition Wilderness trails are considered *easy* due to the hazards of the desert and mountains. All trips require riders and horses to be experienced with travel on mountain, desert, and rough terrain.

Moderate Trip

A *moderate* hike usually involves some off-trail hiking and may require basic route-finding skills. The trip length is less than 10 miles and less than 6 hours hiking time. The abilities to follow rock cairns, use a compass, and read a map are necessary. These treks are for experienced hikers only.

For riders, a *moderate* ride includes trips with stream crossings, narrow trails, and some slick rock sections of trail. The trip usually follows the main Forest Service trail system and does not require off trail riding.

Difficult Trip

A *difficult* hike requires extensive off-trail hiking over rough terrain. Trip length is less than 15 miles, with hiking time less than 12 hours. Hikers will often need excellent route-finding skills and basic *rock-bouldering* techniques. These treks are for very experienced hikers only.

For riders, a *difficult* ride covers portions of non-maintained trails with steep sections, extensive slick rock, loose rock or dirt, and small drops in trail contour. Thick vegetation and lack of use may make the trail difficult to follow.

Very Difficult Trip

A *very difficult* hike has all the characteristics of the *difficult* hike along with the distinct possibility that the hiker may not be able to complete the entire hike in one day. Trip length is less than 18 miles with hiking times less than 14 hours. On a *very difficult* trip, hikers may find the challenge rewarding and inspiring upon completion of a successful hike. On the other hand, hikers may find themselves stranded overnight due to errors in route finding or underestimation of hiking times. Hikers must be familiar with *rock-bouldering* skills. None of the hikes require technical rock climbing equipment. Hikers can extend the *very difficult* hikes to make enjoyable and leisurely overnight hikes. These treks are for expert hikers only.

A *very difficult* trip for riders includes cross-country travel where route conditions are often unknown. Those conditions may make the trip unsafe.

Length and Time

The round-trip or one-way distance and time are based on hiking times. Some loop trips, which have alternate return routes, list only the one-way distance. The length of the trips has been derived from USGS maps using the computer program Terrain Navigator Pro by Maptech. We cross-checked those mileages with various sources including the U.S. Forest Service trail mileages, other hiking books, and maps.

Use the distance for off-trail trips as a guideline, since your route may be slightly different than ours. Time is a more useful measurement for off-trail travel.

Our hiking times include short rest stops and time to enjoy the scenic highlights of the trip. Backpackers carrying heavier packs should expect longer hiking times. Faster and slower hikers will need to adjust the times for their style of hiking. Riders usually travel faster than hikers, but time for saddling up and stops for tightening cinches and adjusting pack animal loads may reduce that advantage.

The elevation change gives you the uphill (indicated by a plus sign, +) and downhill (indicated by a minus sign, -) change for each trip. For loop trips, the uphill and downhill elevation change is the same. On one-way trips, the uphill and downhill elevation change is usually different. Elevation change is not the same as the difference between the high and low points of the trip. For example, if you go up and down two hills, one 1,500 feet high and another 2,000 feet high, the total elevation change is +3,500 and -3,500, expressed in the book as ±3,500 feet. The elevation change for trails with many small fluctuations in elevation may have up to a 10 percent error.

A trail profile of elevation is included with each trip. The profile shows where the major ups and downs occur along the trail.

On one-way Trans-Wilderness trips, the shuttle distance is the one-way road distance you need to drive to place a vehicle at the destination of your trip. You need two vehicles to arrange a shuttle trip or a good friend who is willing to wait for you at your destination. Another way to make a one-way trip is to arrange for two groups to start from opposite trailheads and travel to the other group's vehicle. Be sure both groups have keys to each vehicle. Don't try to exchange keys during the trip.

Maps

In this section, we list the USGS 7.5 minute topographic (topo) maps used for each trip. The scale for the USGS maps is about 2.5 inches per mile. On trips covering more than one map, such as the corners of four maps, you may wish to make or purchase a composite copy of the four USGS maps for a handy area reference. USGS maps are available online from the U.S. Geological Survey at www.usgs.gov.

Reproductions of the 7.5 minute USGS topographic maps in this book are annotated to show the trails and suggested route for each trip. We show numbered Forest Service trails as dashed lines with the trail number in parentheses. Non-maintained trails and *trails of use* are dashed lines, but do not have a number. Off-trail routes are shown as dotted lines. Main roads open to vehicles are shown as solid lines, but roads behind locked gates are shown as trails.

The *Tonto National Forest* map issued by the Forest Service is good for viewing the big picture and the access roads, but is not very useful as a trail guide. The scale is about 0.5 inch per mile.

In addition to the USGS topo maps, we carry two other maps on all trips: *Superstition Wilderness* by Beartooth Maps with a scale of about 1.4 inches per mile, which is based on the USGS topo maps; and *Superstition Wilderness, Tonto National Forest* map issued by the Forest Service with a 1.0 inch per mile scale.

We use GPS coordinates (NAD27) in the degree, minute, and second format (dd mm ss) because we find the format easier to plot on a paper USGS topo map when we are on the trail and back at the office. The *Waypointer Map Scale* from Wide World of Maps (www.maps4u.com) makes the data plotting easy.

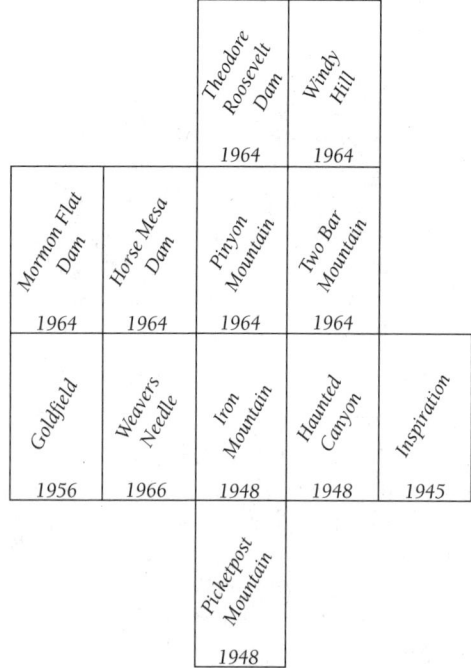

The 7.5 minute USGS topographic maps with the North American Datum 1927 (NAD27) used in this book are shown above. Set your GPS to NAD27.

▬▬▬▬	Main Road (both paved and dirt)
▬▬▬	Secondary Road (dirt)
─ ─ ─ ─	Maintained Trail or Major Trail-of-Use
··········	Off-Trail Route or Abandoned Trail
A	Point of Interest (letters from A to ZZ)
⊙	Point of Interest Location
TH	Trailhead
(109)	U.S. Forest Service Trail Number
FR212	U.S. Forest Road Number (dirt)
⊷	Locked gate or road closed
(60)	U.S. Highway Route Number (paved)
(88)	State Highway Route Number (mostly paved)

Map legend for the annotated topographic maps in this book.

If you prefer to use a different coordinate system, change our numbers by entering them as a waypoint (dd mm ss) in your GPS unit, and then change the GPS unit to read out the waypoint in your desired position format. When you are online, you can use the *Geodetic Tool Kit*, which is described below, for interactive conversion between the UTM format and Latitude/Longitude format.

Over the years, we have noticed that the repeatability of our older field GPS measurements is only good to plus or minus one second. The newer GPS units give better results, but we will have to live with a few old numbers until we verify them in the field again. The GPS coordinates will get you close to your destination, but you will need to complete the route visually.

The 2004 series USGS topo maps modified by the Tonto National Forest were first issued in 2008. Those maps are designed with the NAD83 map datum, which creates an offset when compared to the maps that we use—1940s to 1960s series with NAD27. The longitude offset is about 2 seconds and the latitude offset is about 0.2 seconds. For exact coordinate conversion, NAD83 to NAD27 or NAD27 to NAD83, use the online converter at www.ngs.noaa.gov—select *Geodetic Tool Kit*, NADCON, *interactively compute*...and then enter your coordinates. Another window in the *Geodetic Tool Kit* allows you to convert to and from the UTM position format.

Be sure to set the *map datum* on your GPS to the type of map you are using—NAD27 or NAD83. We estimate that our latitude coordinates (NAD27), shown in this book, will result in a tenth-inch offset (about 200 feet on the ground) to the east of your desired location if plotted on the 2004 series NAD83 maps. If you are using our GPS coordinates to locate your position on the ground, set your GPS map datum to NAD27.

Finding the Trail

Looking for the start of the trail is sometimes the hardest part of a trip. This section helps the hiker and rider get out of the parking lot and onto the correct trail. For trips not starting from a parking lot, a narrative is provided describing the terrain and local landmarks near the beginning of the trip. The trailhead GPS coordinates identify the start of the trail.

The Trip

Here we describe the trip, water availability, and other information necessary to complete the trek. The topographic maps in this book contain point of interest notations identifying the major landmarks. For example, [1-X, 3.2, 4400] indicates point of interest X on Map 1, 3.2 miles from the beginning of the trip, at an elevation of 4,400 feet. Mileage is rounded to the nearest tenth of a mile. For some points of interest, the mileage and/or elevation are not included. We indicate the U.S. Forest Service official trail numbers in parentheses, for example, Reavis Ranch Trail (109). Non-official trails are identified on the maps by the traditional name or a name we have assigned.

History and Legends

We include stories associated with each trip to help you experience the past. In some cases it is impossible to separate history from legend, but we tried to correct misconceptions where we found more reliable information. In many cases, the facts are still being uncovered by dedicated researchers such as Greg Davis of the Superstition Mountain Historical Society. Current research is often discussed on the website www.thelostdutchman.net. Our reference notes, which will guide you to more in-depth reading and research, are shown as superscript numbers in the text. Notes are listed in the back of the book in the section titled Reference Notes to help you find the source of our information.

Ida May Gann's grave at Reevis Mountain School is inscribed, "Ida May Gann. Daughter of W. T. and Alice Gann. Died June 9, 1891. Aged 1 Yr & 9 Ms. Sleep on in peace in this lonely grave." Photo was taken in June 2001.

How To Get There

The boundary of the Superstition Mountains is roughly defined by US60 on the southern side, SR88 in the western and northern regions, and SR188 on the eastern edge. The edges of the Superstition Wilderness are 40 miles east of Phoenix, Arizona, 100 miles north of Tucson, Arizona, and 18 miles west of Globe and Miami, Arizona.

Apache Junction, Arizona, is the closest town on the western side of the mountains. Apache Junction is located next to the southwest corner of the Wilderness where the prominent Superstition Mountains rise from the desert floor to 5,057 feet.

The Superstition Freeway, US60, provides easy access to the Superstition Wilderness from the metropolitan areas of Phoenix, Tempe, Mesa, and Apache Junction. At the eastern end of the Superstition Freeway, US60 continues east as a divided four-lane highway. Stay on US60 to the turnoffs for Hieroglyphic, Peralta, Woodbury, Rogers Trough, Pinto Creek, Haunted Canyon, and Miles Ranch Trailheads. For the Roosevelt Lake area north of Globe, leave US60 in Globe and Miami and turn north on SR188 for Campaign, Tule, Frazier, and Roosevelt Cemetery Trailheads.

For the trailheads north of Apache Junction on SR88—Lost Dutchman State Park, Massacre Grounds, First Water, Canyon Lake, Tortilla Flat, Peters Mesa, Tortilla, Reavis, and Pine Creek Trailheads—use Idaho Road exit 196 on the Superstition Freeway, and drive north on Idaho Road into Apache Junction to connect with SR88. Allow extra driving time on SR88 north of Apache Junction for slow traffic on the winding two-lane road. SR88 is unpaved from the Tortilla Trailhead junction to Roosevelt Dam.

Several Superstition Wilderness trailheads are a short distance from the towns of Globe, Miami, and Roosevelt. For the Miles Ranch Trailhead, drive west on US60 from the towns of Globe and Miami, and use the access on Pinto Valley Mine Road. For trailheads near Roosevelt Lake, go north from Globe and Miami on SR188 to Roosevelt, Arizona, for the Tule, Campaign, Frazier, Roosevelt Cemetery, Reavis, and Pine Creek Trailheads. Roosevelt Lake has very nice camping facilities.

The routes to the popular Rogers Trough and Woodbury Trailheads begin on US60 several miles west of the town of Superior. Forest Service road FR172 to these trailheads offers spectacular views of rugged cliffs and the surrounding Sonoran Desert. Flat areas along FR172 provide easy car camping if you need to rest before your Wilderness trip.

Most trailheads described in this book are accessible by automobile. Some trailheads start next to the paved SR88 and SR188. The trailhead directions indicate when four-wheel drive or high-clearance vehicles are required.

Superstition Wilderness

According to the book, *Geology, Historical Events, Legends and Lore of Superstition Mountain*, by the Superstition Mountain Historical Society, the Indians considered the Superstition Mountains dangerous and a place to avoid. One of the names they gave the mountain was Superstitious Mountain—later the Anglos changed the name to Superstition Mountain.

In 1908, the federal government set aside the Superstition Mountains as a Forest Reserve. The Superstition Primitive Area was established in February 1939 and later upgraded to a Wilderness classification in April 1940. Finally, on September 3, 1964, Congress designated the mountains as the Superstition Wilderness in the National Wilderness Preservation System.

The present size of the Wilderness is 158,345 acres. The north-south distance varies from 9 to 12 miles while the east-west length stretches across 24 miles. Most of the Wilderness is surrounded by the Tonto National Forest except for thirteen sections of Arizona State Trust land along the southwest boundary. One section of private land is adjacent to the Wilderness near Hieroglyphic Canyon.

The Tonto National Forest, U.S. Forest Service, Department of Agriculture manages the Superstition Wilderness. One of the management objectives for the Wilderness is to perpetuate a long-lasting system of high quality wilderness that represents a natural ecosystem. Other objectives are to provide public enjoyment of the resource, to allow for the development of indigenous plants and animals, and to maintain the primitive character of the Wilderness as a benchmark for ecological studies.

High use and human influence on our wilderness lands require the Forest Service to manage the Wilderness by providing wilderness-value education; by prohibiting permanent structures such as campgrounds, buildings, and antennas; by regulating trail use and party size; and by allowing fires to burn only under preplanned conditions.

Hunting, fishing, and trapping in the Superstition Wilderness are managed under state and federal laws. Outfitting and guide services are managed under special use permits with the Tonto National Forest. Livestock grazing is still permitted where grazing existed prior to designation as a Wilderness, but the number of animals is prescribed by the Forest Service.

The Wilderness Act prohibits motorized equipment and mechanical transport in the Superstition Wilderness. The prohibited equipment includes motorcycles, chain saws, generators, mountain bikes, and wagons. Hiking, camping, and horseback riding permits are not required for individuals.

Group size is limited to fifteen people and fifteen head of stock. This rule may limit the number of riders to fewer than fifteen if you have pack animals. Larger groups must be divided into groups of fifteen people or fewer, and they must be separated on the trail by at least thirty minutes. The separated groups must camp out of site of each other. The length of stay is limited to fourteen days.

Current information and publications on the Superstition Wilderness are available from the Tonto National Forest Supervisor's Office in Phoenix, Arizona, and the Mesa Ranger District in Mesa, Arizona. The Mesa Ranger District is the lead district under a consolidated management system with the Globe Ranger District and the Tonto Basin Ranger District. The Tonto National Forest map shows the boundaries for these three districts. Addresses and telephone numbers for these offices are listed in the back of this book under Useful Addresses.

WILDERNESS ETHICS

Take Pictures and Memories—Leave Nothing says it all. *No trace* hiking, riding, and camping are necessary to preserve the Wilderness for future enjoyment. Please join us in preserving the natural and historical heritage of our beautiful Superstition Wilderness.

A small waterfall [23-V] along the abandoned Rock Creek Trail. When the seasonal water flows, this trek described in Trip 26 can make a pleasant outing. A similar waterfall [23-J] is located along the Paradise Trail. Photo was taken in December 2007.

Large groups of hikers and riders have a greater impact on the Superstition Wilderness than small groups. If you have a large group (more than five hikers or riders), stay on the trails—avoid off-trail and cross-country route travel. Riparian zones are the most fragile. Large groups should use previously occupied campsites and avoid establishing new camps. Restoring a campsite to its natural condition is nearly impossible for a large group of campers. Small groups of campers should be able to return a camp to its natural state if they avoid digging holes, cutting vegetation, and building fires. Every attempt should be made to restore the ground cover so the area will look visually appealing to the next group of campers.

Campfires are permitted, and enjoyable on occasion, but we have found that the use of a lightweight backpacker stove is a convenient alternative. Many areas have almost no fuel wood so a stove is often a necessity. If you need to build a fire, use an existing fire site. Do not use a fire ring (a ring of rocks), do not try to burn the unburnable (foil, plastics, metal, etc.), and keep the fire away from cliffs and boulders to avoid coating them with black soot. If firewood is scarce, do not pick the ground clean. Put out campfires with water, not dirt, so they are cold to the touch of your hand.

Pack it in—Pack it out. Everything that you take into the Wilderness must be taken out. If you take food items that don't have a lot of waste and take only the amount you will consume on the trip, you will lighten your load and also reduce the amount of trash that needs to be packed out. Don't bury trash, because animals will dig up the trash and scatter it. Remember that cigarette butts, orange peels, apple cores, and candy wrappers are litter. Unpacking after a day trip or overnight trip is much easier if you store all of your trash in a plastic bag. When you get home, just toss the bag in the garbage. If you include a small plastic bag with your lunch, the bag makes for easy disposal of orange peels, pits, wrappers, etc.

Never vandalize prehistoric sites. Adding graffiti to petroglyphs (prehistoric rock art) or creating your own contemporary petroglyphs may seem artistic at the moment. To the rest of us who enjoy viewing petroglyphs, the new graffiti destroys a piece of history and culture. Trip leaders should suggest that potential graffiti addicts draw in the sand (not on the rock) and then smooth over the sand before leaving. Digging or removing artifacts is not permitted and is prosecutable by law. Even taking potsherds that are exposed on the surface is not allowed. Enjoy them, but leave them for the next person to admire. Sometimes we can damage a prehistoric site by just being there. Loss of vegetation from overuse of an area can increase erosion.

Horse travel in the Wilderness is common and still holds the romance and color of the Old West. The following suggestions will help minimize the effects of stock use and preserve the Wilderness for your next trip. Only tie horses directly to trees for short rest periods. For longer periods, use hobbles, pickets, highlines, or hitch rails. Setting up a picket line between two trees will keep the horses from damaging tree roots and bark. When breaking camp, scatter manure piles to aid decomposition. Pack in your own feed, because natural forage is very limited and grazing stock is not allowed. Avoid using whole grain feeds, which can grow if spilled and compete with the natural vegetation.

Human waste should be buried in a hole four to six inches deep (in soil, not sand) at least 300 feet away from water sources and dry washes. After use, fill the hole with soil. Do not burn or bury the toilet paper. Store the used toilet paper inside the cardboard tube or store the used paper in a plastic bag for disposal when you return home. Preserve the water sources by keeping human waste at least 300 feet from streams, springs, potholes, and dry

Arizona Trail sign at Rogers Trough Trailhead. The Arizona Trail enters the Wilderness here and follows the Reavis Ranch Trail (109) to Reavis Valley. Photo was taken in November 2008.

washes. Do not contaminate the water with soap or any leftover food. Wash dishes and articles with soap away from the stream, not directly in it.

Personal items must not be stored in the Wilderness—it's illegal. Many former and some recent explorers and treasure hunters have stashed equipment and supplies in the Wilderness. Special Forest Order 12-59-R prohibits storing anything in the Wilderness for more than fourteen days. Outfitters and the Forest Service rangers take stashed equipment and supplies out to the trailheads for disposal outside the Wilderness.

Safety and Dangers

Everything you do is your responsibility. Your safety is determined solely by your judgment, skill, condition, and actions. Visiting the Superstition Wilderness carries the individual responsibility of knowing your own abilities. You will need to recognize the potential dangers of outdoor activities without the help of warning signs, handrails, or rangers pointing out the hazards. The hints and suggestions we provide should complement your outdoor skills and not be considered a substitute for proper training and outdoor experience. Be a safe visitor to the Wilderness by knowing your limits. See Useful Addresses in the back of the book for a list of emergency telephone numbers.

The desert mountain-range in the Superstition Wilderness can get very hot. Extreme heat poses a very real threat in the summer when temperatures can reach more than 120 °F in the lower elevations. Always carry adequate water to avoid dehydration or heat exhaustion. See the section on Water that describes the amount of water we carry.

At elevations above 4,800 feet, you will often encounter snow in the winter months. Nighttime temperatures can dip down to -10 °F with daytime temperatures ranging from 20 to 55 °F. To avoid frostbite and hypothermia, be prepared with warm and waterproof clothing.

All trips listed in this book are physically and mentally challenging—even the easy trips. Ascertain your own abilities from previous experience, and know when to abort a trip or modify the original plan.

Off-trail travel, *bouldering*, and climbing are inherently more dangerous than travel on a trail. Injuries due to falling are common. Loose or slippery rocks, on and off the trail, are the primary cause of falls. *Bouldering*, climbing, and travel near cliffs are hazardous and may result in injury or death.

As an individual in a larger group, you must be aware of the inherent danger in this activity and must use your own judgment, based on your own skill level, when confronted with a difficult situation. The responsibility always lies with you as an individual and not with the group. Do not let peer pressure force you into a situation that may be dangerous.

A special caution to horse riders is in order. For your safety, we do not recommend riding off the established trails unless you have considerable experience doing this. Although some riders successfully follow off-trail routes, we have heard that riders have been injured in an attempt to emulate their heroes. The government does not have restrictions on where you may ride, but the Forest Service classifies several steep or rocky trails as "Not Recommended for Horses." The list includes Peralta Trail (102), Boulder Canyon Trail (103), Red Tanks Trail (107), Rogers Canyon Trail (110), Frog Tanks Trail (112), Fire Line Trail (118), Haunted Canyon Trail (203), and Bluff Spring Trail (235). Before you go, consult the Forest Service or your favorite outfitter for current trail conditions. Don't injure yourself or your animal by attempting a ride that is above your ability.

Falling

Injuries due to falling can be a major problem whether it be from slipping on an algae-covered rock in a stream, stumbling on an obstacle in your path, or careening off a precipice. Falling has probably caused more injuries than rattlesnakes and scorpions. The chances of incurring an injury from a fall will increase as you get tired. Lack of attention and declining physical ability are sure signs of danger and increase the likelihood of injury from a fall.

Rattlesnakes

Letting rattlesnakes know you are in their territory will help you avoid an unwanted encounter. We found that a snake stick (any small wooden stick) is handy for beating the brush where you suspect snakes. When you hear that rattlesnake *buzz*, there will be no question whether it is really a rattlesnake. Beating the brush is not a foolproof technique since rattlesnakes don't always buzz, so look around when you're walking, and check nearby vertical walls of stream banks and ravines. Never put your hands or feet where you can't see.

The snake stick is useful for probing overhead rock ledges before you climb up. Also, throwing a small stone in the bushes helps to announce your presence. Forget about trying to shoot a rattlesnake. If you have time to pull out a gun and have a steady enough hand to shoot, you are probably not in danger of a snakebite. Don't kill rattlesnakes; just learn to avoid them.

Venomous Critters

Along with rattlesnakes, hikers and riders need to be aware of scorpions, centipedes, black widow spiders, brown recluse spiders, tarantulas, Gila Monsters, and more. Any venomous bite or sting can be a serious.

Clockwise examples of survey markers for Rae Clark's 1919 Homestead Entry Survey (HES 554), now Miles Trailhead. Bearing tree marked with "6 HES 554 + BT." Sandstone marker for corner #6. Metal capped pipe for corner #1. Limestone marker for corner #2. Photos were taken in December 1998.

Flash Floods

During the rainy season, flash floods are a real danger. Most people don't realize the danger of a flash flood until they see the power and force of the water in action. Camp on high ground. Crossing a flooded stream with water over your knees is dangerous—water at waist level will result in an almost certain swim and possible drowning in the current. Horses may buck you off when crossing a fast moving stream.

Heat and Cold

Heat exhaustion and hypothermia (a drop in body temperature) are potential hazards in the Superstition Wilderness. Extreme changes in weather during a single day and the extremes during the seasons require hikers, riders, and campers to be prepared with the right equipment and provisions. The single most important provision is adequate water. Be sure to read the section in this book on Water. Because of the heat and lack of protection from the sun, heat exhaustion and dehydration are very real dangers. Extreme caution must be exercised between the months of June and September and anytime the temperature exceeds 100 °F.

Firearms

Shooting is not permitted in the Superstition Wilderness except for taking game with a valid hunting license. This means no target shooting. More people are hiking and riding in the mountains than you realize, so you could put the life of another hiker or horse rider in danger with a misdirected shot or the accidental discharge of your gun.

RANCH ROADS AND TRAILS

Homesteaders, ranchers, and miners, beginning in 1876 to the present day, have developed and improved many of the trails and trailheads that we take for granted on our visits to the Superstition Wilderness. After the U.S. Army subdued the Apache in 1873, prospectors began to explore the mountains with greater freedom. They used prehistoric and historic routes that followed major canyons and creeks—Pine Creek, Campaign Creek, Fraser Canyon, Rogers Canyon, Spencer Spring Creek, and Pinto Creek—and connected the routes through passes and saddles in the mountains.

From 1876 through the 1900s, the ranchers in the Superstition Mountains established their headquarters along permanent streams and perennial washes. Many current trailheads are located at the sites of former ranch headquarters or on the roads to present day ranch headquarters. On the west end of the mountains, the ranches were the Weekes Ranch, 3R Ranch, First Water Ranch, and Quarter Circle U Ranch. The ranches in the central mountains were the Tortilla, JF, and Reavis. Many ranches were established on the eastern end of the mountains including the Tony Ranch in Haunted Canyon; Miles Ranch on West Fork Pinto Creek; John Koons Ranch, Jose Periz Ranch, and Horrell JH6 Ranch on Pinto Creek; Spring Creek Ranch on Spring Creek; and the Upper Horrell Ranch and Cross P Ranch on Campaign Creek.

Several ranch and mining roads within the boundaries of the Superstition Wilderness have been converted to trails. Although they have not been maintained as roads, the gentle grade of the former roads tends to make traveling them easier. Examples of the former roads are the Coffee Flat Trail, part of the Second Water Trail, the north end of the Dutchman's Trail, most of the Siphon Draw Trail, the north end of the Bull Basin Trail, portions of the Cuff Button Trail, the Fire Line Trail, and the north segment of the Reavis Ranch Trail.

In 1891, Mr. F. P. Trott reported that he surveyed a route from Mesa to Globe following a route from the Marlow Ranch (Quarter Circle U Ranch) to Little Cottonwood Gulch (Reeds Water) to JF Ranch and over the divide near Rogers Trough. The survey continued down Campaign Creek and connected

Post and pole style corral [38-M] on Rock Creek. The concrete water trough is out of service and the corral wood has mostly rotted. A close-up of the Y Bar B brand inscribed in the concrete is shown on the opposite page. Photo was taken in December 2007.

with the Salt River to Globe Road. The Coffee Flat Trail follows this route to the JF Ranch, and portions of road construction can still be seen in Fraser Canyon, but we do not believe that any construction was done beyond the Rogers Trough area. See page 304 in Trip 42 for more about the survey.

The Dutchman's Trail from First Water Trailhead was the access road to First Water Ranch. At one time, vehicles used the Dutchman's Trail (former Charlebois Trail) to access mines in the Parker Pass area. Another old road following Second Water Trail passed the First Water Ranch, went through Garden Valley, and ended at Cholla Tank.

Many of the former ranch trails have been abandoned since most of the grazing allotments in the Superstition Wilderness are not active. Ranchers had to check each canyon and wash for cattle during the spring and fall roundups so trails were everywhere. Constant use by the cattle and cowboys kept the trails clear of catclaw and brush. Some of those former trails are marked on the 1940s and 1960s topographic maps, but now the only evidence of the overgrown trails is an unused gate in the boundary fence line and sometimes the rounded bed of the track.

Homesteaders and Ranchers

Many early pioneers claimed their ranches as possessory rights on federal government land. They did not own the land, but only had the right of possession to use the land. A possessory right was popular because it avoided the county property tax on the land, although not on the buildings or stock animals.

Romantic tales have portrayed Arizona as the lawless Wild West in the 1880s, but the territorial government, with its laws, courts, and administrative record keeping, was an integral part of society. Some early pioneers had a visit from the county tax man. Tax records show that John LeBarge relinquished his house and corral at his stock ranch in an 1893 sheriff's sale for delinquent tax of $1,290. We do not know the location of LeBarge's ranch, except that his ranch was in Pinal County, but we speculate that his ranch could have been at the site of his 1891 water claim at Cottonwood Spring—three miles southwest of the Marlow Ranch. Elisha Reavis somehow avoided the tax claims against his Superstition Mountain farm in 1893 for $358 and in 1894 for $270. We have not found any record of his payment.

Close-up photo of the Y Bar B brand inscribed on the concrete water trough (opposite page) at the corral [38-M] on Rock Creek. Photo was taken in December 2007.

Archie McIntosh, U.S. Army scout and guide, was one of the first to prove up on an 1884 homestead located at Grapevine Spring on the Salt River just east of the Superstition Mountains. Many other ranchers held on to their possessory rights or transferred the rights by selling their buildings and corrals. Most homesteaders around the Superstition Mountains began to prove up on their claims after 1912 when the residency requirement was reduced from five to three years. The last patent for title to federal land on the edge of the Superstition Wilderness was issued to Edward Horrell in 1923 for the Upper Horrell Place on Campaign Creek.

Ranches consisted of a large acreage of leased Tonto National Forest or Arizona State Trust land and ten acres of private land for the headquarters. Forest Service rules required ten acres of private land for each grazing allotment. Some headquarters, such as the Quarter Circle U, First Water, JF, Tortilla, Reavis, and Two Bar, were established on federal or state land. At a later date, two of those ranch headquarters became private land. In 1919, William Knight received the federal homestead patent for the Reavis headquarters and, in 1947, the Barkley Cattle Company purchased the Quarter Circle U headquarters from the State of Arizona.

The most famous ranch in the Superstitions, the Matt and Alice Cavaness Ranch, plays a role in the Lost Dutchman Mine story. The Cavaness Ranch house was often referred to as the plank house or board house because the building was made from lumber that Matt hauled from Yuma in 1876. George Marlow and Alfred Charlebois were later owners of the Cavaness Ranch, and they operated a meat market in the town of Pinal. Prominent owners of the Cavaness Ranch in later years were Jim Bark, Frank Criswell, and the Barkley family. The ranch is now known as the Quarter Circle U Ranch and is owned by Chuck and Judy Backus.

Elisha M. Reavis established his farm in Reavis Valley in the late 1870s. After Reavis died in 1896, rancher Jack Fraser took over his headquarters along Reavis Creek. The Clemans Cattle Company ran the Reavis and JF operations during the early 1900s. Other owners were John "Hoolie" Bacon and Charles Upton, and later Floyd Stone. Ranch manager for the Clemans Cattle Company, William Martin, Sr., bought the JF portion of the outfit from Bacon and Upton. Billy and Helen Martin bought the ranch from Martin, Sr. and recently George Martin purchased the ranch from his parents, Billy and Helen.

In 1922, William T. Toney homesteaded Tony Ranch on the southeast border of the Wilderness. Even today the private homestead can only be accessed by horse trail. Toney sold to George Taylor in 1924. Later Ann Taylor conferred life estates for the property to rancher Jim Herron and several others. Jim Herron managed the Toney homestead while working for Taylor, and later Jim and Phyllis Herron ran their own operation from the

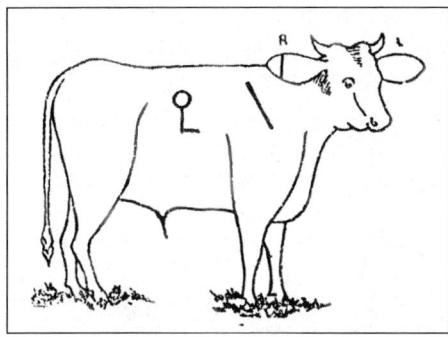

Rae Clark registered this cattle brand and ear mark with the State of Arizona in August 1915. Rae Clark homesteaded the present day Miles Trailhead property. Diagram from Arizona State Brand Book, page 2397. Courtesy of the Arizona State Archives.

Herron Ranch headquarters on Queen Creek near the town of Superior. Tony Ranch was purchased by the Superstition Area Land Trust in August 2008.

Over the mountain to the north of Tony Ranch, Rae Clark homesteaded the wide bench along West Fork Pinto Creek in 1921, which was later known as Miles Ranch—shown as Kennedy Ranch on the topo maps. Not much is known about Rae Clark except that in 1925 he ran the Miami Market on Sullivan Street in Miami. Clark sold to J. Ney Miles in 1924, and Miles owned the ranch for the next twenty-three years. Miles was probably better known for the family's Miles Mortuary business in Miami and Globe. In 1986, the USDA Forest Service purchased forty-two acres of the homestead and incorporated that into the Superstition Wilderness. In 1997, the Forest Service purchased the last ten acre parcel of private land, which is now used for the Miles Trailhead.

Upstream from the Iron Bridge on Pinto Creek, Jose A. Periz received his homestead patent in 1923. Periz was from Jaca, Spain. Hikers and riders can see the ruins of some his buildings along the Haunted Canyon Trail (103) in Pinto Creek. The USDA Forest Service acquired the homestead in a 1969 land exchange with Tennessee Corporation.

John Koons had his headquarters just northwest of the Iron Bridge on Pinto Creek. He ran cattle with the JK brand that he recorded in 1883, but he did not apply for a homestead. He sold his brand to W. T. Rice in 1903. Nothing remains of his operation except for the named landmarks—Coon Spring, JK Mountain, locally named Koons Canyon, and the nearby ruins of the former JK CCC Camp.

Farther downstream on Pinto Creek below the junction with West Fork Pinto Creek, John Horrell located his spread in 1879. The Horrell family brought the JH6 brand with them from California and the property on Pinto Creek has been known as the JH6 Ranch. Marion L. Horrell received the patent for the ranch in 1914, and Ed Horrell received the patent for an adjoining ranch in 1919. The JH6 Ranch still runs cattle and is owned by the L. R. Layton family.

West of present day Roosevelt Lake, several stockmen held possessory rights to the land along Campaign Creek in the 1880s. One of the earliest known ranchers was John Narron. Narron and William T. Gann ran cattle in the area and had possessory rights to the present day Reevis Mountain School property. Edward E. Horrell was the person who eventually proved up on the homestead in 1923. Earl Horrell and his wife Blanche bought the Upper Horrell Place from his father, Ed, in 1928. When Earl's health failed in 1968, he sold the ranch to Earline and James Tidwell—his daughter and son-in-law.

Rock Creek in December 2007 when the stream was flowing with seasonal water. .

Reevis Mountain School bought the property from the Tidwells in 1979, and Peter Busnack now operates the homestead as an organic farm and orchard.[1]

Ed Horrell bought the Luther M. Jackson homestead farther downstream on Campaign Creek, which was formerly known as the Cross P Ranch and now as the J Bar B Ranch. In 1939, Earl Horrell bought the Spring Creek Ranch. The Horrell and Tidwell families ran the three ranches on Campaign and Spring Creeks using the Cross P and Half Diamond Cross brands.[2]

Miners and Prospectors

King Woolsey was one of the early prospectors. He led a prospecting expedition to find minerals in eastern Arizona and along the Salt River in 1864. He wrote "On Tonto Creek we prospected in several places for gold and found color, but not in paying quantities." Although not successful in the exploration for minerals in the Tonto Basin area, he recognized the potential for ranching and farming upstream from Tonto Creek along the Salt River.[3]

James Rogers and his partners were prospecting and mining in Rogers Canyon in 1876 and later shipped gold and silver ore from Pinal to San Francisco. The Woodbury family revived those mines in the early 1900s, but that effort did not seem to be successful.

Sheriff George Shute and Frank Hammon from Globe were prospecting at Gold Gulch in the Pinto Creek area in 1889. Al Sieber had claims on Pinto Creek in 1896 and later sold them for a profit. Modern day prospectors such as John Wilburn found gold and filed claims in Pinto Creek in the 1970s. Copper deposits extending from Pinto Creek to Globe have attracted large scale mining, which is still profitable today. Small scale asbestos and iron mines around the Miles Ranch area had limited success in the 1950s.

On the western edge of the Superstition Wilderness, the Mammoth Mine, discovered in 1893, and the other nearby Goldfield mines were very successful, with some precious metals recovered in recent times. Other large mining operations in the western half of the Wilderness, such as the Carney Mines near Carney Trailhead and the Miller Mines near Tortilla Trailhead, were not as productive.

Mining and Treasure Hunting

The 1964 Wilderness Act closed all wilderness lands to new mineral claims effective January 1, 1984. In the Superstition Wilderness, the Forest Service requires existing valid mining claims to show valuable and locatable minerals. These mineral claims must operate with an approved Notice of Intent and Plan of Operations. The Forest Service has defined several categories of mineral-related activities to help clarify the regulations. Ask the Forest Service or check their website for a copy of the regulations.

HEAT dig at Rogers Spring in November 2004. Workers, left to right, at the head frame and mine shaft are Tom LaMonica, Duane Short, K. J. Schroeder, Jesse Feldman (behind post), and Ron Feldman.

Mining is the extraction of minerals and is subject to the Forest Service rules described above.

Prospecting is only allowed with an approved Plan of Operations. Extraction of a small grab sample is permitted. Anything more than what you can carry in your hands is considered mining.

Gold Panning is considered a type of mining if a mineral is extracted. If a mineral is not extracted, Gold Panning is allowed and is considered Prospecting.

Treasure Trove Hunting is only allowed with a permit from the Forest Service. A treasure trove is defined as money, gems, or precious worked metal of unknown ownership. You must prove that treasure, gems, coins, etc. exist at a particular location before a permit will be issued. If a permit is approved, it is issued for a specific number of days, and the search site is subject to inspection. The only treasure trove permit issued in the Superstition Wilderness was to Ron Feldman's group, HEAT, for excavation at Rogers Spring in 2004. Even though a permit was issued, all equipment and supplies had to be carried into the site by foot or horseback. The mining operation had to be conducted without power tools or power machinery. See Trip 37 (Iron Mountain) on page 279 for more of Feldman's story.

Artifacts that are more than one hundred years old may not be removed under the Archaeological Resources Protection Act. Archaeological sites may not be disturbed. Historic sites and artifacts are government property, and your permit may exclude collection of these items.

Metal Detecting is allowed, but may be considered Mining, Prospecting, or Treasure Trove Hunting depending on what you find.

WATER

It is more convenient on day trips to carry all the water you need rather than purify water found in the creeks and springs. In hot weather, carry some empty containers that can be filled with untreated water—from potholes, springs, and creeks. You can use this untreated water for keeping a bandanna or shirt wet, which will act as your personal evaporative cooler and reduce the amount of water you need to drink. On hot days and in the summer, we freeze plastic bottles of water in advance so we have something cool to drink. On day trips we carry one to four liters of water per person depending on the season and weather. In the summer, four liters per person is a minimum requirement for a day-long trip. Summer heat can make the water so hot it is not very pleasant to drink.

If you are looking for water, check the map for springs and streams. Plan ahead by checking with other people and the Forest Service rangers for the current conditions of springs and water sources. Many springs are seasonal, which means they are dry for long periods of time (months or even years). In the field, observe the color and type of surrounding vegetation. Cottonwood and sycamore trees sometimes indicate water. Green areas may have water or just catch more runoff than nearby areas. Potholes in ravines and intermittent streams are often good sources of water.

Purify all water to be certain it is safe for drinking. Boil water for at least five minutes or use a purifier designed to remove *Giardia, bacteria,* and *viruses*. Some equipment classified as a filter does not remove viruses. Be sure you use a purifier that removes viruses. Always take your water from sources that are impacted by the minimum amount of human and animal traffic.

Although many of the springs developed by the former ranchers and cattlemen are in disrepair, you can often obtain water by following the metal pipes back to the spring. Some of the more reliable water sources are Charlebois Spring, La Barge Spring, Bluff Spring, Hackberry Spring, Rogers Spring, Walnut Spring, Campaign Creek, and Reavis Creek. For the latest information on water conditions, check with the rangers at the Mesa Ranger District in Mesa, Arizona. Their address and phone number are listed in the back of this book under Useful Addresses.

Easy Trips

Here are several easy hike ideas to get you going. If you turn around at our suggested destination or when you get tired, these trips will make ideal easy treks. The difficulty of each trip varies within the easy category. Some of the selections are portions of more difficult trips, so you must read the trip description carefully to identify our suggested turnaround point. The distance and time are given for the round trip. Horse riders can use this as a guide, but they need to read the full description to avoid trips where hikers could scramble over obstacles that would block horses.

Trip	Miles	Hours	Elev.	Destination	Condition
8	0.3	0.5	±60	Cemetery Trail [cemetery]	good trail
9	3.8	3.0	±1,490	Thompson Trail [8-E, 1.9]	good trail
10	2.4	2.5	±310	Cottonwood Trail [8-D, 1.2]	good trail
12	2.4	2.5	±460	Tule Trail [13-D, 1.2]	good trail
13	2.2	2.5	±234	Campaign Trail [14-D, 1.1]	good trail
21	3.0	3.0	±80	Haunted Canyon Trail [22-V, 1.5]	dirt road
24	4.8	5.0	±310	West Pinto Trail [25-M, 2.4]	good trail
25	2.4	2.5	±165	Bull Basin Trail [24-GG, 1.2]	old road
30	1.4	2.0	±280	Paradise Trail [24-K, 0.7]	good trail
38	1.8	2.5	±675	West Pinto Trail [33-PP, 0.9]	good trail

Equipment and Clothing

Equipment and clothing needs will vary from trip to trip, but we can offer some general guidelines. In our day packs for hiking, we each carry a small homemade emergency first-aid kit, flashlight, compass, GPS, camera, toilet paper, knife, maps, pencil, extra bandanna, sunglasses, snacks, and water. On our key chain, we carry a small pliers tool and pointed tweezers. We usually wear quick dry long or convertible pants, long sleeve cotton shirt, bandanna, and some kind of wide brim hat or baseball cap. Loose fitting long pants help protect our legs on cross-country treks and on the lesser traveled trails.

We always add a breathable waterproof jacket with hood, a wool or fleece hat, and liner gloves in the winter and in periods of changing weather. If the weather is cool or really looks nasty, we take polypropylene long underwear tops and bottoms that can be worn under our shirt and pants. In very cold weather, we take a light weight (about one-pound) down jacket. If we expect rain or snow, we take rain pants. We wear wool socks in the winter and summer. Short gaiters on our boots keep the stickers and foxtails out of our socks. Leather gloves protect our hands when bushwhacking.

When riding horseback, we wear denim jeans, long sleeve shirt, bandanna, wide brim western hat (straw in summer, felt in winter), western style work boots, denim jacket, and leather gloves. If the weather looks like rain, we take a full length rain slicker to cover our legs and saddle. In brushy country, we wear leather chaps.

Our first-aid items are stored in a mesh bag that is six inches tall and four inches in diameter. You can also use a small plastic bag. Our emergency first-aid kit contains:

- first-aid antibiotic ointment
- moleskin
- gauze pads
- adhesive tape
- adhesive bandages
- alcohol swab pads
- snake and insect bite extractor kit
- Swiss Army knife with scissors and tweezers
- sunscreen
- Arnica gel
- aspirin
- lip balm
- nail file
- thread and needles
- lighter
- money ($20 or more in small bills and four quarters)

Horse riders will also need to assemble an emergency kit for their horses. For overnight trips, hikers and riders should consult one of the many instructional books on packing and develop their own list of equipment.

Trailheads

These brief descriptions will quickly get you on the road to the trailhead, but the maps and detailed Trailhead descriptions in the trip section of the book will give you a better idea of what to expect. Paved road mileage is rounded to the nearest mile. Roads are suitable for passenger cars except as noted. The GPS coordinates identify the start of the trail from the parking area. Starting with Reavis Trailhead, the trailheads are listed clockwise around the perimeter of the Superstition Wilderness.

Reavis Trailhead

Twenty-eight miles north of Apache Junction on SR88, between mileposts 227 and 228, turn east on FR212 and drive 2.8 miles to end of road. High-clearance vehicle is required. (N33° 33' 23.9", W111° 13' 38.9")

Pine Creek Trailhead

About 33 miles north of Apache Junction on SR88, between mileposts 232 and 233, turn east on FR665 and drive 0.5 mile over the hill to the first water trough. Or, go south on SR88 9 miles from Roosevelt Dam to FR665. High-clearance vehicle is required and sometimes four-wheel-drive is required. (N33° 35' 01.8", W111° 12' 18.5")

Roosevelt Cemetery Trailhead

About 27 miles north of Globe on SR188, between mileposts 242 and 243, turn left (south) into Lakeview Park, then turn right into the paved trailhead parking area. (N33° 40' 02.0", W111° 08' 05.6")

Frazier Trailhead

About 26 miles north of Globe on SR188, between mileposts 242 and 243, turn southwest on FR221 and drive around the power substation to the end of the gravel road. (N33° 39' 43.6", W111° 07' 23.3")

Tule Trailhead

About 20 miles north of Globe on SR188, turn north onto SR188 and go 20 miles to FR449 (J–B Ranch Road) between mileposts 235 and 236. Drive west on FR449 for 2 miles to junction with FR449A. Stay right on FR449 for 1.2 miles to end of road. (N33° 35' 35.9", W111° 04' 32.5")

Campaign Trailhead

Follow directions to Tule Trailhead, but after 2 miles on FR449, bear left on FR449A, and go 5.1 miles to Campaign Trailhead near Reevis Mountain

1. Reavis Trailhead
2. Pine Creek Trailhead
3. Roosevelt Cemetery Trailhead
4. Frazier Trailhead
5. Tule Trailhead
6. Campaign Trailhead
7. Pinto Creek Trailhead
8. Haunted Canyon Trailhead
9. Miles Trailhead
10. Reavis Trail Canyon Trailhead
11. Montana Mountain Trailhead
12. Rogers Trough Trailhead
13. Woodbury Trailhead
14. Peralta Trailhead
15. Dons Camp Trailhead
16. Carney Springs Trailhead
17. Hieroglyphic Trailhead
18. Broadway Trailhead
19. Lost Dutchman State Park Trailheads
20. Crosscut Trailhead
21. Massacre Grounds Trailhead
22. First Water Trailhead
23. Canyon Overlook Trailhead
24. Canyon Lake Trailhead
25. Tortilla Flat Trailhead
26. Tortilla Trailhead

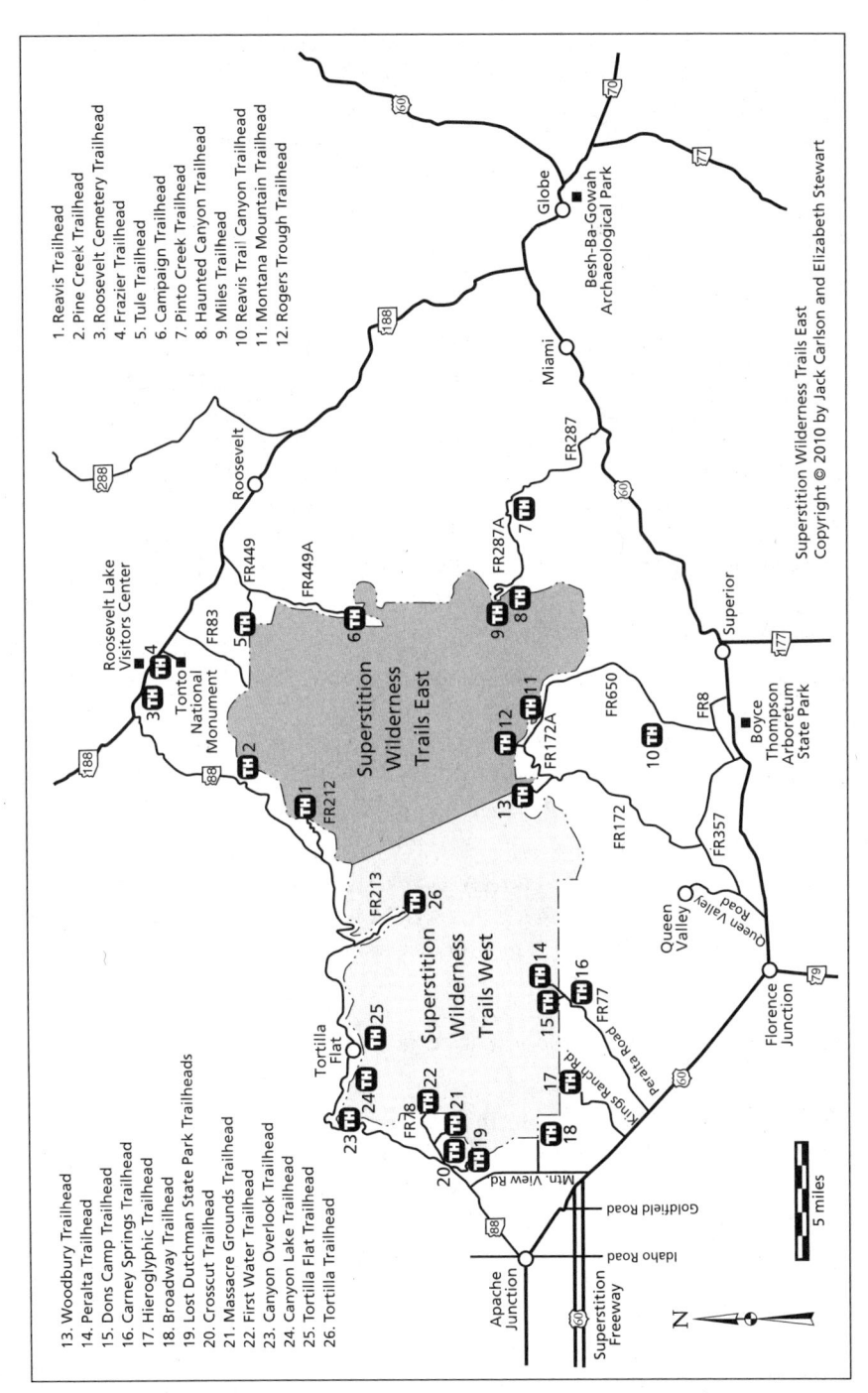

Superstition Wilderness Trails East
Copyright © 2010 by Jack Carlson and Elizabeth Stewart

Trailhead Locator Map

INTRODUCTION   41

School (former Upper Horrell Place). Reevis Mountain School is private property. Since 1994, the Campaign Trail has provided access to the Wilderness by going around the west side of Reevis Mountain School. Deep sand and seasonal water make FR449A a four-wheel-drive road although some high clearance vehicles can make it. (N33° 31' 54.3", W111° 04' 42.1")

Upper Horrell Trailhead (Renamed Campaign Trailhead)

Pinto Creek Trailhead

From Apache Junction, drive 29 miles on US60 to Superior. Continue on US60 for 12 miles to FR287 (Pinto Valley Mine Road) between mileposts 239 and 240. The FR287 junction is 1 mile east of the Pinto Creek highway bridge. Coming from Globe on US60, drive about 4 miles from Miami to the Pinto Valley Mine Road. Drive north on FR287, to the Iron Bridge on Pinto Creek. Before you cross the Iron Bridge, turn left (west) on a dirt road marked as *Trail 203*. Park near the locked gate, but do not block the road. A medium-clearance vehicle is required. (N33° 25' 31.4", W111° 00' 9.7")

Haunted Canyon Trailhead

Follow Pinto Creek Trailhead directions to the Iron Bridge. Cross the Iron Bridge over Pinto Creek, turn left on FR287A in 0.1 mile, go another 3.8 miles, and park in a small pullout on the right (east) side of FR287A. A medium-clearance vehicle is required. (N33° 25' 33.0", W111° 03' 17.3")

Miles Trailhead

Follow Pinto Creek Trailhead directions to the Iron Bridge. Cross the Iron Bridge over Pinto Creek, turn left on FR287A in 0.1 mile, and drive another 5.7 miles to end of FR287A. A medium-clearance vehicle is required. (N33° 26' 14.3", W111° 04' 1.9")

Reavis Trail Canyon Trailhead (Arizona Trail)

From US60 between mileposts 222 and 223, near the Arboretum, take FR357 (Hewitt Station Road) north for a few yards, turn right (east) on FR8 (Happy Camp Road) for 1.8 miles, go left (north) on FR650 for 4.3 miles to the metal *Arizona Trail* sign [37-K]. A high-clearance vehicle is required on this part of FR650—and in wet weather you might need four-wheel-drive. (N33° 21' 09.9", W111° 07' 53.1")

Rogers Trough Trailhead

From Florence Junction, go east 2 miles on US60. Between mileposts 214 and 215 turn north on Queen Valley Road and go 1.8 miles to FR357

(Hewitt Station Road). Go right on FR357 for 3 miles to FR172, and go left 9 miles on FR172 to the junction with FR172A. Continue right for 4 miles on FR172A to end of road—staying left at the junction with FR650. (N33° 25' 19.9", W111° 10' 21.7")

From Superior, go west on US60 to FR357 (Hewitt Station Road) between mileposts 222 and 223. Turn right onto dirt FR357. Go 5 miles on FR357 to FR172, turn right on FR172, and use the directions above. High-clearance vehicle is required on FR172. After seasonal rains, steep and rocky sections of FR172A make this a four-wheel-drive road.

Montana Mountain Trailhead

Follow directions for Rogers Trough Trailhead to the junction with FR172A and FR650. Go right (east) on FR650 for 2 miles to Montana Mountain Trailhead, which is marked by a wooden sign *Trail 509*. FR650 always requires four-wheel-drive. (N33° 24' 19.6", W111° 09' 22.3")

Woodbury Trailhead

Follow directions to Rogers Trough Trailhead to the junction with FR172A. From the FR172A junction, bear left and continue on FR172 for 1.4 miles to the end of the road. High-clearance vehicle is required on FR172. (N33° 24' 33.8", W111° 12' 19.5")

JF Ranch Trailhead (Relocated to Woodbury Trailhead)

Peralta Trailhead

Eight miles east of Apache Junction on US60, between mileposts 204 and 205, turn north onto Peralta Road, FR77, and go 7.2 miles to end of road. (N33° 23' 51.2", W111° 20' 49.6")

Dons Camp Trailhead

Eight miles east of Apache Junction on US60, between mileposts 204 and 205, turn north onto Peralta Road, FR77. Go 7 miles on Peralta Road. Turn left at the Lost Goldmine Trail sign, and drive west across the large parking area to the Lost Goldmine Trail kiosk. (N33° 23' 32.3", W111° 21' 12.0")

Carney Springs Trailhead

Eight miles east of Apache Junction on US60, between mileposts 204 and 205, turn north onto Peralta Road, FR77, go 6 miles, and park in a small area along Peralta Road that is bounded by metal posts and a steel cable. Carney Springs Road was closed to vehicle traffic in June of 2006. (N33° 23' 08.7", W111° 21' 44.7")

Hieroglyphic Trailhead

Six miles east of Apache Junction on US60, between mileposts 202 and 203, turn north on Kings Ranch Road and go 2.8 miles to Baseline Avenue. Turn right (east) on Baseline Avenue for 0.25 mile. Turn left (north) on Mohican Road for 0.3 mile, then left (west) on Valleyview Road. Valleyview Road meanders into Whitetail Road, which intersects Cloudview Avenue. Go right (east) on Cloudview Avenue for about 0.5 mile to the large parking lot for Lost Goldmine Trail. (N33° 23' 23.2", W111° 25' 26.0")

Broadway Trailhead

Three miles east of Apache Junction on US60, between mileposts 199 and 200, turn north on Mountain View Road and go 1.6 miles to Broadway Avenue. Turn right (east) on Broadway for 1 mile until the road curves and turns into South Broadway lane. Park on the left (north) in the small unsigned parking area. (N33° 24' 28", W111° 28' 34")

Lost Dutchman State Park Trailheads

Five miles north of Apache Junction on SR88, between mileposts 201 and 202, turn east into the Lost Dutchman State Park. (N33° 27' 33.2", W111° 28' 45.4")

Crosscut Trailhead

Five miles north of Apache Junction on SR88, between mileposts 201 and 202, turn east on FR78 (First Water Road) and drive 0.6 mile. Park on the right (south) side of FR78 in the signed parking area. (N33° 28' 16", W111° 28' 08")

Massacre Grounds Trailhead

Five miles north of Apache Junction on SR88, between mileposts 201 and 202, turn east on FR78 (First Water Road) and drive 1 mile. On unsigned FR28 turn right (south) and drive 0.7 mile to end of road. Park at the fence. (N33° 28' 02.2", W111° 27' 23.5")

First Water Trailhead

Five miles north of Apache Junction on SR88, between mileposts 201 and 202, turn east on FR78 (First Water Road) and go 2.6 miles to the end of the road. (N33° 28' 47.7", W111° 26' 32.1")

Canyon Lake Trailhead

Fifteen miles north of Apache Junction on SR88, between mileposts 211 and 212, park in the Canyon Lake Marina parking lot on the north side of fence adjacent to SR88. (N33° 32' 02", W111° 25' 20")

Tortilla Flat Trailhead

Seventeen miles north of Apache Junction on SR88, between mileposts 213 and 214, park at Tortilla Flat or on vehicle pullouts down the road near milepost 214. Tortilla Flat is private property. Obtain permission from the store manager before parking at Tortilla Flat. We park near milepost 214. (N33° 31' 50.6", W111° 22' 51.5")

Tortilla Trailhead

Twenty-four miles north of Apache Junction on SR88, between mileposts 221 and 222, turn right and park in the parking area at the start of FR213, or take four-wheel-drive road FR213 to the Old Tortilla Headquarters area. (N33° 29' 33.2", W111° 17' 14.2")

Ella Mary Toney, sitting in the chair, with five of her eight children. Starting from the lower left going clockwise, the children are; Delbert, Leona, Gladys, unknown friend, Ophie, and Ellis. Wilda and Lloyd are not present and Boyd was not born yet. See page 189 for a photo of Ella Mary at the homestead in Haunted Canyon and page 196 for the story of the William Toney homestead. Photo taken circa 1915. Courtesy of Betty Porter Gilbert, granddaughter of William and Ella Mary Toney.

Reavis Trailhead

The Reavis Trailhead is off SR88, between mileposts 227 and 228, about 28 miles northeast of Apache Junction and 14 miles southwest of Roosevelt Dam. From SR88, turn east on FR212. Drive uphill 2.8 miles to the end of FR212.

FINDING THE TRAILHEAD

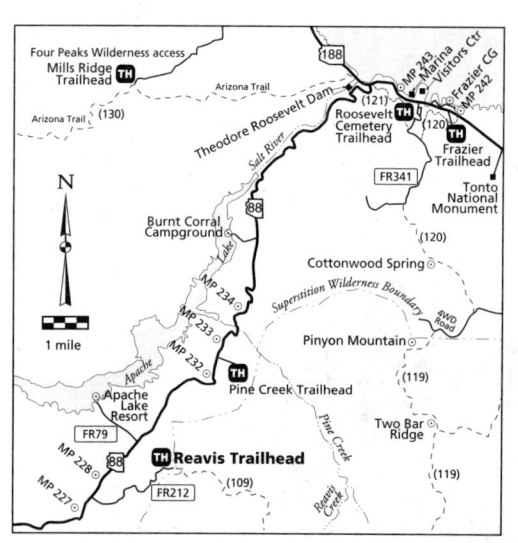

From the town of Apache Junction on SR88, travel another 12 miles past Tortilla Flat to FR212. From Roosevelt Lake on SR88, look for FR212 about 1.6 miles southwest of the Apache Lake Resort Road. FR212 is a one lane, dirt road with several eroded sections that requires a high-clearance vehicle. The 3,700-foot trailhead elevation provides a panoramic view of the Salt River Canyon and Apache Lake to the northwest.

FACILITIES

The trailhead has a hitching post for horses and a small parking lot. Bring your own water. Apache Lake Resort is nearby and has full facilities—motel, restaurant, bar, boat launch, and boat rental.

THE TRAILS

Only one trail begins at this trailhead, the Reavis Ranch Trail (109). From the road barricade [1-A, 0] at the end of FR212 (N33° 33' 23.9", W111° 13' 38.9"), a good trail follows the abandoned road to Reavis Ranch [3-I, 9.3].

The popular Reavis Falls Trail branches off the Reavis Ranch Trail at an unsigned junction [1-X, 3.2] (N33° 32' 45.5", W111° 11' 24.6") and continues to Reavis Falls [2-R, 6.1].

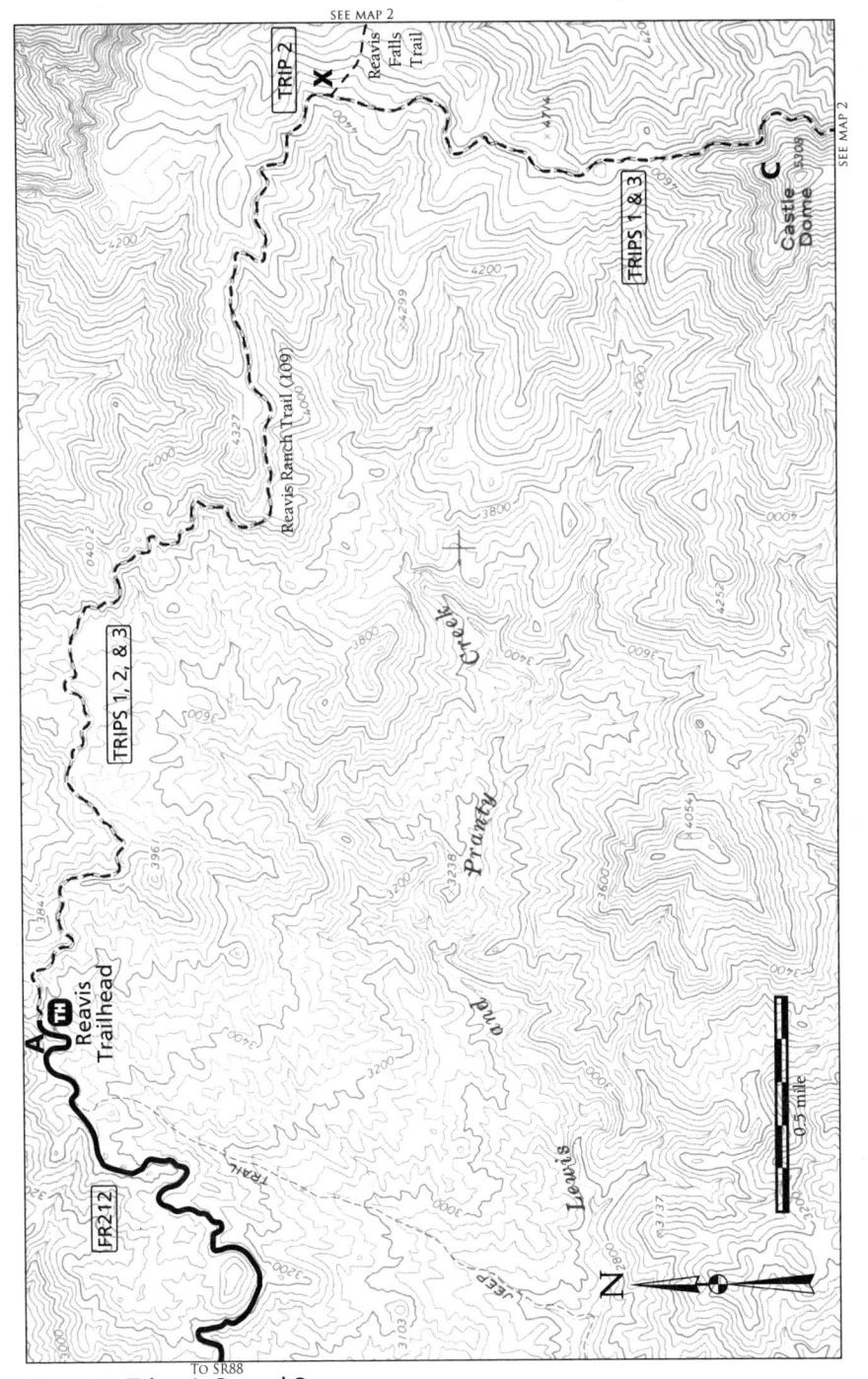

Map 1 – Trips 1, 2, and 3.

Trip 1

REAVIS RANCH FROM REAVIS TRAILHEAD

The Reavis Ranch trip makes a fine two to three day trek to a beautiful and historic region in the Wilderness. The tall ponderosa pine, black walnut, sycamore, cottonwood, and alligator juniper trees make this valley a pleasant destination. The Reavis Ranch house burned in November 1991, but the nearby orchard still produces apples each fall. Several miles north of the ranch are the 196-foot Reavis Falls on Reavis Creek, and to the south is Circlestone ruin next to Mound Mountain.

ITINERARY

From the Reavis Trailhead, follow the Reavis Ranch Trail (109) to Reavis Ranch. Return the same way.

DIFFICULTY

Moderate 2 or 3 day trip for hikers and riders. Elevation change is +1,910 and -650 feet one way.

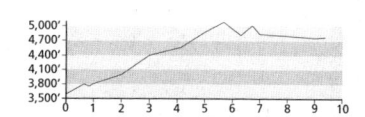

LENGTH and TIME

9.3 miles, 5 hours one way.

MAPS

Arizona USGS topo maps NAD27: Pinyon Mountain, Iron Mountain, Horse Mesa Dam. Superstition Wilderness Beartooth map, grids K8 to N11. Maps 1, 2, and 3.

FINDING THE TRAIL

Trailhead map is on page 46. Trail 109 starts beyond the FR212 road barricade (N33° 33' 23.9", W111° 13' 38.9") and follows the former Reavis Ranch Road.

THE TRIP

Begin with Map 1 on page 47. From the Reavis Trailhead [1-A, 0], Reavis Ranch Trail follows the abandoned road to the site of Reavis Ranch [3-I, 9.3]. Before Castle Dome, a well-worn unmaintained trail [1-X, 3.2] leads to Reavis Falls [2-R]. See Trip 2 for the Reavis Falls Trail description.

Reavis Ranch house in 1924 was made out of wood. The pond was located at the left. Photo by J. D. Jones, April 5, 1924. Courtesy of the Tonto National Forest Service.

Castle Dome [2-C, 4.4], on the west side of the road, is the landmark signaling the upcoming Windy Pass and some up and downhill sections of road. Just past Windy Pass is Plow Saddle [2-D, 6.4], marked by wooden trail signs, where you can use the Plow Saddle Trail (287) to cut across to the Frog Tanks Trail (112). Farther along the Reavis Ranch Trail, the signed Frog Tanks Trail meets Reavis Ranch Trail at a well-marked intersection [4-E, 7.7].

Continuing on the Reavis Ranch Trail, the road turns south along a fence line and begins to parallel Reavis Creek. At the first open grassy area, to the east, you will see a very large group-camping area under a canopy of black walnut, ponderosa pine, and sycamore trees [3-F, 8.3]. This is the first easy access to Reavis Creek where you can often find water. Portions of Reavis Creek may be dry, but we have always found water in two places on the creek—at the Reavis Gap Trail crossing and the Reavis Ranch Trail crossing near the Fire Line Trail.

Farther south on the Reavis Ranch Trail, the signed Reavis Gap Trail (117) enters from the east [3-G, 8.9]. The apple orchard is on the east side of the Reavis Ranch Trail [3-H, 9.0] a short distance south from this trail junction. The site of the Reavis Ranch house [3-I, 9.3] is on a bench above and to the west of the trail. Only the cement floor of the ranch house remains today. South of the ranch house is another orchard to the east of the trail. The trail continues south, passes through a forest of southwestern locust trees, crosses Reavis Creek, and intersects the signed Fire Line Trail (118) on the east bank [3-J, 9.6].

Apple orchard at Reavis Ranch in October 2000. Of the 600 trees that were planted in this orchard, 208 were still standing in December 2003.

Since Reavis Ranch is a popular destination, you might find other people here, but you have plenty of room for camping along the two-mile corridor by Reavis Creek. Fewer people camp south of the Fire Line Trail, so you can find some solitude in this area among the towering ponderosa pine trees. North of the Reavis Gap Trail on an unnamed trail to Government Corral you can find large campsites that are rarely used. These camps lie on the east side of Reavis Creek. The trip description ends here, but you should consult Trip 2 (Reavis Falls) and Trip 3 (Reavis Falls from Reavis Ranch) for more ideas. Return by the same route.

DAY TRIPS FROM REAVIS RANCH

We describe six day trips from Reavis Valley. Circlestone ruin should be your first choice. The other trips will help you explore the country for future trips. The trek to Reavis Falls from Reavis Ranch is a tough one.

      1. Circlestone Prehistoric Ruin. Circlestone ruin [3-O, 6010], about 2.5 miles from the Reavis Ranch Trail at the junction with the Fire Line Trail, is on a lower knoll just northeast of Mound Mountain. The elevation change

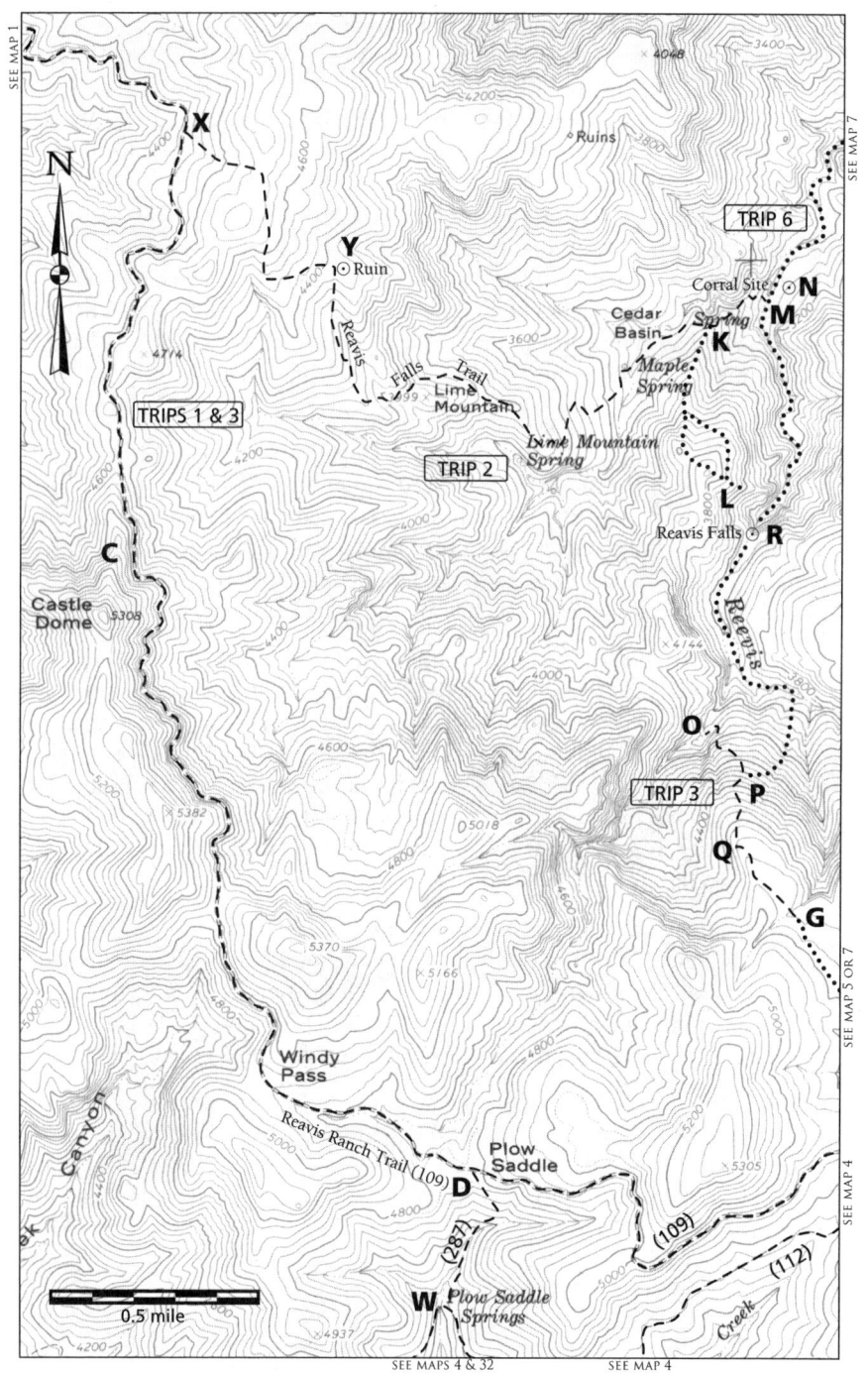

Map 2 – Trips 1, 2, 3, and 6.

is 1,160-feet to the ruin, but the trip is worth the effort to see this unusual ruin and for the view from the top. From the Reavis Ranch Trail [3-J, 0], take the Fire Line Trail (118) uphill. Whiskey Spring [3-B, 0.8] (N33° 29' 15", W111° 08' 35") is on the right, but is not visible from the trail. After reaching the pass [3-K, 1.2], continue down the trail one-half mile and look for the unsigned Allen Blackman Trail marked by several large rock cairns [3-L, 1.7] (N33° 29' 15", W111° 07' 54") on the right (south). The Allen Blackman Trail goes uphill steeply at first, then contours along the east side of the ridge before striking out across the ridge line to Circlestone [3-O, 2.5, 6010]. Circlestone ruin is on the top of a knoll partially hidden among a growth of manzanita and large alligator junipers. Please don't camp or build fires in or around the ruin. Allow about three hours for the round trip.

2. Boulder Peak. To get to the Boulder Peak benchmark from the Reavis Ranch Trail [4-G, 0], take the Reavis Gap Trail (117) east to Boulder Pass [4-M, 1.2]. The pass would be a good turnaround point for an easier trip. Backtrack on the trail a little bit from the pass to get on the southwest side of the Boulder Pass Butte. Go cross-country up the gully on the west side of the butte and then move farther west to the brass marker [4-N], which is dated 1946. Horse riders may have difficulty on the cross-county part of the trip.

3. Pine Creek and Walnut Spring. From the Reavis Ranch Trail [4-G, 0], take the Reavis Gap Trail (117) to Boulder Pass [4-M, 1.2]. Continue on Reavis Gap Trail down to the Pine Creek crossing [4-P, 2.5] where you may find some water. Explore upstream on the left side from the Pine Creek crossing. See Trip 19 (Upper Pine Creek) for more information on this area. Horse riders could extend the trip by continuing on the Reavis Gap Trail to the Two Bar Ridge Trail [15-T, 3.3] for a ride over to Walnut Spring [15-W, 3.8]. See Two Bar Ridge Trail, Trip 20.

4. Ponderosa Pine Forest. If you came to Reavis Valley from the north, take Reavis Ranch Trail south from the Fire Line Trail (118) junction [31-J, 0]. Continue on the Reavis Ranch Trail through the ponderosa pine forest for about a mile to the large juniper tree [31-N, 1.0] (N33° 28' 37", W111° 09' 34"). Return the same way. Allow about 1.5 hours for the 2 mile round trip.

5. Plow Saddle Loop. If you came to Reavis Valley from the south, go north on the Reavis Ranch Trail from the Reavis Gap Trail (117) junction [4-G, 0]. Turn left (southeast) on the Plow Saddle Trail (287) [4-D, 2.5], turn left (southeast) on the Frog Tanks Trail (112) [4-W, 2.9], turn right (east) and connect with Reavis Ranch Trail [4-E, 4.4] for the completion of the 5.6 mile loop to Reavis Valley [4-G, 5.6].

6. Reavis Falls. Take Trip 3 (Reavis Falls from Reavis Ranch). The country along the route is pretty, and you don't have to go all the way to Reavis Falls.

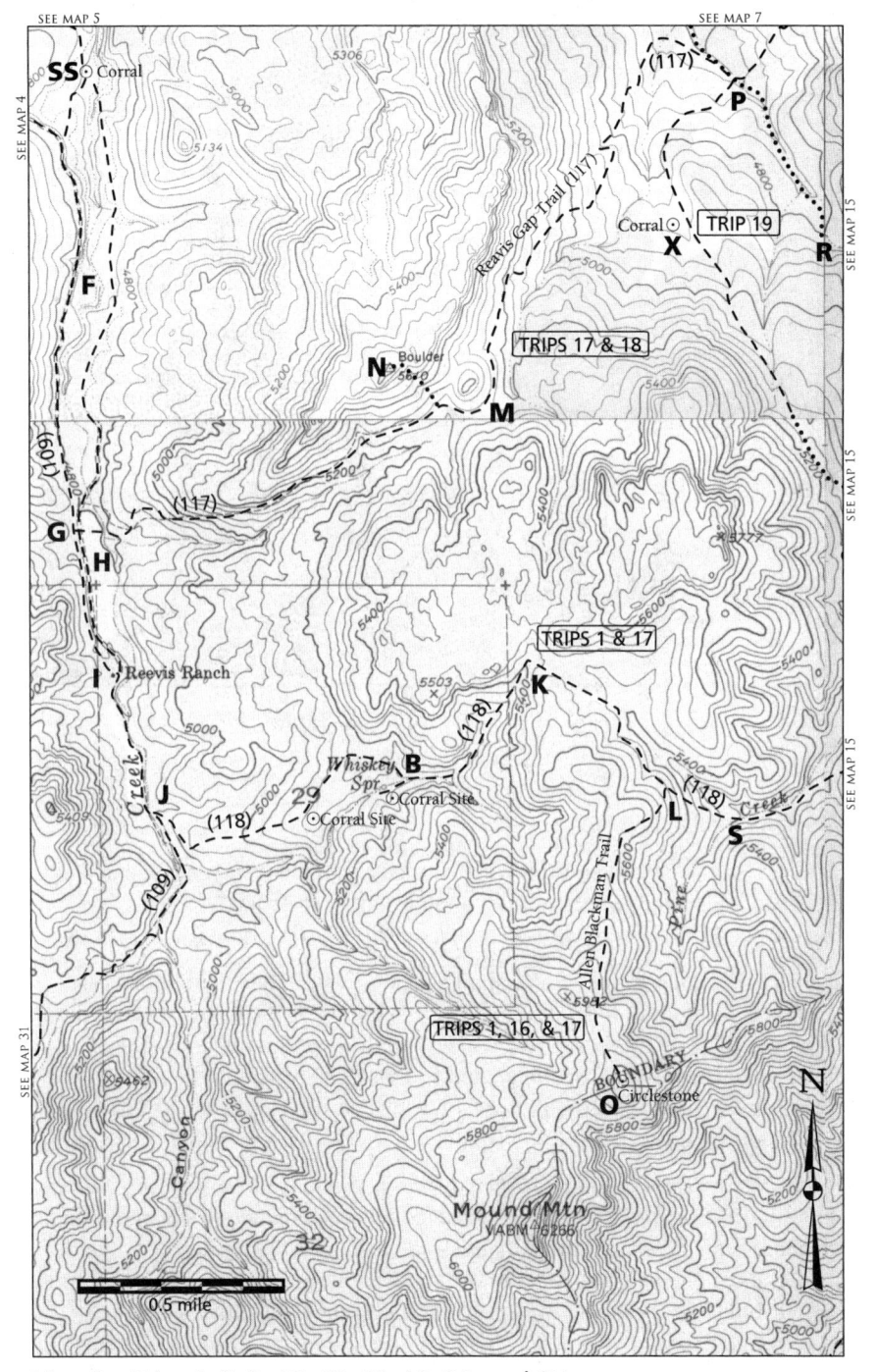

Map 3 – Trips 1, 2, 3, 16, 17, 18, 19, 34, and 35.

Apples from Reavis Ranch orchard. The apples are usually small, but they taste good. Photo taken in October 2000.

HISTORY AND LEGENDS

Evidence of the Salado culture, which ended about AD 1450, is present in Reavis Valley and the surrounding mountains. One such structure, Circlestone [3-O], makes an excellent side trip when visiting the Reavis area.

Located on a small knoll at an elevation of 6,010 feet and northeast of Mound Mountain, Circlestone is reached by a trail blazed by the late Allen Blackman. The ruin is constructed of a three-foot-wide sandstone wall. The diameter of the not-quite-circular ruin is about 133 feet with the outline of a 17-foot-by-17-foot building in the center.[4] Circlestone dates to AD 1250–AD 1300.[5] Some experts believe Circlestone to be celestially oriented.

In *Circlestone: A Superstition Mountain Mystery*, Swanson and Kollenborn describe Circlestone ruin in complete detail while analyzing the structure with experts from many scientific disciplines. Their book is available at the Superstition Mountain Museum in Apache Junction. The diagrams in their book will help you understand the layout of the ruin.

In later years, the Yavapai and Apache occupied the land in Reavis Valley, but Elisha Reavis was the person who established individual rights to

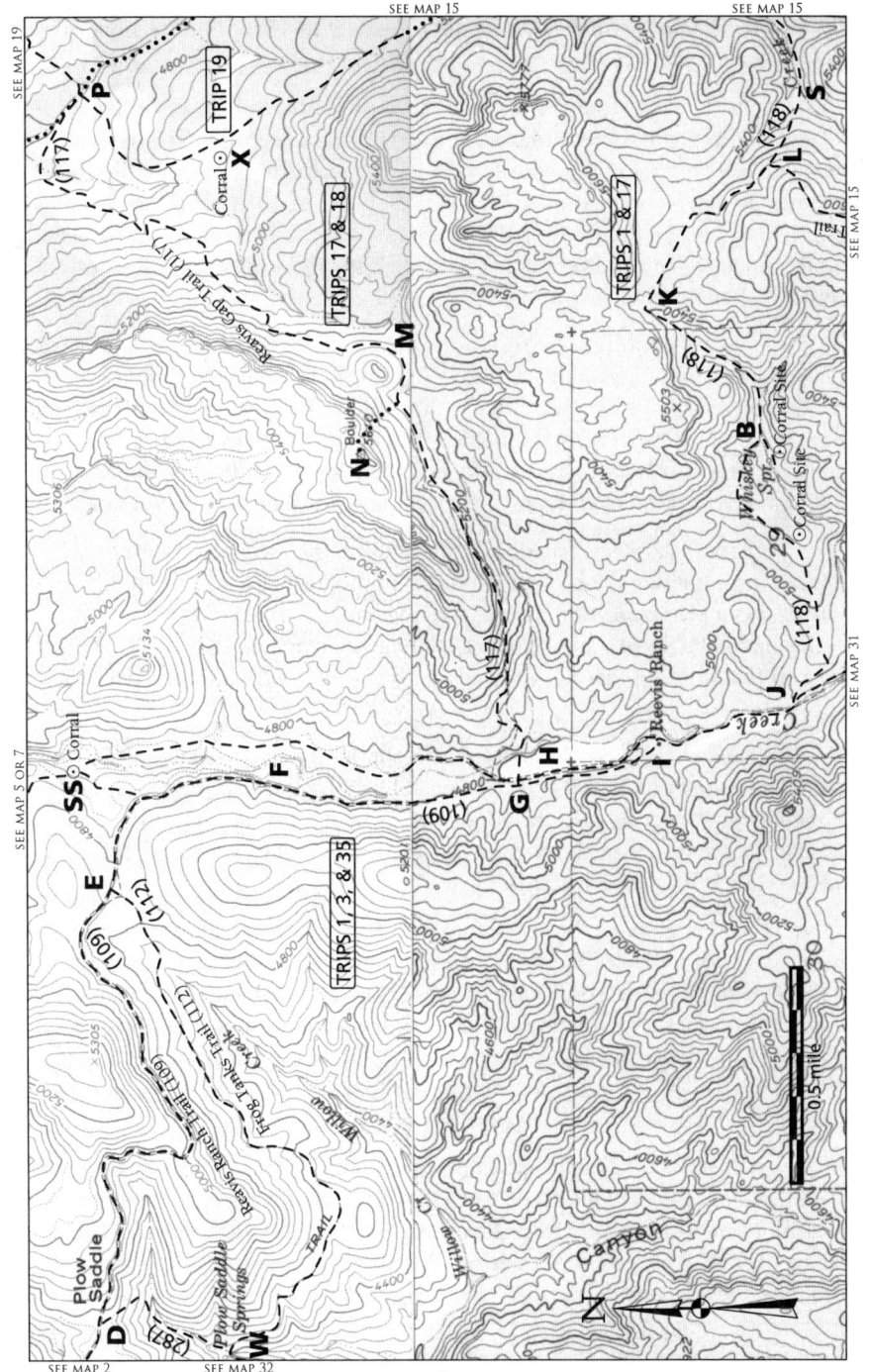

Map 4 – Trips 1, 2, 3, 17, 18, 34, and 35.

Reavis Trailhead—Trip 1. Reavis Ranch from Reavis Trailhead 55

the valley when he settled along Reavis Creek about 1876. For the story of Elisha Reavis, see Trip 34 (Rogers Trough to Reavis Ranch) on pages 262-264.

John J. "Jack" Fraser is prominent in the history of Reavis Valley. Fraser was living at Silver King as early as 1881 and had an interest in some Mineral Hill District mines with Robert Bowen and others. He won fifty head of cattle in an election bet at Silver King, probably in 1884, since he registered his JF brand on February 11, 1885. He began running the fifty head of cattle on the open range and eventually established his JF headquarters 7 miles southwest of Reavis Valley at the head of Fraser Canyon.[6]

Another important person in the history of Reavis Valley and Jack Fraser's operations was William "Billy" Knight. For part of his childhood, he lived at Silver King where his father, John Knight, ran a mercantile store. Billy kept the post office records and helped in the store. His father moved the store to Tempe in 1889 or 1890. Billy attended Tempe Normal School, and in 1892 he traveled to the JF Ranch for a visit and hired on with Jack Fraser.[7]

After Elisha Reavis died in 1896, Fraser expanded his ranching operation to include the possessory rights of the former Reavis farm. Reavis Ranch was a prime location for ranching, farming, and tourists because the valley had good spring water and a cool summer climate. About 1897, Fraser burned the building that Reavis used and replaced it with a cabin on a bench above the old cabin site.[8]

Fraser developed the property as a tourist pack-trip destination named Bloomerville. In 1899, the *Arizona Daily Gazette* reported four hardy Phoenicians venturing into the Superstitions on a hunting trip. Their snowy January horse ride took them to the Rogers Canyon cliff dwellings and to Reavis Ranch for a visit with Mr. Fraser.[9]

Billy Knight was the ranch foreman in 1910 when Jack Fraser sold his possessory rights for the JF and Reavis Ranches to William J. Clemans. Clemans and his three sons, Earle, Mark Twain, and William, Jr. continued with the summer resort theme and tried to promote the area with the new name of Pineair. By the 1920s interest diminished in Pineair, partly because of its remoteness, with the last mention in a 1924 newspaper article promising new road construction with support from the Tonto National Forest.[10]

William "Bill" Martin, Sr. came over from Globe in 1913 and hired on with foreman Billy Knight at the Clemans Cattle Company. His father, Arch Martin, brought his family from Texas and eventually settled on a ranch at Cherry Creek. After his father's death, Bill Martin, Sr., cowboyed for Henry Mounce and worked at other jobs before heading over to the Reavis Ranch.[11]

In 1909, Billy Knight, a United States citizen, initiated the homestead process for the Reavis property. Jack Fraser and Earle Clemans did not apply for the homestead, but they vouched for and supported Knight in the long process to obtain the legal title to the land. Billy Knight finally received the title for the sixty-five acres of Reavis Ranch in 1919.[12]

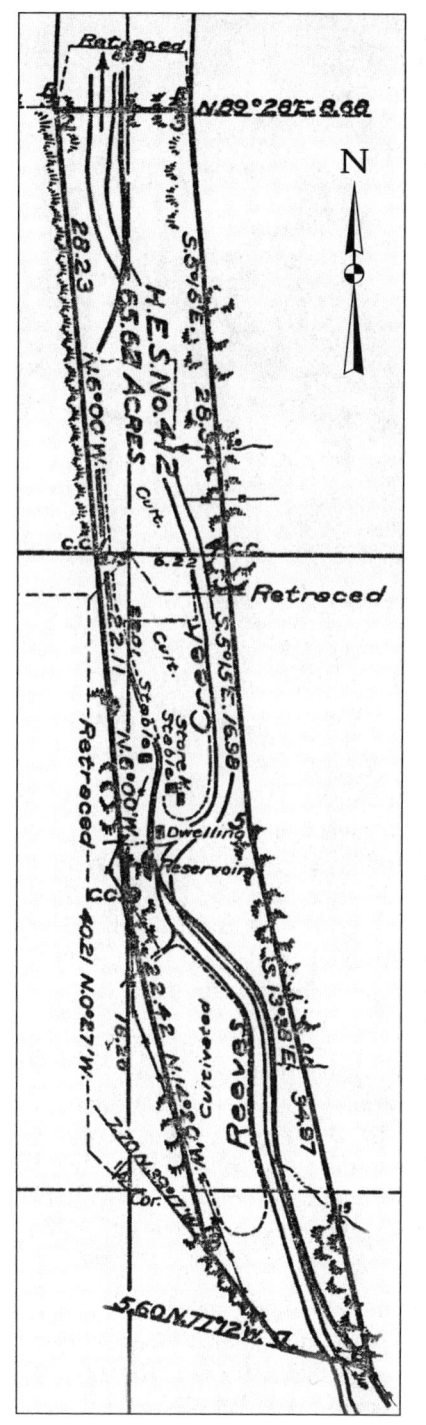

In 1913, Knight married Eunice Riggs who was a relative of the Clemans family. Eunice spent several years at both the JF and Reavis Ranches and recorded her experience in a journal, which was reprinted in the *Superstition Mountain Journal*, Volume 14, 1996. Herman Petrasch was working for the JF when Eunice arrived in 1914. She said he was a "carpenter, builder, cement and pipe man and water developer...On the side he was a prospector."[13] Bill Martin, Sr., moved up to the foreman job when Eunice and Billy Knight left the Reavis in 1915 to help Clemans with farms and ranches in the Florence area.

The wooden house that Jack Fraser built at Reavis burned in the mid 1930s. Two cowboys employed by Mark Twain Clemans replaced that house with a sandstone and adobe structure. Only the cement floor and stone walls of the building remained after the Clemans house burned in a November 1991 fire. The stone walls were taken down in January 1994.

Mark Twain Clemans is credited with planting six hundred apple trees, and subsequent owners Floyd

Homestead Entry Survey (HES 412) for William Knight's homestead at Reavis Ranch. The survey was completed on Feb. 10, 1916. Knight received the land patent on January 16, 1919. Survey map from the BLM, Phoenix Office.

Reavis Ranch circa late 1920s or early 1930s. The man standing on the right with the lead rope could be Ellis Toney, son of William Toney. The names of the other people are unknown. Courtesy of the Tonto National Forest, the Martin Ranch, and the Martin family. Photographer unknown.

and Lucille Stone planted more trees. The surviving trees usually produce apples each fall.

The Reavis Ranch was comprised of four headquarters areas—Reavis, JF, Tortilla, and Queen Creek. In 1946, the Reavis Ranch was divided with the desert portion on Queen Creek going to Bill Martin, Sr. At the same time, John Bacon and Charlie Upton purchased the JF, Tortilla, and Reavis portions. "Hoolie" was John Bacon's nickname, and Forest Service Trail (111) bears his name today—the Hoolie Bacon Trail. Construction on the Reavis Ranch Road, begun in 1910, was finally finished in 1947 by Bacon and Upton.[14]

When Bacon and Upton decided to sell in 1952, Bill Martin, Sr., bought the JF and Tortilla Ranches—the divided portions were now being described as ranches. Floyd "Stoney" Stone and his wife Lucille Bacon purchased the Reavis in 1955. Lucille was the adopted daughter of Hoolie Bacon. Martin then sold the Tortilla Ranch to the Stones who retained the JF brand for the Reavis and Tortilla while Martin used the J Slash A on the JF and Queen Creek Ranches.[15] See Trip 34 (Rogers Trough to Reavis Ranch) for more on the Martin Ranch history.

In 1966, the Stones sold all the private land on the Reavis Ranch—the Billy Knight homestead of 65.62 acres—to the Tonto National Forest in a trade for the IV Ranch, which is near Reavis Trailhead. The Billy Knight homestead was incorporated into the Superstition Wilderness in 1967.[16]

Trip 2

REAVIS FALLS

Reavis Falls is a spectacular destination in a remote part of the Superstition Wilderness. An unmaintained trail marks the way into the narrow canyon below the 196-foot waterfall. Reavis Creek provides water for people and stock.

ITINERARY

From the Reavis Trailhead, take Reavis Ranch Trail (109) for 3.2 miles to the unsigned Reavis Falls Trail. Descend to Reavis Creek and proceed up canyon to Reavis Falls. Return the same way.

DIFFICULTY

Difficult 1 or 2 day trip for hikers and riders. Elevation change is +1,600 and -1,790 feet one way.

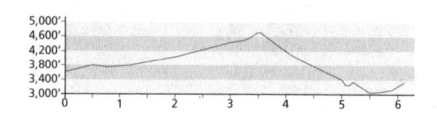

LENGTH and TIME

6.1 miles, 6.5 hours one way.

MAPS

Arizona USGS topo maps NAD27: Pinyon Mountain. Superstition Wilderness Beartooth map, grids K8 to M9. Maps 1 and 2.

FINDING THE TRAIL

Trailhead map is on page 46. Trail 109 starts from the parking lot at the end of FR212 (N33° 33' 23.9", W111° 13' 38.9") and follows the abandoned Reavis Ranch Road.

THE TRIP

Start on Map 1 on page 47. From the Reavis Trailhead [1-A, 0], follow Reavis Ranch Trail (109) as the trail winds its way around the ridges. Use Castle Dome Peak [1-C] as a landmark since the Reavis Falls Trail junction is about 1 mile north of Castle Dome Peak. When the Reavis Ranch Trail turns south for a long stretch, near the headwaters of Lewis and Pranty Creek, you are near the unsigned Reavis Falls Trail [1-X, 3.2]. The Reavis Falls Trail junction is easy to miss, so look closely for small rock cairns on the left (east) side of

Reavis Falls Trail [1-X] heads uphill when it branches left (east) from the Reavis Ranch Trail (109) at a small rock cairn. The peak of Castle Dome can be seen on the horizon. Photo taken in March 2008.

the Reavis Ranch Trail. From the Reavis Trailhead, you will reach the Reavis Falls Trail junction [2-X, 3.2] (N33° 32' 45.5", W111° 11' 24.6") in about 1 hour and 20 minutes.

If you pass through a barbed wire fence line on the Reavis Ranch Trail or if you have gone south of Castle Dome Peak, you have missed the Reavis Falls Trail and you need to backtrack on the Reavis Ranch Trail.

The Reavis Falls Trail [2-X, 3.2] branches off to the left (southeast) from the Reavis Ranch Trail and goes up a grassy hill on a narrow, but well-worn track. Follow the trail as it goes through an open gate and cut fence, crosses a low pass, heads south and downhill, and then turns east toward a large juniper tree and a stone ruin [2-Y, 3.9]. At the prehistoric ruin, the trail makes a sharp turn to the right (south) and goes down the right side of a ravine, heading south, on the northwest side of Lime Mountain. The trail crosses Lime Mountain Pass [4.3] to the north side of Lime Mountain following the Lime Mountain ridge east and then northeast to Maple Spring [5.1]. Lime Mountain resembles a hogback ridge, not a mountain.

A cement slab at Maple Spring was probably the site of a concrete water trough—the remains are about 75 feet to the east near the wash. The wash here may have running water in the wet seasons. The trail becomes vague after crossing the small wash, but you can follow the rock cairns. Continuing northeast, up and over a small ridge [2-K, 5.3], and down the steep hill takes you to Reavis Creek [2-M, 5.5] (N33° 32' 24.7", W111° 09' 58.1"). Horse riders will have to leave their stock on the east side of Reavis Creek, when they first enter the creek, since the downed and overhanging trees make traveling a challenge going upstream even while walking. Reavis Creek usually has water from this junction up to the falls.

Follow Reavis Creek to the right (south) going upstream and staying on the left (east) bank for the first few hundred yards. Some signs of a trail exist along the streambed, but the 0.6 mile up the creek is slow going as you climb around rocks and duck under branches.

The canopy of cottonwood, oak, willow, and walnut trees along Reavis Creek makes this a cool and shady place to camp in the hotter months, but in the winter the air can be a bit damp and cold. The trail goes through most of the campsites, so you might not get the privacy you expected in this remote canyon.

The trip ends at the base of Reavis Falls [2-R, 6.1] (N33° 31' 57", W111° 09' 59") where you have plenty of room to eat lunch and relax for the return trip. Water cascades through a slot in the cliff above, but when the water level is low, the water only dribbles down the right face of the cliff. Return the same way.

OPTIONAL TRIP

To get to the west rim for a bird's-eye view of Reavis Falls, backtrack on Reavis Falls Trail from Reavis Creek 0.2 mile to the high point [2-K] on the trail. Look to the left (south) for some short wooden posts in the ground—the remains of a former fence line. Head uphill (south) and follow the faint trail and remains of the fence posts to the top for a view of Reavis Falls. We saw horse tracks along the former fence line. The lower viewpoint [2-L] is on a steep slope (not suitable for horses), so use caution when scrambling on the hillside. This optional round trip will add about 1 mile to your trek with a steep 500-foot elevation gain.

From our vantage point [2-L] on the west rim of Reavis Creek, it looks like it is possible to head across the top of the ridge going farther south and then heading east to the top of Reavis Falls. We did not see any cliffs or obstacles that would block this route, but we have not field checked this approach to the falls.

For other routes to Reavis Falls, see Trip 6 (Pine Creek to Reavis Falls) and Trip 3 (Reavis Falls from Reavis Ranch).

View of Reavis Falls from the west rim of Reavis Creek Canyon at location [2-L] in Trip 2. Only a small trickle of water flows over the cliff. The debris pile, that probably broke off the right side of the cliff, can be seen at the bottom of the falls. Photo was taken in March 2008.

HISTORY AND LEGENDS

We do not known who was the first to discover Reavis Falls, but Nyle Leatham wrote a story that describes the modern day discovery. Allen Blackman told Tom Kollenborn about the falls sometime in 1982 or 1983, and shortly after, Tom and Bud Lane rode horseback to check out the falls. Nyle suggested that the falls be named Kollenborn Falls, and to this day, some people badger Tom about the naming idea, even though Tom did not want his name used. We believe that Tom is the only person to have measured the height of the falls—196 feet.[17]

The November 1993 issue of *Arizona Highways* features an article on Reavis Falls by Stan Smith with photographs by David Elms, Jr. The photographs and article are worth reviewing if you plan to attempt this trek. On our first trip in 1998, we hiked to the falls on a route suggested by David. A very wide angle lens for your camera will help you get a top-to-bottom photo of the falls. His photos from the west rim were taken near the location [4-L] described in our Optional Trip.[18]

Charles Liu, in *60 Hikes within 60 Miles, Phoenix*, notes that the large pool at the base of Reavis Falls was buried by a rock slide in January 2004.[19] On our last trip to the falls in March 2008, we noticed that a small pool was forming, but the water was running downstream under the rubble. It looked like the slide broke off the hill on the west side of the falls, which may have been undercut by seeping water. Only the top of the large boulder—where hikers posed for photos—is sticking out of the debris. Until the rubble is washed downstream, the rock slide has temporarily shortened the height of the falls by 15 or 20 feet.

The Reavis Falls Trail, from the ruin [2-Y] near the large juniper tree heading downslope and across Lime Mountain, may be a prehistoric route. We noted the outline of several ruins along the trail to Maple Spring. This arrangement of settlements on a ridge and the points of ridges, all connected by a trail, follows a similar pattern of habitation that we have observed in other parts of the eastern Superstition Mountains.

Trip 3

REAVIS FALLS FROM REAVIS RANCH

Abandoned trails and cross-country travel take you to the top of Reavis Falls. Travel through brushy forests, over grassy mesas, and into cavernous Reavis Canyon will make this a challenge to seasoned trekkers. The 196-foot waterfall on Reavis Creek is a spectacular destination in a remote part of the Wilderness.

ITINERARY

From the Reavis Ranch area, take Reavis Ranch Trail (109) to Government Corral. Use abandoned trails and cross-country travel to drop into Reavis Canyon. Follow Reavis Creek to the top of Reavis Falls. Return the same way.

DIFFICULTY

Very difficult 1 day trip for hikers and riders. Elevation change is +190 and -1,550 feet one way.

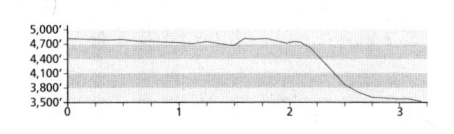

LENGTH and TIME

3.1 miles, 5 hours one way.

MAPS

Arizona USGS topo maps NAD27: Pinyon Mountain, Iron Mountain. Superstition Wilderness Beartooth map, grids N11 to M9. Maps 2, 3, and 5.

FINDING THE TRAIL

Take Trip 1 to [3-G] as described on pages 48 to 50. The trip starts at the wooden trail sign [3-G, 0] (N33° 29' 46", W111° 09' 23") on the Reavis Ranch Trail (109) at the junction with the Reavis Gap Trail (117).

THE TRIP

Start on Map 3 on page 53. The route takes you through the forest and over the mesas on the west side of Reavis Creek for most of this trek. Horse riders will have to leave their mounts on the mesa [5-Q, 2.2] before the descent into Reavis Canyon. This trip does not go into the bed of Reavis Creek until you are close to Reavis Falls.

From the Reavis Gap Trail (117) junction [3-G, 0], follow the Reavis Ranch Trail (109) for 1 mile going north. Before the trail curves left (west) take the second road track heading downhill to the right (east). In 2003, we saw a short signpost (without a sign) near the road track. We think this was the signpost for the former Government Corral and Government Camp. From the road track, take one of the many trails in the area and head north for 0.1 mile to a wooden corral (Government Corral) [5-SS, 1.1]. If you had difficulty finding Government Corral, this trip might not be for you, since the route finding becomes extremely difficult later in the trip. Be sure you remember how to retrace your route back to camp.

From the center of Government Corral, head north through the corral gate and look for a faint trail marked by rock cairns and maybe horse tracks. Take the trail to the top of the hill and continue on an almost completely overgrown trail. Watching for rock cairns, following the curved bed of the old trail, and using your map, compass, and GPS will help you through this area. We have been lost here several times!

At a small ravine [5-I, 1.5], you will notice some trail construction heading west as the route ascends the north side of the ravine. At the top of the hill, the trail goes through a prehistoric ruin. Do not remove anything from the archaeological site. From the ruin, set a cross-country course across

Government Corral [5-SS] along route to the top of Reavis Falls. Photo was taken in December 2004.

the grassy slope heading northwest to a collapsed gate in a fence line [5-G, 1.9]. The gate in the fence line can be identified from a distance by the white soil in the area.

Stay along the left (west) side of the mesa, and head northwest to the edge of the mesa. Near the north edge of the mesa, you should see rock cairns leading down to the start of an overgrown, but well-defined trail [5-Q, 2.2] (N33° 31' 21", W111° 10' 03"). Don't drop off the mesa before finding the trail. Horse riders should leave their horses on the mesa.

Continue down the trail to a switchback [5-P, 2.4] (N33° 31' 28", W111° 09' 58"). From here go cross-country down a steep slope to Reavis Creek. This is a rough bushwhack, and you need to mark your route so you can return the same way. If you follow the trail from [5-P, 2.4] farther downhill, the trail leads to a steeply eroded bank that perilously drops off into Reavis Creek. Don't risk climbing the eroded bank into Reavis Creek. Boulders could pull out of the dirt cliff. The trail, which you do not want to follow, ends in Plow Saddle Canyon [5-O] in another 0.2 mile at three 50-foot waterfalls that block access to Reavis Creek.

In 1985, horse riders head across the mesa to the top of the switchback trail [5-Q] leading down to Reavis Creek and Reavis Falls in Trip 3. Riders left to right: unknown, Arkie Johnston, Tony Backus, Jerry Walton, and Bill Smith. Photographer unknown. Courtesy of Bill Smith.

Map 5 – Trips 1, 2, 3, 6, and 35.

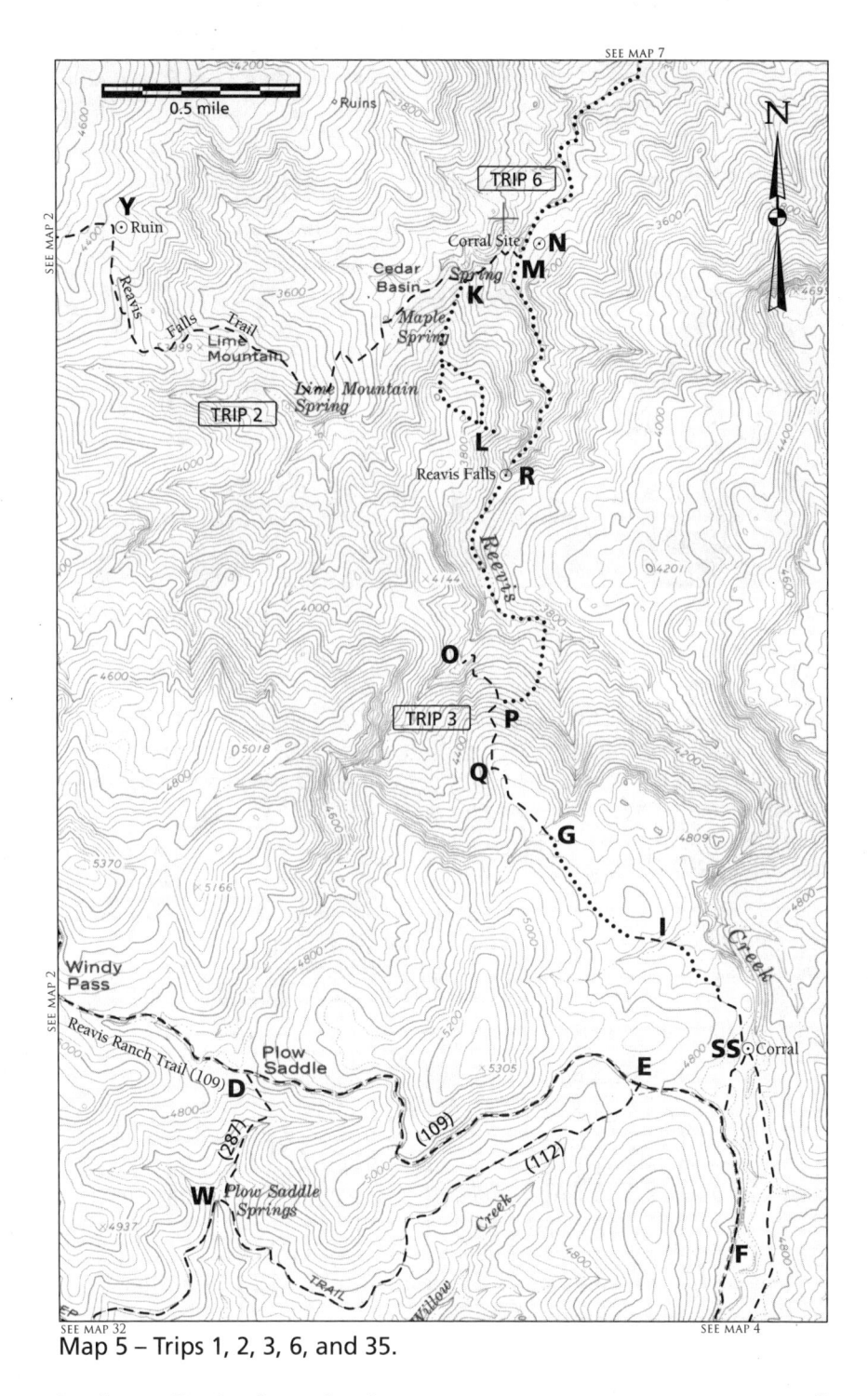

Reavis Trailhead—Trip 3. Reavis Falls from Reavis Ranch 67

Bill Smith at the top of Reavis Falls. See Trip 3 for the route description. Photographer unknown, 1985. Courtesy of Bill Smith.

Once in Reavis Creek, follow the game trail, which is often on the left (west) bank, to the top of Reavis Falls [5-R, 3.1] (N33° 31' 57", W111° 09' 59"). The creek usually has some water, but the water often goes underground at the waterfall. Return the same way.

HISTORY AND LEGENDS

Ken Nelssen worked for the Tonto Basin Ranger District from 1954 to 1979. He said his trail crews camped at Government Corral while working on the trails and trail signs in the Reavis Valley. He would get them started by showing the young crew members how to cook on an open fire, and then he left them in the Reavis area to do the trail work.[20]

In 1985, Arkie Johnston, who was working for Chuck Backus at the Quarter Circle U Ranch, guided Backus, Bill Smith, Merlin Yeager, Jerry Walton, Tony Backus, and Paul Russell on a horse pack trip to Reavis Valley. The Reavis Ranch house was still standing at that time and they made that their headquarters for the trip. From Reavis Ranch, they made a day trip to the top of Reavis Falls using the route we described for this trip. They rode their horses to the grassy mesa [5-Q], went on foot down the abandoned trail to Reavis Creek, and continued downstream to Reavis Falls.[21] See Trip 2 for the discovery story of Reavis Falls.

PINE CREEK TRAILHEAD

Pine Creek Trailhead is east of SR88, between mileposts 232 and 233, about 33 miles northeast of Apache Junction and 9 miles southwest of Roosevelt Lake Dam. Go east on FR665 and drive 0.6 mile over the hill to the first water trough. FR665 is 1.1 miles southwest of the Pine Creek Bridge on SR88.

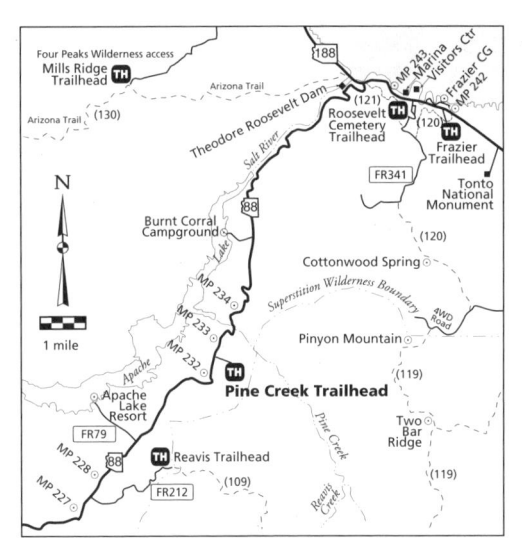

FINDING THE TRAILHEAD

Go north on SR88 about 2.5 miles past the Apache Lake Marina Road. Or, from Roosevelt Lake, go south on SR88 9 miles. When you turn east on the signed FR665, between mileposts 232 and 233, you will see a metal corral [6-A] ahead. Continue through the gate on the left side of the metal corral. FR665 goes 0.6 mile up and over a hill to a concrete water trough and the unsigned trailhead area [6-B] (N33° 35' 01.8", W111° 12' 18.5").

FR665 is a one lane, dirt road with eroded sections requiring a high-clearance vehicle and possibly four-wheel-drive if the road is not maintained. Park at the metal corral [6-A] (near N33° 35' 22", W111° 12' 32") if your vehicle or trailer can't negotiate FR665. Don't block access to the corral.

We have also parked our vehicle on either side of the Pine Creek Bridge [6-K] on SR88, but there is not much room to pull off the road. Parking along the road is somewhat hazardous. For a short walk up Pine Creek from the bridge, it might be okay to park along the road for a while, but for any day trip or overnight trip, it is best to park on FR665 where you can avoid the traffic and you have plenty of room to unload stock animals.

FINDING THE TRAIL

The route heads northeast from the concrete water trough [6-B] (N33° 35' 01.8", W111° 12' 18.5") near the end of FR665 and shortly turns east.

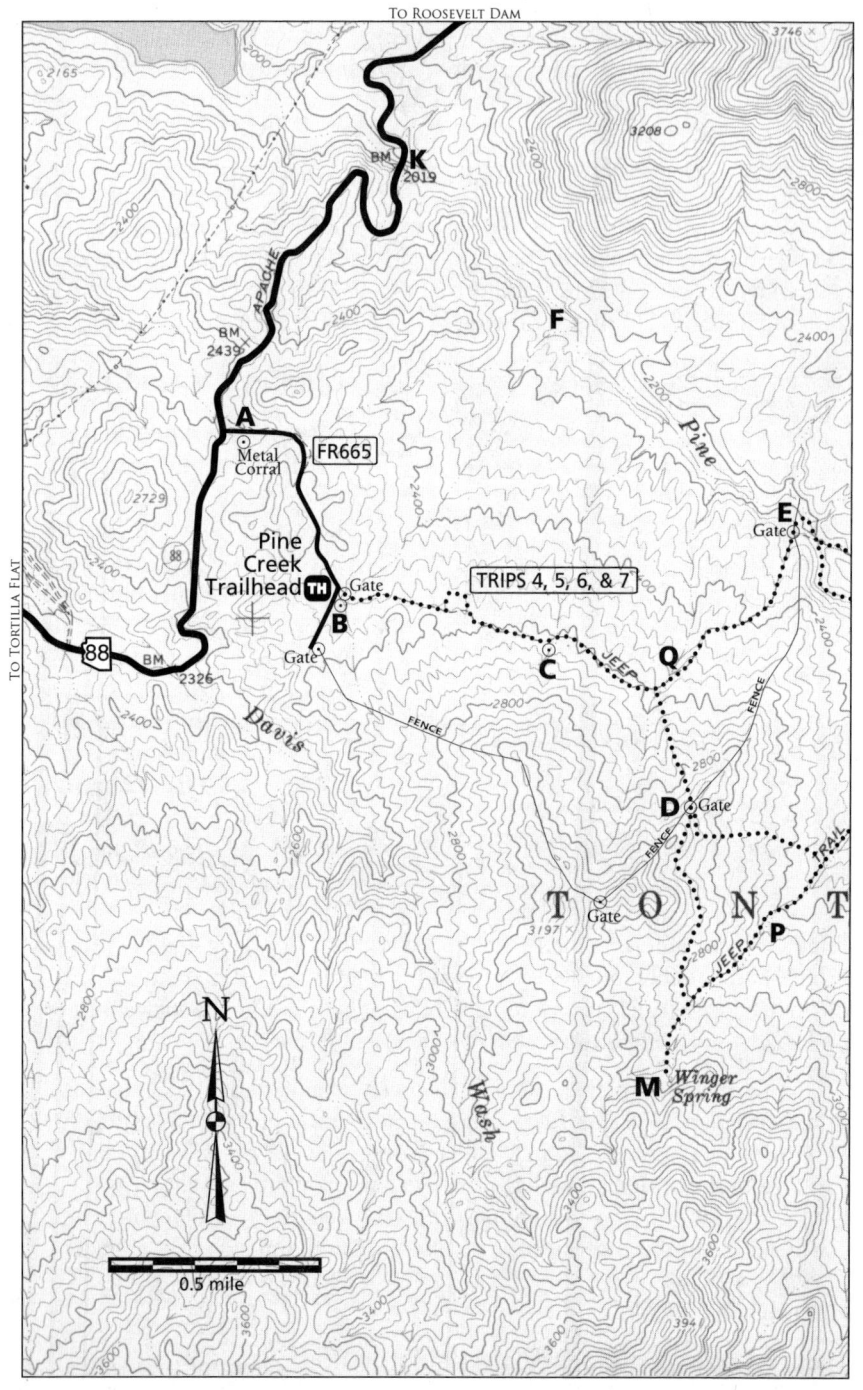

Map 6 – Trips 4, 5, 6, and 7.

Map 6 continued – Trips 4, 5, 6, and 7.

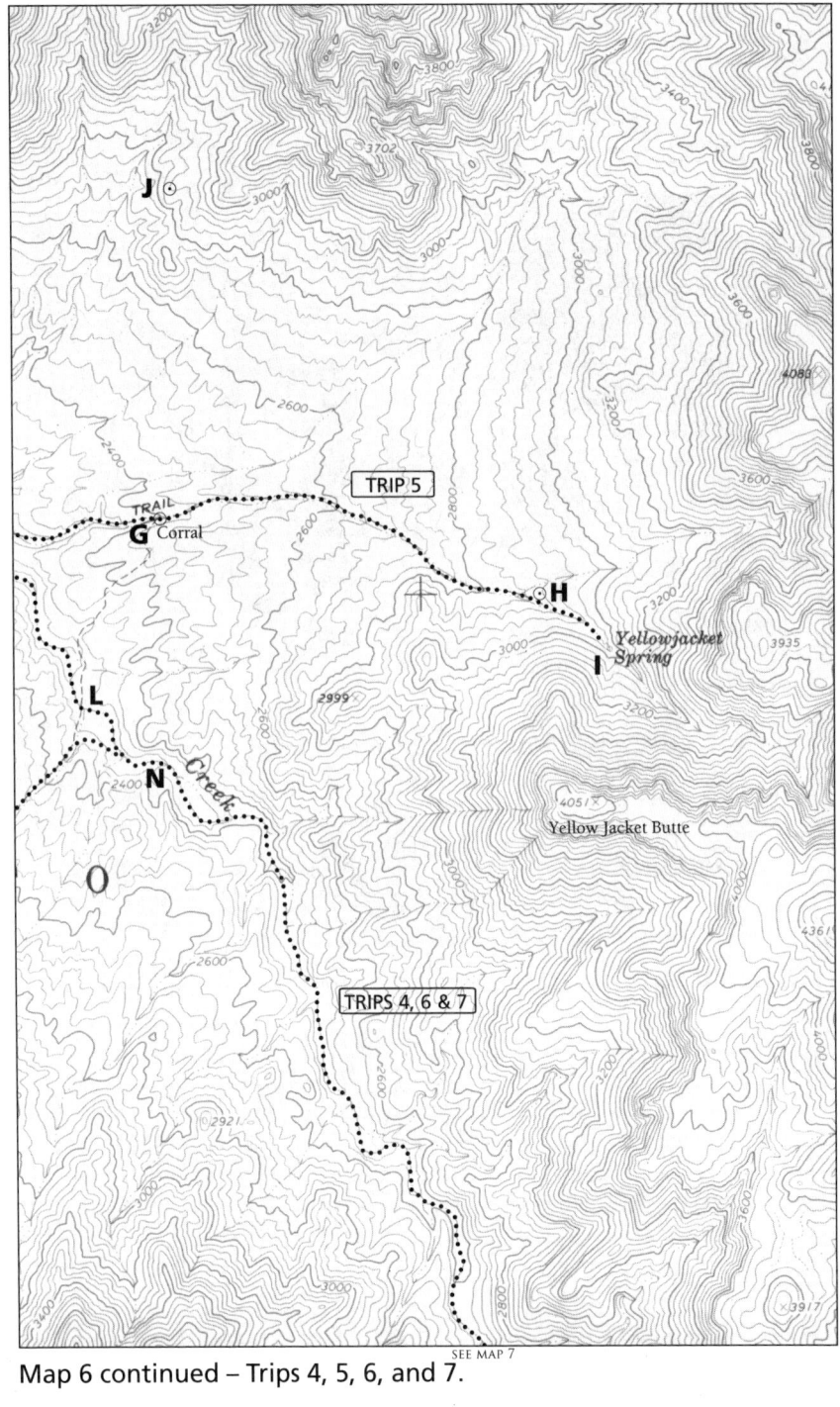

Lower Pine Creek near the former Jeep Road crossing [6-E]. Photo was taken in April 2008.

FACILITIES

No facilities are located at the Pine Creek Trailhead. Do not park next to the water trough, fences, gates, corral, or on the road. Ranch operations require access to all of these range improvements. Cattle may dent your vehicle if you park too closely. Bring your own water. The water troughs may be dry if no cattle are in the pastures.

Trip 4

LOWER PINE CREEK

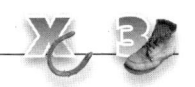

Lower Pine Creek is a historic area where the military once camped in 1872, and early pioneers used the trails to reach the high country. The trip involves mostly cross-county travel through sandy washes and across deeply cut ravines. Pine Creek has seasonal water.

ITINERARY

From the concrete water trough on FR665, go east on the track of a former jeep trail to Pine Creek. Continue up Pine Creek to the junction with Reavis Creek. Return the same way.

DIFFICULTY

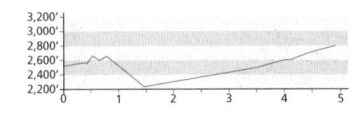

Difficult hike. Not recommended for horses. Horse riders may not be able to negotiate the steep ravines and rocky canyons. Hikers can scramble through the ravines and creek bed. Elevation change is +690 and -420 feet one way.

LENGTH and TIME

4.8 miles, 6.5 hours one way.

MAPS

Arizona USGS topo map NAD27: Pinyon Mountain. Superstition Wilderness Beartooth map, grids L7 to M8. Maps 6 and 7.

FINDING THE TRAIL

Trailhead map is on page 69. The route starts near the end of FR665 at the concrete water trough [6-B] (N33° 35' 1.8", W111° 12' 18.5").

THE TRIP

Start on Map 6 on page 70. The trip follows an abandoned road that is shown as *jeep trail* on the Pinyon Mountain USGS topo map. The jeep trail is now not much more than a vague route that is washed out by the eroding granite hillside. Crossing the deep V-shaped gullies on your route makes traveling slow and tedious.

From the Pine Creek Trailhead [6-B, 0] near the end of FR665, head northeast from the concrete water trough and go through the adjacent closed gate. The sandy wash goes northeasterly, but you want to head more easterly. Within 100 yards of the gate, you should see evidence of the former jeep trail on your right, now an unsigned route, which begins in a southeast direction and then turns to the east. Heading toward Yellow Jacket Butte will keep you going in the correct direction. The sandy wash running northeast will take you to a downstream area of Pine Creek, and you can use this wash as a return route from Pine Creek, which is described later in this trip as Option 1.

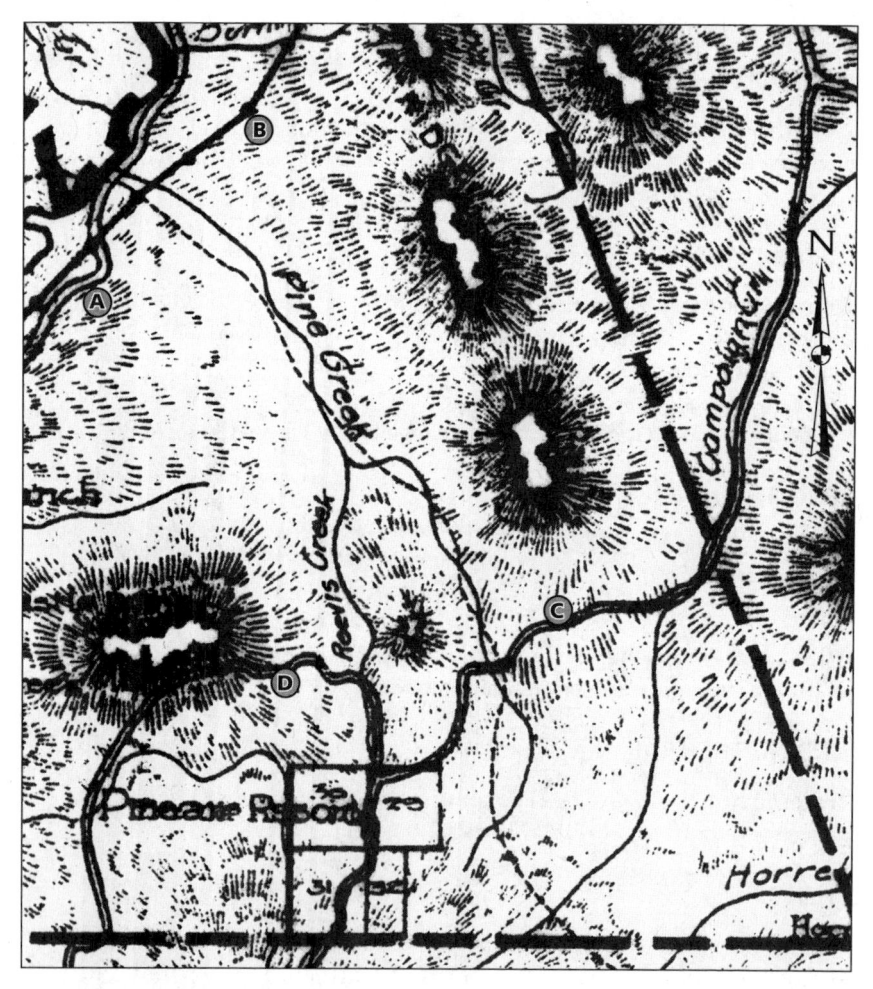

Map of Central Arizona by F. N. Holmquist, 1916. Remnants of the trail (small dashed line) shown along Pine Creek remain today, but the trail is difficult to follow. The map shows the former Roosevelt Road and now Apache Trail (A), Transmission Line (B), Reavis Gap Trail (C), Reavis Ranch Trail (D). Pineair Resort was located at Reavis Ranch. Courtesy of Arizona State Archives, Map Room.

Following the former jeep trail, you pass a metal Wilderness boundary sign [6-C, 0.6] (N33° 34' 57.1", W111° 11' 46.0") as you make your way across the V-shaped gullies. The trick to staying on the route is to imagine the route as a road and only go where a jeep could have gone.

As an optional route, we sometimes leave the former jeep trail when the route turns north into a wide wash. Here we turn southeast and climb up the hill to a gate in the barbed wire fence [6-D] (N33° 34' 37.1", W111° 11' 25.5"). From the gate, we head downhill going cross-country to Winger Wash. This route is not any easier than sticking with the former jeep trail—they are both tedious treks. If you miss the gate at [6-D], either climb over the fence or look for the gate—do not cut any fences. In 1999, we followed a trail through the gate, but in 2008, the trail was not visible.

We continue the trip description at the wide wash where the jeep trail begins to meander in a northerly direction [6-Q, 1.0]. The route goes down the center of the wide wash and out of the wash on the right bank onto the former road cut (N33° 34' 53.1", W111° 11' 27.8"). The route continues across the top of a ridge and then drops, to the right, into another wash.

Following the wash in a northerly direction, you come to a water-gap fence across the wash, which hikers can cross by standing on a large flat rock in the middle of the wash. Horse riders can go through the gate here [6-E, 1.5] (N33° 35' 10.9", W111° 11' 8.6"). Don't open the gate unless you absolutely need to open it. The gate is a long stretch of heavy fence, and the gate may be difficult to close. Pine Creek is just beyond the wire fence and gate. The former jeep trail goes into the creek here, heads upstream a little way, and continues up a wash on the left (east).

Once you arrive at Pine Creek [6-E, 1.5], you have several trip options. (1) Go downstream (northwest) 0.8 mile to the sandy wash [6-F, 2.3] (N33° 35' 34.4", W111° 11' 42.2") that heads uphill and southwest to the Pine Creek Trailhead [6-B, 3.2]. If you miss the turn at the sandy wash, you end up at the Pine Creek Bridge on SR88 [6-K, 2.9]. From the bridge, another 1.1 miles, mostly uphill on SR88, takes you to the metal corral [6-A, 4.0] and to the beginning of the trip [6-B, 4.6]. (2) Continue on the track of the jeep trail to Yellow Jacket Spring [6-I, 3.2] as described in Trip 5 (Yellow Jacket Spring). (3) Follow the cross-county route up Pine Creek to the junction of Reavis Creek [7-S, 4.8], which is the destination of this trip (Trip 4).

Continuing the Trip 4 description from where we first arrived at Pine Creek [6-E, 1.5], head upstream (southeast) in the bed of Pine Creek. Horse riders will have trouble in Pine Creek due to the narrow, slick rock canyon. Large cottonwood trees dot the course of the normally dry creek and make a nice place for a rest or lunch. Winger Wash comes in from the right (south) [6-L, 2.1], and you can make a 1.1 mile side trip up to Winger Spring [6-M].

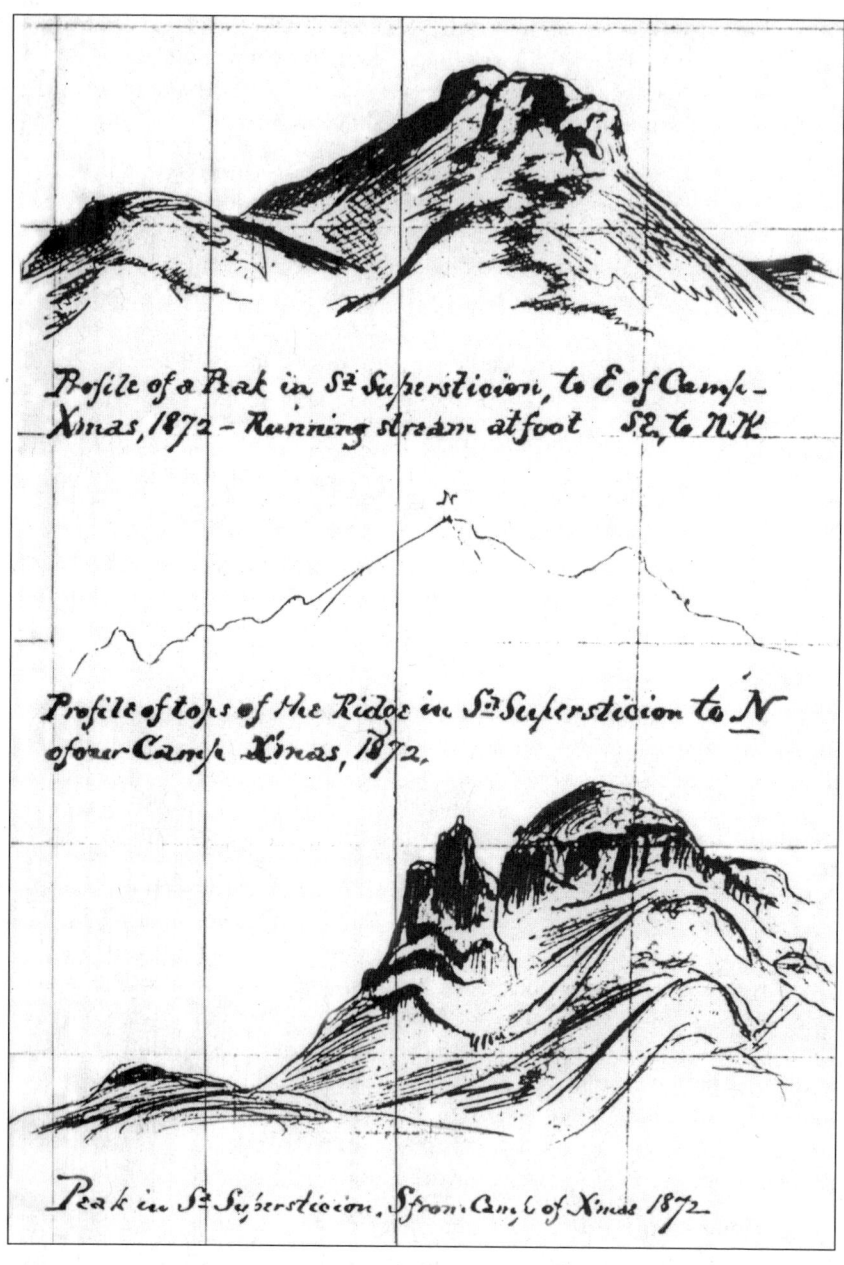

Profile of a Peak in S⁴ Supersticion, to E of Camp Xmas, 1872 – Running stream at foot S.E. to N.W.

Profile of tops of the Ridge in S⁴ Supersticion to N of our Camp Xmas, 1872.

Peak in S⁴ Supersticion, S from Cam, 6 of Xmas 1872

Page from John G. Bourke's diary showing the three sketches he made on December 25, 1872 from his camp on Pine Creek. We estimate that his camp [6-N] was just upstream (south) on Pine Creek from the junction with Winger Wash. We named the top sketch Yellow Jacket Butte. We named the butte with the pinnacle-like formation in the lower sketch Bourke's Butte, although he incorrectly noted the butte as Weavers Needle on one of his maps. Map from ASU Hayden Library, Special Collections.[22]

Lower Pine Creek near Winger Wash [6-L] with Bourke's Butte on the horizon. The butte in this photo is similar to the lower sketch on the opposite page that John Bourke made on December 25, 1872 and labeled "Peak in Sierra Superstition, South from Camp of Xmas 1872." Photo taken in May 2008.

When the creek is dry in the lower section, we have found water in the creek as we proceeded upstream. A pour-off in the bed of Pine Creek at a large pool of water [7-TT, 4.4] (N33° 33' 20", W111° 09' 48") blocks travel up the creek bed, which we bypassed on the right (south). A good trail on the right takes you to the top of a ridge overlooking the creek where horse riders will have to end their trip. The trail seemed to end at the top of the ridge, but we continued, bushwhacking down a steep dirt slope—holding onto the side of a cliff and the vegetation. We didn't check for a possible route on the north side of the pour-off.

Continue up the potholed bedrock of Pine Creek to the junction of Reavis Creek [7-S, 4.8] where this trip ends. Seasonal water collects in the potholes here.

If you are camping in this rugged area, check the east bench farther upstream on Pine Creek [7-V] (N33° 33' 02", W111° 09' 12") for a flat campsite. The 1916 Pine Creek Trail goes through that camp and also goes through a gate or cut fence [7-UU] (N33° 33' 07", W111° 09' 29") on a nearby ridge

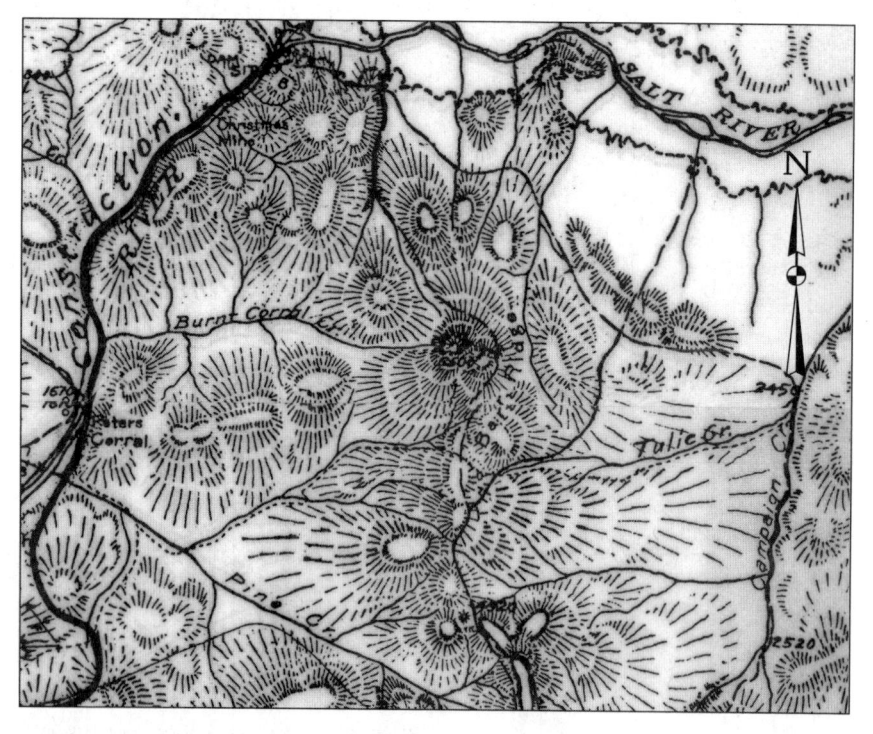

Map shows a trail (dashed line) on Pine Creek and Tulie [sic] Creek that could have been used by the 1872 U.S. Army Military Campaign. USGS Reconnaissance Map of Country between Salt River Reservoir and Phoenix, A. P. Davis, Engineer, July 1903. Courtesy of Arizona State Archives.

to the northwest of the camp. Following Reavis Creek from the junction with Pine Creek for 1.6 miles will take you to Reavis Falls [7-R] as described in Trip 6 (Pine Creek to Reavis Falls).

HISTORY AND LEGENDS

The 1916 *Map of Central Arizona* by F. N. Holmquist on page 74 shows a trail that follows Pine Creek from the Salt River to the headwaters of Pine Creek. We have traced the trail on the ground from the Fire Line Trail down to the junction with Reavis Creek. Just below Reavis Creek, the terrain opens up and many possibilities exist for the course of the trail, but the trail probably used the low benches on either side of the creek. Well-known people used this trail and their stories are told elsewhere in this book—Jacob Waltz (page 89), Elisha Reavis and Matt Cavaness (page 262).

In 1872, the U.S. Army came over Two Bar Ridge from Tule Creek and descended into Pine Creek drainage for their December 25 camp. Major Brown's men could have entered Pine Creek on the trail shown on the A. P. Davis 1903 *USGS Reconnaissance Map of Country Between Salt River Reservoir and Phoenix*. From the 1903 map on the opposite page, the trail looks like it might have gone north of Yellow Jacket Spring, but we have not field checked that route into the hills for signs of a trail yet. Author and outdoorsman Bruce Grubbs hiked through the steep hills south of the 4,083-foot elevation notation on the Pinyon Mountain topo map, so he may have been near the route of the old trail.[23]

On December 25, 1872, Major Brown probably camped [6-N] on Pine Creek just upstream from the junction with Winger Wash. The three sketches on page 76 that John Bourke drew of the surrounding mountains match this location. Captain Burns was camped one-half mile to the west, which was probably in Winger Wash [6-P]. According to Bourke's diary entry for December 26, scouts came into camp with news that a fresh trail had been found. The decision was made here in Pine Creek to combine the commands of Brown and Burns totaling 220 fighting men and proceed across the Salt River to the Yavapai stronghold. The battle, which took place on December 28, would later be referred to as the Skeleton Cave Massacre. See History and Legends (Tule Trailhead, page 117) for more of the military campaign in this area and Bourke's map on page 121.

At Winger Spring the inscription on the concrete and rock water trough reads *Winger Spring Trough, made by E. Daley, July 31, 1919*. We have not been able to find any history relating to Winger Spring or E. Daley.

Trip 5

YELLOW JACKET SPRING

The trip to Yellow Jacket Spring takes you across hillsides of decomposing granite that are dotted with saguaro cactus. The open landscape provides sweeping views of the mountains surrounding the Lower Pine Creek valley. Yellow Jacket Spring usually has water.

ITINERARY

From the Pine Creek Trailhead, follow a former jeep trail to Pine Creek. Continue east, following the route of the old jeep trail to Yellow Jacket Spring. Return the same way.

DIFFICULTY

Difficult hike. Not recommended for horses because of the deeply cut ravines. Elevation change is +900 and -430 feet one way.

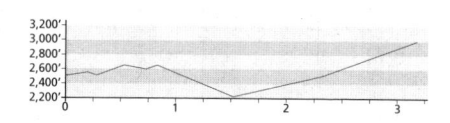

LENGTH and TIME

3.2 miles, 2 hours one way.

MAPS

Arizona USGS topo map NAD27: Pinyon Mountain. Superstition Wilderness Beartooth map, grids L7 to N7. Map 6.

FINDING THE TRAIL

Trailhead map is on page 69. The route starts near the end of FR665 at the concrete water trough [6-B, 0] (N33° 35' 01.8", W111° 12' 18.5").

THE TRIP

Start on Map 6 on page 70. From the Pine Creek Trailhead [6-B, 0], follow the directions in Trip 4 (Lower Pine Creek) to Pine Creek [6-E, 1.5].

  From Pine Creek, head east on the route of the former jeep trail by following the wash that leads to Yellow Jacket Spring. We only found short stretches of the jeep road, so following the Yellow Jacket Spring Wash is the easiest route. If you came down Winger Wash, go cross-country, heading north and northeast until you intercept Yellow Jacket Spring Wash near a corral [6-G] on the north side of the wash.

The route takes you by a corral [6-G, 2.0] on the north bank of Yellow Jacket Spring Wash, which you might not be able to see from the wash. Continuing east, you will find Yellow Jacket Spring water trough and corral [6-H, 3.0] (N33° 35' 00", W111° 09' 43") on the north side of the wash. You can follow the water pipes from the trough to Yellow Jacket Spring [6-I, 3.2], which is in a narrow ravine farther to the east. Return the same way.

While traveling in the Lower Pine Creek valley, you probably have been curious about the white quartz outcrop [6-J] (N33° 35' 47", W111° 10' 33") on the eastern hillside. On one trip, we hiked over to the outcrop to get a closer look. We didn't see any evidence of mining at the outcrop, and from our observation, the quartz did not contain silver or gold.

HISTORY AND LEGENDS

Rancher Dwight Cooper, who brands the Hay Hook, told how he cleaned out the Yellow Jacket Spring. When we were at the spring, we noticed the opening was only about one foot high, which led to a larger chamber inside. He said he kept the entrance small to keep the javelina and other animals out. When his children were small, he had them muck and pull out the roots from the chamber of the spring. The spring was chilly inside with cold water running from the ceiling. When the children came out of the spring, he had a warm blanket waiting for them and quickly wrapped them in it. That was many years ago. The children are adults now—having outgrown that advantage of being small.[24]

Jack Carlson looking at water flowing out of hole under cliff at Yellow Jacket Spring [6-I]. Jan. 2002.

Trip 6

PINE CREEK TO REAVIS FALLS

Traveling up Pine Creek brings you to the junction with Reavis Creek where the water has cut through bedrock to form a narrow canyon. Trekking on these game and former cowboy trails is a true Wilderness experience in this seldom traveled region that takes you to Reavis Falls.

ITINERARY

From the Pine Creek Trailhead, follow a cross-country course, which eventually traces the bed of Pine Creek to the junction of Reavis Creek. Go cross-country up Reavis Creek to Reavis Falls. Return the same way or make a loop to Reavis Trailhead.

DIFFICULTY

Difficult 2 or 3 day trip. Elevation change is +970 and -420 feet one way. Not recommended for horses due to the rough terrain and lack of trails.

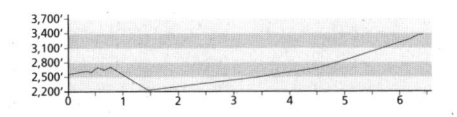

LENGTH and TIME

6.4 miles, 9 hours one way.

MAPS

Arizona USGS topo maps NAD27: Pinyon Mountain. Superstition Wilderness Beartooth map, grids L7 to M9. Maps 6 and 7.

FINDING THE TRAIL

Trailhead map is on page 69. The route starts near the end of FR665 at the concrete water trough [6-B] (N33° 35' 01.8", W111° 12' 18.5").

THE TRIP

Start on Map 6 on page 70. From the Pine Creek Trailhead [6-B, 0], follow the directions in Trip 4 (Lower Pine Creek) to Reavis Creek. From the junction with Pine Creek [7-S, 4.8], the trek up Reavis Creek to Reavis Falls is straightforward creek bushwhacking. Seasonal pothole water near the junction of Pine Creek and Reavis Creek makes the area here a good spot for a base camp although flat ground for tents is limited.

The first landmark on the trek up Reavis Creek is the former corral [7-N, 5.7] (N33° 32' 28", W111° 09' 54") on the left (east) side of the creek. The corral posts were burned, but some of the wire and metal survived. This open space at the corral would make a good place to camp in the otherwise thick underbrush along the creek. A faint trail leads out of the south end of the corral area and meets Reavis Creek near the remains of a dugout building, which looks like a rock wall (N33° 32' 24", W111° 09' 56"). If you can't find the faint trail, continue south in the bed of Reavis Creek where you will soon see the popular Reavis Falls Trail [7-M, 5.8] (N33° 32' 24.7", W111° 09' 58.1") coming in on the right (west) from the Cedar Basin and Maple Spring area. A large broken cottonwood tree in Reavis Creek stands near the junction with the Reavis Falls Trail. The stone wall of the dugout (mentioned earlier) is on the left (east) just up canyon from the junction with Reavis Falls Trail.

Approaching Reavis Falls, Reavis Creek becomes heavily wooded and the hiking is slower than you might expect as you negotiate your way around downed trees, pools of water, and rock outcrops. Reavis Falls is at the south end of the box canyon where the trip ends [7-R, 6.4] (N33° 31' 57", W111° 09' 59"). Return the same way to Pine Creek Trailhead or end the hike at Reavis Trailhead using the Reavis Falls Trail and Reavis Ranch Trail (109) as described in Trip 2 (Reavis Falls).

HISTORY AND LEGENDS

Rancher John "Hoolie" Bacon was removing the wild cattle from his range in Pine Creek because they were eating forage that his cattle needed. Bob Wallauer was helping Hoolie roundup the wild cattle and had a wild cow tied to a juniper tree near the junction of Pine and Reavis Creeks. With the cow tied securely to the tree by her horns, Hoolie sawed off the ends of the horns to reduce the danger of getting gored. He then showed Bob how to keep the cow dallied close to his horse and set the wild cow free. It was a race down canyon until the cow settled down and learned how to follow behind Bob's horse, Danny Boy. Bob brought the cow down Pine Creek through that rough country to the corral for branding and shipment to the sale auction.[25]

Rancher Billy Martin said they called the corral [7-N] along Reavis Creek the Pine Creek Corral even though the corral was not on Pine Creek. That may have been near the area where Bacon and Wallauer were rounding up the wild cattle.

Trip 7

MIDDLE PINE CREEK

Pine Creek is a little known area of the Superstition Wilderness. In the 1800s, Pine Creek was used as a corridor to connect the Salt River to the Reavis Valley. The rough abandoned trail that runs the length of Pine Creek will help you explore this region of the Wilderness. Pine Creek has seasonal water.

ITINERARY

From Pine Creek Trailhead, follow a cross-country course, which eventually traces the bed of Pine Creek to the junction with Reavis Creek. Continue up Pine Creek to the junction with Beanie Burrito Canyon. Take optional trips to the chockstone in Pine Creek, Walnut Spring, or Klondike Spring. Return the same way or make a loop to Frazier, Tule, Campaign, or Reavis Trailhead.

DIFFICULTY

Difficult 3 to 5 day hike. Not suitable for horses due to lack of trails and rough country. Elevation change is +1,170 and -480 feet one way to [7-X]; add ±920 for Option 1 loop; add +1,336 for Option 2 to Walnut Spring; add +1,590 and -160 for Option 2 to [15-P]; add +820 and -90 for Option 3 to [7-KK].

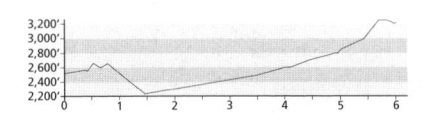

LENGTH and TIME

6.0 miles plus optional trips, 1.5 days plus optional trips one way.

MAPS

Arizona USGS topo maps NAD27: Pinyon Mountain, Two Bar Mountain. Superstition Wilderness Beartooth map, grids L7 to N9. Maps 6, 7 and 15.

FINDING THE TRAIL

Trailhead map is on page 69. The route starts near the end of FR665 at the concrete water trough (N33° 35' 01.8", W111° 12' 18.5").

THE TRIP

Start on Map 6 on page 70. From the Pine Creek Trailhead [6-B, 0], follow the description in Trip 4 (Lower Pine Creek) to the junction with Reavis Creek

[7-S, 4.8]. We defined Middle Pine Creek as the stretch of creek upstream from Reavis Creek to the chockstone [7-C] that forms a box canyon in Pine Creek northwest from Walnut Spring.

One way to enjoy Middle Pine Creek is to set up a camp and make day trips through this remote area. Two options for campsites in this rough country are on the high benches above the creek, [7-V] and [7-E].

Following the course of the 1916 Pine Creek Trail is a matter of cross-country travel with occasional sightings of trail construction or a rock cairn. The old trail is difficult to follow and your progress may only be one-quarter to one-half mile per hour.

An open gate [7-UU] in the fence (or maybe just a cut fence) on the ridge, east of the junction with Reavis Creek, is possible evidence of the former 1916 Pine Creek Trail. From the junction of Reavis and Pine Creeks [7-S, 4.8], head east toward the flat bench where a trail passes through a former campsite [7-V, 5.2], which is located next to the ramp that takes you down to creek level. Going upstream in the bed of Pine Creek, look for another ramp [7-Y, 5.3] that will take you up to the next high bench. This ramp is upstream from a red cliff on the left (northeast side) of the creek bed. The old trail passes a possible camp area [7-E, 5.6], crosses a deep ravine [7-F, 5.9], and eventually takes a ramp down to the creek level near the junction of Pine Creek and Beanie Burrito Canyon [7-X, 6.0] where you will find a flat camp area on the bench directly to the south. A large saguaro cactus above the camp area is marked with a rectangular cut, which probably indicates the direction of the 1916 Pine Creek Trail.

To help you locate the 1916 Pine Creek Trail, we have selected several coordinates along the trail, listed from north to south.

Open gate or cut fence	[7-UU]	(N33° 33' 07", W111° 09' 29")
Camp area	[7-V]	(N33° 33' 02", W111° 09' 12")
Ramp	[7-Y]	(N33° 33' 00", W111° 09' 06")
Camp area	[7-E]	(N33° 33' 01", W111° 09' 00")
Trail	[7-]	(N33° 32' 59", W111° 08' 47")
Trail	[7-]	(N33° 32' 56", W111° 08' 44")
Deep ravine	[7-F]	(N33° 32' 51", W111° 08' 40")
Ramp	[7-]	(N33° 32' 48", W111° 08' 41")
Ramp	[7-]	(N33° 32' 43", W111° 08' 38")
Switchback trail	[7-D]	(N33° 32' 33", W111° 08' 33")

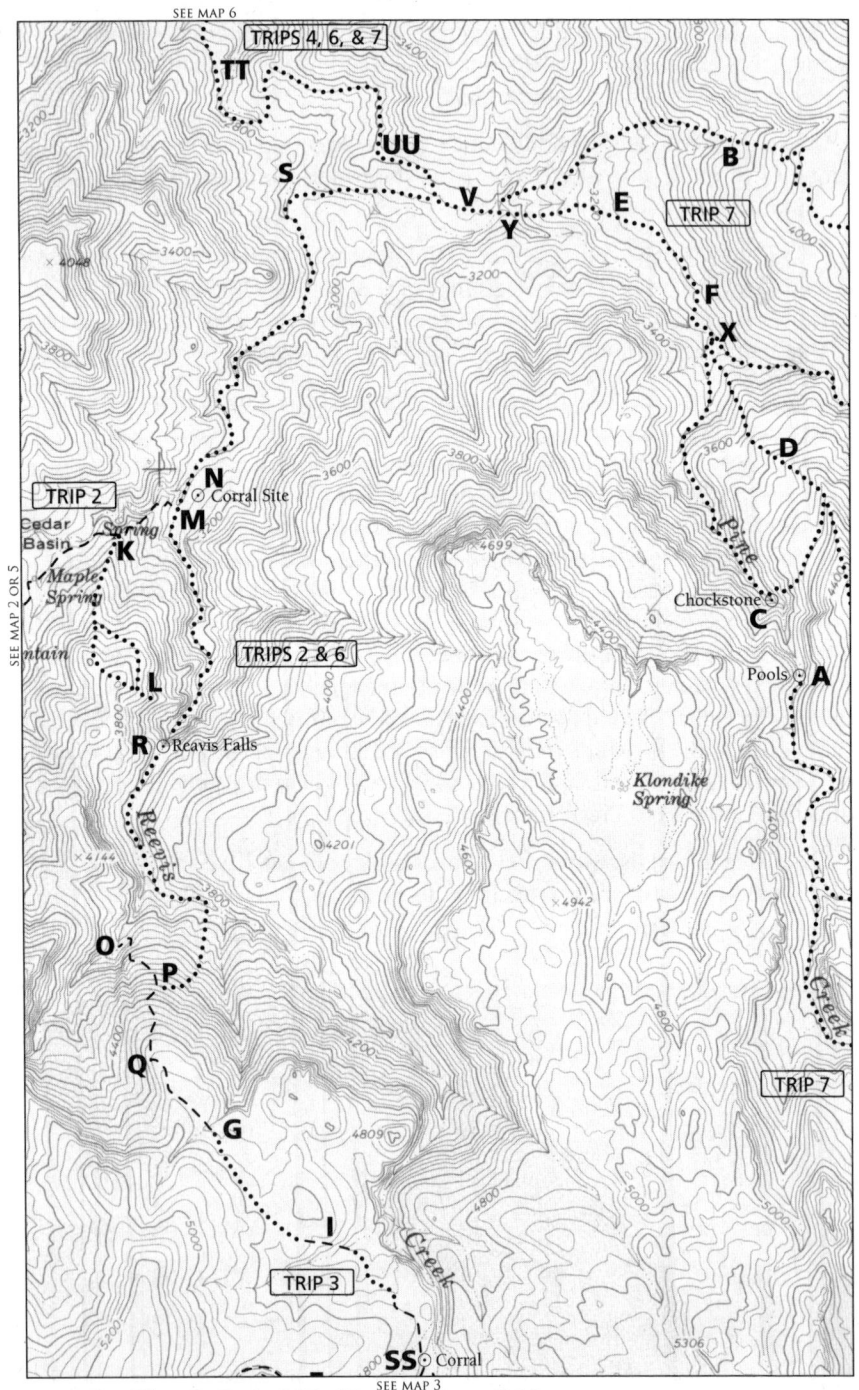

Map 7 – Trips 2, 3, 4, 6, 7, 17, 18, 19, and 20.

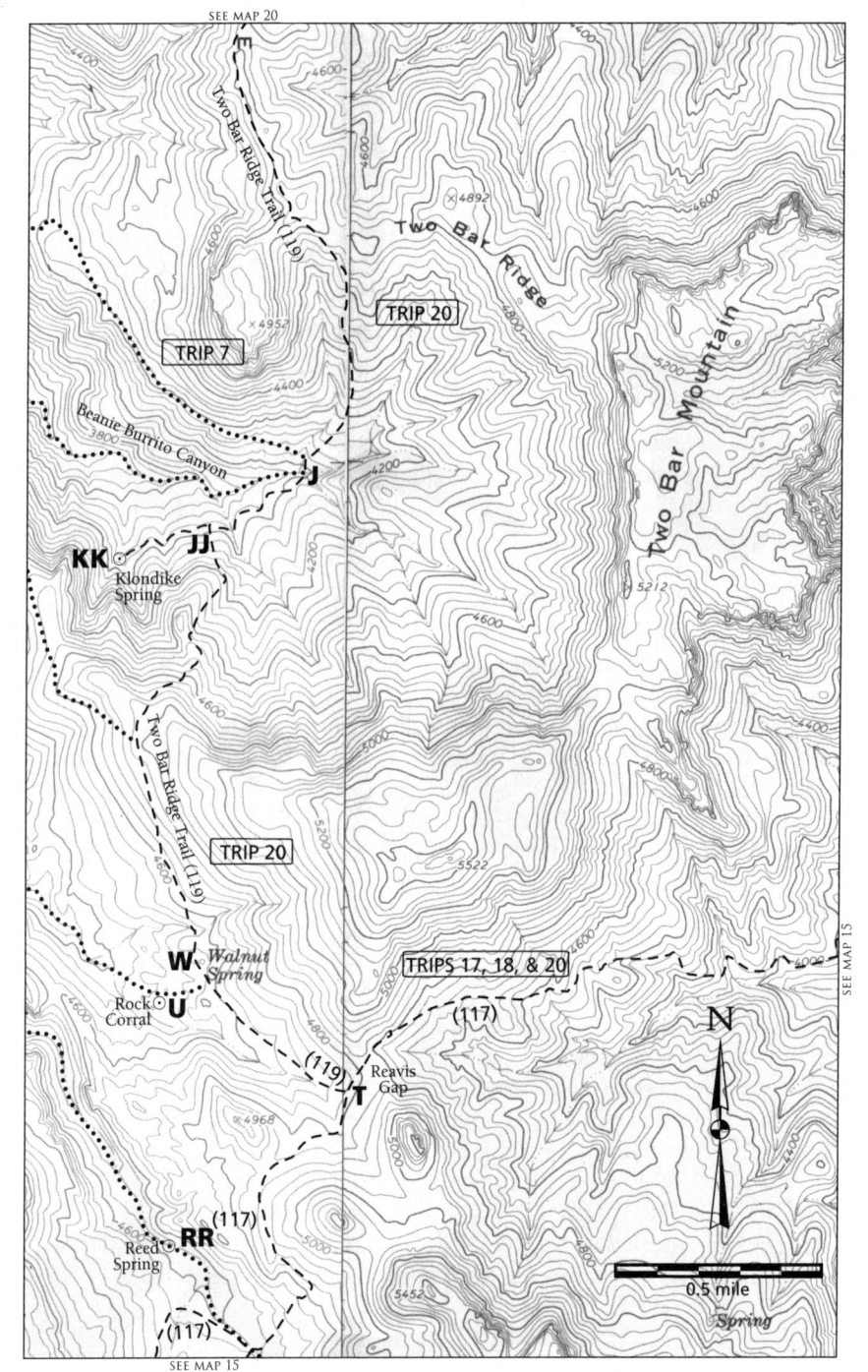

Map 7 continued – Trips 2, 3, 4, 6, 7, 17, 18, 19, and 20.

From the junction of Pine Creek and Beanie Burrito Canyon [7-X, 0], you have three day trip options—Continue up Pine Creek to the chockstone, go to Walnut Spring, or go to Klondike Spring.

Option 1. Pine Creek to chockstone. From [7-X, 0], no significant obstacles block your travel upstream in Pine Creek until you reach the chockstone in a narrow part of the canyon [7-C, 0.7] (N33° 32' 14", W111° 08' 28"). You can retrace your trip back down Pine Creek from the chockstone, but a more interesting return route (cross-country) is to go up a steep bank to the left (east) and return down the hillside. Follow the dotted line on Map 7 for our route. You may pass the remains of the 1916 switchback trail on the hill [7-D, 1.2], but the switchback is of little use as a trail now, due to erosion and lack of maintenance. The loop trip ends back at Pine Creek [7-X, 1.5].

Option 2. Go to Walnut Spring. Find the ramp, south of [7-X, 0], that leads up to the bench, then tackle the hill that is defined by Pine Creek and Beanie Burrito Canyons, heading south. Tracings of the 1916 Pine Creek Trail are visible on the ground once in a while [7-D, 0.3], but trying to follow the old trail is not useful in making travel easier to go up the hill. Head in a southeasterly cross-country direction, and connect with the Two Bar Ridge Trail that takes you south (right) to Walnut Spring [7-W, 1.7]. If you want to trace the route of the 1916 Pine Creek Trail farther upstream, from [7-D, 0.3] go in a more southerly direction, and enter Pine Creek around the 4,240-foot elevation level. Large pools in the bedrock, downstream around the 4,080-foot elevation [7-A], could be a refreshing diversion on a hot day. Faint traces of the old trail continue south following the low benches of Pine Creek, passing Reed Spring [7-RR, 2.6], and connecting to the Reavis Gap Trail where the old trail crosses Pine Creek [15-P, 2.9]. The continuation of the 1916 Pine Creek Trail from the Reavis Gap Trail [15-P] is described in Trip 19 (Upper Pine Creek).

Option 3. Go to Klondike Spring. Going up Beanie Burrito Canyon from the junction with Pine Creek [7-X, 0] is easy creek bed walking. We expected to see a spring in the bed of Beanie Burrito Canyon one-half mile up canyon at a large cottonwood tree, but no water surfaced there. Potholes in the wash east of the cottonwood tree collect runoff and rainwater. To approach Klondike Spring, pick up the Two Bar Ridge Trail at the Beanie Burrito Canyon crossing [7-J, 1.2]. Go right (south then west) on Two Bar Ridge Trail to the junction with the unsigned Klondike Spring spur trail [7-JJ, 1.5] (N33° 32' 22", W111° 07' 50"). From that junction, going farther west to the spring area [7-KK, 1.8] (N33° 32' 19", W111° 08' 04") is a bushwhack. Don't count on Klondike Spring for water, which is only a seep in the ravine.

Return the same way for Option 3, or try a rough cross-country route starting at [7-J, 2.4], and go up the hillside north of Beanie Burrito Canyon by following our dotted line on Map 7. If your route takes you to the big drainage with a steep gully, try the game crossing we happened to find [7-B, 3.8] (N33° 33' 10", W111° 08' 36"). Returning to a possible camp at [7-V, 4.5] ends the day trip.

More planning options are possible by combining ideas from adjacent trip descriptions. Instead of returning to the Pine Creek Trailhead, you could plan loop trips to Campaign Trailhead, Tule Trailhead, FR83, Frazier Trailhead, or Reavis Trailhead. Trip 19 (Upper Pine Creek) describes the Walnut Spring area and upstream along Pine Creek to the Fire Line Trail. If you have camped on either of the benches mentioned earlier, [7-V] and [7-E], you could consider a day trip to Reavis Falls. See Trip 6 (Pine Creek to Reavis Falls) for that route description.

HISTORY AND LEGENDS

Tales of the Lost Dutchman Mine might seem out of place in the eastern Superstition Wilderness, but Barry Storm told a story about Jacob Waltz traveling though the region. Waltz was reported to have stayed at the Blevins cabin, which we believe was located near the present site of the Windy Hill Campground at Roosevelt Lake. When Blevins returned from a trip to Globe, his son told him of their overnight guest who had just departed. Blevins followed Waltz and tracked him to a little flat just south of the junction of Reavis and Pine Creeks. That flat [7-V] could have been along the 1916 Pine Creek Trail near the camp area, which we described in the above trip. The tracks abruptly ended on the flat, and Waltz's route from the flat was never determined. Barry Storm's story ends with Waltz arriving a short time later in Tucson with $1,600 in gold ore.[26]

Roosevelt Lake Area

The Roosevelt Lake Area is the location of several trailheads, campgrounds, a visitor center, the post office, and restaurants. Use the campgrounds as a base camp while day hiking, riding, enjoying Roosevelt Lake, or visiting the Tonto National Monument cliff dwellings. From Apache Junction at Idaho Road, on US60, drive east 49 miles to SR188 on the west side of Globe. From Globe, go north on SR188 for about 15 miles.

FINDING THE TRAILHEADS

Four trailheads provide access to the Superstition Mountains from SR188. To reach Tule Trailhead, turn southwest from SR188, between mileposts 235 and 236, onto FR449. Follow FR449 to the parking area at the end of the road. On the way to the Tule Trailhead, take FR449A if you want to go up the mountain to the Campaign Trailhead near Reevis Mountain School. Frazier Trailhead is on the south side of SR188 between mileposts 242 and 243. Roosevelt Cemetery Trailhead is south of SR188 between mileposts 242 and 243 across the highway from the Roosevelt Lake Visitors Center. Detailed directions and maps for the trailheads are in the individual trailhead sections.

FACILITIES

The description of facilities along SR188, listed from south to north, begins at milepost 233 just before Pinto Creek and extends north to milepost 245 just beyond Roosevelt Lake Bridge. Roosevelt Lake Resort near milepost 233 offers food and lodging. The Spring Creek complex of businesses—gas station, restaurant, convenience store, golf course office, RV park, motel, and boat repair—is across the highway from the Roosevelt Post Office between mileposts 233 and 234. Farther north on SR188, between mileposts 234 and 235, the Roosevelt Estates Road leads to a small community and restaurant.

  The Tonto National Forest operates several nice campgrounds at Roosevelt Lake. Purchase a campground pass (Tonto Pass) at a Forest Service office or at a local store in advance of your stay. Passes are not sold at the campgrounds. The first campground going north on SR188 is Schoolhouse Recreation Area between mileposts 235 and 236.

  The next campground is Grapevine Group Use Site between mileposts 236 and 237, which is available only with advance reservations. Grapevine Bay Campground is located at the end of Grapevine Road. The size of this campground varies with lake level since it is located on the shore.

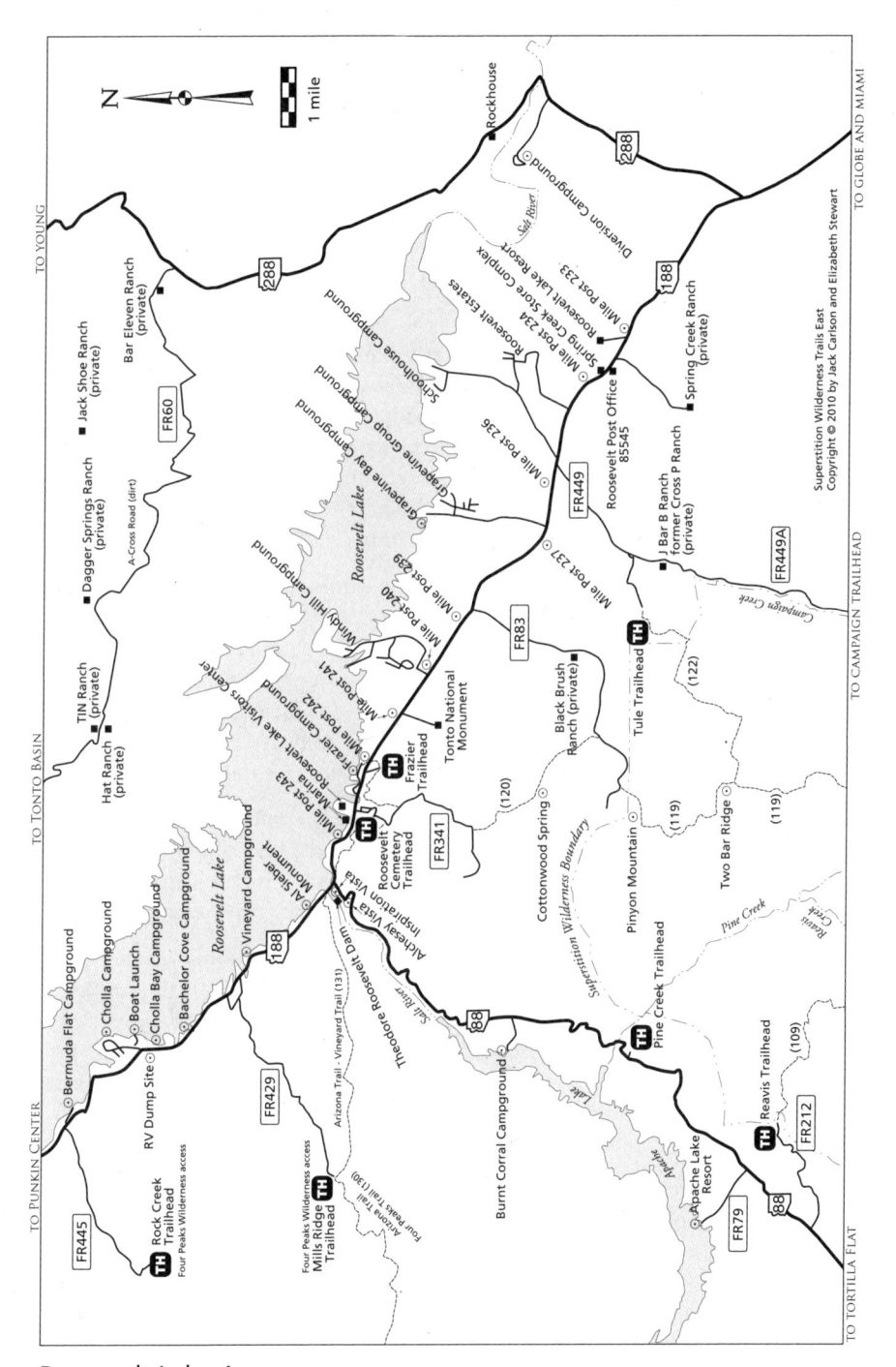

Roosevelt Lake Area.

Windy Hill Recreation Site, between mileposts 240 and 241 on SR188, is a large campground with 347 camp units. The campground has flush toilets, showers, potable water, and shade ramadas. We use this campground when we visit the area.

Tonto National Monument is located between mileposts 240 and 241. You can tour the lower cliff dwelling, which was occupied by the Salado people about seven hundred years ago. The upper cliff dwelling is only open for visitation several times each year. Picnicking, but no camping, is permitted in the park.

Cottonwood Day Use Site, Frazier Equestrian Campground, and Frazier Group Site are located between mileposts 242 and 243 on the north side of SR188. These sites sit across the road from the Frazier Trailhead and between Tonto National Monument and the Roosevelt Lake Visitors Center. Equestrians can camp here and make connections to Cottonwood Trail (120), Thompson Trail (121), Arizona Trail, or Frazier Trailhead via a horse trail that passes through a tunnel under SR188 near milepost 242.

At the turnoff for the Roosevelt Lake Visitors Center, between mileposts 242 and 243, you will find a convenience store near the entrance to the Roosevelt Lake Marina. The Tonto National Forest operates Roosevelt Lake Visitors Center, which has a nice museum—displaying wildlife, dam construction, and pioneers—adjoining the reception area and gift shop. The staff can help you with all your questions. The Roosevelt Cemetery Trailhead is on the south side of SR188 across from the Visitors Center.

The Arizona Trail and Thompson Trail (121) come down the hill on the south side of SR188, between mileposts 244 and 245, just before you reach Roosevelt Lake Bridge. The small trail signs are difficult to see from the road, but you might be able to see the green metal gate part way up the hill.

The Roosevelt Lake Bridge near milepost 244 was completed in 1990. Before the bridge was built, vehicles traveled on a road across the top of the dam. Roosevelt Dam was completed in 1911, and extensive renovations were completed in 1996. For good views of the dam, drive southwest 0.4 mile on SR88 to Inspiration Vista and another 0.6 mile to Alchesay Vista, which has rest rooms. Farther south on SR88 are the Pine Creek and Reavis Trailheads, which we describe in another section of this book.

The Arizona Trail via the Vineyard Trail (131) continues on the northwest side of the Roosevelt Lake Bridge and heads west to the Four Peaks Wilderness. Connections to other trailheads in the Four Peaks Wilderness can be made from SR188 as you continue north. The book *Arizona Trail: The Official Guide,* by Tom Lorang Jones, describes the Arizona Trail, which extends from Mexico to Utah.

A stone monument memorializes Al Sieber on the Roosevelt Lake side of SR188, north of the bridge, at milepost 245. Sieber, former chief of scouts for the U.S. Army in the 1800s, died during the construction of the Roosevelt Dam road in 1907. The monument marks the approximate location of his accidental death. Sieber is buried at the Globe Cemetery, in Globe, where his grave is marked with another handsome stone monument.

Continuing north on SR188 you have more choices for campgrounds, which include boat launches, rest rooms, and an RV dump site. These recreation areas are right on the shoreline of Roosevelt Lake, which is convenient for fishermen and boaters.

HISTORY AND LEGENDS[27]

The two maps in this section of the book will help you find the historic sites. The *Roosevelt Lake Area* map on page 91 shows the present day ranches and communities that were homesteaded in the early 1900s. The *Homesteads Submerged by Roosevelt Lake* map on page 95 shows the late 1800s homesteads along the Salt River.

The Salado culture declined around AD 4500, but the Salado left their mark on the Roosevelt area with the cliff dwellings at Tonto National Monument and many archaeological sites in the region. The Yavapai and later the Apache inhabited the region until the U.S. Army moved them onto reservations in the 1870s.

Grapevine Spring is identified on an 1869 map with its location on the south side of the Salt River and east of Tonto Creek. In 1864, King S. Woolsey named the spring when he was leading an expedition of gold prospectors and men to remove the Apache from the region. He wrote, "…we moved to the inviting point, and named it Grape Vine springs. About the springs are at least two-thousand acres of good tillable land, and the water is sufficient for very large herds of stock."[28]

One of the first homesteaders in the Roosevelt area was Henry Armer who established a ranch at Grapevine Spring on the south bank of the Salt River about 1876. Later, probably in 1878 or 1879, he moved across to the north side of the river, just east of Windy Hill, where he proved up on two homesteads covering 74 and 160 acres. He received both of those land patents in 1891.[29]

Another early homesteader was Archie McIntosh, a guide for the army. He served with General Crook during the military campaign to remove the Yavapai and Apache from the Superstition Mountains and surrounding territory in 1872. His knowledge of the country probably helped him select the prime location for his ranch with permanent water and a fertile floodplain along the Salt River.

McIntosh's homestead affidavit shows that he settled at Grapevine on March 6, 1876. He described his improvements on the land as "one double log house, one single log house, one stone house, 80 acres under fence, 35 acres in cultivation, and a ditch one-half mile long." McIntosh received his patent for the 80 acres on the banks of the Salt River at Grapevine Spring (also called Black Mesquite Spring) in 1884, and in 1891 he received the patent for an adjoining 80 acres.[30] Grapevine Group camping site at Roosevelt Lake covers the southern end of his former homestead.

McIntosh was born in Michigan to a Scottish father and a Chippewa mother in 1834. McIntosh's second marriage was to Domingo who was from the San Carlos Reservation. Together they ran cattle on the Grapevine Spring homestead and branded the DO, which was registered in Domingo's name in 1882. Their son Donald attended school at Grapevine and later at the Carlisle Indian School in Pennsylvania.[31]

Henry and Lucinda Armer lived near McIntosh and they listed Grapevine as the location for the birth of their son Preston Armer in 1878. Archie's wife Domingo (sometimes spelled Dominga) was the midwife for Lucinda.[32]

The community of ranches near McIntosh's homestead was known as Salt River. Across the river from McIntosh, the Armer Post Office was established at the Armer Ranch, which handled mail between 1884 and 1895. Lucinda Armer was the postmaster. Some other homesteaders that received patents for their homesteads between 1885 and 1895 included Frank Cline, James Hocker, Edmund Kenton, George Danforth, John Vinyard, Peter Robertson, Joseph Flippen, and Elizabeth Gordon. See the *Homesteads Submerged by Roosevelt Lake* map for the locations of these and other homesteads.

Most of the private property along SR188 was homesteaded in the late 1800s and early 1900s. The rules varied over the years, but homesteaders generally had to live on the land for three to five years and have it under cultivation. When they *proved up* on the homestead requirements, they were issued a patent, which gave them title to the property.[33] Theodore Roosevelt Dam construction started in 1903 and by the time the dam was completed in 1911, the U.S. government had bought the twenty-five land patents in the Salt River community that were to be covered by Roosevelt Lake when the water backed up behind the dam. Only the few homesteads on higher ground around the lake remain in private ownership today.[34]

The name of the Salt River community changed over the years with specific locations being noted as Grapevine, Catalpa, Livingstone, Roosevelt, and Kirby. Livingstone, the site of the engineers camp for Roosevelt Dam, was named for the Livingston family. Postmarks and maps show the spelling of

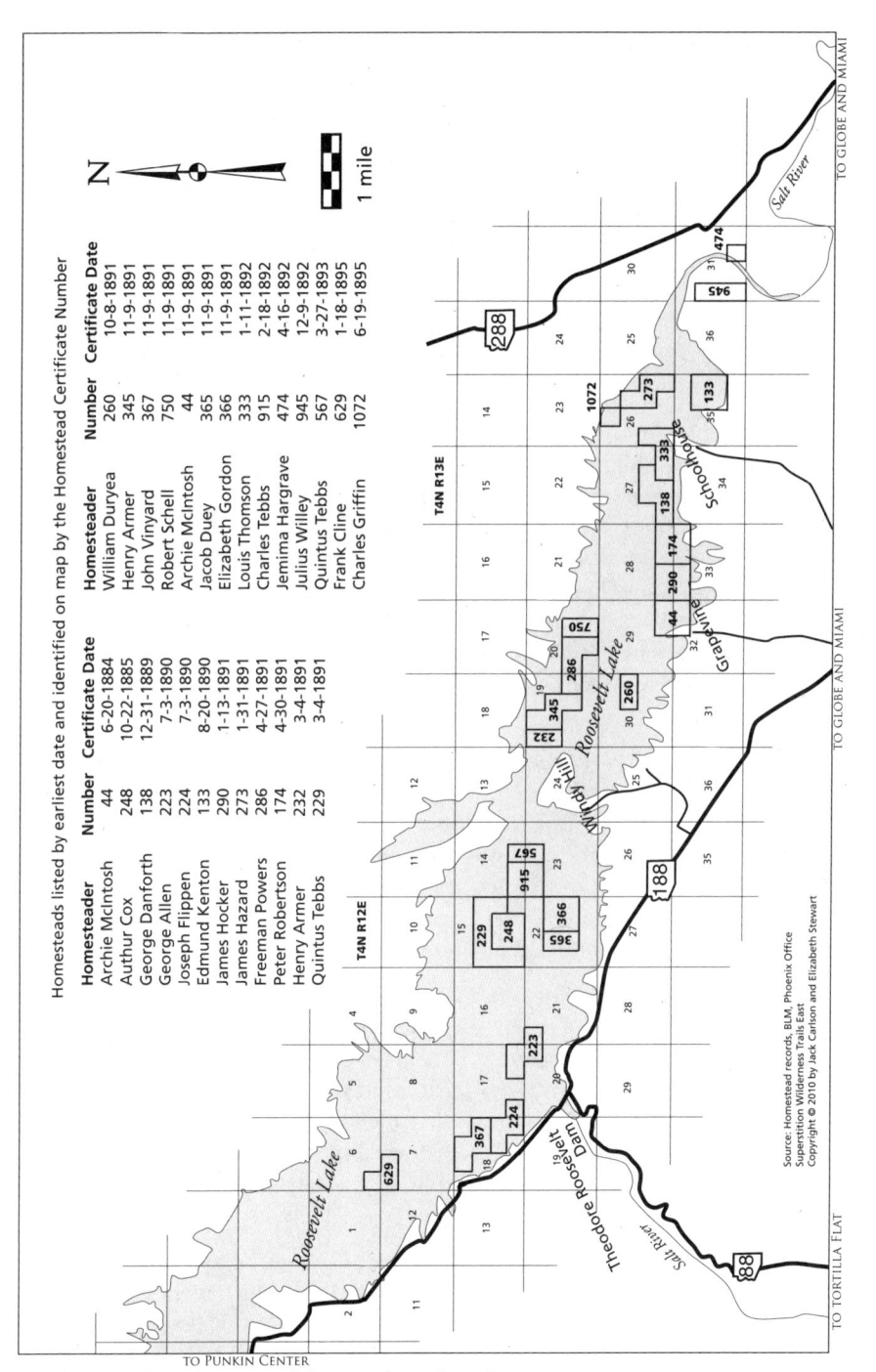

Homesteads listed by earliest date and identified on map by the Homestead Certificate Number

Homesteader	Number	Certificate Date	Homesteader	Number	Certificate Date
Archie McIntosh	44	6-20-1884	William Duryea	260	10-8-1891
Authur Cox	248	10-22-1885	Henry Armer	345	11-9-1891
George Danforth	138	12-31-1889	John Vinyard	367	11-9-1891
George Allen	223	7-3-1890	Robert Schell	750	11-9-1891
Joseph Flippen	224	7-3-1890	Archie McIntosh	44	11-9-1891
Edmund Kenton	133	8-20-1890	Jacob Duey	365	11-9-1891
James Hocker	290	1-13-1891	Elizabeth Gordon	366	11-9-1891
James Hazard	273	1-31-1891	Louis Thomson	333	1-11-1892
Freeman Powers	286	4-27-1891	Charles Tebbs	915	2-18-1892
Peter Robertson	174	4-30-1891	Jemima Hargrave	474	4-16-1892
Henry Armer	232	3-4-1891	Julius Willey	945	12-9-1892
Quintus Tebbs	229	3-4-1891	Quintus Tebbs	567	3-27-1893
			Frank Cline	629	1-18-1895
			Charles Griffin	1072	6-19-1895

Homesteads Submerged by Roosevelt Lake.

the town as Livingstone, with an e, unlike the family name Livingston. The post office at Livingstone was in service from 1896 to 1907.

The Salt River community was initially in Yavapai County, included in Maricopa County in 1871, and finally made part of Gila County in 1881. That year Charles Livingston was the first to register his V brand in the newly formed county. Globe was in Pinal County from 1875 to 1881. Livingston did not prove up on a homestead. He was the school census marshal for Grapevine in 1886-87.

The present day Roosevelt Estates property was homesteaded by Isaac Johnson in 1919. Chester Cooper homesteaded a 15-acre extension to the south in 1923.

Alma LeCornu Kerby settled in the Roosevelt area in 1905 and received the 1913 homestead patent for 80 acres at the present day Roosevelt Lake Resort community. He submitted this homestead request with his name spelled as Kirby and the Land Office questioned his application. Using the name of L. A. Kerby, he had received a homestead patent for 160 acres near Pima (west of Safford) in 1893 and the Land Office wanted to clarify if Kerby and Kirby were the same person—which they were and the application was accepted. Alma Kerby seemed to freely interchange the use of Kirby and Kerby since we found school records using Kirby, but birth and death certificates using Kerby.

In 1913, Forest Ranger W. M. Cohea reported that Kerby's "Claim is used as a road house and for a little store. It would be impossible for anyone to make a living depending on the store and road house," which implied that the agricultural use of the land was important.[35] Kerby raised wheat, barley, potatoes and garden truck. His improvements included a three-room house, a one-room house, a store house, a barn, a chicken house, a hay house, and a well. He had four horses and one hundred chickens, but no cattle were present.

Kerby's homestead patent was issued in the name of Alma Kirby and his road house along the main road was referred to as Kirby. The Kirby post office, sometimes called Kirby Station, was in service from 1914 to 1917, and Alma's wife Amelia was the postmaster. Amelia was born in Utah and raised her nine children on the homestead. She died in 1951. Alma was born in England, a rancher by trade, and died in 1915. They are both buried in the Globe Cemetery.[36]

Robert J. Whalley homesteaded Dwight Cooper's Hay Hook Ranch property in 1920. Whalley died in 1944 on another of his ranches on the Globe-Winkelman highway. He was the son of William Whalley who established the Whalley Lumber Company in Globe. The William Whalley home on Maple Street in Globe was on the 2001 Annual Home and Building Tour.[37]

Luther Jackson with his wife Annie and children at their house on Pinto Creek near Roosevelt Lake. He worked on the Roosevelt Dam Project as an inspector for the Power Canal. The photo was taken in March 1909 and is labeled "Ditch Rider Luther Jackson with family at Pinto Creek." Courtesy Salt River Project Archives and U.S. Reclamation Service, HAER AZ-4-14. Photographer unknown.

Henry R. Tarr initiated a 1911 homestead filing for the land straddling Pinto Creek, just south of SR188. In 1908, he recorded a brand that looks like 2 *Lazy H*. Frank Thomas was later interested in the property, but it was William R. E. Lee who received the patent in 1923. We think this is the property that was exchanged with the Forest Service for the tract of land where the Spring Creek Store and business complex are located. Ranchers Jim and Earline Tidwell built the Spring Creek Store here in the early 1970s.[38]

Luther M. Jackson received the patent for the Cross P Ranch, now known as the J Bar B Ranch, in 1925. He branded the Cross P and the Bar V Bar. Rancher A. J. Henderson's daughter, Annie, married Jackson in 1904. When they had their third child in 1914, they were living in Livingstone, and Luther was a Power Canal inspector for the Roosevelt Dam Project. The Power Canal supplied water to the run the generators that provided electricity for Roosevelt Dam construction and for commercial sale.[39]

Blevins Cemetery is located in the Windy Hill Recreation Site, but none of the grave markers have names. Two unrelated Blevins families settled here in the Salt River community with the early pioneers.

Frazier's Store was located on Tonto Forest land and operated under a Special Use Permit at the SR188 junction with the Roosevelt Lake Visitors Center. See History and Legends in Frazier Trailhead for more about the Frazier family.

Roosevelt Cemetery Trailhead

Roosevelt Cemetery Trailhead is next to SR188 across the road from the Roosevelt Lake Visitors Center, between mileposts 242 and 243, about 27 miles northwest of Globe. Turn south into the Lakeview Park and within 100 feet, turn right into the Roosevelt Cemetery Trailhead parking lot.

FINDING THE TRAILHEAD

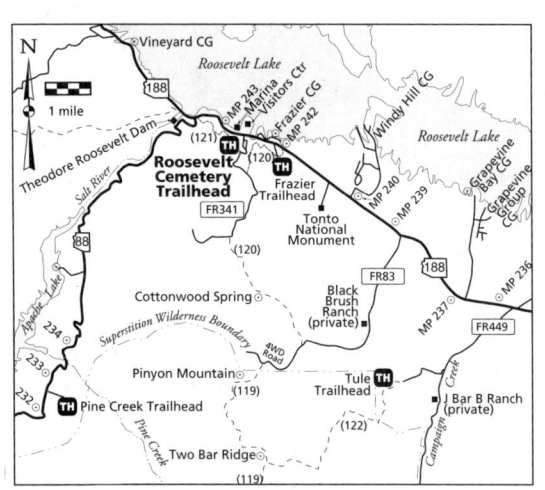

Drive about 2 miles north of the Tonto National Monument entrance on SR188 and turn left into the Lakeview Park mobile home park. Turn right on the first road, within 100 feet of the highway, and park in the Roosevelt Cemetery parking lot. The Lakeview Park is directly across the highway from the entrance to the Roosevelt Lake Visitors Center.

FACILITIES

The Roosevelt Cemetery Trailhead has no facilities except for parking. A small convenience store, on the north side of SR188, is located within walking distance. Roosevelt Lake Visitors Center is nearby. Bring your own water.

THE TRAIL

Only one trail begins at this trailhead, Roosevelt Cemetery Trail (255). The paved trail begins on the southwest side of the parking area (N33° 40' 2.0", W111° 08' 5.6") and heads up a small hill to the Roosevelt Cemetery. The paved trail ends at the cemetery entrance. A dirt trail continues uphill to the Thompson Trail (121), which is part of the Arizona Trail system. At the Thompson Trail, a pedestrian gate blocks stock animals from entering or exiting the Roosevelt Cemetery Trail.

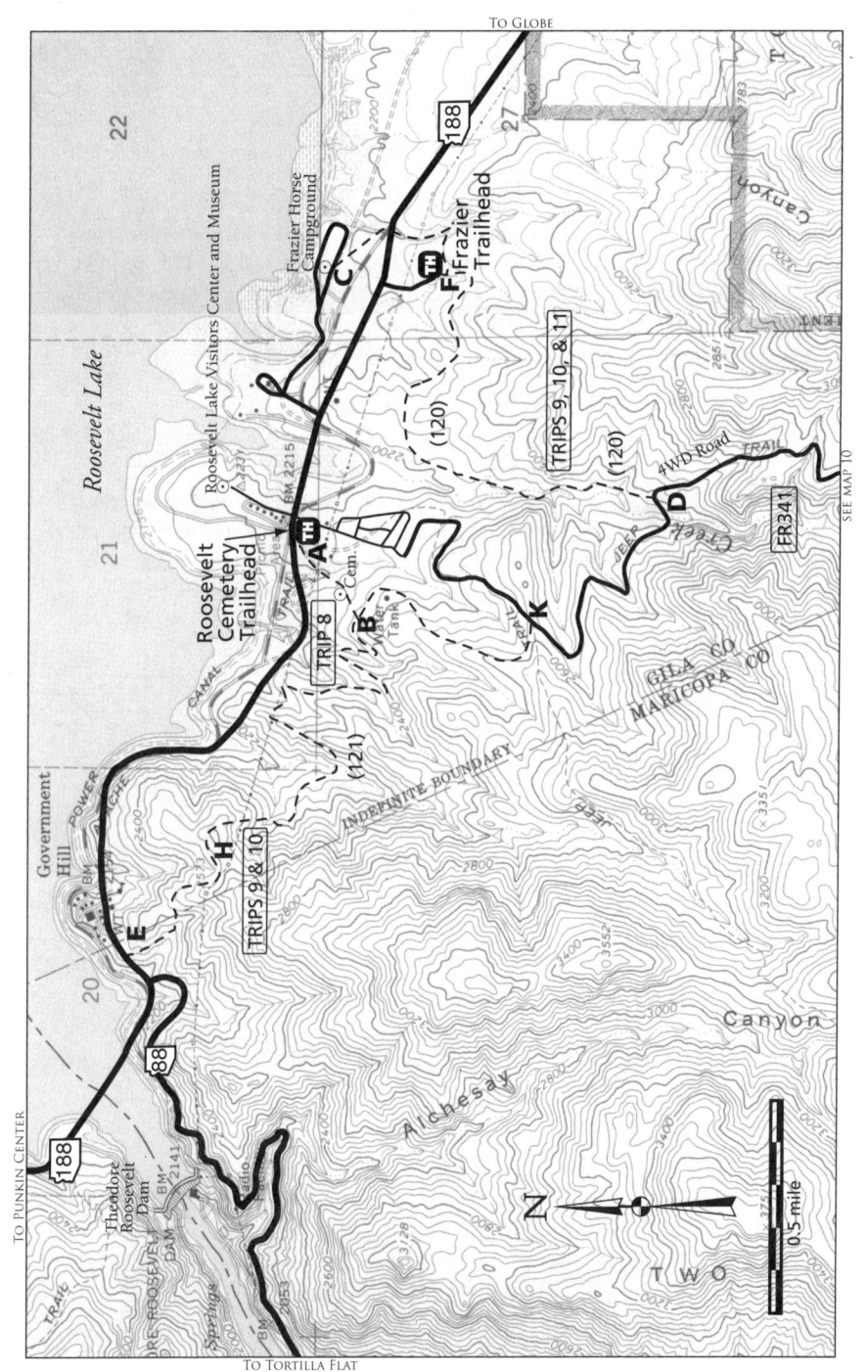

Map 8 – Trips 8, 9, 10, and 11.

Trip 8

ROOSEVELT CEMETERY TRAIL

The Roosevelt Cemetery Trail takes you to the cemetery for construction workers at Roosevelt Dam, local ranchers, and homesteaders. The earliest grave is dated 1905, and the most recent is dated 1911. Some graves are marked with elaborate monuments, but most are only marked with mounds of stone or wooden crosses. The view of Roosevelt Lake makes this a fine location for a final resting place.

ITINERARY

From the Roosevelt Cemetery Trailhead, follow the paved path southwest, uphill, to the cemetery. Return the same way, or continue uphill to the intersection with the Thompson Trail (121) and the Arizona Trail.

DIFFICULTY

Easy. Elevation change is +60 feet one way. The paved path is not recommended for horses.

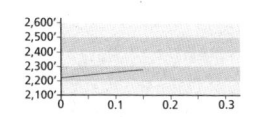

LENGTH and TIME

0.15 mile, 15 minutes one way.

MAPS

Arizona USGS topo map NAD27: Theodore Roosevelt Dam. Superstition Wilderness Beartooth map, grid N4. Map 8.

FINDING THE TRAIL

Trailhead map is on page 98. The trail starts at the southwest corner of the parking lot.

THE TRAIL

Start on Map 8 on page 99. From the Roosevelt Cemetery Trailhead [8-A, 0] (N33° 40' 2.0", W111° 08' 5.6"), the Roosevelt Cemetery Trail follows the paved path through the mesquite trees to the cemetery entrance within 0.15 mile. The cemetery is on an open hillside and the entrance is marked by a plaque and stone monument. Return on the same path, or continue uphill on a dirt trail for another 0.1 mile to the trail intersection with Thompson Trail (121), which is also the Arizona Trail. The pedestrian gate [8-B] at this

Roosevelt Dam during the dedication by Theodore Roosevelt in 1911. The spectators are standing on the roadway, which went across the top of the dam. Apache Lodge is on the point of land in the upper right corner of the photograph. Courtesy of Gregory Davis, Superstition Mountain Historical Society, Postcard Collection. Photographer unknown.

intersection does not allow stock animals to pass through. To connect to the Thompson Trail and Arizona Trail, stock animals can use FR341, which runs through the Lakeview Park, or they can use Frazier Trailhead [8-F]. Hikers can also use those two access points to make a loop trip.

HISTORY AND LEGENDS

More than thirty people died during the construction of Roosevelt Dam, from 1903 to 1911. Many of those people are buried in the Roosevelt Cemetery. The largest headstone is inscribed "In memory of John Loser, a native of Germany. Killed April 25, 1908. One of the unforeseen costs of the Roosevelt Dam. Erected by fellow workmen." The base of his gravestone reads "Stone Cutter."

Only eighteen graves are identified in the cemetery. Documented dates of burial are between 1905 and 1910, but the historical literature indicates that the local residents used the cemetery until the 1920s.[40] According to a story in *The Arizona Republic*, many headstones have been removed or stolen.[41]

Trip 9

THOMPSON TRAIL

The Thompson Trail (121) is part of the Arizona Trail. The Thompson Trail connects SR188 near the Roosevelt Lake Bridge to the Cottonwood Trail (120) at Thompson Spring. The trail provides a bird's-eye view of Roosevelt Lake as the trail contours around some low hills. At its north end, you have a view down to the blue-painted Roosevelt Lake Bridge. At its south end, the Thompson Trail traverses FR341 until it connects with Thompson Spring.

ITINERARY

From the Roosevelt Cemetery Trailhead, follow the paved path to the Roosevelt Cemetery and continue up the hill on a dirt trail to the junction with Thompson Trail (121). Go right (north) on the Thompson Trail to its end at SR188. Return the same way, or make a loop by returning on SR188.

DIFFICULTY

Easy hike. Moderate horse ride. Elevation change is +780 and -710 feet one way.

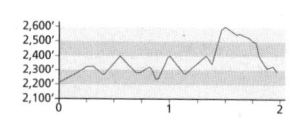

LENGTH and TIME

1.9 miles, 1.5 hours one way.

MAPS

Arizona USGS topo map NAD27: Theodore Roosevelt Dam. Superstition Wilderness Beartooth map, grid N4. Map 8.

FINDING THE TRAIL

Trailhead map is on page 98. For hikers, start at the Roosevelt Cemetery Trailhead [8-A], and take the Roosevelt Cemetery Trail. For horse riders, start on FR341 or Cottonwood Trail at Frazier Trailhead [8-F] where the trails are open to both horse riders and hikers.

THE TRIP

Start on Map 8 on page 99. From the Roosevelt Cemetery Trailhead [8-A, 0], hikers can go uphill, past the cemetery, to the junction with the Thompson Trail [8-B, 0.2]. The wooden sign here marks the intersection. Going left 0.6 mile (southeast) takes you to the junction with FR341 [8-K] where horse

After passing through the green gate, the Thompson Trail (121) ends on SR188. The Arizona Trail continues north on an elevated section of SR188, goes across Roosevelt Lake Bridge, and heads left uphill on the Vineyard Trail (131) toward the Four Peaks Wilderness. Photo taken in December 2001.

riders can pick up the trail. Hikers turn right (northwest) at the wooden sign, which leads to SR188 near Roosevelt Lake Bridge in 1.7 miles.

The Thompson Trail contours around several hills and parallels SR188 about 200 feet above the roadway. This is a good trail for people who want to hike on the Arizona Trail, but still want to be close to civilization. The desert terrain is open with sections of the trail offering some nice stands of saguaro cactus and ocotillo. If you travel here after a rain when the ocotillo are dressed out in green leaves, the long stalks make a good picture frame for photographs of the sailboats on Roosevelt Lake.

One section of the trail, which has been constructed with earth and wooden steps, is steep. Horse riders will want to avoid this section by following the bypass route marked by a signpost with the horse logo. The bypass horse trail joins with the hiking trail in the next ravine to the north.

When the trail reaches its high point at a pass [8-H, 1.5], you get your first view of Roosevelt Lake Bridge. This is a good turnaround point for a shorter trip, or you can continue down to the green gate next to SR188 [8-E, 1.9] near the south end of Roosevelt Lake Bridge. Return on the same trail.

Some hikers make a 1.2 mile return trip to the trailhead [8-A, 3.1] using highway SR188 because it is flatter. If you walk along the highway, stay off the paved surface. Do not ride your horse along the highway. There is no parking or vehicle pullout on SR188 at the north end of Thompson Trail.

FRAZIER TRAILHEAD

The Frazier Trailhead is off SR188, between mileposts 242 and 243, 26 miles northwest of Globe—about 1.2 miles north of Tonto National Monument and about 0.7 mile south of Roosevelt Lake Visitors Center. Turn southwest on FR221, and drive about 0.1 mile to the parking area.

FINDING THE TRAILHEAD

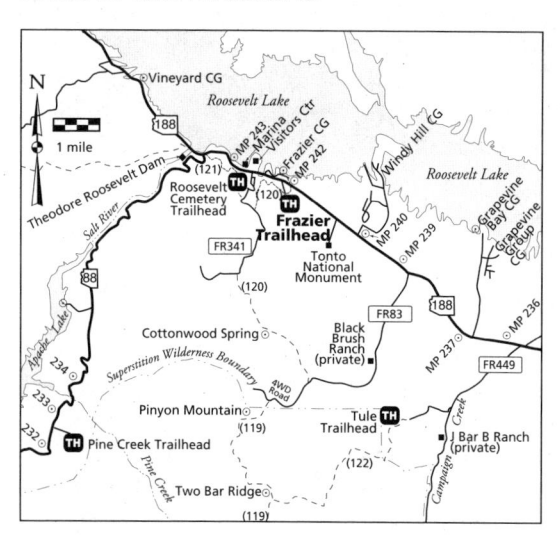

Drive about 1.2 miles north of the Tonto National Monument entrance on SR188, and turn left on FR221. The dirt road takes you around the right side of the Frazier Power Station and a wooden corral. The road ends at the trailhead parking lot. From the Frazier Horse Campground, you can reach the Frazier Trailhead by a horse trail and tunnel that go under SR188.

FACILITIES

No facilities exist at the trailhead except for pull-through parking. Camping, water, rest rooms, and equestrian facilities are available on the north side of SR188 at the Frazier Recreational Site, 0.4 mile away by horse trail.

THE TRAIL

Lower Cottonwood Trail (120) begins on the southwest side of the parking area (N33° 39' 43.6", W111° 07' 23.3") and heads west toward Cottonwood Creek. Within a few yards, near the wooden trail sign, a trail branches to the left (east) and goes to the Frazier Recreation Site in 0.4 mile where you can camp with your horses. Trail 120 continues south along Cottonwood Creek and joins FR341 at Thompson Spring in 1.2 miles.

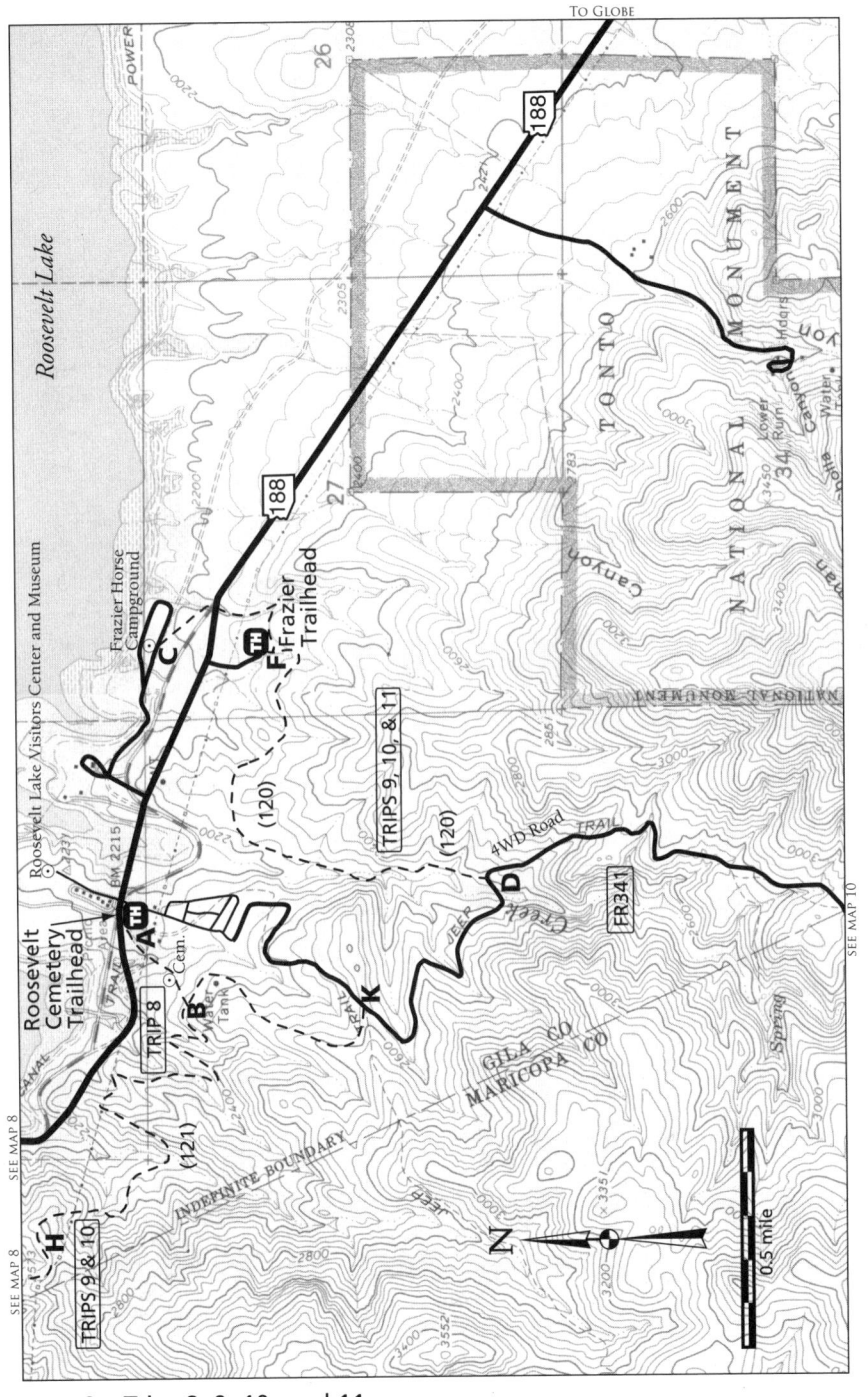

Map 9 – Trips 8, 9, 10, and 11.

FRAZIER TRAILHEAD 105

HISTORY AND LEGENDS

Frazier Trailhead is named for Thaddeus "Thad" and Stella Frazier who owned and operated the Frazier Store at Roosevelt. The store was in operation from the early 1900s, when Roosevelt Dam was under construction, to 1969 when the store closed. The Fraziers leased about two acres of land from the Tonto Forest through a Special Use Permit, which was assessed by the government as a fixed fee and percentage of sales fee. Originally the store was situated below the dam during construction. Later, the store and resort were located on the Apache Trail (former SR88), at the present day junction of SR188 and the turnoff to the Roosevelt Lake Visitors Center. Their facilities included a general store, post office, lunch counter, filling station, and tourist cabins. In a newspaper article, Stella Frazier said, "Groups such as the Dons Club...stopped here for lunch...We have fed as many as 450, cafeteria-style, on the Dons' visits."[42]

Stella Frazier was the daughter of rancher George Pemberton and his wife, Sallie, who had a ranch on the south side of the Salt River near the Frazier Store. The Pembertons were early pioneers, and their ranch is identified on an 1889 Gila County map. Stella married Thad T. Frazier in 1908. Mrs. Frazier was appointed postmaster for Roosevelt in 1916 and served as postmaster until 1958. Thad died in 1964, and Stella died in 1971.[43]

Store owner and merchant, Thad T. Frazier is often confused with rancher John J. Fraser who owned the Reavis Ranch and Fish Creek Station. References to J. J. Frazier in early 1900s newspaper articles are probably misspellings and should read J. J. Fraser.

Frazier's Store at Roosevelt, Arizona. Courtesy of Gregory Davis, Superstition Mountain Historical Society, Postcard Collection. Photographer and date unknown.

COTTONWOOD TRAIL TO ROOSEVELT LAKE BRIDGE

Near the end of this trip, the trail overlooks the blue-painted Roosevelt Lake Bridge, but nearby hills block the view of Roosevelt Dam. The trip begins by going up Cottonwood Canyon, which makes a nice out-and-back trip if you do not want to go far. The trip connects with FR341 and Thompson Trail at Thompson Spring where large cottonwood trees dot the canyon. Farther on, the Thompson Trail contours along low hills and provides a fine view of Roosevelt Lake. The Thompson Trail is part of the Arizona Trail.

ITINERARY

From Frazier Trailhead, follow Cottonwood Trail (120) and Thompson Trail (121) to an overlook for Roosevelt Lake Bridge. Return the same way, or make a loop using SR188.

DIFFICULTY

Easy hike and moderate horse ride. Elevation change is +1,100 and -1,090 feet one way.

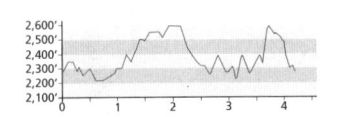

LENGTH and TIME

4.2 miles, 2.5 hours one way.

MAPS

Arizona USGS topo maps NAD27: Theodore Roosevelt Dam, Windy Hill. Superstition Wilderness Beartooth map, grids O4 to N4. Map 8.

FINDING THE TRAIL

Trailhead map is on page 104. The trail starts at the southwest corner of the Frazier Trailhead parking lot and is identified by a wooden trail sign. Frazier Equestrian Campground riders can connect with this trip by taking the horse trail from the campground.

THE TRIP

Start on Map 8 on page 99. From the Frazier Trailhead [8-F, 0] (N33° 39' 43.6", W111° 07' 23.3"), Lower Cottonwood Trail (120) intersects the horse trail from the Frazier Horse Campground within a few yards. Add about 0.4

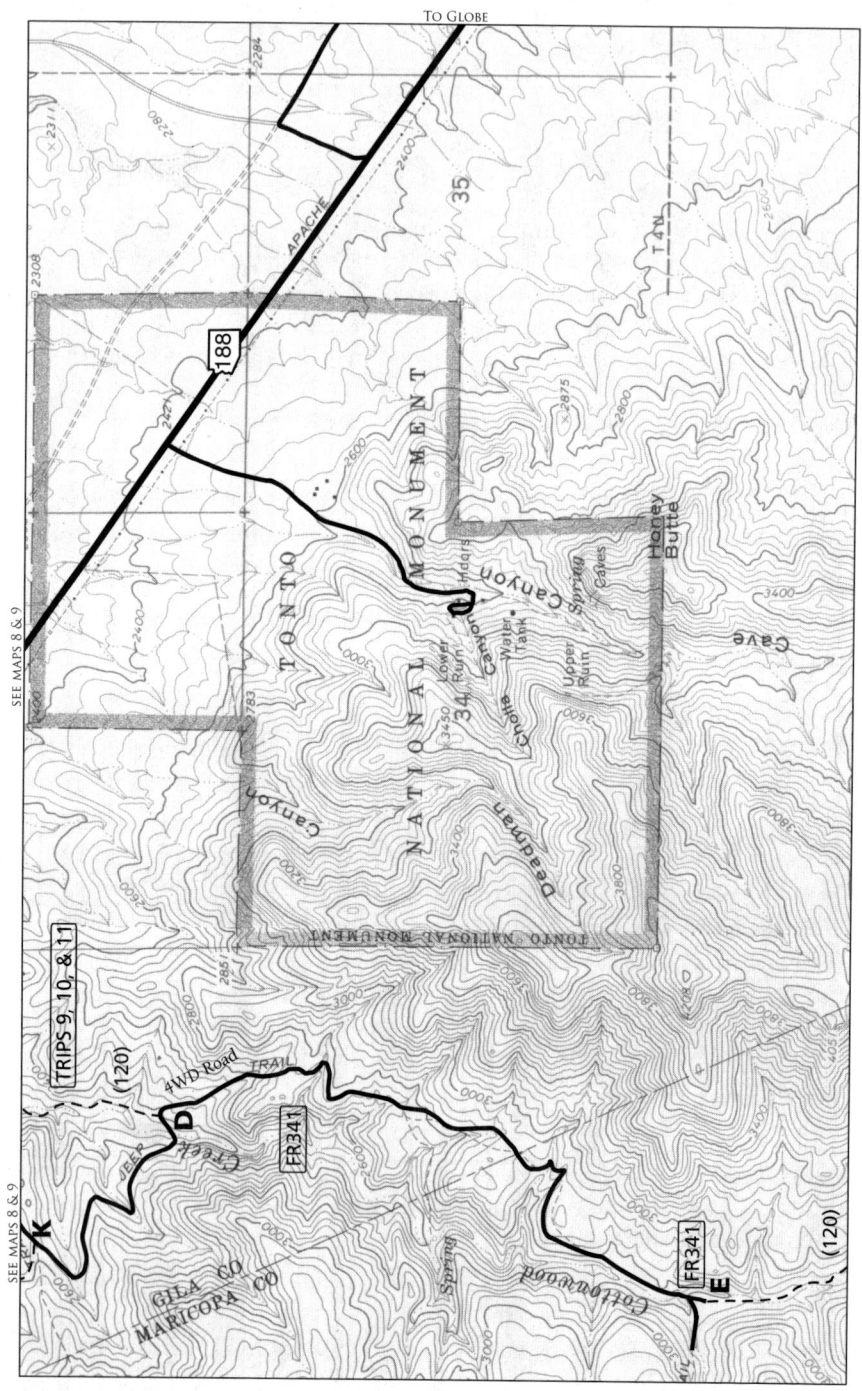

Map 10 – Trips 9, 10, and 11.

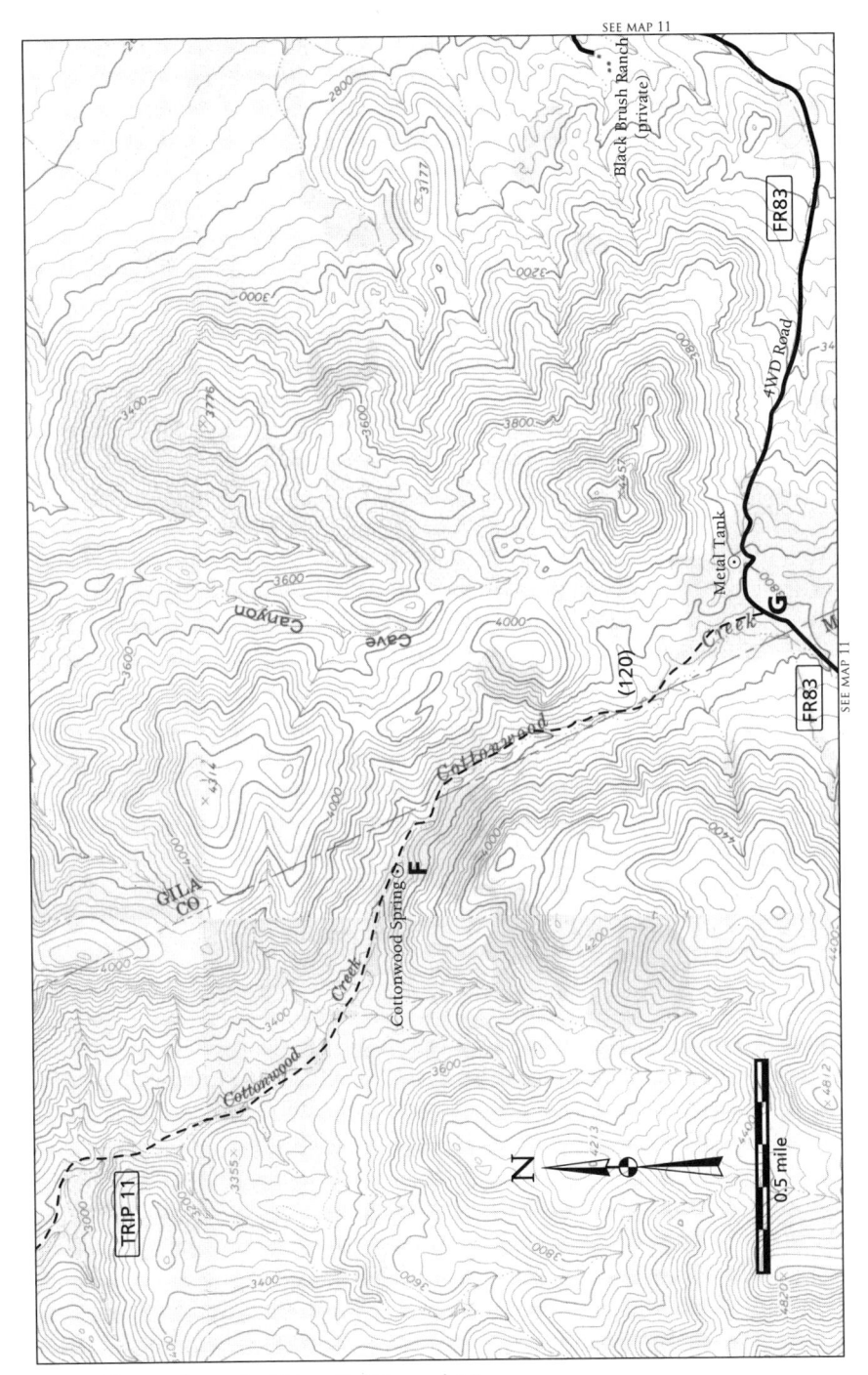

Map 10 continued – Trips 9, 10, and 11.

mile to the trip if you start from the campground [8-C]. Lower Cottonwood Trail continues to Cottonwood Canyon and meets dirt road FR341 [8-D, 1.2] at Thompson Spring. The Arizona Trail is aligned with FR341 in this area. Thompson Spring is a good turnaround point for a short trip. Stock animals can usually find water in the wash here.

The trail and road at Thompson Spring have duplicate names, so the directions can get confusing. From Thompson Spring, Upper Cottonwood Trail goes left (south) and follows dirt road FR341 up a very steep hill, but our trip goes right (northwest) following dirt road FR341 (also named Thompson Trail and Arizona Trail) up a less steep hill.

Continue northwest (and north) to the top of the hill where the Thompson Trail and the Arizona Trail branch to the west from FR341 [8-K, 1.9]. For a shorter trip, you can follow Forest Road FR341 downhill to SR188 and the Roosevelt Cemetery Trailhead parking lot where you can park a shuttle vehicle [8-A, 2.7].

Thompson Trail (121) and the Arizona Trail continue west, following the contour of the hillside. At the junction with the Cemetery Trail (255) [8-B, 2.5], you can make another shorter trip (blocked to stock animals) by taking the Cemetery Trail (255) to the Roosevelt Cemetery Trailhead parking lot [8-A, 2.7] and your shuttle vehicle.

Farther to the west on the Thompson Trail, at a Y in the trail, stock animals should take the left trail to avoid the stairs on the right portion of the trail. The left trail is marked with a horse logo sign. Both trails merge at a stock water tank that might have water. Hikers can travel either trail.

When you see the blue-painted Roosevelt Lake Bridge [8-H, 3.8], the Thompson Trail begins to descend to SR188 [8-E, 4.2]. The first view of Roosevelt Lake Bridge makes a good turnaround point if you want to avoid the trek back up the hill from SR188. At the end of the Thompson Trail, there is no room along SR188 to park a shuttle vehicle.

Hikers can make a loop back to the Roosevelt Cemetery [8-A, 5.4] or Frazier Trailheads [8-F, 6.2] using SR188 as the return. Stock animals should return on the Thompson Trail and not use SR188. Traffic moves fast on SR188, so you must stay off the pavement, stay inside the guardrail, and walk facing traffic.

HISTORY AND LEGENDS

Robert Mason, author of the books *Verde Valley Lore*, *MORE Verde Valley Lore*, and *The Burning*, recounted a November 1868 military patrol from Fort McDowell. Samuel L. Potter, Acting Topographic Engineer, wrote, "The following morning, that of the 28th, the lookout having observed smoke

A Hay Hook Ranch cow grazes the prickly vegetation along the Cottonwood Trail (120) south of the Frazier Trailhead. The view is toward the Lakeview Park community across from the Roosevelt Lake Visitors Center. The photo was taken in April 2000 when the water level in Roosevelt Lake was low.

arising from a canyon to the southward, the Cavalry portion of the command, under Bvt. Lt. Col. G. B. Sanford, proceeded to the place, I accompanying it. After crossing the Rio Salinas (Salt River), at the junction therewith of Tonto Creek, we climbed the Mesa on the southern bank, and galloped about two miles nearly due south to a canyon, which proved to be the one from which the smoke had been seen ascending. From hence, after killing one Apache, the command returned by the same trail to the crossing of Salt River, near which on an elevated point of the mesa, I found a good station for observations, and therefore took many compass bearings." The location of the encounter could have been on Cottonwood Creek.[44]

Also, see the History and Legends section of Trip 8 (Roosevelt Cemetery Trail). For the history of the Roosevelt Lake Bridge and Dam, see the section of the book titled Roosevelt Lake Area.

Trip 11

COTTONWOOD TRAIL TO FR83

Cottonwood Trail and the Arizona Trail follow four-wheel-drive road FR341 for a steep uphill climb and then strike off into some lesser traveled country. Oak and cottonwood trees line the intermittent water in Cottonwood Creek as the trail approaches Cottonwood Spring. Beyond the spring, the canopy of trees opens up, the water disappears, and the Cottonwood Trail continues though desert country where it connects with four-wheel-drive road FR83.

ITINERARY

From the Frazier Trailhead, follow the Cottonwood Trail (120) to FR83. Return the same way, or make a shuttle via FR83. Arizona Trail users can continue to the end of FR83 and the Superstition Wilderness boundary to connect with Two Bar Ridge Trail (119).

DIFFICULTY

Moderate hike and horse ride. Elevation change is +1,780 and -280 feet one way.

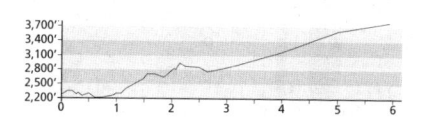

LENGTH and TIME

5.9 miles, 4 hours one way.

MAPS

Arizona USGS topo maps NAD27: Theodore Roosevelt Dam, Windy Hill, Pinyon Mountain, Iron Mountain. Superstition Wilderness Beartooth map, grids O4 to O6. Maps 9, 10, and 11.

FINDING THE TRAIL

Trailhead map is on page 104. The trail starts at the southwest corner of the Frazier Trailhead [9-F] parking lot.

THE TRIP

Start on Map 9 on page 105. From the Frazier Trailhead [9-F, 0] (N33° 39' 43.6", W111° 07' 23.3"), follow Cottonwood Trail (120) to Cottonwood Canyon. This portion of Cottonwood Trail is sometimes referred to as Lower Cottonwood Trail.

Continue upstream in Cottonwood Canyon to Thompson Spring and dirt road FR341 [9-D, 1.2]. Go left on dirt road FR341. For the next 1.6 miles, dirt road FR341, Cottonwood Trail (120), and the Arizona Trail all follow the same track. Cottonwood Trail (120) is also referred to as Upper Cottonwood Trail as it proceeds south from Thompson Spring. FR341 is extremely steep for the first half mile or so, then levels off somewhat.

Cottonwood Trail (120) and the Arizona Trail bear left (south) leaving FR341 at the corral and water tank [10-E, 2.8]. From the corral, the trail stays close to the bottom of Cottonwood Creek where you may find running water. The trail makes frequent creek crossings in the tree lined wash as it continues to gradually gain elevation.

Cottonwood Spring [10-F, 4.7] is marked by a wooden sign, but the spring does not seem to have a specific location. The water trough is out of service, but water can be found in the bed of Cottonwood Creek. Cottonwood Spring is a pleasant area with large sycamore and cottonwood trees. The spring would make a good turnaround point for your trip.

As the trail heads upstream from Cottonwood Spring, the water in Cottonwood Creek begins to disappear, and the vegetation transitions to the Sonoran desert's saguaro and prickly pear cacti with wide open vistas.

Nearing the intersection with FR83, Cottonwood Trail (120) turns into a wider track and meets dirt road FR83 at [11-G, 5.9]. From this intersection, you have three options. First, return the same way to Frazier Trailhead [9-F]. Second, continue on FR83 and the Arizona Trail by going up the mountain to the right (southwest) another 1.3 miles to connect with the Two Bar Ridge Trail (119) [11-H] in the Superstition Wilderness. Third, make a shuttle by parking a vehicle 2.0 miles down dirt road FR83 at the junction near Two Bar Ranch (private), or 3.9 miles down FR83 near its intersection with SR188 [11-K]. FR83 is narrow and considered a four-wheel-drive road as it goes uphill south and west of the Two Bar Ranch (also known as the Black Brush Ranch). Park well off the road, and do not block the road, since ranchers and others frequently use FR83.

HISTORY AND LEGENDS

Rancher Dwight Cooper, who brands the Hay Hook, built the water storage tank at the top of the hill [10-E] where Cottonwood Trail (120) leaves FR341. He also built the storage tank [near 10-G] on FR83 near the south end of the Cottonwood Trail, which is supplied with water that is pumped across the canyon from the west. He has established an impressive water improvement with these storage tanks and troughs.[45]

Eagle Scout candidate Michael Wagstaff, from Troop 678 in Tempe, and his crew installed the self-closing gate on the Cottonwood Trail just north

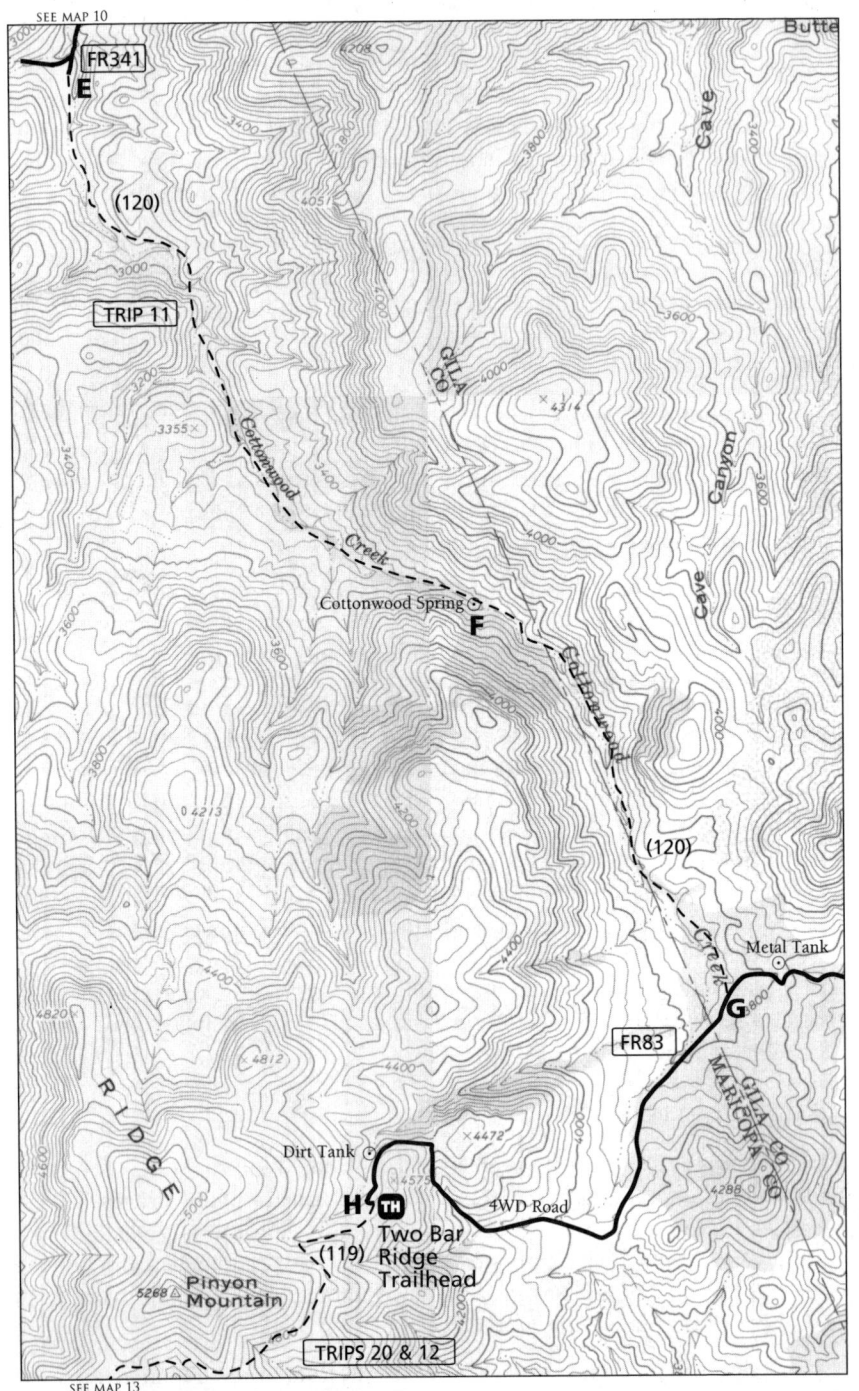

Map 11 – Trips 11, 12, and 20.

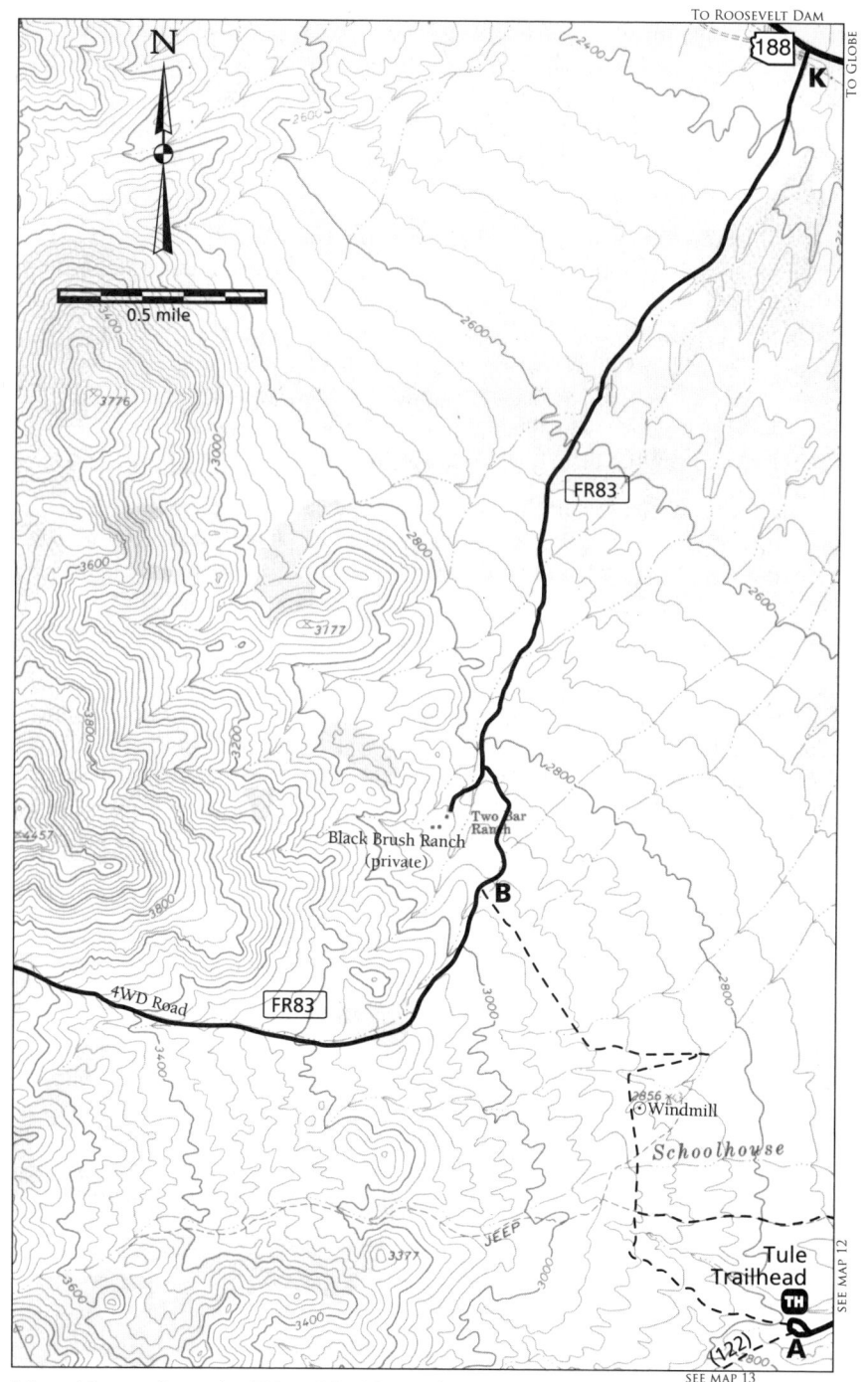

Map 11 continued – Trips 11, 12, and 20.

of Cottonwood Spring.[46] The handle to open the gate is horse rider friendly, so you do not have to dismount to pass through the gate. This gate marks the boundary between the Roosevelt and School House grazing allotments. We saw several wooden signs along the Cottonwood Trail that were inscribed with "Gila County Mountaineers, Adopt a Trail Program," but we have not found any information on that group.

The Two Bar Ranch is also known as the Black Brush Ranch and the Black Bush Ranch. Some maps and signs use the name Black Bush Ranch, but former ranch owners, the Schulzes and the Bacons, said they always called the place Black Brush Ranch.[47] Archie McIntosh was an early rancher in this general area who obtained a patent on nearby land in 1884 at Grapevine Spring, which was noted as Black Mesquite Spring next to his name on the 1880 and 1881 maps.[48] The Black Brush and Black Bush names may have been derived from the Black Mesquite Spring name.

Earl E. Bacon was in the area about 1874 running several businesses including the hot springs at the Roosevelt Dam site. After Roosevelt Dam was built and the waters began to rise, Bacon moved his operation over to the Two Bar Ranch and the Grapevine areas where they branded the Two Bar.[49]

John and Helen Schulze bought the Two Bar Ranch from Neil Lyall and ran it and their ranch near Miami. Helen said that John and she both held full time jobs besides working on the two ranches. She said the Bacons built a house at the headquarters and used some of the redwood lumber that lined the old Power Canal that was used during the Roosevelt Dam construction. The boards were in the ceiling of the house, and as the building warmed in the morning and cooled at night, the boards would creak, making an eerie sound. They had three men rebuilding the concrete water tank at the Black Brush headquarters, and she told them that they could sleep in the house, but they declined. She said the creaking sounds aroused their superstitions, so they slept out on the lawn.[50]

John Schulze said they often had grass fires on the range. Trying to make use of the available feed, he would send the cattle down to Roosevelt Lake to graze on the bottom land where the new grass came up as the lake receded in the dry spells, but the Forest Service did not approve. After one fire, he noticed a green spot on the hill behind the headquarters and had a crew drive a pipe 90 feet horizontally into the hill to tap the water. They got a good flow of water about the size of your thumb.[51]

TULE TRAILHEAD

From Apache Junction at Idaho Road, drive east on US60 for 49 miles to SR188, on the west side of Globe. From Globe, go north on SR188 for 20 miles to FR449 (J Bar B Road) between mileposts 235 and 236. FR449 is 2 miles north on SR188 from the Spring Creek Store. Drive west on FR449 for 2 miles to its junction with FR449A. Stay right on FR449 for 1.2 miles to the end of the road. Tule is locally pronounced "Two-lee."

FINDING THE TRAILHEAD

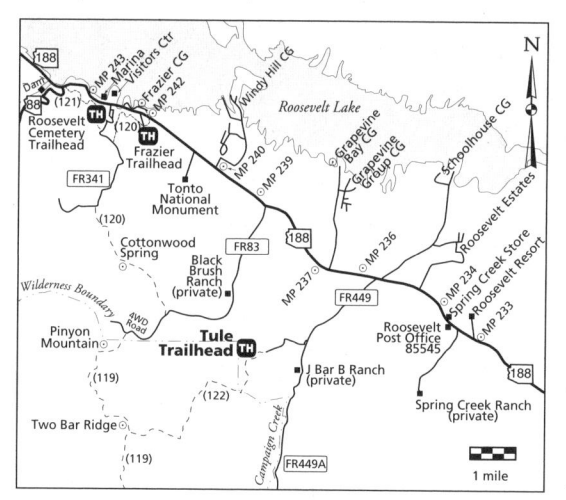

The FR449 road is well marked and easy to follow. Bear right at the junction with FR449A, go up and over a steep, but small hill, and follow the dirt road with a gravel overlay. FR449 ends at a turnaround and small parking area posted with information and trailhead signs.

FACILITIES

No facilities are located at the Tule Trailhead except for a small parking area. Bring your own water. See the section titled Roosevelt Lake Area for visitor facilities along nearby SR188.

THE TRAIL

Tule Canyon Trail (122) begins from the south side of the parking area (N33° 35' 35.9", W111° 04' 32.5") and is marked with a wooden trail sign. From the trailhead you have a clear view of Two Bar Mountain across the open desert.

HISTORY AND LEGENDS

General Crook's aide-de-camp, John Bourke, kept a diary of his field notes for the Apache campaign in Arizona and mentions his travels through the eastern Superstition Mountains. On December 11, 1872, an expedition under the command of Major Brown left Camp Grant on the San Pedro River with

Tule Trailhead in December 2000. Two Bar Mountain is at the top of the photograph. Tule Trail (122) heads across the flat toward Two Bar Mountain, then turns right at Tule Canyon and reaches Two Bar Ridge Trail (109) on the ridge, which is off the right side of the photograph.

thirty-one Indian Scouts, companies L and M of the 5th Cavalry, a pack train of sixty mules, and several guides. General Crook remained at Camp Grant and did not go on this march. On December 23, the expedition came down the Salt River and turned up the dry creek bed of Pinto Creek. Although Bourke wrote that they were on Pinto Creek, they probably camped on Spring Creek downstream from the present day Spring Creek Ranch where they found wood, water, and grass.[52] See Bourke's map on page 121.

On December 24, the camp moved over to the Tule Spring area where they found water running over the rocks, but then sinking into the sand. They probably rode the upper section of the present day Tule Trail to reach Two Bar Ridge on December 25. From the ridge, they descended into Pine Creek making camp [6-N] about two miles upstream from the present day SR88 bridge across Pine Creek. Captain James Burns with his company G of the 5th Cavalry was camped nearby—one-half mile to the west, probably in Winger Wash [6-P]. Major Brown and Captain Burns discussed their military plans while at Pine Creek, and Mike Burns, the captive Yavapai child of Captain Burns, confirmed the location of the Skeleton Cave rancheria during that conversation.

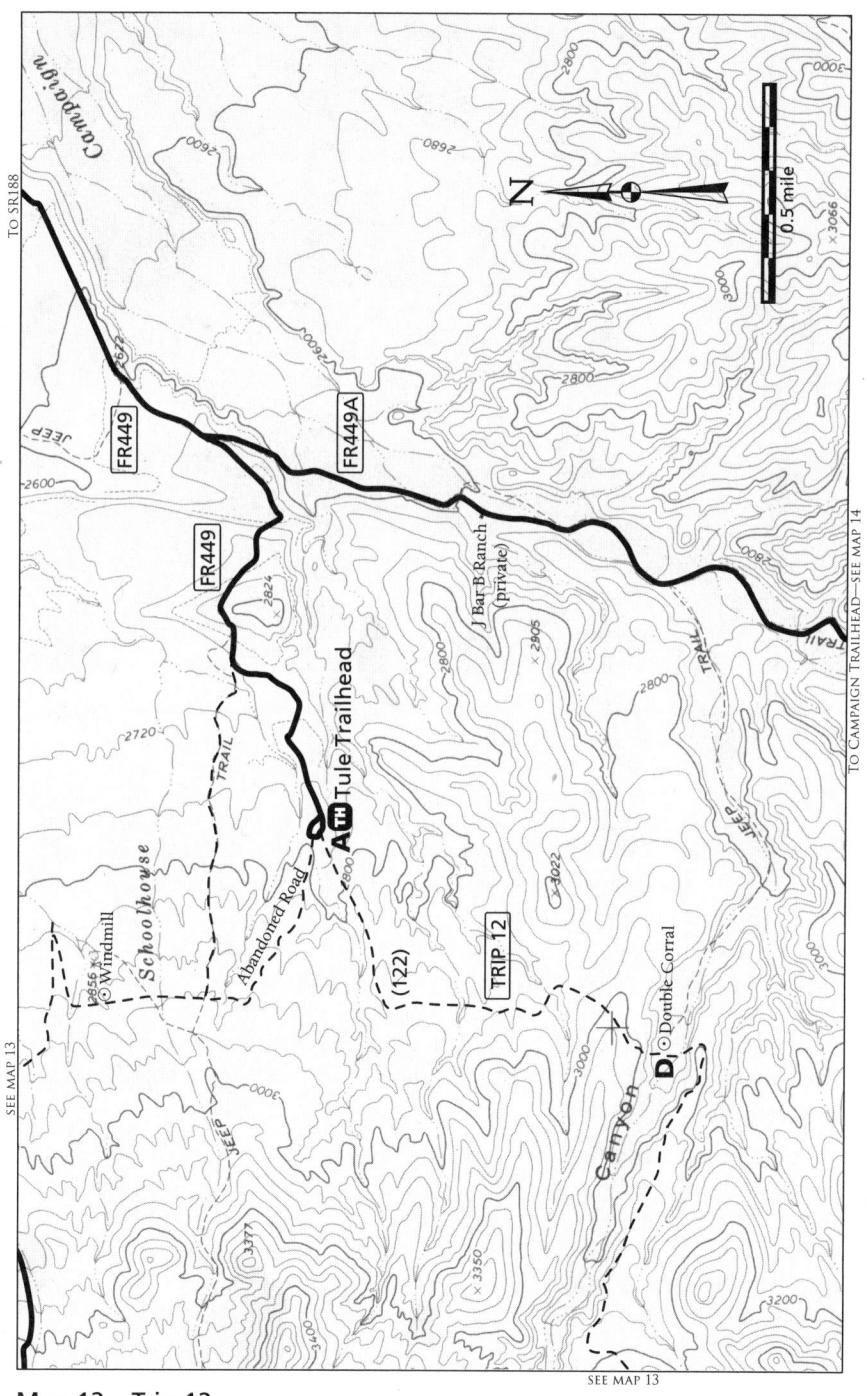

Map 12 – Trip 12.

The trail blaze cut into this old juniper tree on Two Bar Ridge marks the route of the Two Bar Ridge Trail (119). Photo was taken in November 2000.

On December 26, the combined force of 220 fighting men crossed to the north side of the Salt River and camped downriver. On December 27 they went farther west, and after resting a bit, they moved out at eight o'clock p.m. without making camp that night. Just after midnight they reached the summit. Advancing slowly and waiting for sunup on December 28, they stumbled on the rancheria and the battle began. Seventy-six Yavapai were killed and fifty-seven taken prisoner in the five-hour battle, now referred to as the Skeleton Cave Massacre. Only one Army scout, a Pima, was killed. They arrived in Camp McDowell with their prisoners on December 29 for the completion of the march.

Trip 4 (Lower Pine Creek) on page 79 contains more of the story about the December 25, 1872, army camp in Pine Creek. See Miles Trailhead on page 206 for a description of the army's march from Mason's Valley through Pinto Creek and the West Fork Pinto Creek areas in March 1873. John Bourke's description of the January 1873 march is on page 225 and his map is on page 226.

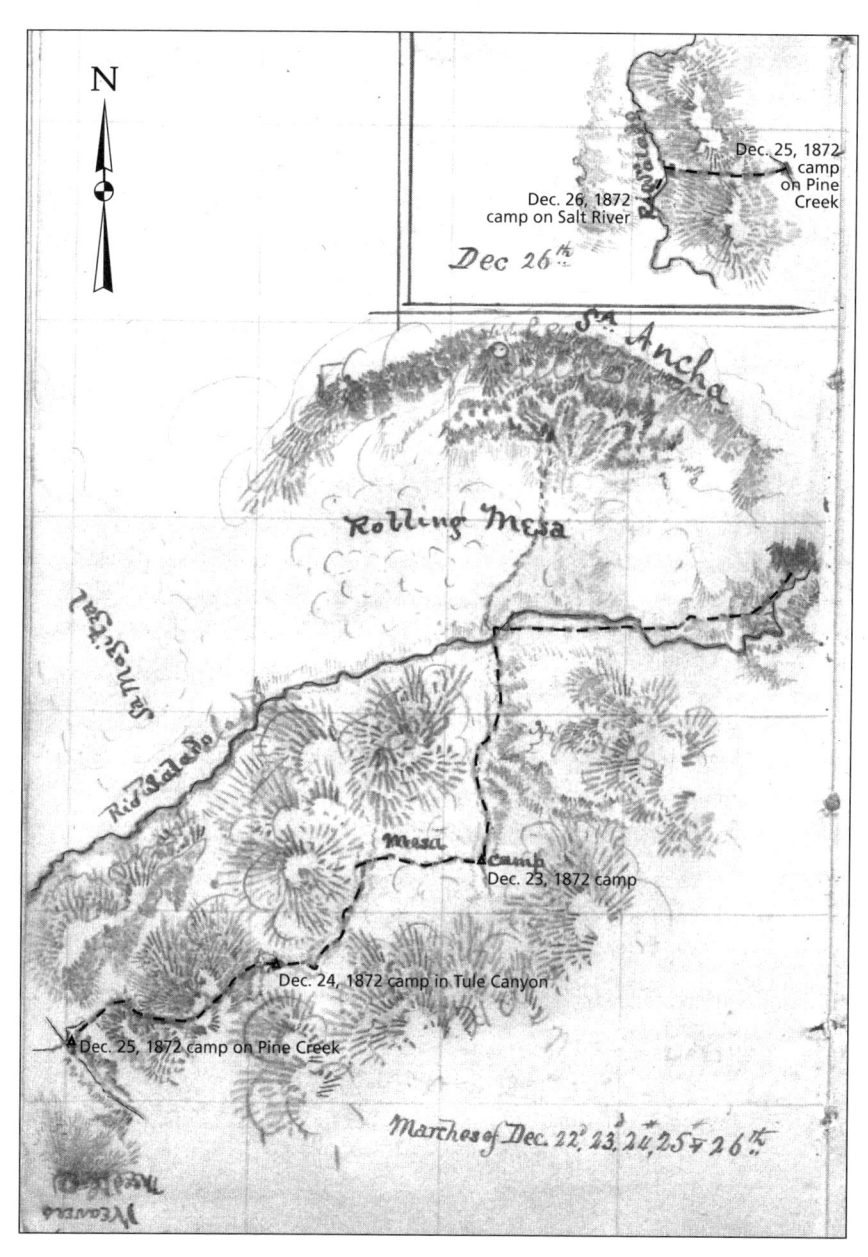

Page from John G. Bourke's diary showing the Army's marches from December 22 to 26, 1872. Several place names are familiar: Rio Salado (Salt River), Sierra Ancha and Sierra Mazitzal. On December 22, they left the Salt River, headed south on Pinto Creek, and most likely made their December 23 camp on Spring Creek or Pinto Creek. The butte labeled Weavers Needle in the lower left corner is not Weavers Needle. It is the formation that we named Bourke's Butte, which Bourke sketched at his Pine Creek camp. We overlaid dashed lines for the trail and streams. We also added the typeset dates for his camps and the north arrow. Map from USMA Library, Special Collections, West Point, NY.[53]

Trip 12

TULE TRAIL TO TWO BAR RIDGE

The Tule Trail takes you up the hill to the Two Bar Ridge Trail where you will enjoy a view in all directions from the narrow ridge. You can look down into the Pine Creek drainage, and farther to the west you can see Apache Lake.

ITINERARY

From the Tule Trailhead, follow the Tule Trail (122) to Two Bar Ridge where Tule Trail meets the Two Bar Ridge Trail (119). Return the same way, or make a loop using Two Bar Ridge Trail, FR83, and cross-country travel back to the Tule Trailhead.

DIFFICULTY

Moderate hike. Difficult horse ride due to sections of steep and narrow trail. Elevation change is +2,120 and -180 feet one way.

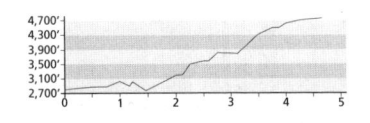

LENGTH and TIME

4.7 miles, 4.5 hours one way.

MAPS

Arizona USGS topo maps NAD27: Pinyon Mountain, Two Bar Mountain. Superstition Wilderness Beartooth map, grids P7 to O8. Map 13.

FINDING THE TRAIL

Trailhead map is on page 117. The beginning of the trail is marked with a wooden sign on the south side of the parking lot (N33° 35' 35.9", W111° 04' 32.5"). The Tule Trail (122) goes south to Tule Canyon before making a sharp turn toward the west and your destination on the ridge.

THE TRIP

Start on Map 13 on page 125. From the Tule Trailhead [13-A, 0], the Tule Trail is marked with large rock cairns. The first mile heads south across a relatively flat area dense with Sonoran desert vegetation. The trail drops into Tule Canyon near Double Corral and a tall water tank [13-D, 1.2]. The older part of Double Corral is built with long timbers and makes a good setting for photographs. Many years ago, we saw goldfish in the water trough here, but on recent trips they had vanished. The Bar V Bar brand, registered by rancher Luther Jackson in 1908, which appears on the cement water trough, is the name of the grazing allotment—Bar V Bar.

The trail crosses Tule Canyon, usually a dry sandy wash, on the upstream side of Double Corral. A Superstition Wilderness boundary sign marks the Tule Trail as it goes up out of the wash onto the south bank of Tule Canyon. An older eroded trail goes up the hill starting from the right side of the sign, but if you look closely through the mesquite trees on the left, you will see a much better trail heading around the south end of the small hill.

Once you are up on the south bank of Tule Canyon, it is easy going again as the trail turns west with good views in all directions. At about the 2.0 mile mark, the trail turns south into the first ravine and starts uphill toward a low ridge where horse riders may have difficulty with loose rocks on the narrow trail. We saw fewer saguaros and more juniper trees as we gained elevation.

From the ridge line, about mile 2.3, we could see light green foliage, probably cottonwood trees, to the west in the ravine below. We assume the green foliage was at the Lost Dutchman Spring and off in the distance to the

Double Corral in Tule Canyon. The cement water trough between the two corrals is inscribed with the Bar V Bar brand. Tule Canyon wash is above the corrals and the Tule Trail heads across Tule Canyon on the right side of the round corral. Photo taken in 2000.

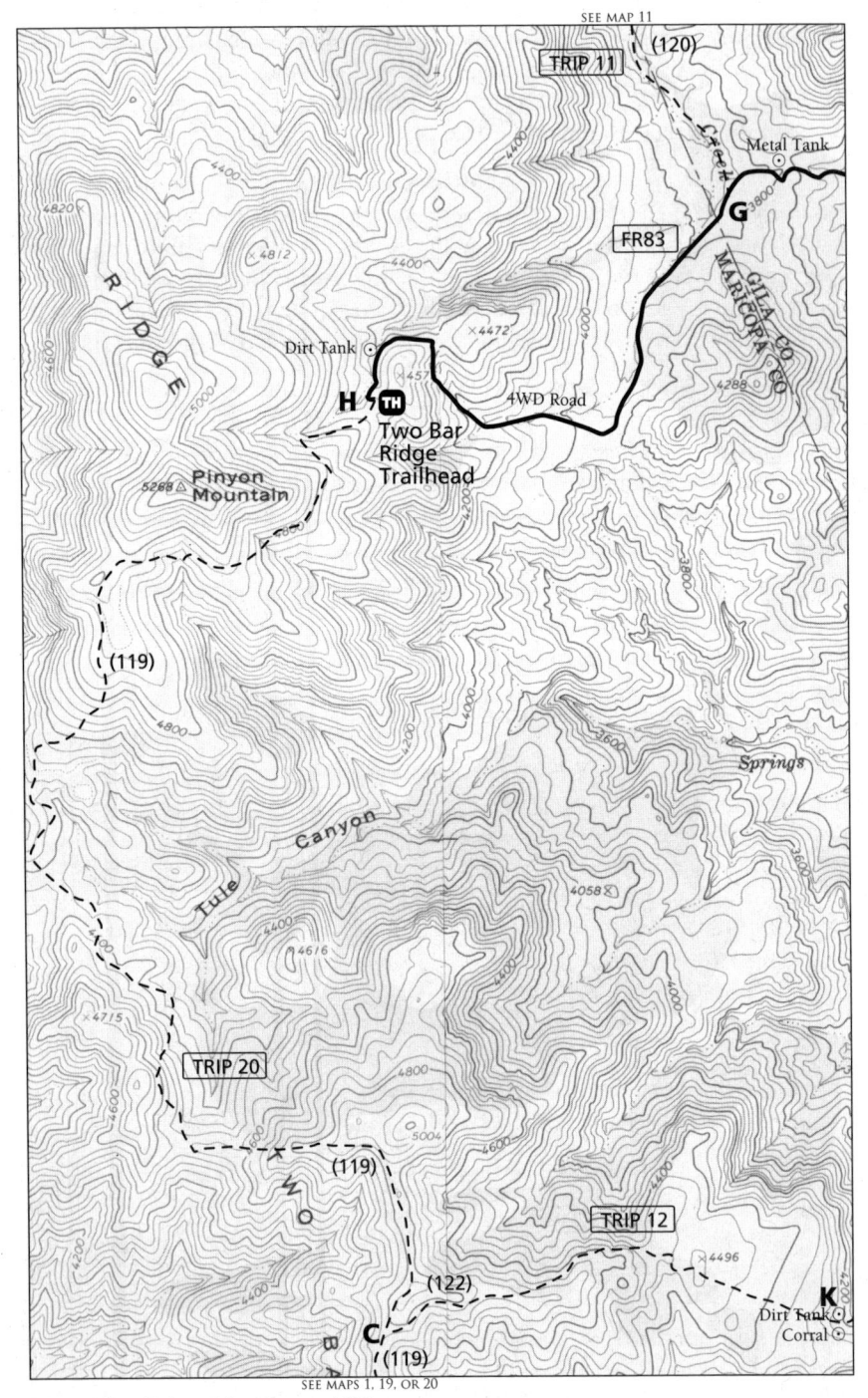

Map 13 – Trips 11, 12, and 20.

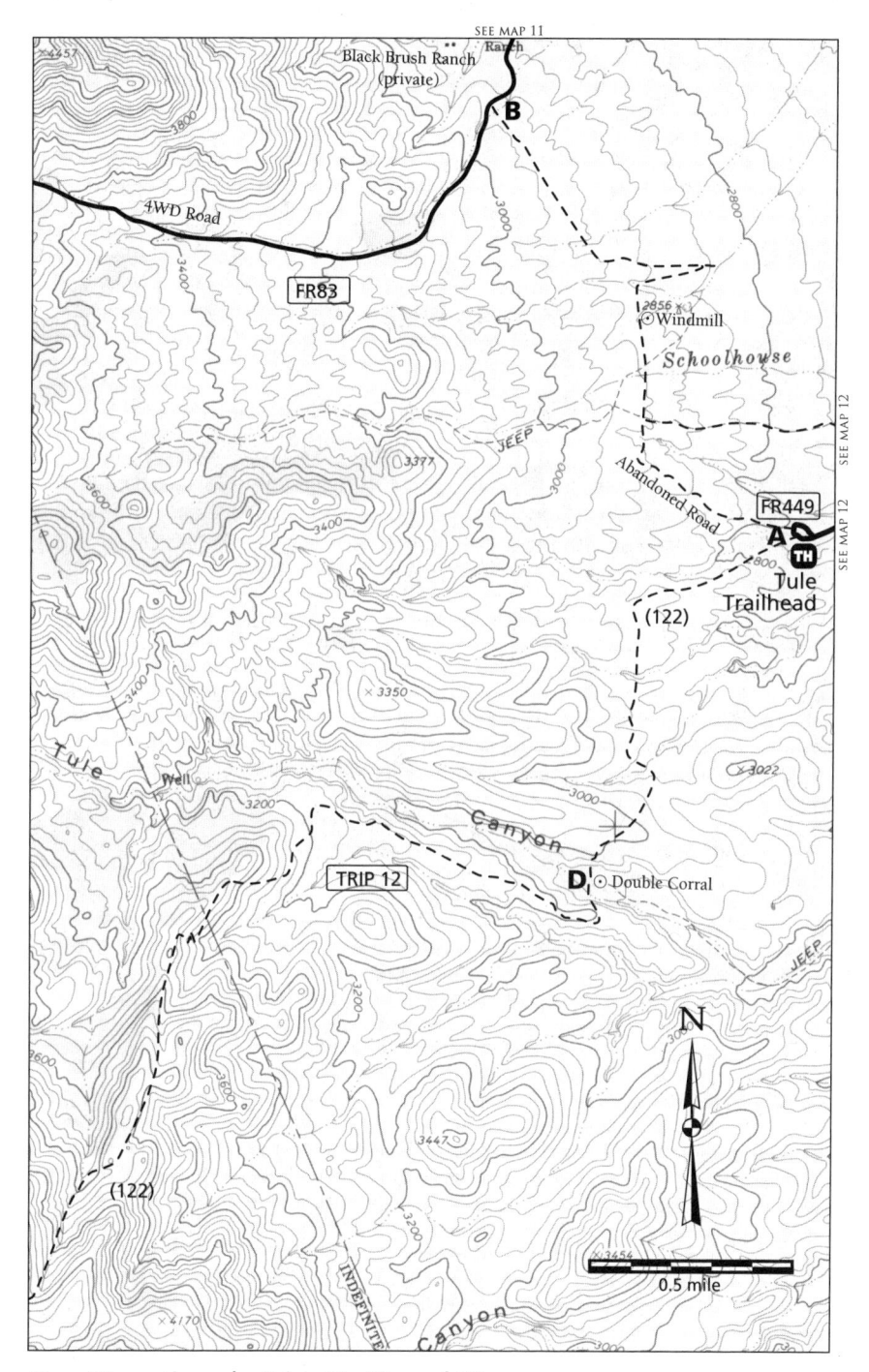

Map 13 continued – Trips 11, 12, and 20.

north was Tule Spring. The Tule Trail does not go to Lost Dutchman Spring or Tule Spring and it looks like it would be a rugged cross-country trek to get there.

After a rain you might find potholes of water in the upper part of Lost Dutchman Spring ravine where the trail comes close to the bed of the ravine. At the top of Lost Dutchman Spring ravine, the trail takes a sharp turn to the right (west) at a large dirt water tank [13-K, 3.5]. The water is usually muddy here. This dirt tank and the trough at Double Corral are the only places to water a horse along this trail. South of the dirt tank is a barbed wire corral and some flat areas that would be good for camping. Continuing uphill to the west, the trail is difficult to follow across an open area, but you will find enough rock cairns to maintain the direction of the trail.

A pinyon pine tree is the next landmark on the trail at about mile 3.8 at the 4,480-foot elevation. The Tule Trail continues uphill as it snakes its way through some low hills until it finally tops out and connects with the Two Bar Ridge Trail (119) on a sloping rocky ridge [13-C, 4.7] (N33° 34' 01", W111° 07' 39"). A wooden trail sign marks the trail intersection.

We expected to see more pinyon tress or even some ponderosa pines on Two Bar Ridge, but the landscape is more like an open high desert with grasses, juniper trees, sotol, yucca, scrub oak, and hedgehog cactus. To the northwest you can see the rugged drainage of Pine Creek, and farther in the distance, a small slice of Apache Lake appears below the cliffs of the Four Peaks Wilderness area. Using our binoculars we could see the road cut for the Reavis Ranch Trail (109) in the Castle Dome area.

You can end your trip at the wooden trail sign, or you can go a short distance in either direction on the Two Bar Ridge Trail. This stretch of the Two Bar Ridge Trail is the only place where you can look over both sides of the ridge. From the junction [13-C] of the Tule and Two Bar Ridge Trails, the closest reliable water is at Walnut Spring [7-W], which is 3.4 miles to the south on Two Bar Ridge Trail. Return to the Tule Trailhead the same way, or consider the more difficult alternate route described below.

ALTERNATE RETURN ROUTE

A much longer return trip can be made by going north (right) on the Two Bar Ridge Trail (119) to the Superstition Wilderness boundary where it meets FR83 [13-H, 8.1]. From the Wilderness boundary, follow FR83, a steep four-wheel-drive dirt road, downhill. Go by the junction with the Cottonwood Trail [13-G, 9.4] and the nearby metal water tank. When you reach a gate [13-B, 11.2] across FR83, go southeast on a cross-country route following old roads and trails to the Tule Trailhead [13-A, 13.0]. Our cross-country route, shown on Map 13, uses dirt roads, some of which have been abandoned. You need to scout this cross-country route in advance, since you will probably have to travel the last part in the dark. The only water along this return loop is seasonal water in the dirt tanks along FR83.

HISTORY AND LEGENDS

See the History and Legends on page 117 in Tule Trailhead for the story of the U.S. Army's march through this area. Their December 24, 1872, camp may have been at Tule Spring—several days before their famous December 28 battle at Skeleton Cave on the north side of the Salt River.

Frank Hammon worked the fall 1887 roundup for Bob Pringle's Flying H brand. Pringle's range was over on Cherry Creek, north of the Salt River. Hammon's place was on nearby Coon Creek where he also ran cattle. In his diary, Hammon wrote that the rodeo (roundup) was gathering cattle behind William Gann's place (probably the Spring Creek Ranch), and they camped at Pete Gann's place (maybe Gans Hole Spring) on October 11. The next day the rodeo camped below the narrows on Campaign Creek where an 1889 map shows a Gann Ranch. On October 13, they gathered between Campaign Creek and Tule Spring. The following day they drove the gathered cattle down to Pemberton's place, which was on the south side of the Salt River across from the Armers' place. Gathering and branding continued in the canyons to the north, and Hammon drove twenty-four of the Flying H cattle over to Cherry Cheek on October 21.[54]

Two Bar Ridge Trail (119) near the junction with Tule Trail (122) follows the top of Two Bar Ridge through the high desert vegetation. Photo was taken in November 2000.

CAMPAIGN TRAILHEAD

From Apache Junction at Idaho Road, drive east on US60 for 49 miles to SR188, on the east side of Globe. In Globe, go north on SR188 for 20 miles to FR449 (J Bar B Road) between mileposts 235 and 236. FR449 is 2 miles north on SR188 from the Spring Creek Store. Drive west on FR449 for 2 miles to the junction with FR449A. Take FR449A left for 5.1 miles to Campaign Trailhead near Reevis Mountain School.

FINDING THE TRAILHEAD

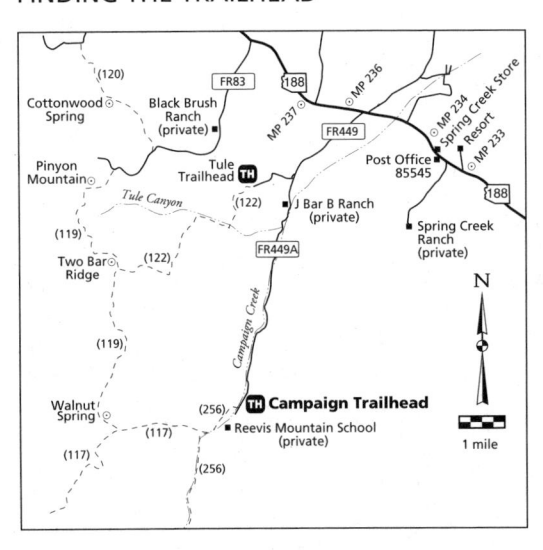

FR449 is well marked to the junction with FR449A. FR449A is a four-wheel-drive road that follows the bed of Campaign Creek. FR449A may be impassable during periods of heavy rain. In the dry season, a high-clearance vehicle will work in ideal weather and road condition. Avoid the deep, soft sand. Following the signs to Reevis Mountain School will keep you on FR449A to Campaign Trailhead.

FACILITIES

The Campaign Trailhead (former Upper Horrell Trailhead) has no facilities except for a small parking area. You must purify drinking water from the creek and all springs in the area, or bring your own water.

THE TRAILS

Campaign Trail (256) begins at the parking area (N33° 31' 54.3", W111° 04' 42.1"), goes south on FR449A, and is marked with a wooden trail sign where the trail leaves FR449A on the right (west) side of the road. In the spring of 1994, the Campaign Trail was realigned so that it goes around the west side of Reevis Mountain School on the west side of Campaign Creek. Do not use the trail that passes through the Reevis Mountain School (private property). Reavis Gap Trail (117) branches off to the right (west) at a signed trail intersection about 1.1 mile south on the Campaign Trail from the trailhead.

HISTORY AND LEGENDS

The private property near Campaign Trailhead, now the Reevis Mountain School and former Upper Horrell Place, has a long history of ranching. John C. Narron was probably the first to establish his headquarters here. Later the Ganns and then the Horrells made this their home. Three ranches in the area, the Upper Horrell Place, the Spring Creek Ranch, and the former Cross P Ranch all played a part in the history of the area.

Ownership records are sketchy in the late 1800s when squatters rights were bought and sold—sometimes without recorded titles, but the official homestead papers in the early 1900s shed light on the people that were living here.

John Narron left Kansas and arrived in Arizona between 1880 and 1883. In Kansas, he was friends with Milo C. Webb who also migrated to the Tonto Basin area. The Webb family became a respected ranching family in Arizona.[55]

In 1886, John and Angeline "Adis" Narron's four children—Alice, Annie, Willie, and Lillian—were attending school in the town of Livingstone on the south bank of the Salt River. Charles Livingston was the school census marshal who kept the records.[57]

Narron branded the N and bought and sold other brands over the years. Like other ranching parents, he registered a brand, the Y J, for three of his children, Annie, W. T., and Lillian, in 1888. In 1892, he purchased three-hundred head of cattle with various brands from his son-in-law William Gann for $2,000.[56]

Marriages between neighboring ranch families were common, and land holdings were often passed down to the children. The Narrons' three girls married local ranchers. The youngest, Lillian, married Charles E. Chilson on December 29, 1900, in Payson. His brother, John C. Chilson, married Emily Jane Gann at the Spring Creek Ranch. Emily's father, Andrew Gann, who lived in the area, was the brother of ranchers William Gann and Pete Gann.[58]

Narron's second oldest daughter was Annie. She married John See on March 3, 1889. Tragically, her husband shot and killed her at her sister's Spring Creek Ranch on May 18, 1892. Her father, John Narron, sister Alice, Alice's husband William Gann, and Annie's six-month-old son were present when she was shot. Sheriff J. Henry Thompson thought John See was

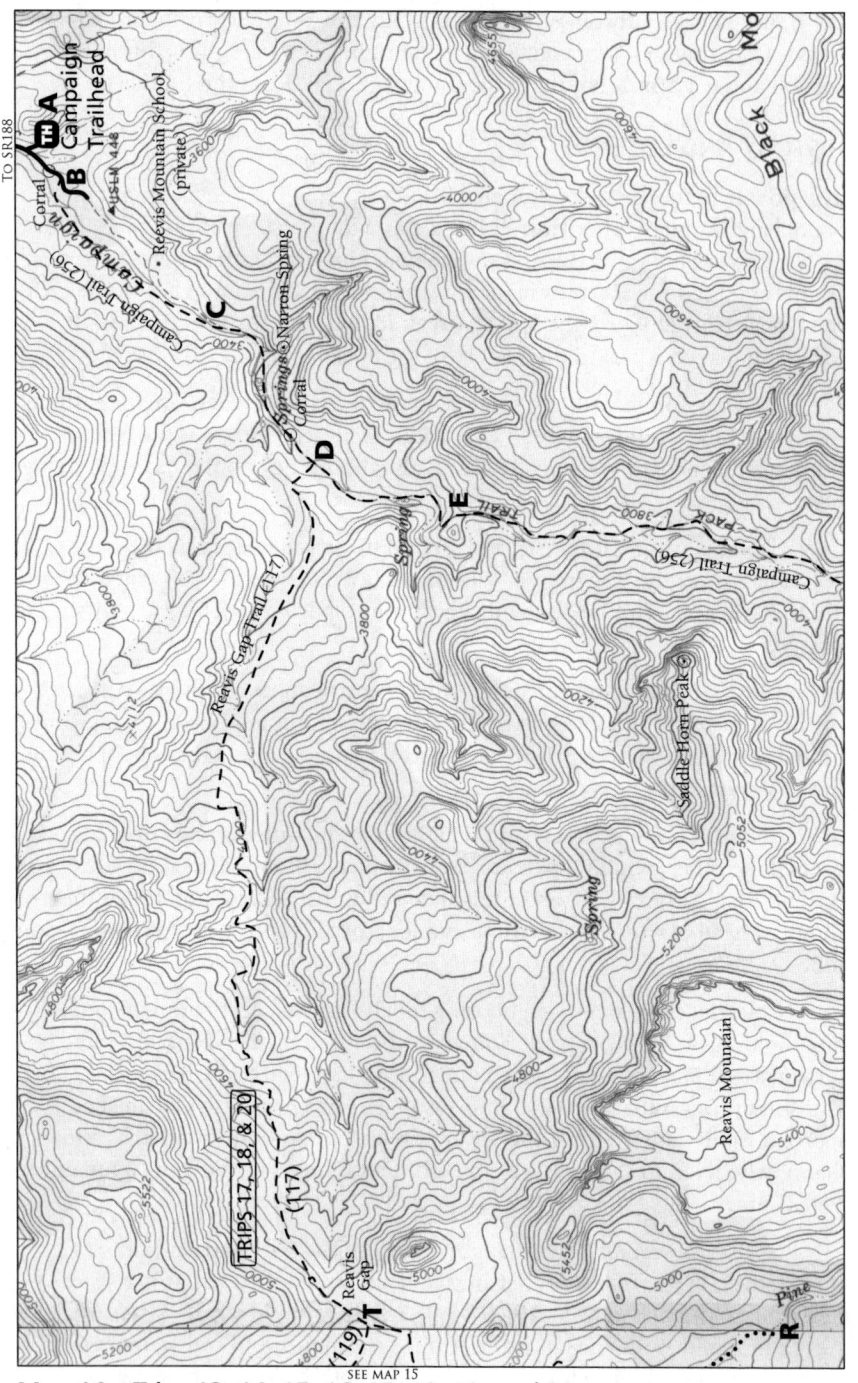

Map 14 – Trips 13, 14, 15, 16, 17, 18, 19, and 20.

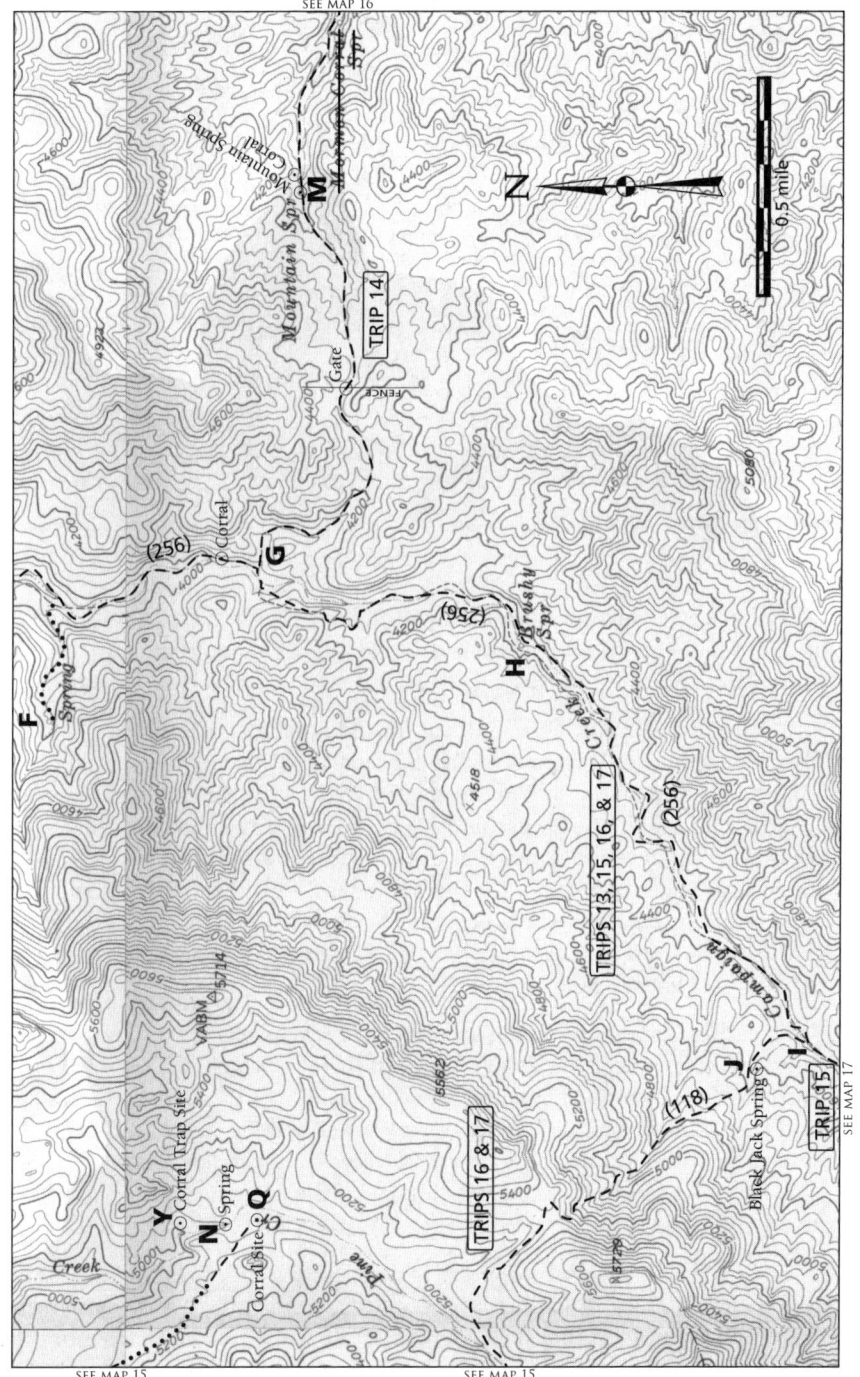

Map 14 continued – Trips 13, 14, 15, 16, 17, 18, 19, and 20.

Campaign Trailhead 131

Ephraim "Pete" Gann with his horse Rowdy, circa 1890s in California. Courtesy of Denise Cortelyou.

involved in a stage holdup, and Annie was helping the sheriff with information about the robbery. John must have found out and taken revenge. She is buried near the ranch. John See fled to Mexico and was never apprehended.[59]

Alice (Martha Alice Narron) was the oldest of the children. She married local rancher William Thomas Gann at Grapevine on January 9, 1887, and is listed on the school census with William as the guardian for two of his children from another marriage.[60] Alice and William's daughter, Ida May, died from eating honey that contained a bee stinger.[61] She is buried with a handsome gravestone at the old homestead, now the Reevis Mountain School. Ida's gravestone reads, *Daughter of W. T. and Alice Gann, died June 9, 1891, aged one year and 9 months, Sleep On In Peace In This Lonely Grave*. See page 20 for a photo of her gravestone.

William Gann was buying and selling property in Globe in 1880 and had married his second wife Emily Knudson there on September 19, 1881.[62] Some of William Gann's brands were the Diamond X, GAN, Quarter Circle V, and Hat. William and his brothers, Travis and Ephraim, carried out many transactions with local ranchers for cattle, brands, and land. William and Emily were divorced on December 1, 1886, shortly before he married Alice Narron. Alice and William were running the Spring Creek Ranch in 1892 when her sister Annie was killed at the ranch.[63]

Pete Gann and his bother Travis returned to their father's ranch in the San Joaquin Valley of California along with Pete's wife Laura Horrell about 1887 or 1888. Another brother Isaac was living at the California ranch. The last record showing a member of the Gann family in Gila County is in 1897 when William sold the Quarter Circle V branded cattle to his son Teddie. William and Alice Gann settled in Los Angeles County, California and were living there in 1900. Alice's family, the Narrons, moved back to Kansas around 1900.[64]

The History of Tonto notes that the Cooper brothers bought the Gann outfit, although the book does not give a date. The Cooper brothers left Arizona shortly after buying the Gann outfit, but Ruth Cooper remained at Salt River and married Earl E. Bacon. They had four children, Grant, Earl, John, and Ruth. John, nicknamed Hoolie, was the owner of the Reavis Ranch in the mid 1900s.[65]

Traces of the stockade-style log cabin—logs placed vertically instead of laid horizontally—from the Narron era ranch were still visible in 1979 when

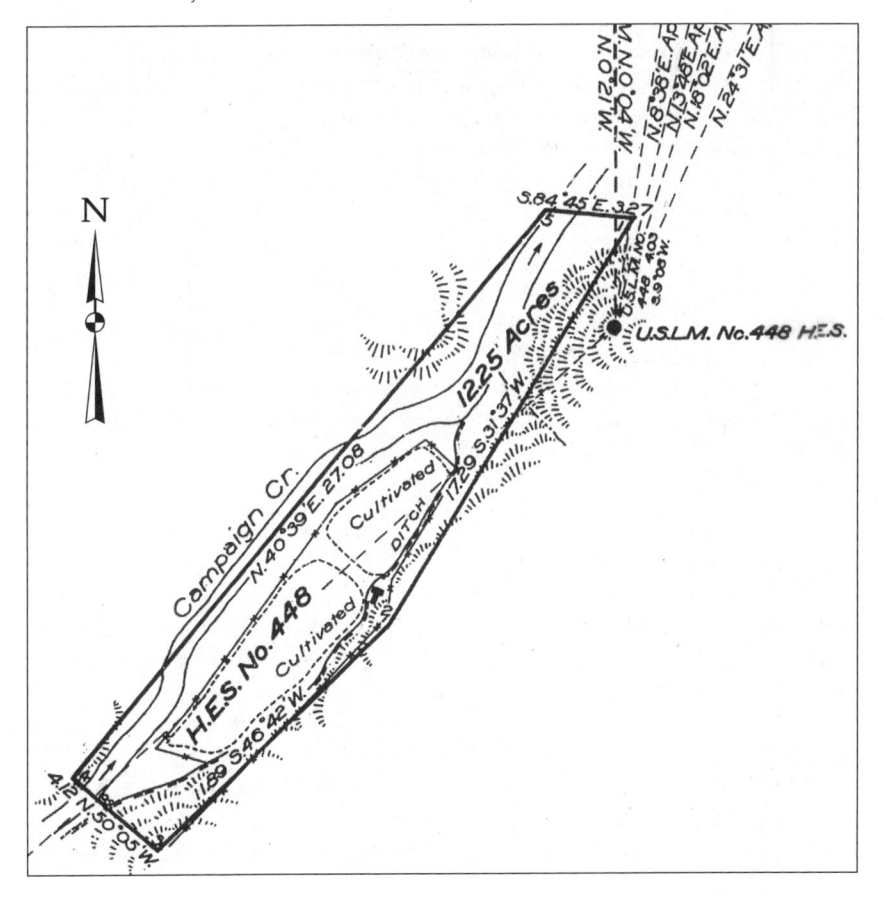

Homestead Entry Survey (HES 448) for Edward Horrell's homestead (the present day Reevis Mountain School) shows the T-shaped log dwelling. The survey was completed on April 14, 1916. Horrell received the land patent on November 12, 1923. Map from BLM, Phoenix Office.

Peter Busnack started the Reevis Mountain School. The 1916 homestead survey describes the building as a T-shaped log dwelling with two rectangular sections, one 24-by-16 feet and the other 24-by-18 feet (see survey map on page 133).[66]

Starting in 1909, ranchers such as Mrs. E. A. Hocker, Harry Shute, and Grover Wright were trying to prove up on the Campaign Creek homestead, but it was Ed Horrell who received the patent for the 12-acre Upper Horrell Place in 1923.[67] Later, Ed Horrell bought the Luther Jackson homestead on the lower part of Campaign Creek, which was known as the Cross P Ranch (now the J Bar B). Ed's son, Earl Horrell, a graduate of the University of Southern California in accounting, bought the Upper Horrell Place from his father in 1927 and made that his headquarters with his wife Blanche Carter.[68]

In 1939, Earl and Blanche bought the Spring Creek Ranch from George Henderson and made it their Half Diamond Cross (or Rafter Cross) headquarters, which was often referred to as the Lower Ranch. Earl and Blanche's daughter, Earline, married James Tidwell in 1959, and they managed all three ranches after Earl passed away in 1978. Earl was still active with cattle buying at the Bixby auction a few years before he died. See History and Legends on pages 178 to 180 in the Pinto Creek Trailhead section of this book for the early history of the Horrell family.

Upper Horrell still retains its name on many of the maps, but the former Horrell Ranch has been the Reevis Mountain School since 1979. John Goodson was a colleague of Jim Tidwell at the University of Arizona, and John arranged the purchase of the ranch from Jim and Earline.[69] John established the ranch as a non-profit school and farm—a division of the Pateman-Akin-Kachina Foundation. Peter "Bigfoot" Busnack and John Goodson are the founders of the Reevis Mountain School of Self-Reliance.

At the quiet farm and sanctuary on Campaign Creek, Peter is reliving some of the same adventures Elisha Reavis experienced more than one hundred 100 years ago. With his partners at Reevis Mountain School, he grows fruit, herbs, and vegetables on the farm at the edge of the Wilderness. Peter teaches the student interns his knowledge of herbal remedies, farming, construction, wilderness survival, and outdoor skills. The farm sells its produce, fruit, and herbal remedies in nearby towns including Globe and Tempe. Peter and the school are well-known for their classes on botanical medicine, self-healing, and plant identification. We learned our plant identification skills from Peter over the years and hope we do justice to his patient instruction. The Reevis Mountain School website, www.reevismountain.org, tells more about the school, classes, and overnight stays.

Trip 13

CAMPAIGN TRAIL TO FIRE LINE TRAIL

Campaign Creek is a scenic and quiet area of the Wilderness. You can spend the day or plan an overnight pack trip with side trips to Circlestone ruin or Horrell Creek. The trail follows Campaign Creek and it is mostly flat with a gentle grade. The thick canopy of tall sycamore trees provides shade in the warmer months and a colorful display in the fall. Several water sources in the area make this a good trip in all but the driest seasons.

ITINERARY

From the Campaign Trailhead, follow the Campaign Trail (256) to Fire Line Trail (118). Return the same way.

DIFFICULTY

Easy hike. Moderate horse ride. Elevation change is +1,340 and -60 feet one way.

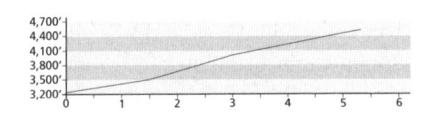

LENGTH and TIME

5.3 miles, 3.5 hours one way.

MAPS

Arizona USGS topo maps NAD27: Two Bar Mountain, Haunted Canyon. Superstition Wilderness Beartooth map, grids P9 to O11. Map 14.

FINDING THE TRAIL

Trailhead map is on page 128. The trail starts at Campaign Trailhead (N33° 31' 54.3", W111° 04' 42.1") and goes south on dirt road FR449A. Before reaching the Reevis Mountain School gate, the Campaign Trail goes right (west) and crosses Campaign Creek.

THE TRIP

Start on Map 14 on page 130. From Campaign Trailhead [14-A, 0], go south on FR449A, passing through a wooden corral, to reach the trail sign for Campaign Trail (256). At the trail sign [14-B, 0.1], turn right (west), cross Campaign Creek, and continue up a hill as the Campaign Trail skirts the edge of the Reevis Mountain School property. From the trail, you have a bird's-eye view of the farm and extensive orchard. You might see a small herd of javelina in the orchard picking up scraps of fruit that fell from the trees.

The trail descends to creek level, crosses to the east side of Campaign Creek [14-C, 0.7], then follows the creek, meandering from one side to the other. Narron Spring, where Reevis Mountain School obtains its water, is located on the east bank (avoid the poison ivy here).

After passing through a corral, you will see a wooden sign that marks the Reavis Gap Trail (117) coming in from the right (west) [14-D, 1.1]. This is a good turnaround point or a nice rest area if you are on a leisurely trip. Campaign Creek normally has water here, but the creek is usually dry a short distance upstream. Be sure to purify your drinking water from the creek, or bring your own water. The creek supports a thick stand of cottonwood, sycamore, and walnut trees. If you take the Reavis Gap Trail, which is mostly uphill, from Campaign Creek, you will reach the Two Bar Ridge Trail (119) junction [14-T] in another 2.4 miles, Pine Creek [15-P] in 3.2 miles, and the Reavis Ranch Trail (109) junction [18-G] in 5.7 miles.

Trip 13 continues on the Campaign Trail, follows the right bank of the creek for a short distance, then stays on the left bench as the trail climbs over the neck of a ridge [14-E, 1.5] to avoid obstacles in the creek where the stream water originates. Campaign Creek is usually dry beyond this ridge, except for Brushy Spring farther along in the trip.

We named Saddle Horn Peak on our Map 14 for the prominent rock outcrop on the west hillside near mile 2.1 in the trip. Hiker and outdoorsman John Fritz calls the outcrop Skeleton Peak for the skull face at the top of the peak and a spine on the left side, just above our saddle horn image.[70]

You can take a side trip up to an unnamed spring [14-F] on the west side of the canyon. Water from the ravine disappears underground when it meets Campaign Creek. A livestock trail takes you up the left (south) side of the ravine for about 0.3 mile to the source of the water.

When the trail passes through a fence and wire corral, you are about 0.1 mile from the former trail junction [14-G, 3.2] (N33° 29' 43", W111° 05' 40") with the abandoned Pinto Peak Trail. This intersection, where the former K.R.N. *Trail* sign was posted, is not easy to recognize. If you are interested in the abandoned Pinto Peak Trail, look for a rock cairn marking the trail as the trail heads east, going up a ravine and over the ridge to Horrell Creek. If you are looking for water, you might find a water seep about 0.1 mile up the old Pinto Peak Trail at an out-of-service cement water trough. Another 1.1 miles takes you to a more reliable water source at Mountain Spring on the east side of the ridge in the Horrell Creek drainage. See Trip 14 (Mountain Spring and Horrell Creek) for the description.

Peter "Bigfoot" Busnack harvesting potatoes in the vegetable garden at the Reevis Mountain School, which is near the Campaign Trailhead on Campaign Creek. The farm is dominated by a large fruit orchard. Photo was taken in April 1998.

This trip continues south on the Campaign Trail, which crosses to the right side (west) of the creek, goes up a deep cut in the west bank of Campaign Creek, and climbs a small hill that bypasses the narrows in the creek. The trail descends to a flat bench that has room for camping.

Farther upstream, the trail follows the east bench, which becomes wider, and you will find flat places to camp under the tall sycamore trees. We saw the ruins of a corral in this area, which is just downstream from Brushy Spring.

Brushy Spring [14-H, 4.0] is aptly named as the spring is a brushy area in the bed of Campaign Creek where water surfaces for a short distance along

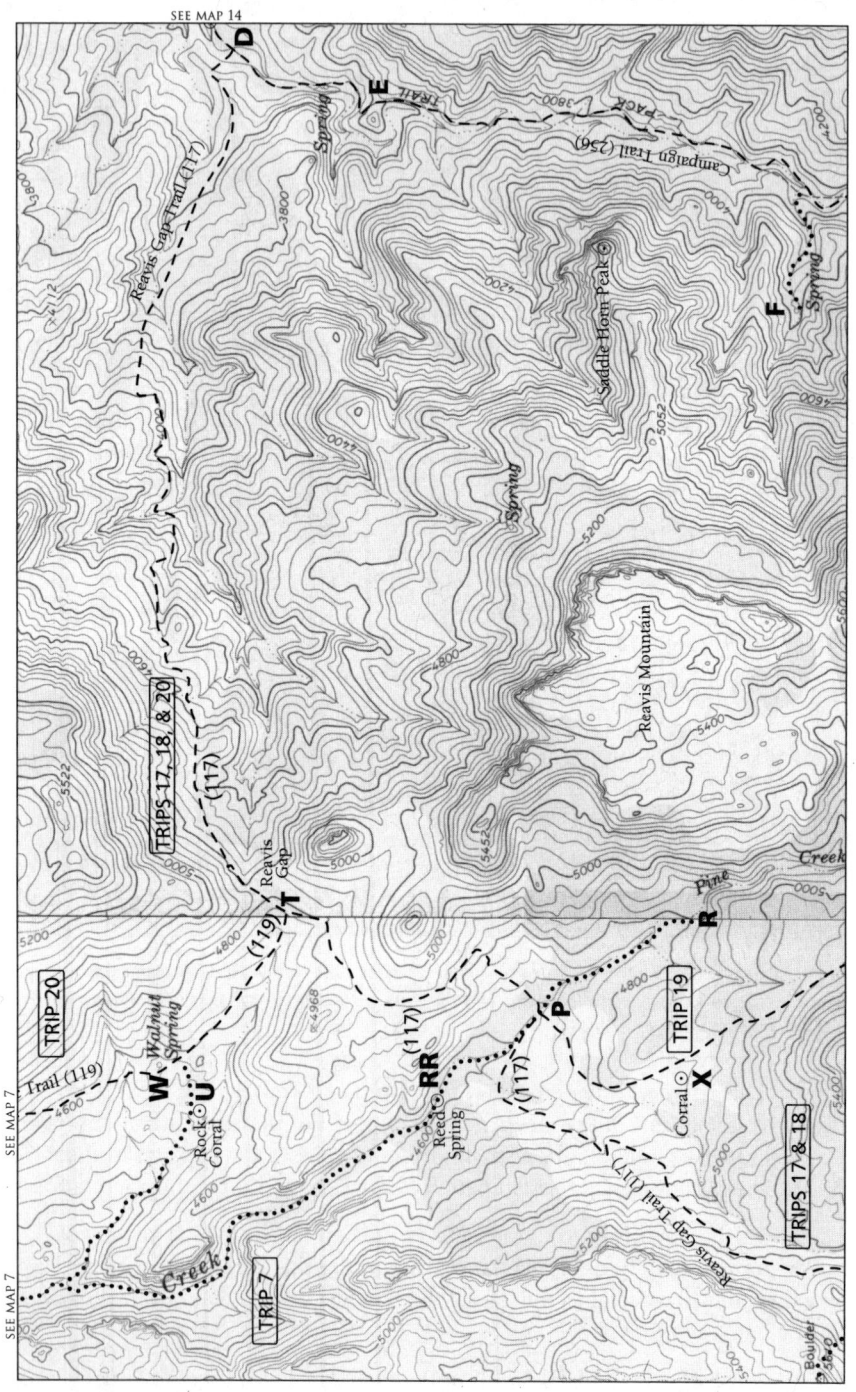

Map 15 – Trips 1, 7, 13, 15, 16, 17, 18, 19, and 20.

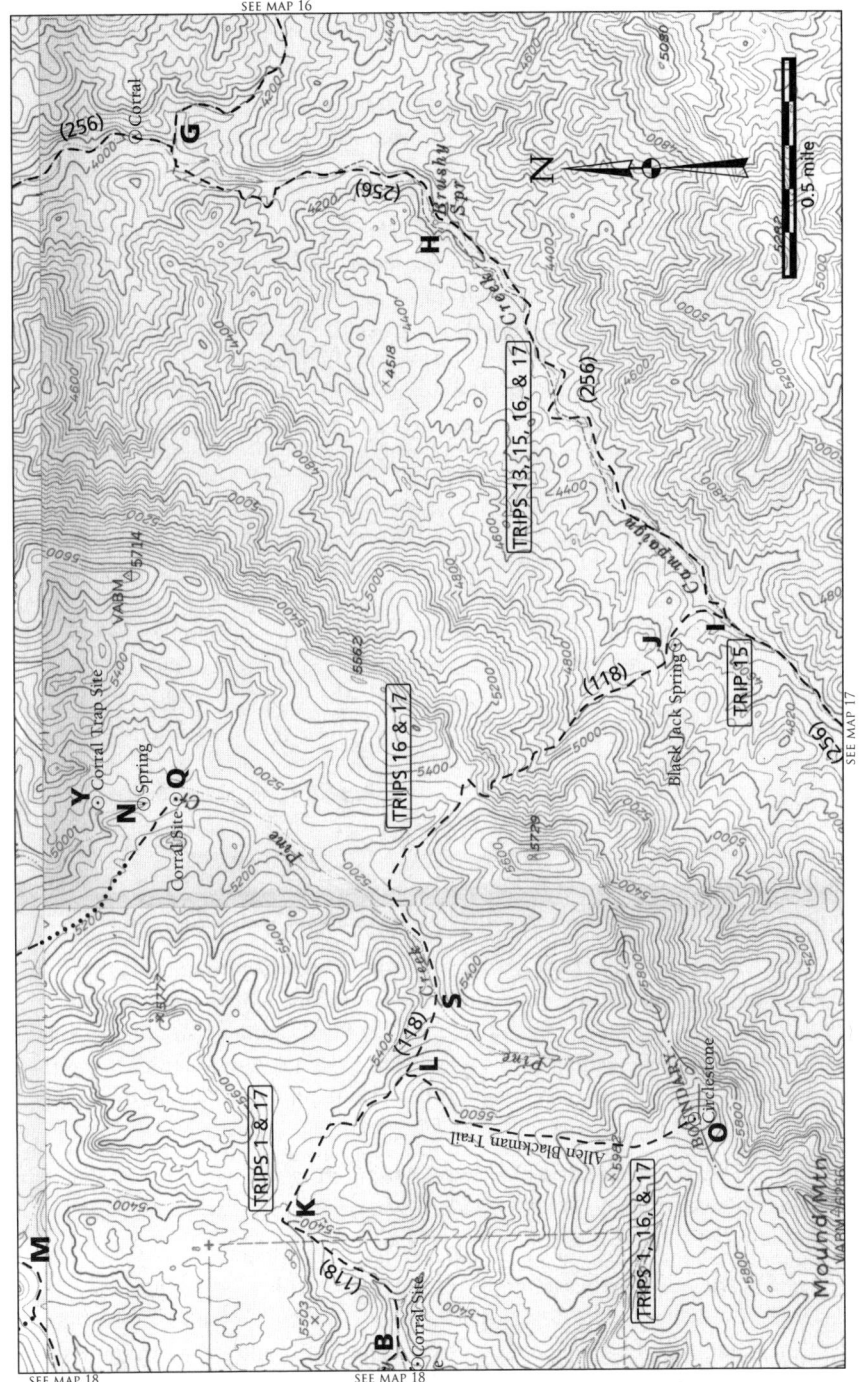

Map 15 continued – Trips 1, 7, 13, 15, 16, 17, 18, 19, and 20.

the normally dry creek bed. We found the best water about 0.1 mile upstream from the map location of the spring.

Upstream from Brushy Spring, the trail favors the south bank making only a few crossings. A steel cable across Campaign Creek signals the nearby junction with the Fire Line Trail (118). The trail, now on the left (south) bank, goes through an open gate and enters a stand of ponderosa pine trees where the Campaign and Fire Line Trail junction is marked with a wooden sign [14-I, 5.3]. The trail sign is next to a large ponderosa pine tree, which makes the sign difficult to see when traveling from the south. The trail junction makes a nice turnaround point or a place to take a break, since both the Campaign and Fire Line Trails begin their uphill climbs from here. The trip ends here. Return the same way. The optional side trips described below can lengthen your day trip or make an extended camping trip enjoyable.

OPTIONAL SIDE TRIPS

1. Circlestone Ruin. Starting on the Fire Line Trail, the round trip to Circlestone ruin is 4.8 miles. From the Campaign Trail [15-I, 0], go west on the steep Fire Line Trail up to Black Jack Spring [15-J, 0.2], and then up to the saddle at mile mark 0.8. Drop into the Pine Creek drainage where you can find some nice campsites under the ponderosa pines. Pine Creek is usually dry at the Fire Line Trail crossing [15-S, 1.4], but a spring [15-N] in the creek bed, about 0.9 mile down canyon at elevation 5,040, might be a possible source of water. Continue on the Fire Line Trail as the trail goes uphill out of the Pine Creek drainage to the junction with the unsigned Allen Blackman Trail [15-L, 1.6] (N33° 29' 15", W111° 07' 54"). Turn left (south) at the rock cairns, and follow the well-worn Allen Blackman Trail to Circlestone ruin [15-O, 2.4]. See Trip 34 (Rogers Trough to Reavis Ranch) and Trip 16 (Campaign Trail to Circlestone) for more details on Circlestone.

2. Pinto Divide. Starting from the Fire Line Trail junction [17-I, 0], the Campaign Trail takes you up to the divide [17-K, 1.8] that separates Campaign Creek and West Fork Pinto Creek. The Campaign Trail is an uphill climb, and the trail is sometimes brushy. You can continue downhill from the divide, heading southeast, to the end of the Campaign Trail where it meets West Fork Pinto Creek at Oak Flat [17-N, 4.4].

3. Reavis Ranch Loop. See Trip 17 for a 16.1 mile trip through Reavis Ranch. From Campaign Creek [15-I], the distance to Reavis Ranch [3-I] is 3.6 miles.

4. The Bruce Grubbs Loop. Author Bruce Grubbs, in *Backpacking Arizona* (Campaign Creek Loop), describes an interesting loop trip that takes you on Campaign Trail to Oak Flat, West Pinto Trail to Rogers Trough, Reavis Ranch Trail to Reavis Ranch, and Reavis Gap Trail for his 29.9 mile loop.[71]

5. **Variation of the Bruce Grubbs Loop for Horse Riders.** Stockmen that want to use chuck-wagon support for their food and camp gear can use the trailhead access roads. Start at Campaign Trailhead (FR449A), camp the first night at Miles Trailhead (FR287A), second night at Rogers Trough Trailhead (FR172A), third night at Reavis Ranch (no access road here), fourth night at Two Bar Ridge Trailhead (FR83), and the last night at Frazier Equestrian Campground by Roosevelt Lake (SR188).

HISTORY AND LEGENDS

In 2000, we found a broken trail sign on the ground at the junction of the Campaign Trail and old Pinto Peak Trail. One of the names on the wooden sign read *K.R.N. Trail*. We traced the name on the sign to Kenneth R. Nelssen

Pine needles and cones cover the ground at the junction of the Campaign Trail (256) and the Fire Line Trail (118). This scenic area under a stand of tall ponderosa pine trees is a good place to take a break or have lunch. Photo taken February 2000.

who worked for the Tonto Basin Ranger District from 1954 to 1979. In the 1950s or early 1960s, he was making improvements to the trails in the Upper Horrell area when rancher Earl Horrell told him about an old trail that went up Campaign Creek connecting the Reavis Gap Trail to the Pinto Peak Trail. Ken followed the blazes on the trees and flagged the overgrown trail. Someone suggested that they use Ken's initials for the trail name, but after the signs were installed, the agency decided that naming trails after living Forest Service employees might not be good policy. The trail was eventually renamed the Campaign Trail. Kevin McCombe of the Forest Service recovered the trail sign and donated the sign to the Superstition Mountain Museum in 2002.[72]

    Many older maps show Pinto Peak Trail (213), but the 2001 revision of the Tonto National Forest map was the first to reflect the abandonment of a portion of that trail and the renaming of the rest of the Pinto Peak Trail as the Campaign Trail (256). The old Pinto Peak Trail started at Oak Flat on West Fork Pinto Creek and climbed over the divide to Campaign Creek. It then went down Campaign Creek for 3.9 miles, turned east, went over the ridge to Mountain Spring, and ended a little beyond Mormon Corral. The portion of the trail from Mormon Corral to Campaign Creek has been abandoned as an official trail for maintenance purposes, but you can still use it. The rest of the trail, all the way to Oak Flat, has been renamed Campaign Trail (256).

    The steel cable across Campaign Creek near the junction with the Fire Line Trail was probably used to carry a water pipeline from Black Jack Spring [15-J] across Campaign Creek to some water troughs. The boundaries of three grazing allotments—Reevis, Campaign, and Brushiest—were partitioned so all the cattle could water here. The notation on some older maps indicates that those water troughs may have been named Lower Campaign Spring. The Reevis allotment was headquartered at Reavis Ranch, the Campaign allotment at the Upper Horrell Place, and the Brushiest allotment at Miles Ranch.

Trip 14

Mountain Spring and Horrell Creek

This trip follows the abandoned portion of the former Pinto Peak Trail (former 213) that extends from Campaign Creek over the ridge into Horrell Creek. Horrell Creek is usually dry, but several springs along the trail provide water—Mountain Spring being the most reliable. Corrals, water troughs, and a windmill on this active grazing allotment make good subjects for western photographers.

ITINERARY

From the Campaign Trailhead, follow the Campaign Trail (256) for 3.2 miles, and turn left (east) on the unmarked and unmaintained trail. Follow the trail to the top of the ridge and down into Horrell Creek. Return the same way.

DIFFICULTY

Easy hike. Moderate horse ride. Elevation change is +1,170 and -670 feet one way.

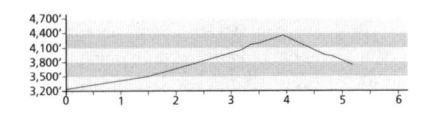

LENGTH and TIME

5.2 miles, 4 hours one way.

MAPS

Arizona USGS topo maps NAD27: Two Bar Mountain, Haunted Canyon. Superstition Wilderness Beartooth map, grids P9 to P11. Maps 14 and 16.

FINDING THE TRAIL

Trailhead map is on page 128. The Campaign Trail starts at Campaign Trailhead (N33° 31' 54.3", W111° 04' 42.1") and goes south on dirt road FR449A. Before reaching the Reevis Mountain School gate, the Campaign Trail goes right (west) and crosses Campaign Creek. See below for the Horrell Creek turnoff.

THE TRIP

Start on Map 14 on page 130. From the Campaign Trailhead [14-A, 0], follow Trip 13 (Campaign Trail to Fire Line Trail) for the first 3.2 miles. At the unsigned trail junction [16-G, 3.2] (N33° 29' 43", W111° 05' 40"), turn left

Mormon Corral on Horrell Creek. Since the well casing is collapsed, the windmill is inoperable and the covered water tank in the corral is empty. Photo was taken in February 2000.

(east) and head up the ravine on the former Pinto Peak Trail. Within 0.1 mile, you may find a seep of water at a broken cement water trough on the left side of the trail. Pass through a gate in the fence on the ridge [3.8], and continue downhill into the Horrell Creek drainage.

Mountain Spring [16-M, 4.4] is the first spring you pass. The water pipe is in a corral on the left (north) side of the trail. Water usually runs out of the pipe onto the ground and does not fill the tanks or troughs. This seems to be a fairly reliable spring. Down canyon from Mountain Spring, the springs noted on the maps do not produce as much water as Mountain Spring.

Several of the springs are mislabeled on the USGS Haunted Canyon topo map, which we have corrected on our Map 16. The Superstition Wilderness maps by the Forest Service and Beartooth show the correct names for the springs.

The trip ends at Mormon Corral and the Wilderness boundary [14-N, 5.2] where you might find the corrals and abandoned windmill interesting to photograph. Return the same way. You can continue down Horrell Canyon as far as you like on the dirt road FR306 and FR305, but do not rely on these roads for vehicle access.

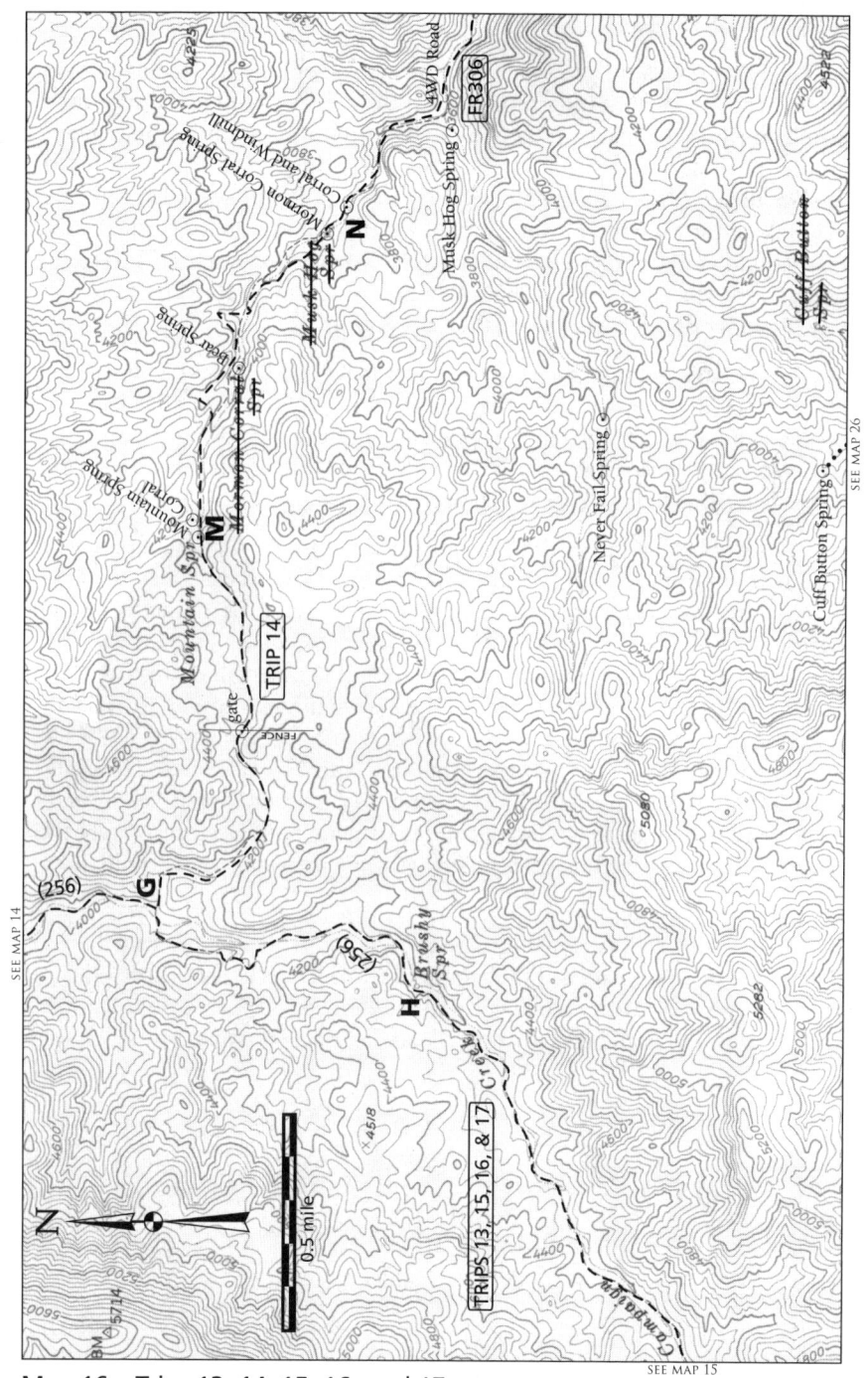

Map 16 – Trips 13, 14, 15, 16, and 17.

HISTORY AND LEGENDS

In the 1980s, Howard H. Horinek was the manager of the JH6 Ranch working for owner L. R. Layton. Intermittent water flow from Mountain Spring was a problem. Horinek and Danny Avendano dug up the Mountain Spring underground pipeline and leveled the pipe from the spring box to the corral to remove the air locks that sometimes stopped the water flow. At that time, they maintained the tank full of water, which fed the water troughs. Horinek and Pilar Maldonado Ochoa packed in material to repair that water tank, which was built by the CCC in the 1930s. A similar water tank [26-JJ] built by the CCC is at Sycamore Spring along the Cuff Button Trail.

We have not seen the concrete water trough at Bear Spring, but Horinek said he knew that was the name of the spring because the Bear Spring name was inscribed in the concrete. Former ranch owner John Anderson told Horinek that the Mormon Corral Well, down canyon a short distance, was abandoned because it had a collapsed well casing.[73]

Neighboring rancher Bill Bohme told Howard Horinek about an old road that ran from Punkin Center to Silver King. Howard described the road as going by Mountain Spring, turning south at Mormon Corral, crossing Cuff Button Corral, following Cuff Button Trail to the top of the hill, and then heading southwest to Miles Ranch. We have not checked all of this route, but Howard said he saw clear signs of the road south of Mormon Corral and found wagon wheel cuts in the bedrock between Never Fail Spring and Cuff Button Spring. A 1916 map shows a trail in the area he described. The trail on the 1916 map is an extension of the trail that goes up Pine Creek from the Salt River. Although the landmarks on the map are not placed accurately, the road Horinek described may be the trail that the map maker was trying to depict.[74]

Horrell Creek is named for the Horrell family that homesteaded the JH6 Ranch on Pinto Creek at the mouth of Horrell Creek. See History and Legends in the Campaign Trailhead and the Pinto Creek Trailhead for stories about the Horrell ranchers on pages 134 and 178 respectively.

Campaign Trail to West Fork Pinto Creek

The Campaign Trail follows the tree-lined Campaign Creek to its headwaters, then goes up and over the Campaign–Pinto Creek Divide. Traveling downhill into West Fork Pinto Creek, the open country provides good views of the surrounding mountains. Once in West Fork Pinto Creek at Oak Flat, you will find seasonal water and abundant trees—Arizona cypress, sycamore, and cottonwood. Several trails from Oak Flat make extended pack trips possible.

ITINERARY

From the Campaign Trailhead, follow the Campaign Trail (256) to West Fork Pinto Creek and the West Pinto Trail (212) at Oak Flat. Return the same way, or link up with other trails.

DIFFICULTY

Difficult hike. Difficult horse ride. Elevation change is +2,160 and -1,720 feet one way.

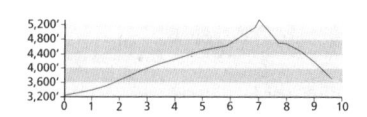

LENGTH and TIME

9.7 miles, 7 hours one way.

MAPS

Arizona USGS topo maps NAD27: Two Bar Mountain, Haunted Canyon, Iron Mountain. Superstition Wilderness Beartooth map, grids P9 to O13. Maps 14 and 17.

FINDING THE TRAIL

Trailhead map is on page 128. The trail starts at Campaign Trailhead (N33° 31' 54.3", W111° 04' 42.1") and goes south on dirt road FR449A. Before reaching the Reevis Mountain School gate, the Campaign Trail goes right (west) and crosses Campaign Creek.

THE TRIP

Start on Map 14 on page 130. From the Campaign Trailhead [14-A, 0], follow Trip 13 (Campaign Trail to Fire Line Trail) for the first 5.3 miles to the junction with the Fire Line Trail [17-I, 5.3]. At the junction with the Fire Line

Ranch owners Blanche and Earl Horrell at the Upper Horrell Place on Campaign Creek. Photographer unknown, circa 1920. Courtesy of Earline Horrell Tidwell.

Trail, a lunch stop or camp under the tall ponderosa pines might be in order, although the tent site is small and close to the trail in the narrow section of canyon. Water is usually available at Black Jack Spring [17-J], 0.2 mile uphill on the Fire Line Trail.

This trip continues on the Campaign Trail, with the trail staying flat and mostly on the left (south) side of the normally dry Campaign Creek until the trail takes a switchback up the north side of the bank to avoid an upcoming bend in the creek. Upper Campaign Spring, marked on some maps, did not have water when other springs in the area had water, so it is probably not worth the bushwhack up the ravine to check the spring for water. Eventually the trail leaves the creek bed and begins the climb to the divide [17-K, 7.1] where you have a very good view into the West Fork Pinto Creek. The divide is another good turnaround point for those on a shorter trip.

From the divide, go downhill on the Campaign Trail until it meets the normally dry West Fork Pinto Creek at Oak Flat. Just before you reach the creek, you will see a large wooden corral on your left (east). The corral is still usable, although the closest water is the seasonal water in the creek.

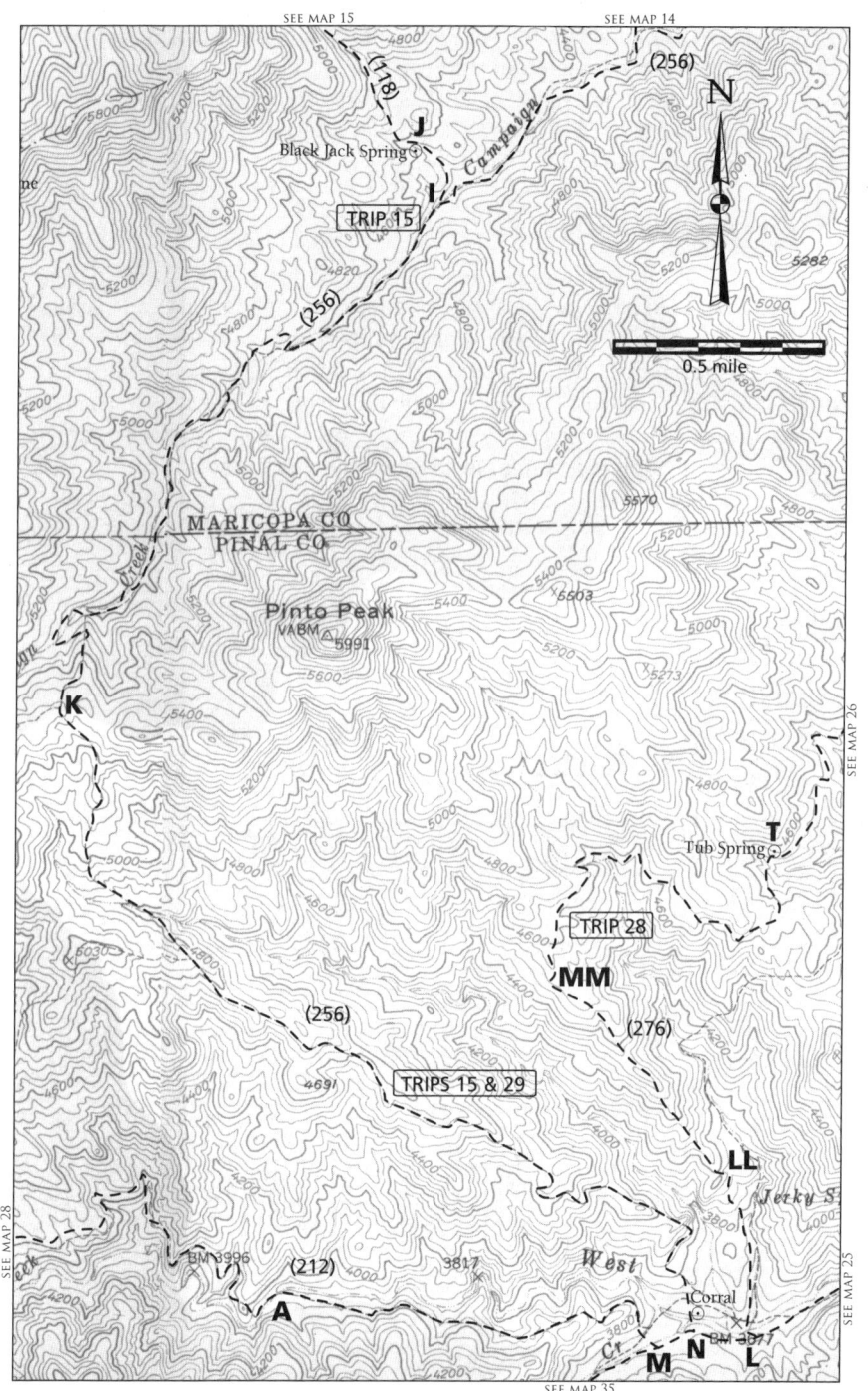

Map 17 – Trips 13, 15 and 29.

Campaign Trailhead—Trip 15. Campaign Trail to West Fork Pinto Creek

The Campaign Trail ends on the south side of the creek where it meets the West Pinto Trail at a wooden trail sign [17-N, 9.7]. Return the same way, or continue on a connecting trail. See Trip 24 (West Pinto Trail to Oak Flat), Trip 27 (Spencer Spring Creek), and Trip 28 (Cuff Button Trail) all in the Miles Trailhead section of the book for things to do in the Oak Flat area.

HISTORY AND LEGENDS

In January 2002, the sign at the divide was packed out on the Campaign Trail by Kevin McCombe of the Tonto National Forest, Tonto Basin District. He donated the sign to the Superstition Mountain Museum along with other old signs removed from the Wilderness. The wooden sign was engraved with these words and mileages, *Campaign–Pinto Cr. Divide, Miles Ranch 5, Upper Horrell Ranch 7*. The Forest Service does not show mileages on the newer signs and usually only posts signs at the start and end of the trails.

Former trail sign at the Campaign Creek and West Fork Pinto Creek Divide [17-K]. It was removed by the Forest Service and donated to the Superstition Mountain Museum in January 2002. Photo was taken in March 1997.

Trip 16

Campaign Trail to Circlestone

Circlestone ruin is one of the most interesting prehistoric sites in the Superstition Wilderness. Much speculation and analysis about the site will spark your interest in the origin of this mountaintop structure.

ITINERARY

From the Campaign Trailhead, follow the Campaign Trail (256) to Fire Line Trail (118). Take Fire Line Trail and Allen Blackman Trail to Circlestone. Return the same way.

DIFFICULTY

Difficult one day hike or horse ride. Moderate two day hike or horse ride. The Forest Service does not recommend the eastern section of the Fire Line Trail for horse travel because the trail is steep. Elevation change is +2,990 and -200 feet one way.

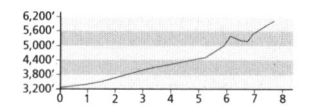

LENGTH and TIME

7.7 miles, 5 hours one way.

MAPS

Arizona USGS topo maps NAD27: Two Bar Mountain, Haunted Canyon, Iron Mountain. Superstition Wilderness Beartooth map, grids P9 to N11. Maps 14 and 15.

FINDING THE TRAIL

Trailhead map is on page 128. The trail starts at Campaign Trailhead (N33° 31' 54.3", W111° 04' 42.1") and goes south on dirt road FR449A. Before reaching the Reevis Mountain School gate, the Campaign Trail goes right (west) and crosses Campaign Creek.

THE TRIP

Start on Map 14 on page 130. Although some hearty travelers can make it to Circlestone and back in one day, most people will enjoy the trip as an overnight trek by camping around the Brushy Spring area. From Campaign Trailhead [14-A, 0], use Trip 13 (Campaign to Fire Line Trail) for the first segment of the trip to the junction of the Fire Line Trail [14-I, 5.3].

From the wooden sign [15-I, 5.3] at the junction of the Campaign Trail and Fire Line Trail (118), go right (north) across the normally dry Campaign Creek and begin the uphill climb. Not far up the trail, at the place where the trail crosses the first ravine to the left, look for a metal water trough at Black Jack Spring [15-J, 5.5] that is buried in the ground. The trough is out of service and may not be easy to see. The spring box is up the ravine a few feet from the trough and is covered by some flat rocks and rebar. Be sure to purify the water. Even if you do not need water now, check the condition of the spring for a possible water stop on the return trip.

From Black Jack Spring, the Fire Line Trail becomes very steep as the trail heads up to the pass. The Forest Service literature notes that "the eastern section of the trail is very steep and eroded, and not recommended for horses." As the trail drops into the Pine Creek drainage, you will enter a large stand of ponderosa pines—their needles cover the ground making this an

An exterior wall at Circlestone ruin. Note the large stones. Photo was taken in December 2004.

View to the south of an exterior wall at Circlestone ruin with the peak of Mound Mountain in the background. Photo was taken in February 2000.

inviting place. Although the Pine Creek is normally dry at the Fire Line Trail crossing [15-S, 6.7], you may find water at a spring [15-N] down canyon 0.9 mile just beyond a former corral [15-Q].

From the Pine Creek crossing [15-S, 6.7], the Fire Line Trail begins another uphill ascent that turns into an ill-defined route sparsely marked by rock cairns. The trail soon changes to a wide track, and the distance is not far to the junction with the Allen Blackman Trail that is marked with several large rock cairns on the left (south) (N33° 29' 15", W111° 07' 54") [15-L, 6.9]. From the Allen Blackman Trail junction, another 1.7 miles takes you to the end of the Fire Line Trail near Reavis Ranch.

Our trip goes left (south) on the Allen Blackman Trail and heads uphill, steeply at first, and then levels off as the trail contours around a hill to gain the ridge. The trail ends at Circlestone ruin [15-O, 7.7], which is easily recognized by its high rock walls on top of the ridge. Mound Mountain, 0.5 mile farther to the south of Circlestone, is not easy to approach through the thick vegetation. We have not done it, but others have made the bushwhack to the top of Mound Mountain. Return the same way. See Trip 34 (Rogers Trough to Reavis Ranch) for more about Circlestone ruin.

Trip 17

CAMPAIGN TRAIL TO REAVIS RANCH LOOP

The Reavis Ranch loop makes a good three night pack trip to a beautiful and historic region in the Wilderness. Reavis Creek provides water for people and stock. Several springs along the trails give a choice of camps if you are not camping in Reavis Valley. An easy side trip, from the Fire Line Trail, can be made to Circlestone ruin, near Mound Mountain.

ITINERARY

From the Campaign Trailhead, take Campaign Trail (256), Fire Line Trail (118), and Reavis Ranch Trail (109) to Reavis Ranch. Return on the Reavis Gap Trail (117) and Campaign Trail (256).

DIFFICULTY

Difficult hike and very difficult horse ride for the 3 or 4 day trip. The Forest Service does not recommend the eastern section of the Fire Line Trail (118) for horse travel because the trail is steep. The Reavis Gap Trail is also steep. Elevation change is +2,540 and -950 feet to Reavis Valley. The return to Campaign Trailhead is +770 and -2,350 feet on the Reavis Gap Trail.

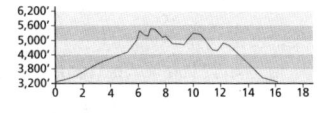

LENGTH and TIME

Total 16.1 miles. Reavis Valley is 8.9 miles and 10.5 hours. Add 7.2 miles and 8.5 hours to complete the loop back to Campaign Trailhead.

MAPS

Arizona USGS topo maps NAD27: Two Bar Mountain, Pinyon Mountain, Haunted Canyon, Iron Mountain. Superstition Wilderness Beartooth map, grids P9 to N11, and N11 to P9. Maps 14, 15, and 18.

FINDING THE TRAIL

Trailhead map is on page 128. The trail starts at Campaign Trailhead (N33° 31' 54.3", W111° 04' 42.1") and goes south on dirt road FR449A. Before reaching the Reevis Mountain School gate, the Campaign Trail goes right (west) and crosses Campaign Creek.

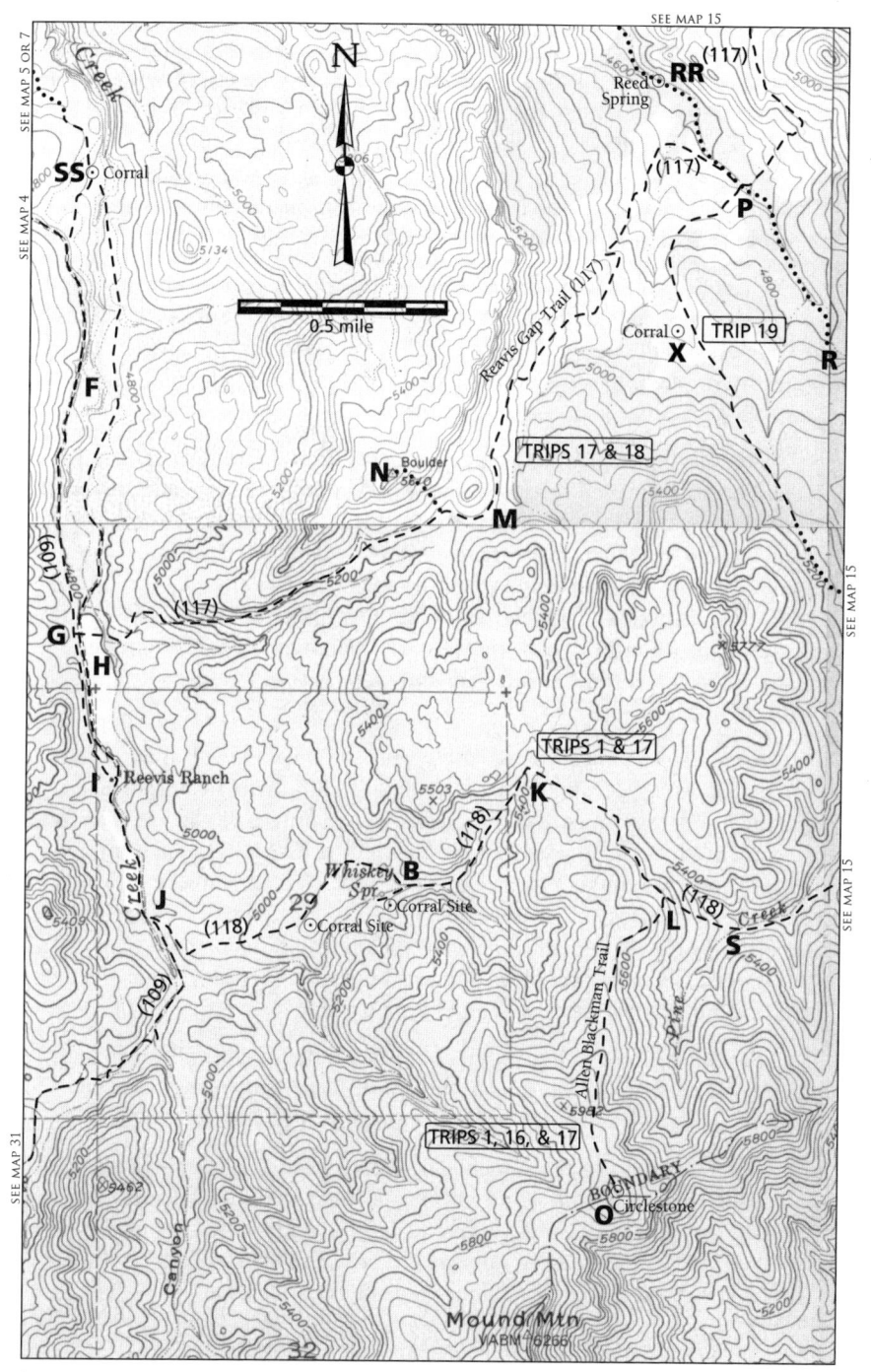

Map 18 – Trips 1, 16, 17, 18, 34, and 35.

THE TRIP

Start on Map 14 on page 130. The advantage of taking the Campaign and Fire Line Trail to Reavis Ranch is the gentle grade of the Campaign Trail for the first five miles. In comparison, the Reavis Gap Trail takes on the uphill grade immediately. The disadvantage of using the Campaign and Fire Line Trails is that the total up and down elevation change and the distance traveled is a little larger than that of the Reavis Gap Trail.

From the Campaign Trailhead [14-A, 0], follow Trip 13 (Campaign Trail to Fire Line Trail) to the junction with the Fire Line Trail [14-I, 5.3]. Pine Creek is usually dry at the Fire Line Trail crossing [15-S], so plan ahead for your water needs by considering Brushy Spring [15-H] and Black Jack Spring [15-J] as water sources.

Cross the normally dry Campaign Creek on the Fire Line Trail [15-I, 5.3], and begin the uphill section of the trip. As the Fire Line Trail crosses the first drainage, look to the left (west) for Black Jack Spring [15-J, 5.5]. The out-of-service galvanized water trough is probably the first thing you will notice on the left side of the trail. The spring box, which is a few feet up the dry wash, is partially hidden and covered with flat rocks and rebar. You can insert your water filter hose in the small opening to obtain water. Be sure to purify all water as some springs are known to harbor microscopic critters harmful to humans.

After a steep climb, you reach the pass and head downhill into the Pine Creek drainage [15-S, 6.7] where you will find inviting camping places under the ponderosa pines, but no reliable water sources. If you are spending some time in Pine Creek, you could go down Pine Creek 0.8 mile from the Fire Line Trail crossing to a former corral [15-Q] and beyond where the dry creek makes a turn into a narrow canyon heading northwest. We have seen water [15-N] near the former corral, but the narrow canyon, downstream, in Pine Creek is a more probable source of water. See Trip 19 (Upper Pine Creek) for more information on Upper Pine Creek.

From Pine Creek [15-S, 6.7], continue on the Fire Line Trail as the trail climbs uphill again. Sections of the uphill climb become washed out here, so you need to follow the sparsely placed rock cairns.

Several large rock monuments [15-L, 6.9] (N33° 29' 15", W111° 07' 54") on the left (south) side of the trail mark the start of the Allen Blackman Trail that takes you to Circlestone ruin [15-O]. A side trip to Circlestone ruin from here is 0.8 mile, about 30 minutes one way. See Trip 34 (Rogers Trough to Reavis Ranch) and Trip 16 (Campaign Trail to Circlestone).

The Fire Line Trail continues up and over another pass and comes down the hill to a small ravine where Whiskey Spring [18-B, 7.8] (N33° 29'

Reavis Creek is usually dry upstream from Reavis Ranch, but the creek normally has year-round water at the Fire Line Trail crossing, the Reavis Gap Trail crossing, and in the Reavis Falls area. This photo was taken about 0.5 mile downstream from the Reavis Gap Trail crossing in October 2000.

Jack Carlson at camp on the Fire Line Trail near Reavis Ranch. Photo was taken in December 2004.

15", W111° 08' 35") is located. Whiskey Spring and the former corral area are on the left (south) side of the Fire Line Trail. The spring, where you can often find water, is a two-minute walk on a faint path leading from the Fire Line Trail. If the water at Whiskey Spring is a little stagnant, check for clear water farther down the wash where the water runs over bedrock.

The Fire Line Trail ends at the signed junction [18-J, 8.6] with the Reavis Ranch Trail (109). Reavis Creek normally has water here. Go left (south) a few hundred feet to find the best place to filter drinking water from the creek.

The trip continues to the right (north) on the Reavis Ranch Trail and immediately crosses Reavis Creek where the low bank makes watering your animals very convenient. Reavis Ranch Trail stays on the left (west) side of Reavis Creek and heads north across the former homestead with plenty of campsites for large and small groups.

The site of the former ranch house [18-I, 8.9] is on the left (west) side of the trail, up on a higher bench. The apple orchard [18-H, 9.2] is on the right (east) side of the trail as you continue north. Trip 34 (Rogers Trough to Reavis Ranch) and Trip 1 (Reavis Ranch from Reavis Trailhead) describe the Reavis Valley.

At the north end of the apple orchard, our trip goes right (east) on the Reavis Gap Trail (117) at a signed junction [18-G, 9.3]. The trail junction is on the left (west) side of the meadow and may not be easy to see. To start on the Reavis Gap Trail, find the trail sign at the junction with the Reavis Ranch Trail, then head east across the meadow, through the tall grass that obscures the trail. Cross Reavis Creek, which usually has water here, and follow the rock shelf by the creek around to the right where the Reavis Gap Trail becomes well defined.

The terrain is uphill to Boulder Pass and then downhill into the Pine Creek drainage, where Reavis Gap Trail crosses Pine Creek [18-P, 11.8]. If the creek is dry here, look upstream about 0.2 mile for water in the bed of the creek. Two nice campsites under the ponderosa pines flank the creek crossing. Trip 19 (Upper Pine Creek) describes the Upper Pine Creek area.

The Reavis Gap Trail meets the signed junction [15-T, 12.6] with the Two Bar Ridge Trail (119) on an open grassy slope. Walnut Spring [15-W], a reliable water source, is 0.5 mile from here. Trip 7 (Middle Pine Creek) and Trip 20 (Two Bar Ridge Trail) describe the Walnut Spring area.

Within a short distance, the trail passes over the grassy ridge of Reavis Gap and begins the long, downhill and steep trek to Campaign Creek where the Reavis Gap Trail meets the Campaign Trail (256) at a wooden sign [15-D, 15.0]. The trip turns left (north) and retraces the first part of the trip on the Campaign Trail to the Campaign Trailhead [14-A, 16.1] where this loop trip ends. Trip 18 (Reavis Gap Trail to Reavis Ranch) describes the Reavis Gap Trail.

In *Backpacking Arizona*, Bruce Grubbs describes a Campaign Creek Loop that passes Reavis Ranch. He rates this a three-day, moderate trip, on lesser-traveled trails. Our Trip 17, described above, follows his two-day shortcut route, although we think three days (two nights) would make a more relaxed, but still challenging trip. Grubbs' Fire Line Loop trip in *Hiking Arizona's Superstition and Mazatzal Country* describes the trip in the reverse direction.[75]

HISTORY AND LEGENDS

See the History and Legends section in Trip 1 (Reavis Ranch from Reavis Trailhead) on pages 54 to 58, Trip 34 (Rogers Trough to Reavis Ranch) on pages 262 to 264, and Trip 19 (Upper Pine Creek) on page 168.

Trip 18

REAVIS GAP TRAIL TO REAVIS RANCH

The pack trip to Reavis Ranch on the Reavis Gap Trail is a strenuous uphill trek to Reavis Gap where you reach the high country. An intermediate stop on the trail at Pine Creek or an off-the-trail stop near Walnut Spring can add variety to the trek if you have been to Reavis Valley before.

ITINERARY

From the Campaign Trailhead, follow the Campaign Trail (256) and Reavis Gap Trail (117) to Reavis Ranch. Return the same way, or make a loop on the Fire Line Trail (118) and Campaign Trail (256).

DIFFICULTY

Difficult hike and very difficult horse ride for the 2 or 3 day trip. The eastern part of Reavis Gap Trail is steep. Elevation change is +2,350 and -770 feet one way.

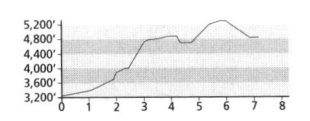

LENGTH and TIME

7.2 miles, 8.5 hours one way.

MAPS

Arizona USGS topo maps NAD27: Two Bar Mountain, Pinyon Mountain, Iron Mountain. Superstition Wilderness Beartooth map, grids P9 to N11. Maps 4, 14, and 15.

FINDING THE TRAIL

Trailhead map is on page 128. The trail starts at Campaign Trailhead (N33° 31' 54.3", W111° 04' 42.1") and goes south on dirt road FR449A. Before reaching the Reevis Mountain School gate, the Campaign Trail goes right (west) and crosses Campaign Creek.

THE TRIP

Start on Map 14 on page 130. From the Campaign Trailhead [14-A, 0], follow Trip 13 (Campaign Trail to Fire Line Trail) to the junction with the Reavis Gap Trail [14-D, 1.1] at the wooden trail sign. Campaign Creek will be your last source to obtain and filter water for a while.

Benchmark on top of Two Bar Mountain shows elevation of 5519 feet.

Go right (north and then west) on the Reavis Gap Trail as the trail climbs up to an exposed ridge. The trail is a steep climb the whole way to Reavis Gap. A few flat spots on the trail, where you and your stock can catch your breath, seem to be prehistoric building sites, so we believe the trail is probably several hundred years old. If you see an artifact, feel free to snap a photograph, but leave the artifact where you found it.

Reavis Gap is a wide grassy pass on the trail at the top of the climb. You probably won't have the energy to trek to the high point on Two Bar Mountain, which is to the right (north), but you can impress your friends by knowing that the brass marker at the peak shows an elevation of 5,519 feet instead of the 5,522 feet printed on the map.

The junction with the Two Bar Ridge Trail (119) [15-T, 3.5] is marked with wooden trail signs on a grassy slope with open views to Four Peaks in the north. Walnut Spring [15-W] is 0.5 mile downhill on the Two Bar Ridge Trail and the slope of the hill is a bit flatter in that area so you might find a

Photo was taken from the Benchmark 5519 on top of Two Bar Mountain in December 1999. You can see Reavis Gap (flat area in foreground) and Reavis Gap Butte on the left.

suitable campsite there. See Trip 19 (Upper Pine Creek) for things to do in the Upper Pine Creek area.

Pine Creek [15-P, 4.3] is the next landmark on the Reavis Gap Trail. Campsites on either side of the creek crossing are shaded by towering ponderosa pine trees. More campsites, upstream, on the east side of the creek will get you away from the trail. You can usually find some water at this crossing. If the water does not look good, you can check upstream (south) where we often find more and better water for filtering. If your party is tiring and lacking stamina, you might consider setting up camp at Pine Creek and continuing the trip to Reavis Valley as a day trip.

The last uphill section of the Reavis Gap Trail begins at the Pine Creek crossing and tops out at Boulder Pass [4-M, 5.6]. The bushwhack (no trail) to the benchmark on Boulder Peak [4-N] is a little tedious. The best approach is to go up the gully on the west side of the butte near the pass. Then after gaining elevation, move farther west to the brass marker. The marker is dated 1946, but it is not inscribed with the elevation.

The last leg of the Reavis Gap Trail crosses Reavis Creek where you can usually find water. The low bank on the creek here provides an easy place to water stock. From the creek, the trail goes across the grassy meadow in Reavis Valley and ends at the signed junction with the Reavis Ranch Trail (109) [4-G, 6.8]. Reavis Ranch house site [4-I] is 0.4 mile to the left (south). The apple orchard [4-H], which comprises the trees you see on your left (southeast), bears fruit in the fall. From the trail sign, great camping is available in either direction along the Reavis Ranch Trail. See Trip 1 (Reavis Ranch from Reavis Trailhead) and Trip 34 (Rogers Trough to Reavis Ranch) for more information on Reavis Valley.

HISTORY AND LEGENDS

Almost all stories describing the death of Elisha Reavis mention that the news was brought to the town of Florence, but we often forget that the community of Salt River, now mostly under Roosevelt Lake, was much closer. That is why prospector James Delabaugh came down Reavis Mountain to Narron's Ranch with the word that Elisha Reavis had died.

Delabaugh contacted John C. Narron on May 5 or 6, 1896, at Narron's Ranch (now Reevis Mountain School), and Narron assembled a small party from the community of Salt River to investigate the Reavis death. F. M. Cooper, A. J. Henderson, and Narron proceeded up the mountain where they found the decomposed body of Reavis.[76] Since the shortest trail from Narron's Ranch to the Reavis farm was the Reavis Gap Trail, these men probably used the Reavis Gap Trail to get to the farm. They would have taken the Reavis Ranch Trail south to the place where Reavis died, now called Grave Canyon.

See Trip 34 (Rogers Trough to Reavis Ranch) for more about Reavis, and to learn how to find his grave site. See History and Legends in Campaign Trailhead for the background story on John Narron.

Old signs at the junction of Reavis Gap Trail (117) and Two Bar Ridge Trail (119) near Reavis Gap. Note the Reevis spelling with two e's. When the trail signs were upgraded, the Tonto Forest donated these signs to the Superstition Mountain Historical Society. Photo was taken in October 2000.

Upper Pine Creek

Walnut Spring in the Upper Pine Creek area forms the hub of several day trips from a base camp in this remote section of the Superstition Wilderness. Treks using abandoned trails, cross-country routes, and stream side paths link with the Two Bar Ridge and Reavis Gap Trails to provide opportunities for exploring the Pine Creek drainage, which has seasonal water.

ITINERARY

From the Campaign Trailhead, follow the Campaign Trail (256) and Reavis Gap Trail (117) to Pine Creek or the Walnut Spring area where you make camp for several day trips. Return the same way.

DIFFICULTY

Difficult hike and very difficult horse ride for this 4 or 5 day trip. Elevation change is +1,590 and -270 feet to Walnut Spring one way.

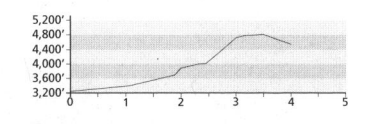

LENGTH and TIME

4.0 miles, 4.5 hours to Walnut Spring. The approximate day trip mileage from your camp is mentioned in the trip description.

MAPS

Arizona USGS topo maps NAD27: Two Bar Mountain, Pinyon Mountain, Haunted Canyon, Iron Mountain. Superstition Wilderness Beartooth map, grids P9 to N9. Maps 14, 15, 19, and 20.

FINDING THE TRAIL

Trailhead map is on page 128. The trail starts at Campaign Trailhead (N33° 31' 54.2", W111° 04' 42.1") and goes south on dirt road FR449A. Before reaching the Reevis Mountain School gate, the Campaign Trail goes right (west) and crosses Campaign Creek.

THE TRIP

Start on Map 14 on page 130. From the Campaign Trailhead [14-A, 0], follow Trip 13 (Campaign Trail to Fire Line Trail) to the start of the Reavis Gap Trail

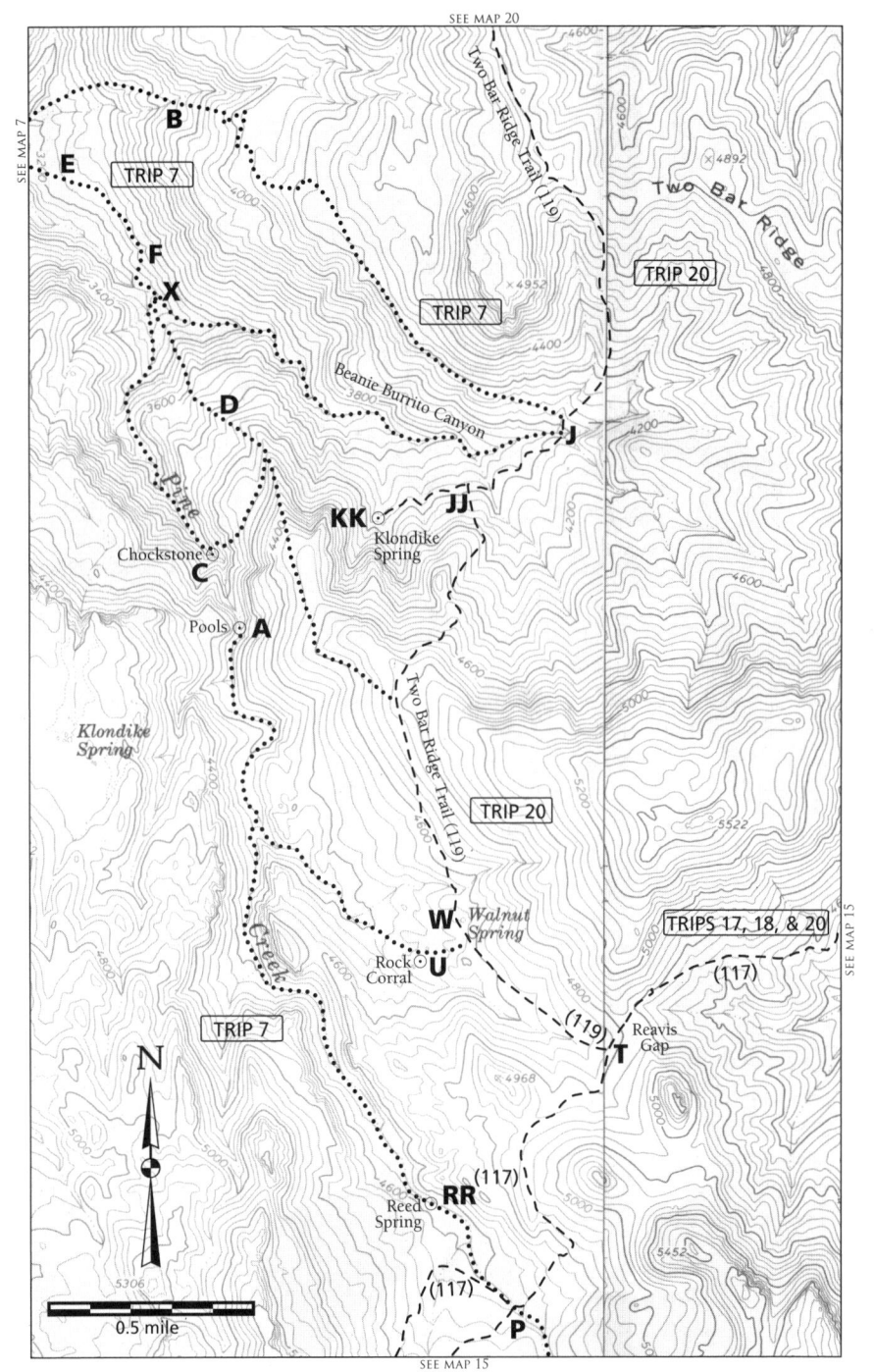

Map 19 – Trips 7, 17, 18, 19, and 20.

CAMPAIGN TRAILHEAD—TRIP 19. UPPER PINE CREEK   165

These logs are all that remain of the corral [15-Q] in Upper Pine Creek, about 0.8 mile down canyon from the Fire Line Trail crossing. Photo taken in December 2000.

[14-D, 1.1]. Then head uphill on the Reavis Gap Trail using the description in Trip 18 (Reavis Gap Trail to Reavis Ranch) to the junction with Two Bar Ridge Trail [19-T, 3.5] near Reavis Gap.

On the Reavis Gap Trail at the junction [19-T, 3.5] (N33° 31' 13", W111° 07' 29") with the Two Bar Ridge Trail, turn right (north) and head downhill to find a campsite. When we come to this area near Walnut Spring (N33° 31' 29", W111° 07' 50") [19-W, 4.0], we usually set up camp and then make day trips. Be sure to camp 0.25 mile away from Walnut Spring so you do not disturb the wildlife that may be using the spring. Campsite selection is a personal thing, and you have many choices here. You can camp in the open grassy areas, on a ridge, in a hollow along Pine Creek, or you can hide among the hoodoo rocks. You can also camp at the Pine Creek [19-P] crossing on the Reavis Gap Trail if you prefer a more wooded location.

We outlined three day trips from your camp near Walnut Spring [19-W] to get you started. Horse riders may want to modify our suggestions and stick to the maintained trails, since cross-country travel along Pine Creek is very rough.

The first day, you can make a counterclockwise loop going up Pine Creek and returning on the Reavis Gap Trail. If you have not located the Rock Corral [19-U], look for the corral about 0.2 mile southwest from Walnut Spring. From Rock Corral, head down the Walnut Spring Wash (northwest) to Pine Creek. Follow Pine Creek downstream to a deep pool of water [19-A, 1.3] in the bedrock. The pool and a chockstone [19-C] in the creek block travel farther downstream. Retrace your trip up the creek going past a seep spring that we named Reed Spring [19-RR, 3.0]. The trail shown on the 1916 Holmquist map probably followed Pine Creek here. When you reach the Reavis Gap Trail [15-P, 3.3], you can return to your camp near Walnut Spring to complete the 4.6 mile loop. Continuing from the Reavis Gap Trail crossing [15-P], if you had more time and energy, you could follow the left (east) side of Pine Creek on a faint trail up the creek a short distance until the canyon narrows [15-R]. You will find nice campsites under the trees here, but you will have to share them with the black bears that seem to frequent this area.

On the second day, you can take the Two Bar Ridge Trail to the junction [20-C, 3.4] (N33° 34' 01", W111° 07' 39") with the Tule Trail (122) on an out-and-back trip. Horse riders could continue farther on the Two Bar Ridge Trail or even ride downhill a short distance on the upper end of the Tule Trail. Either on the way out or the way back, make a detour (0.6 mile round trip) to Klondike Spring [19-KK] by taking a faint trail to the west at an unsigned trail junction [19-JJ] (N33° 32' 22", W111° 07' 50") with the Two Bar Ridge Trail. We have never found usable water at the spring—only damp ground or a trickle over the rocks. Down the wash from the spring, several wooden posts remain standing from a former corral or trap. Return the same way for a total day trip of 7.4 miles.

On the third day, take the Reavis Gap Trail over to the Pine Creek crossing [15-P, 1.3]. Cross Pine Creek to the southwest side, follow the Reavis Gap Trail through the campsite under the tall ponderosa pines, and turn left (south) at a small ravine within 100 feet of the campsite. Follow the ravine, mostly on the left side, going uphill while looking for rock cairns that will lead you to a deeply eroded trail. A GPS reading on the eroded trail is (N33° 30' 34", W111° 07' 55"). A wooden corral [15-X, 1.4], across the way (west) on the grassy hillside, can been seen as you continue uphill. Rock cairns mark the trail as it enters the brushy, tree-covered hilltop. The faint trail is missing in places and is not easy to follow. The trail eventually leads you to a stack of logs from the former corral [15-Q, 2.8] (N33° 29' 43", W111° 07' 14") on Pine Creek. From the former corral, 0.8 mile will take you up Pine Creek to the Fire Line Trail crossing [15-S]. Return the same way, or continue down Pine Creek to the remains of a trap corral [15-Y, 3.0]. From the trap corral, follow an even more difficult trek on the east side of Pine Creek over rugged terrain (not suitable for horses) to the Reavis Gap Trail [15-P, 4.0]. The return to the Walnut Spring [15-W, 5.3] area completes the 5.3 mile trip.

HISTORY AND LEGENDS

Peter Busnack told us when he first visited Walnut Spring in the 1970s, the spring was a twelve-foot deep well that was cribbed with logs. When the Forest Service eliminated the range improvements in the area, they hired rancher Dwight Cooper to remove the well and water troughs. Dwight said that the money was so good for the job, he could not refuse the work. The spring was a muddy hole after that, so Peter cleaned the spring out, and since then the spring has been a reliable water source for more than twenty years.

We gave the name Upper Pine Creek Trail to the old trail beginning near the Pine Creek crossing [15-P] on the Reavis Gap Trail. That trail heads uphill, goes south, stays on the west side of Pine Creek, and descends to the site of a former corral [15-Q] on Pine Creek, close to the Fire Line Trail. Rancher Billy Martin said that he remembered the Upper Pine Creek Trail as always being a rough trail, and it was never in good shape. This trail could be the same trail shown on the 1916 *Map of Central Arizona* by F. N. Holmquist.

We are not sure of the U.S. Army's exact route, which John Bourke wrote about, but we think the army crossed the Two Bar Ridge near the Tule Trail junction and then headed down to Pine Creek. When you are up on the ridge, you can speculate how the army might have made its descent on a route that sixty pack mules could negotiate. See History and Legends in Tule Trailhead for the army's march through the eastern Superstition Mountains.

Remains of the post and wire corral [15-X] along the Upper Pine Creek Trail. View to the south toward the Reavis Gap Trail as the trail climbs to Boulder Pass [15-M]. Photo was taken in December 2001.

Two Bar Ridge Trail

Two Bar Ridge Trail is part of the Arizona Trail and, with other trails, connects the Reavis Ranch area to Frazier Trailhead on SR188. Two Bar Ridge Trail can be used while exploring the Pine Creek drainage, and the reliable Walnut Spring makes extended stays in the area possible. Only about one mile of the Two Bar Ridge Trail is actually on Two Bar Ridge, but that short distance provides distant views to the east and west.

ITINERARY

From the Campaign Trailhead, follow the Campaign Trail (256) and Reavis Gap Trail (117) to Two Bar Ridge Trail (119), and camp in the Walnut Spring area. Return the same way, or make a through trip to Frazier Trailhead.

DIFFICULTY

Difficult hike and very difficult horse ride for this 2 or 3 day trip. Elevation change is +1,590 and -270 feet to Walnut Spring one way, +2,260 and -2,290 feet from Walnut Spring to FR83 [20-H].

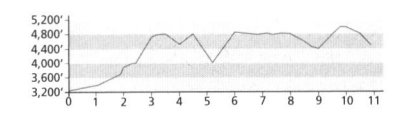

LENGTH and TIME

4.0 miles, 4.5 hours one way to Walnut Spring. Add 6.8 miles to go to FR83.

MAPS

Arizona USGS topo maps NAD27: Two Bar Mountain, Pinyon Mountain. Superstition Wilderness Beartooth map, grids P9 to N9, and N9 to N7. Maps 14, 15, 19, and 20.

FINDING THE TRAIL

Trailhead map is on page 128. The south end of the Two Bar Ridge Trail starts at the Reavis Gap Trail [19-T] (N33° 31' 13", W111° 07' 29").

THE TRIP

Start on Map 14 on page 130. From the Campaign Trailhead [14-A, 0], follow Trip 13 (Campaign Trailhead to Fire Line Trail) to [14-D, 1.1] and Trip 18

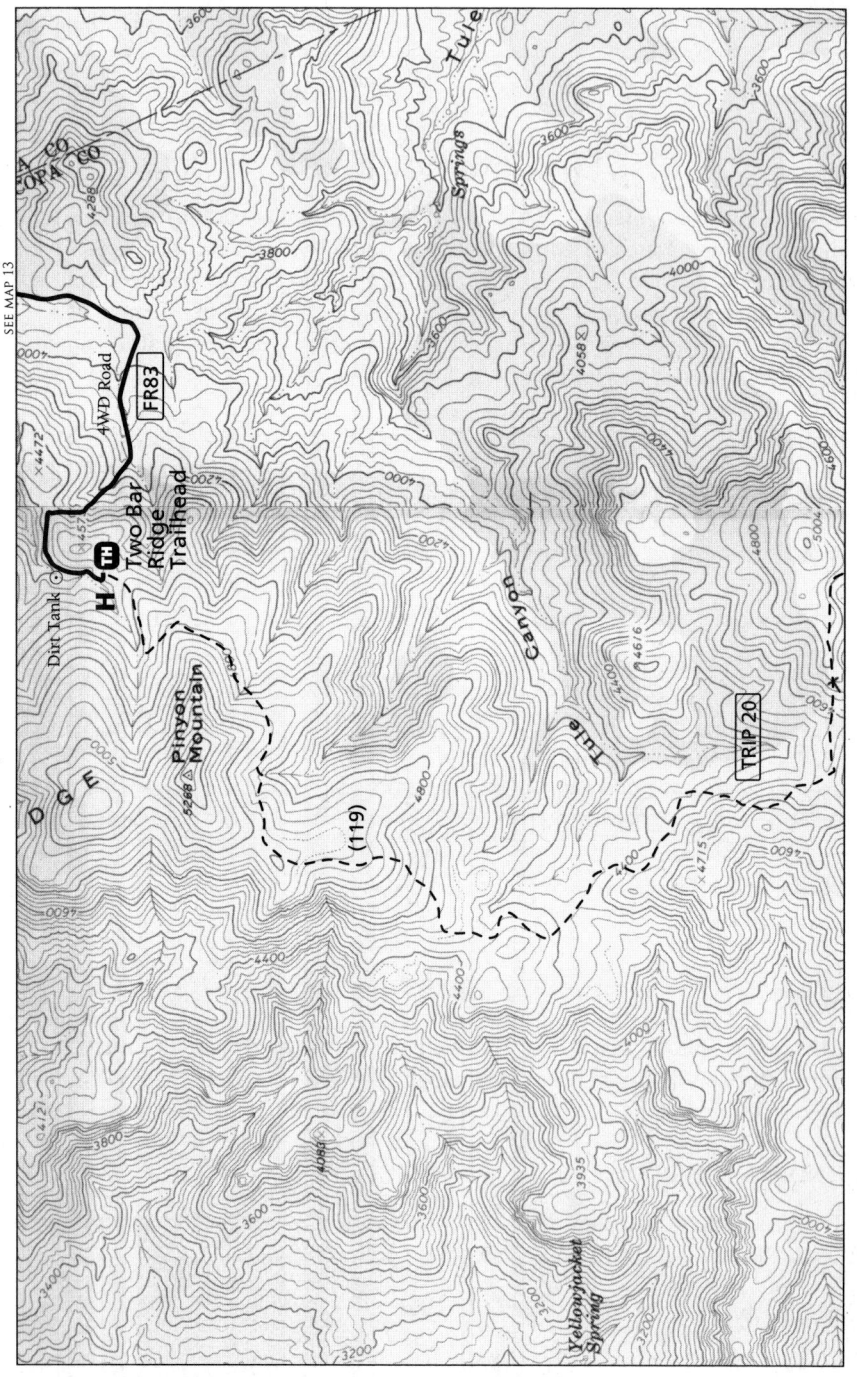

Map 20 – Trips 19, 20, and 12.

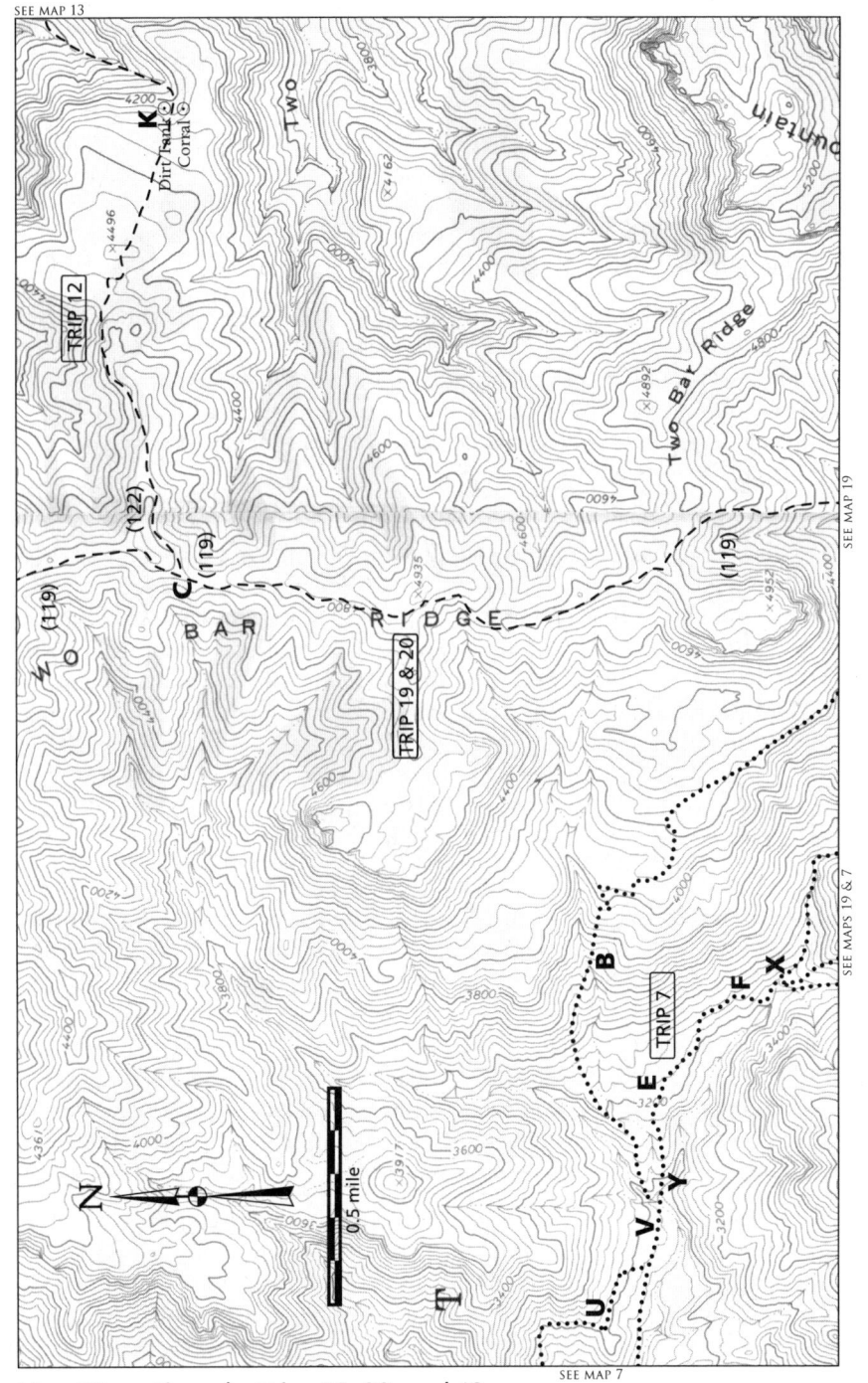

Map 20 continued – Trips 19, 20, and 12.

(Reavis Gap Trail to Reavis Ranch) to get to the south end of Two Bar Ridge Trail [19-T, 3.5]. The History and Legends described in those trips will enhance your trip experience.

Walnut Spring [19-W, 4.0], a reliable water source, will be your first stop on the trail, which is 0.5 mile north of the junction with the Reavis Gap Trail. Trip 19 (Upper Pine Creek) describes the area, camping, and things to do around Walnut Spring. Trip 7 (Middle Pine Creek) gives you more options, but they may be too far north to cover on this trip.

From Walnut Spring, the Two Bar Ridge Trail heads north and drops into a deep drainage. Going down this hill [19-JJ], Kelly Tighe and Susan Moran described the difficulty they had on this section of steep trail in there book *On the Arizona Trail*. Their pack burro, Beanie, slipped off the trail here and landed upside down, but was not hurt. They nicknamed this canyon Beanie Burrito Canyon.[77]

At the bottom of the trail in Beanie Burrito Canyon, the Two Bar Ridge Trail goes right (east) at an unsigned junction [19-JJ, 5.2] (N33° 32' 22", W111° 07' 50"). In the late 1990s, we saw a wooden sign for Klondike Spring leaning against a bush here, but in December 2000 we noticed it had disappeared. A faint trail, which heads left (west), goes to Klondike Spring [19-KK] (N33° 32' 19", W111° 08' 04"). A brushy 0.3 mile bushwhack takes you to the spring area, which is dotted with sycamore trees. We have never been able to get water at this site—only a small trickle of water over the rocks or just damp ground—since the water improvements have not been maintained. We looked for the spring box, but could not find it in the tangle of vines. Wooden corral posts mark the downstream end of the spring area.

Down canyon about one-half mile or more in Beanie Burrito Canyon from the Two Bar Ridge Trail crossing, you may find pockets of rainwater that collect in the bedrock near cottonwood trees. Climbing out of Beanie Burrito Canyon, the Two Bar Ridge Trail finally reaches Two Bar Ridge. Here you begin about a mile of ridge line travel where you can enjoy the distant views. The signed Tule Trail junction [20-C, 7.4] (N33° 34' 01", W111° 07' 39") marks your progress along the ridge. If you are on an out-and-back trip, the Tule Trail junction sign would be a good turnaround place. Taking the Tule Trail (122) down to Tule Trailhead [13-A] is 4.7 miles, and Trip 12 (Tule Trail to Two Bar Ridge) describes that trail and history.

Continuing north on the Two Bar Ridge Trail, the trail leaves the open ridge, bends left (west), and drops down on the east side of Two Bar Ridge to the Tule Canyon headwaters. This section of the trail is very remote and isolated, and as a result, we don't have much on-the-ground experience here. If you have enough water for a dry camp, you can find several flat places in the passes along the trail to camp.

Tent camp among the hoodoo boulders just west of the Two Bar Ridge Trail and Walnut Spring in December 2000. Reavis Gap Butte is on the right and Reavis Gap is in the notch on the horizon.

The terrain to the northwest is very rugged, and the first time we were here, we looked into those canyons and hoped that the trail ahead did not drop into that country. It didn't. Bruce Grubbs found a route into that terrain as described in his Lower Pine Creek trip in *Hiking Arizona's Superstition and Mazatzal Country*. His route went down the steep hills south of the 4,083-foot elevation notation on the Pinyon Mountain topo map.[78] Fortunately, the Two Bar Ridge Trail turned away from the rugged canyons at about the 4,500-foot elevation and began the uphill climb toward Pinyon Mountain.

After contouring around the south side of Pinyon Mountain, the Two Bar Ridge Trail passes through the Wilderness boundary gate. The Two Bar Ridge Trail continues down a switchback where the trail meets FR83 [20-H, 10.8]. Follow FR83 downhill on a steep and rough dirt road, and bear right at an intersection. You will pass two dirt water tanks, which may have seasonal runoff water—probably muddy. The concrete water troughs along FR83 for the Two Bar Ranch cattle operation may not have water if they are not running cattle in this pasture.

Farther down FR83 where the terrain is flatter, the junction with Cottonwood Trail (120) is marked with a small sign [11-G, 12.1], and the trail heads off to the left (north). From FR83 on the Cottonwood Trail, Cottonwood Spring [11-F] is 1.2 miles, which usually has water, and Frazier

View to the north along the Two Bar Ridge Trail in December 2000. Four Peaks is on the left horizon.

Trailhead [9-F] is 5.9 miles. See Trip 11 (Cottonwood Trail to FR83) for the Cottonwood Trail description.

If you continue down FR83 from the junction with Cottonwood Trail (120) to paved highway SR188 [11-K], you will travel another 3.9 miles. See Trip 12 (Tule Trail to Two Bar Ridge, "Alternate Return Route") if you want to go cross-country to Tule Trailhead [11-A]—about 3.6 miles from the junction of FR83 and Cottonwood Trail (120).

Pinto Creek Trailhead

From Apache Junction at Idaho Road, on US60, drive 29 miles to Superior. Continue east toward Miami and Globe on US60 for 12 more miles. One mile east of the Pinto Creek highway bridge, turn left (north) on FR287 (Pinto Valley Mine Road) between mileposts 239 and 240. If you are coming from Miami, drive west on US60 for 4 miles to FR287. Follow the public roads, FR287 and FR287A, across the BHP mining operations to the Pinto Creek Trailhead near the Iron Bridge on Pinto Creek.

FINDING THE TRAILHEAD

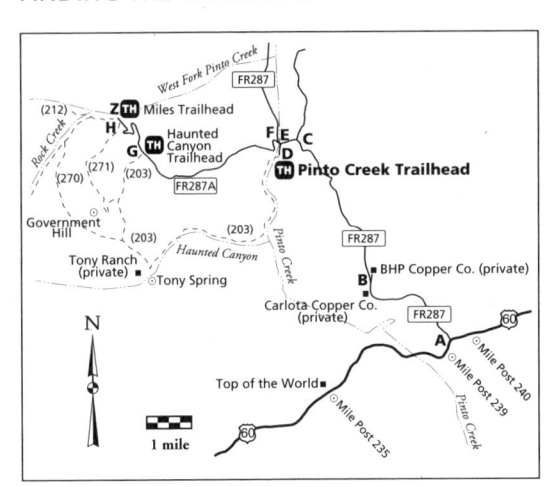

Our Pinto Creek Trailhead is often referred to as the Lower Trailhead for the Haunted Canyon Trail. FR287 takes you across the facilities of the BHP Copper Company and along several large mine-tailing ponds. FR287 is not the most-traveled road in the area, and the FR287 intersections with the BHP roads may not be obvious—signs get knocked down and some people steal them—but BHP tries its best to keep the road marked for public access. Follow the signs marked *Public Access*, and do not drive on any roads marked *Active Mining Area*. The route of FR287 may change to accommodate mine operations, so you need to pay close attention to the road signs and speed limit.

From US60 [A, 0], drive north on paved FR287 for 2.8 miles to the BHP entrance [B, 2.8], and bear left as FR287 turns into a dirt road. Continue on dirt FR287 through the BHP property following the *Public Access*, *Haunted Canyon*, and *JH6 Ranch* signs. Turn left at the cattle guard and locked gate [C, 6.7] for the JH6 Ranch. Continue on FR287 to the Iron Bridge at Pinto Creek [E, 7.2]. Before you cross the Iron Bridge, turn left (south), look for the Haunted Canyon Trail (203) sign, and continue to the locked gate [D, 7.4] (N33° 25' 31.4", W111° 00' 9.7"). Park near the locked gate, but do not block the gate or the road. A medium-clearance vehicle is required. Allow extra driving time for getting lost on the first section of the road [B, 2.8 to C, 6.7].

FACILITIES

The Pinto Creek Trailhead does not have any facilities. Horses are blocked by the gate across the road, but they may be able to find a way around the gate by riding near the creek. Bring your own water.

THE TRAIL

The large sign for the Haunted Canyon Trail (203) marks the approximate location of the trailhead. Some people refer to this as the Lower Trailhead. From the locked gate [21-D, 0], Trail 203 follows the road going south, crosses to the right (west) side of Pinto Creek, and continues to the end of the road at a small corral [21-V, 1.5]. At the corral, the trip goes right (southwest), through a barbed wire gate on the unsigned Trail 203.

HISTORY AND LEGENDS

Pinto Creek is shown on John Bourke's military maps that he drew during the Apache Campaign of 1872 and 1873. Al Sieber, Chief of Scouts, was on that campaign.[79] Military men took advantage of their familiarity with the mountains, and in 1879, Sieber staked two gold and silver claims in the Mazatzal Mountains. In 1896, Sieber filed several mining claims on Pinto Creek. One of his copper claims on Pinto Creek was named the Hal and Al, which was described as being one-quarter mile east of Banker's Arastra on the East Fork of Pinto Creek. The East Fork may be the present day Gold Gulch that enters Pinto Creek at the Iron Bridge, or it may be a tributary farther to the south. In 1901, Sieber sold ten of his mining claims to E. P. Shanley of Globe for $2,000.[80]

Tom Kollenborn related a story about Jacob Waltz prospecting in Pinto Creek about 1872. Waltz had a dry washer built for him in the town of Florence that could be packed on a burro. Kollenborn said it was no secret to the people of Florence that Waltz was working in Pinto Creek. John D. Mitchell's story of the dry washer in *Lost Mines and Buried Treasures Along the Old Frontier* has Waltz working a tributary of Pinto Creek—probably the West Fork Pinto Creek below Iron Mountain.[81]

Sheriff George Shute and Deputy Frank Hammon prospected in Gold Gulch for a few days in 1889. Shute bought a dry washer and with Hammon, Allison, and Middleton struck out from Globe to look for placer gold in the Pinto Creek area. As a group, they were only panning $1 to $5 of gold each day when wages per man would be $3.50 per day at the local mines. Hammon decided the project was not profitable.[82]

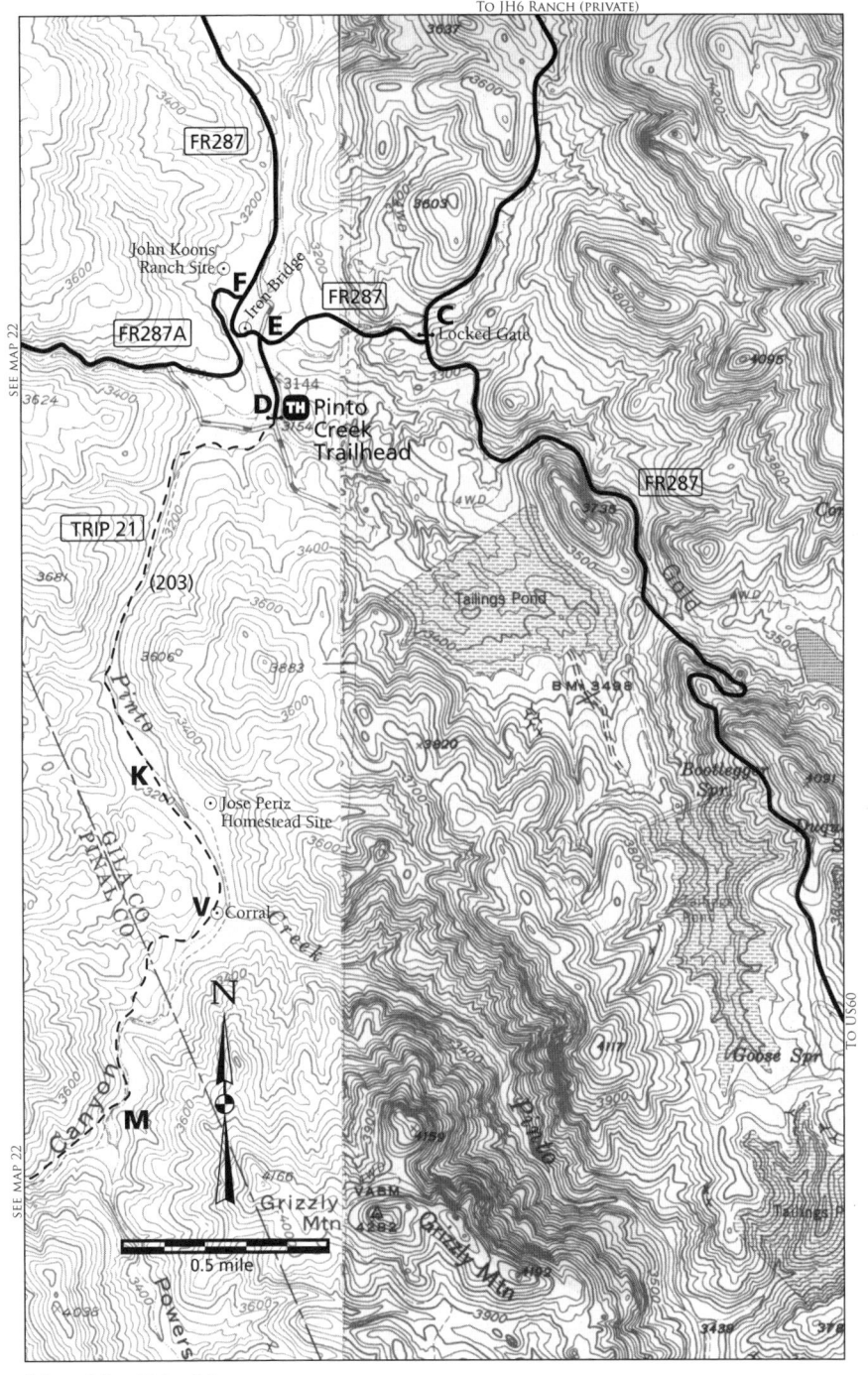

Map 21 – Trip 21.

Pinto Creek Trailhead 177

John Wilburn staked two mining claims (Bedrock 1 and Bedrock 2) on Pinto Creek south of the Iron Bridge in 1973. He found flakes of gold and small nuggets the size of watermelon seeds and traced the source of the gold to Gold Gulch, which enters Pinto Creek at the Iron Bridge, but he was not able to work the gulch because it was on mining company property. John said he found coarse gold along a 3,000-foot section of the creek, but not much above or below his claims. During one week in 1980, he and Frank Clark took out about seven ounces of coarse gold from John's claims using a large scale portable washing plant. Gerard "Cap" Bebeau staked the Mucho Oro claim downstream from Wilburn. About three hundred feet of Cap's claim showed placer gold. Wilburn and Bebeau worked together on the claims using dredging equipment. In 1986, Wilburn sold his two claims to the Mesa Roadrunner Prospecting Club.[83]

You may see some painted names on the concrete foundation of the Iron Bridge such as Diamond 1 through Diamond 4. Those claims were staked by Earl "Lane" Shoebridge, who later sold them for a large sum of money. John Wilburn said Shoebridge's claims were on the upstream end of his claims and were worthless because there wasn't any significant gold above his claims.[84] If you plan to pan for gold in Pinto Creek, be sure you know the location of the existing claims. You don't want to be a claim jumper.

Many landmarks west of the Iron Bridge on Pinto Creek are named for rancher John Koons—JK Mountain, Coon Spring, Koon Canyon, and the former JK CCC Camp. The Koons Ranch headquarters was northwest of the junction of FR287 and FR287A, but nothing remains at the site today.

John Koons witnessed the recording of several 1876 mining claims in the Globe Mining District, which was the earliest date that we uncovered his name. At age thirty, he appears on the 1882 Gila County Enumeration Census, but he must have registered in 1880, since other records establish his birth date as about 1850. Koons ran cattle with his JK brand in Gila County in 1883, but it wasn't until 1897, when he registered the brand with the Territory of Arizona, that he identified his range as Pinto Creek in Gila County. In 1903, he sold his brand to W. T. Price of Globe, and that is the last record we have for him.[85] Several maps continued to show the Koons Ranch on Pinto Creek through the 1920s.

Farther downstream on Pinto Creek at the junction with Horrell Creek, John W. Horrell established the JH6 Ranch. It was 1879, and John had just arrived in Arizona the year before with his wife Susan and nine of their children—three were born in Texas, and six were born in California. That same year they established the home ranch at Wheatfields on Pinal Creek. He established a one room school in Miami for his children and other local

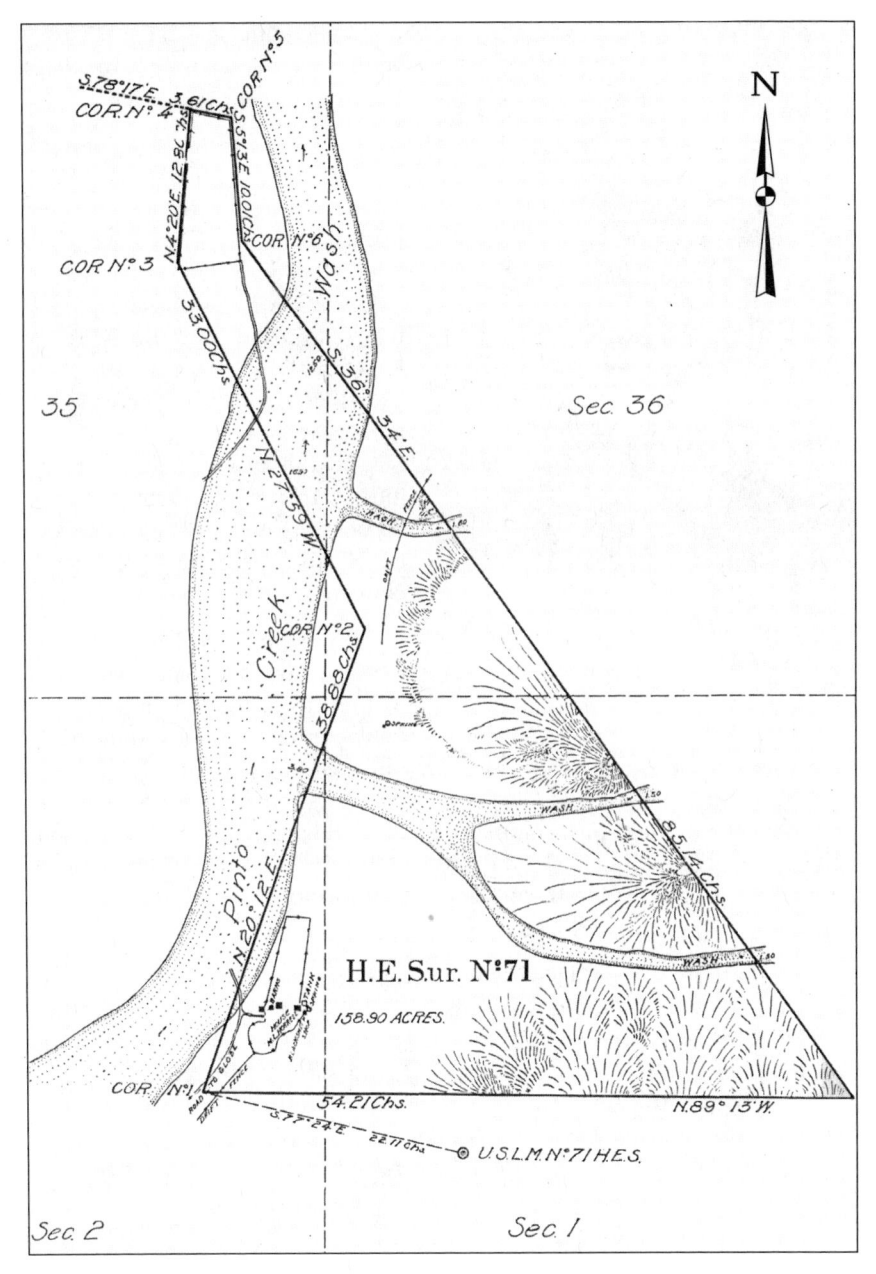

Homestead Entry Survey (HES 71) for Marion L. Horrell's homestead on Pinto Creek. The working cattle ranch is still known as the JH6 Ranch after the brand that John Horrell used in the 1880s. The survey was completed on June 12, 1912. Marion Horrell received the land patent on April 17, 1914. Ed Horrell homesteaded the land on the west side of Pinto Creek next to the JH6 Ranch and received the land patent for HES 441 on July 10, 1919. Map from BLM, Phoenix Office.

residents. John Horrell died in 1894 and his youngest son, Edwin, at age 19, took over the ranch operation.[86]

Susan Horrell, John Horrell's widow, obtained the homestead patent for the Wheatfields property in 1901, which is now known as the Bixby Ranch. One of Susan's older sons, Marion Horrell, received the patent for the JH6 Ranch on Pinto Creek in 1914. The Homestead Entry Survey for the JH6 is shown on page 179. Marion and his wife Laverna spent most of their time in Tempe and Mesa where they pastured some of the Horrell cattle. They had eight children.[87]

Susan Horrell, wife of John Horrell, circa 1880s. Photo by Henry Buehman, Tucson, A. T. Courtesy of Earline Horrell Tidwell.

Edwin Elisha Horrell received a bit of fame in 1899 when he rode his horse from his JH6 Ranch on Pinto Creek to Phoenix for a steer tying event, which he won. Edwin, also known as Ed and Edward, received the patent for the land adjacent to the JH6 Ranch in 1919—now owned by one of the copper mining companies. Ed and his wife Alice Wilson had two sons, Louie and Earl. Ed continued to consolidate his ranch holdings, which is described in History and Legends for the Campaign Trailhead on page 134.[88]

Louie Horrell and his wife, Winnie Foster, ran the JH6 Ranch from the 1920s to the 1970s and advertised commercial and registered Hereford cattle for sale. They were adventurous travelers, going to Europe shortly after World War II in 1949, visiting Guatemala in 1951, and taking commercial airline flights to many cattle grower's events across the country in the 1950s. Louie died in 1985 and Winnie in 1994. The JH6 has been owned by the Anderson family and most recently the ranch is now owned by the L. R. Layton family.[89]

Trip 21

TONY RANCH FROM PINTO CREEK

This trip starts on Pinto Creek near the Iron Bridge and follows the riparian corridor of Pinto Creek and Haunted Canyon to Tony Ranch (private). Year round water in some areas and the canopy of sycamore and Arizona cypress trees make this a pleasant and scenic trip.

ITINERARY

Follow Trail 203 from the locked gate on the road going south beside Pinto Creek. Follow Trail 203 through Haunted Canyon to Tony Ranch. Return the same way, or make a loop or shuttle connection at Haunted Canyon Trailhead or Miles Trailhead.

DIFFICULTY

Moderate hike. Difficult horse ride. Trail is obscure in some places. Not recommended for horses after leaving Pinto Creek, but the stretch of old road along Pinto Creek is a moderate ride. Elevation change is +830 and -80 feet one way.

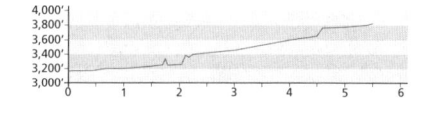

LENGTH and TIME

5.5 miles, 3.5 hours one way.

MAPS

Arizona USGS topo maps NAD27: Haunted Canyon, Inspiration. Superstition Wilderness Beartooth map, grids R13 to Q15. Maps 21 and 22.

FINDING THE TRAIL

Trailhead map is on page 175. From the locked gate (N33° 25' 31.4", W111° 00' 9.7"), follow the dirt road going south.

THE TRIP

Start on Map 21 on page 177 at the Pinto Creek Trailhead [21-D, 0] locked gate. Horse riders can get around the gate by going west along the fence toward Pinto Creek. Hikers can duck under the gate and follow the road going south. The road crosses to the west side of Pinto Creek and stays on the

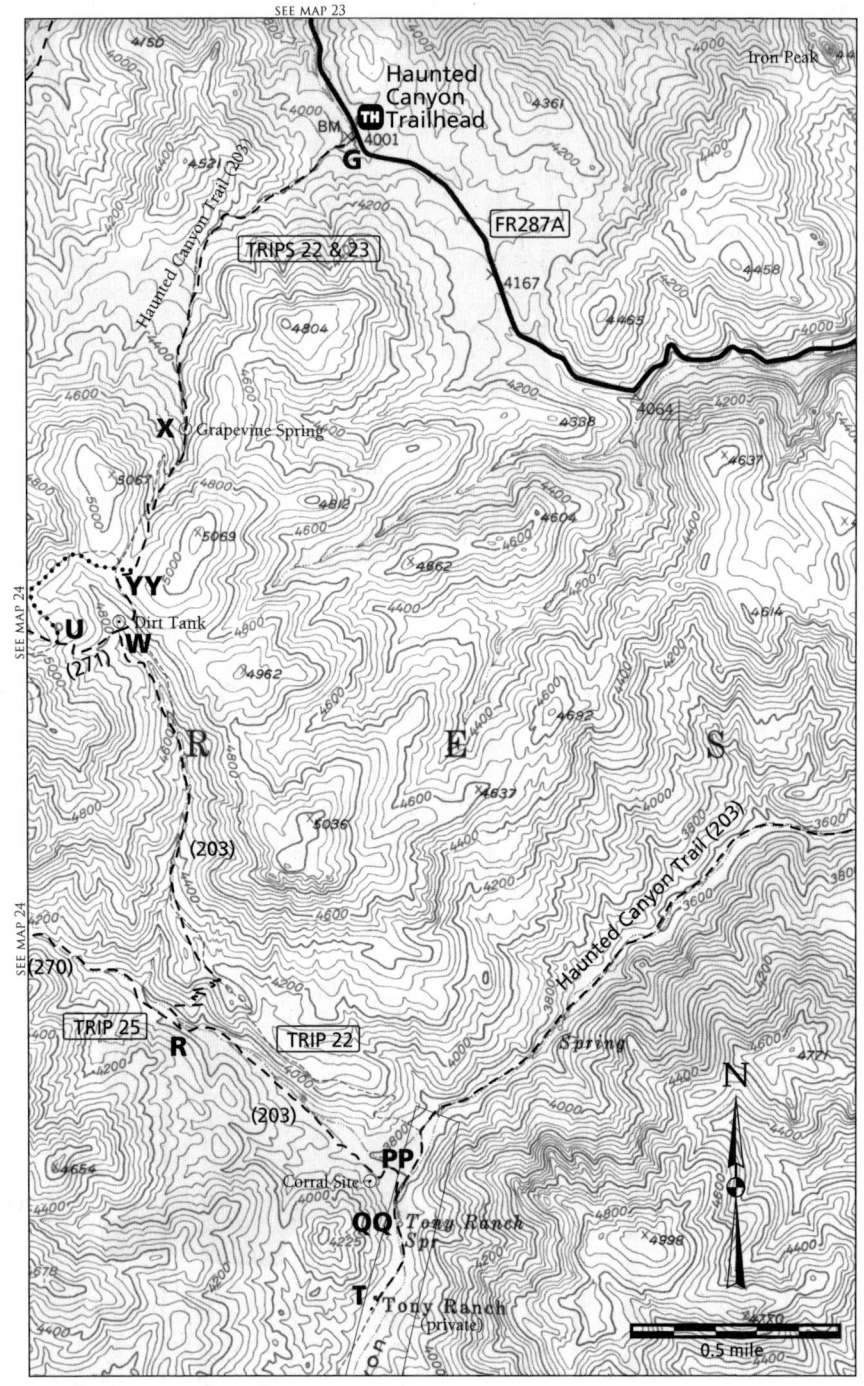

Map 22 – Trips 21 and 22.

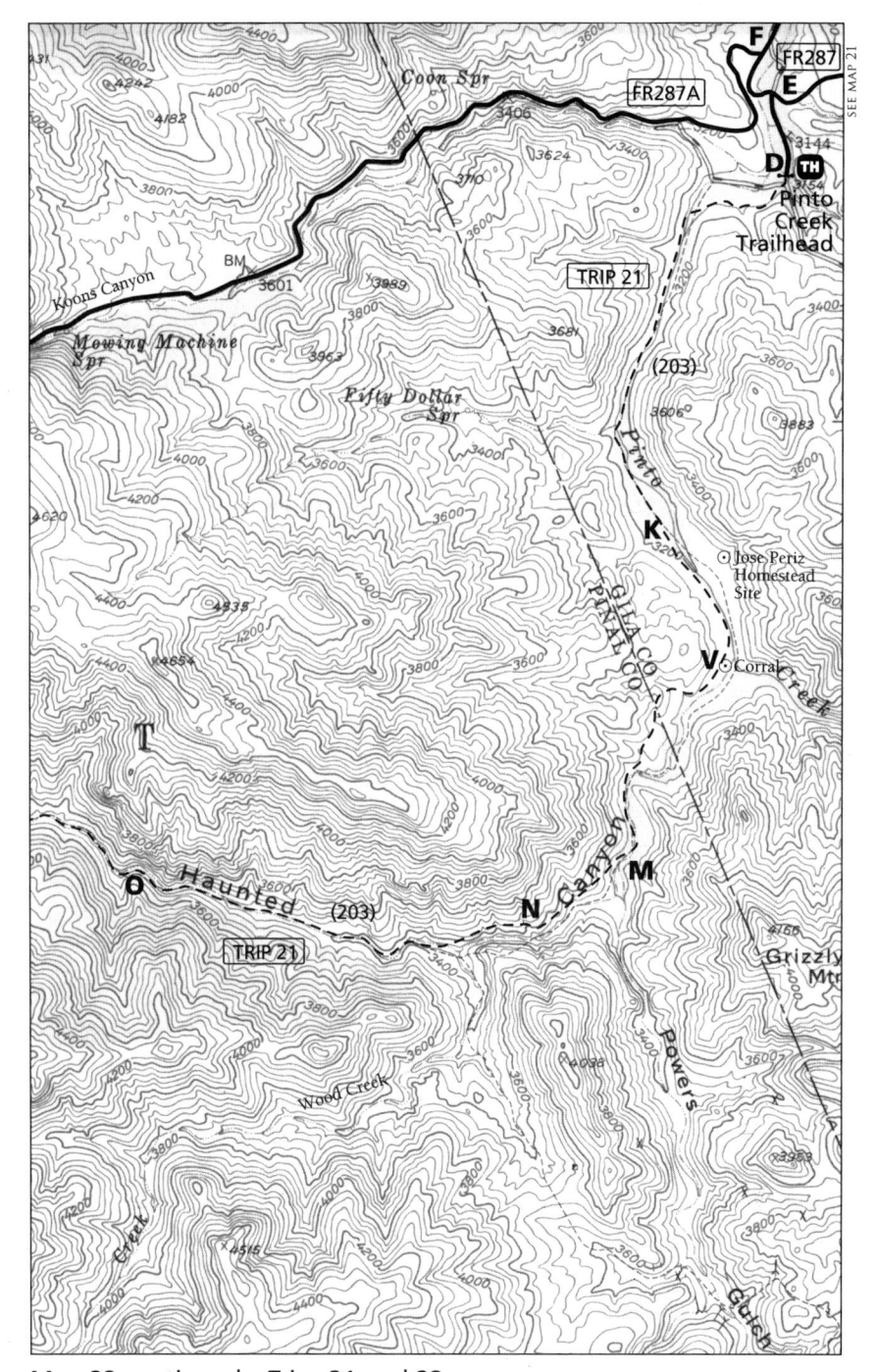

Map 22 continued – Trips 21 and 22.

west bank except for some detours into the creek bed to avoid the washed out areas. This is a pleasant road for a walk or ride under the canopy of tall trees.

The ruins of a wooden building on the right side of the road [22-K, 1.1] are the remains of the Periz homestead. On the left (east) side of the creek, out of sight of the road, is an old log cabin. The road ends at a small corral [22-V, 1.5] where the trip heads right, through a gate in the barbed wire fence. The trip now leaves Pinto Creek and follows a narrow trail into Haunted Canyon that can be steep in places. This would be a good place for horse riders to turn around. For riders, a better trail to Tony Ranch starts from Haunted Canyon Trailhead (Trip 22) on the west end of Trail 203.

Powers Gulch enters Haunted Canyon from the left (south) [22-M, 2.1], but the junction is not easy to see through the trees and vegetation. Haunted Canyon Creek usually has water here, but often is dry as you go up stream. A short side trip up Powers Gulch brings you to a narrow slick rock canyon that may not be passable when wet. The narrows in Powers Gulch might be a good destination for a shorter trip into this region. We have made an off-trail loop through Powers Gulch returning to Haunted Canyon by way of Wood Creek, but that would be best to do on a separate trip.

Haunted Canyon Trail leaves the bottom of the canyon [22-N, 2.3] and heads up a steep hill on the right to avoid a small pour-off in the creek. When the creek is dry, most hikers could jump down the pour-off, but getting up would be difficult.

Wood Creek—visible if you look closely—enters from the left (south) when the trail comes back to creek level. The trail crosses Haunted Canyon Creek several times, and at one spot [22-O, 3.4] you usually have to walk through water between a narrow cut in the cliff. You can scramble around the cliff on the right side (north), but the detour is tough going and not worth the effort to avoid the water.

In the fall, the large yellow and orange leaves of the sycamore trees make this a colorful trip. The smooth-bark cypress trees, which are common in this area of the Superstitions, are green all year.

At a large flat [22-PP, 5.1], which is on the north end of the William Toney homestead, Haunted Canyon Trail (203) turns right (northwest) and heads over Government Hill to Haunted Canyon Trailhead on FR287A in 3.3 miles.

This trip continues south along Haunted Canyon Creek to Tony Ranch Spring [22-QQ, 5.3] (N33° 23' 23", W111° 03' 11") on the left (east) side of the creek. Tony Ranch Spring usually has water and can be identified by some corrugated sheet metal that covers the spring box. Tony Ranch cabin [22-T, 5.5] (N33° 23' 14", W111° 03' 15") is farther south on the right (west) side of a large meadow. The cabin and surrounding 78 acres are private property. Please respect the private property.

Return the same way from the Tony Ranch cabin, or use a shuttle vehicle and end your trip at either Haunted Canyon Trailhead or Miles Trailhead. You have three choices for the shuttle trips. (1) From [22-T], take Trail 203 3.7 miles to Haunted Canyon Trailhead [22-G]. (2) From [22-T], take Trail 203, Bull Basin Trail (270), and West Pinto Trail (212) 6.4 miles to Miles Trailhead [23-Z]. (3) From [22-T], take Trail 203, Paradise Trail (271), and FR287A 5.0 miles to Miles Trailhead [23-Z]. For choice number one, some people hide a bicycle at Haunted Canyon Trailhead [22-G] and ride 4.1 miles on FR287A to complete the loop to Pinto Creek Trailhead [22-D], which is mostly downhill, but there are a few uphill sections.

Elizabeth Stewart walking across the meadow at Tony Ranch. Photo was taken in November 1996.

HISTORY AND LEGENDS

The ruins of the frame building [22-K] along the road are on the former homestead of Jose Ausere Periz. Several other people tried to homestead this property, but they did not meet the government requirements. Charles W. Hardy applied for the homestead in 1910 and had the land surveyed in 1914. Then, Manuel Prieto submitted his application for the homestead in 1915, but he relinquished his rights in 1917. Periz filed his application in 1917, proved up on the five-year requirements, and received his 38-acre land patent on July 24, 1923.[90]

In the affidavit for Periz's homestead, Martha J. Bohme said that she often passed the Periz place and stopped there while looking for cattle in the vicinity. George Rae Clark said that he frequently stopped at the Periz place on his way to his ranch, which was at the present day Miles Trailhead. Clark said that Periz packed supplies up the mountain to his ranch.[91]

The 1914 survey shows three buildings on the Periz homestead—a log storage building, a log dwelling, and a frame dwelling. The existing log building may be one of those described in the survey. The ruin of a frame building along the road is probably the two-room lumber house that Periz built in February 1917. He also had a hay shed, a chicken house, a tool house, a sheet iron stable, and two wells.

Jose Periz was born in Jaca, Spain on August 7, 1880. His wife Josefha Sanchez was also from Jaca, Spain. They had four children, Fidel, Pellarr, Maria, and Aurolia, who lived in Miami, Arizona during the school year. On his Naturalization Certificate, Periz's occupation was listed as a miner. He arrived in the United States in 1912 and obtained his citizenship in 1923, just in time to meet the homestead requirements.[92] Ranchers in the Pinto Creek area referred to a Spanish man nicknamed Frenchy who we believe was most likely Jose Periz.[93]

On April 16, 1969, the U.S. Forest Service obtained the homestead, which had been owned by a mining company, in exchange for other National Forest land.[94] Today the Periz homestead is part of the Tonto National Forest.

Tom Kollenborn has written several articles about the *Cave of a Thousand Eyes* that is supposed to be in the mountains west of Pinto Creek—the location is still a secret. Kollenborn recounts a 1916 newspaper story about Jose Perez (sic) finding gold in a large cave, but upon returning with a mining engineer, no mineralization was found. Homesteader Jose A. Periz may be the person that is described in these newspaper articles. Joe Modock found the same cave in 1935, but he thought the crystals were diamonds. Kollenborn wrote that rancher Frank Moraga was probably the first person to explore the cave in the 1890s when it was known as the Moraga Cave.[95]

In 1911, rancher Pedro Moraga homesteaded 31.9 acres along Pinto Creek two miles south of Horrell Creek and the JH6 Horrell homesteads. He received his land patent in 1919.[96] Pedro was probably the man referred to as Frank in the *Cave of a Thousand Eyes* stories. The Moraga homestead is now owned by one of the copper mining companies.

See History and Legends on pages 196 to 198 for the story about homesteader William Toney and his ranch in Haunted Canyon.

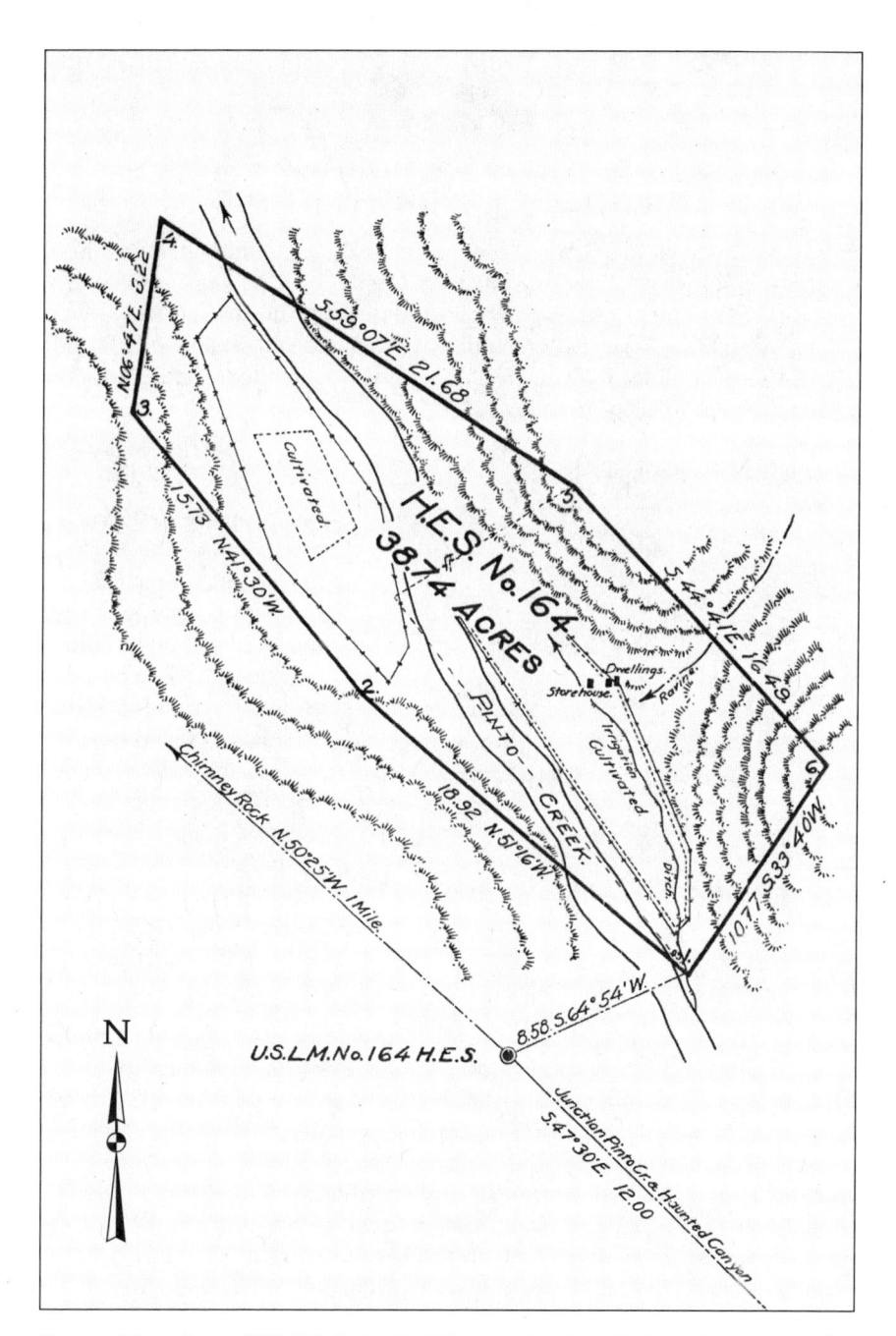

Homestead Entry Survey (HES 164) for Jose Periz's homestead on Pinto Creek, which is now part of the Tonto National Forest. The survey was completed on October 17, 1914. Periz received the land patent on July 24, 1923. Map from BLM, Phoenix Office.

HAUNTED CANYON TRAILHEAD

From Apache Junction at Idaho Road, on US60, drive 29 miles to Superior. Continue east toward Miami and Globe on US60 for 12 more miles. One mile east of the Pinto Creek highway bridge, turn left (north) on FR287 (Pinto Valley Mine Road) between mileposts 239 and 240. Follow FR287 and FR287A to the trailhead. If you are coming from Miami, drive 4 miles west on US60 to the Pinto Valley Mine Road.

FINDING THE TRAILHEAD

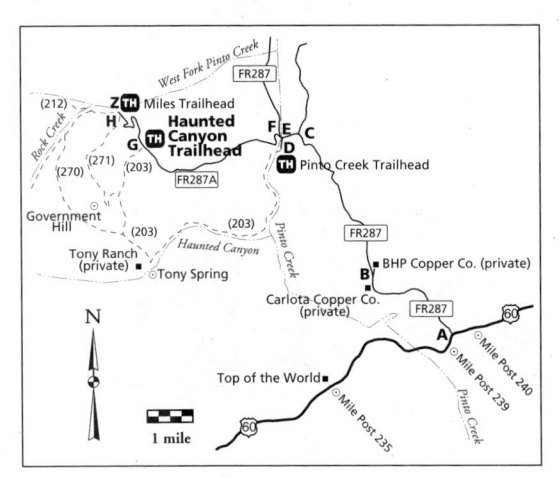

The approach to the trailhead follows FR287 across the facilities of the BHP Copper Company and the mine-tailing ponds. Forest Service road FR287 is a seldom traveled road, and the FR287 intersections with the BHP roads are not always well marked. Follow the signs marked *Public Access*, and do not drive on any roads marked *Active Mining Area*. The route of the public access road may change to accommodate mine operations, so you need to pay close attention to the road signs and speed limit.

From US60 [A, 0], drive north on paved FR287 for 2.8 miles to the BHP entrance [B, 2.8], and bear left as FR287 turns into a dirt road. Continue on dirt FR287 through the BHP property following the *Public Access*, *Haunted Canyon*, and *JH6 Ranch* signs. Turn left (east) at the cattle guard and locked gate [C, 6.7] for JH6 Ranch. Continue on FR287 and cross the Iron Bridge at Pinto Creek [E, 7.2]. At the signed intersection with FR287A [F, 7.3], take FR287A west to the Haunted Canyon Trailhead on FR287A [G, 11.1], which is often referred to as the Upper Trailhead for the Haunted Canyon Trail. If you went too far and missed the trailhead, backtrack from Miles Trailhead about 1.9 miles on FR287A. A medium-clearance vehicle is required. Allow extra driving time for getting lost on the first section of the road through the mine operations [B, 2.8 to C, 6.7].

188   SUPERSTITION WILDERNESS TRAILS EAST

FACILITIES

The Haunted Canyon Trailhead has no facilities except for a small parking area. Bring your own water.

THE TRAIL

The sign, *Trail 203*, for the Haunted Canyon Trailhead parking lot (N33° 25' 33.0", W111° 03' 17.3") is on the right (east) side of FR287A. The Haunted Canyon Trail (203) begins across the road from the parking area.

Ella Mary Toney in 1916 at Haunted Canyon feeding her chickens in foreground. Note the fruit trees. The 1971 inscription written on the back of the photo by her daughter, Gladys V. Porter, reads, "My mother at Haunted Canyon, 12 miles from Superior, Arizona. The year is 1916 before she passed away on December 11, 1920 in Superior. She is in front of the house with her few chickens." Courtesy of Betty Porter Gilbert, granddaughter of Ella Mary Toney.

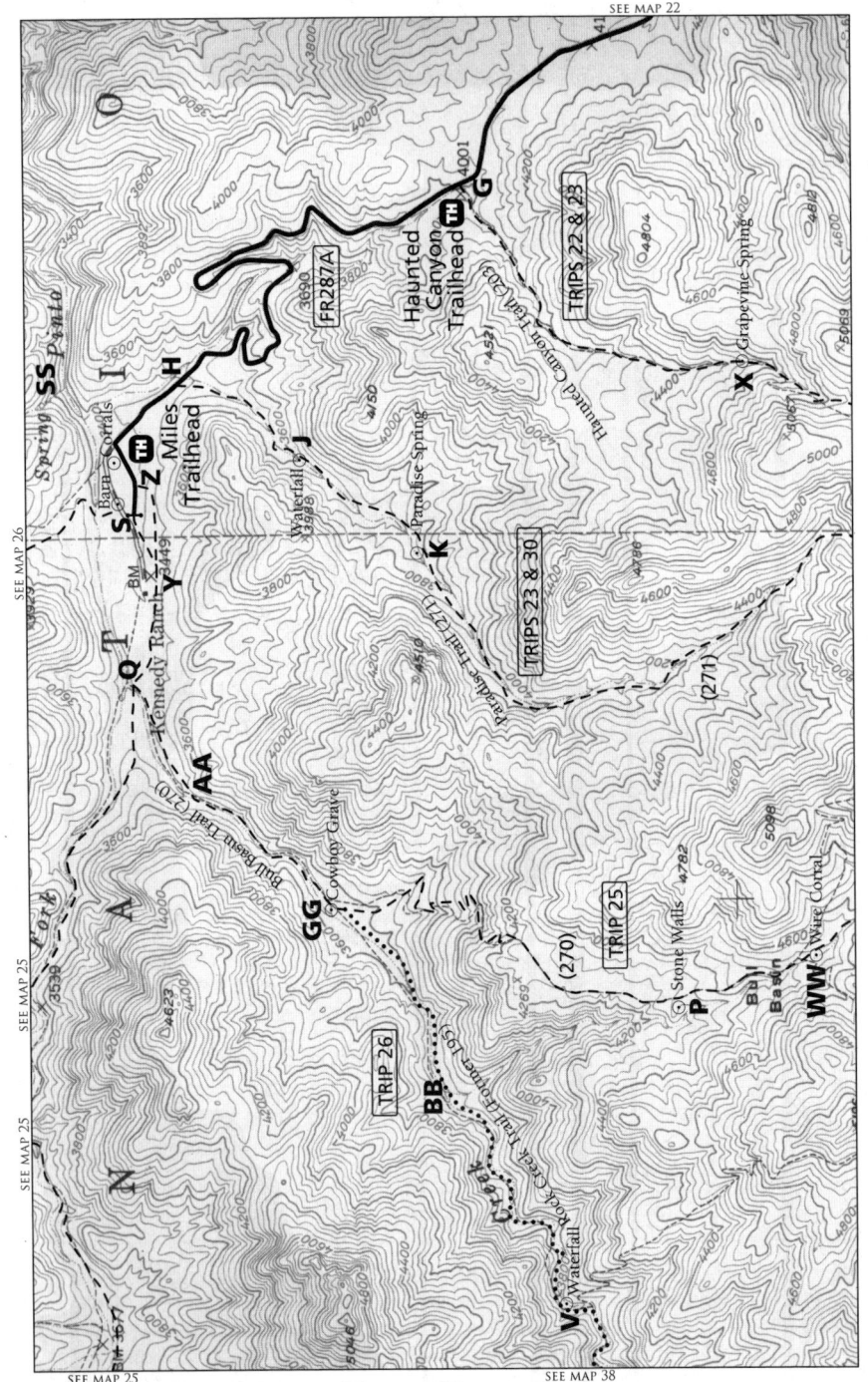

Map 23 – Trips 22, 23, 25, 26, and 30.

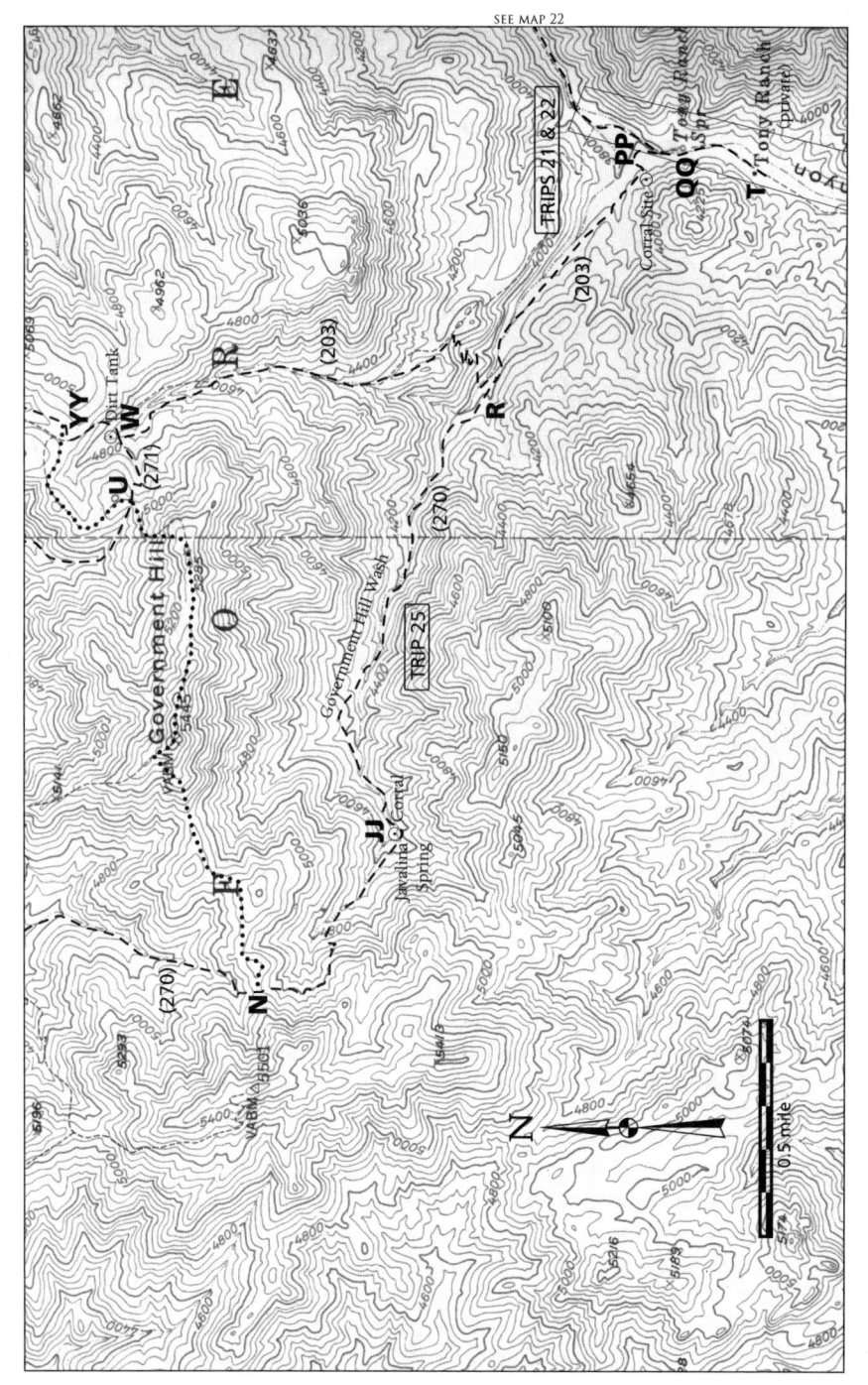

Map 23 continued – Trips 22, 23, 25, 26, and 30.

HISTORY AND LEGENDS

Rancher Ephraim "Pete" Gann is credited with naming Haunted Canyon—probably sometime in the 1880s. He spent the night in the canyon during an intense rain storm. Geraldine Craig recounted his adventure by writing, "The wind, the rain, the roar of the running water, the rolling rocks, and after the rain, the hooting of owls all combined made him feel that the place was truly haunted..."[97]

Pete Gann married Laura Horrell in Globe, Arizona Territory, in 1883. They were both from well-established ranching families. Pete was the brother of William T. Gann, and Laura was the sister of Ed Horrell. In the 1880s, Pete and William had ranches in the Campaign Creek area near Salt River, while the Horrells had ranches on Pinto Creek and in Wheatfields. Pete and Laura lived in Wheatfields along Pinal Creek just south of Globe. In 1885 Pete registered the Club cattle brand. Since it was common for ranching families to register a cattle brand in their child's name, in 1887 he registered the GAN brand for his oldest son, Walter, who was about three years old.[98]

Laura Horrell Gann and Ephraim "Pete" Gann, circa 1890s. Photo by Barton M. Houston, Sacramento, CA. Courtesy of Denise Cortelyou, granddaughter of Laura and Ephraim.

Pete and Laura moved to Mono County, California, where their third child, Hilda, was born in 1890. They settled in Lake County and are buried near Clearlake, California. Pete died in 1932, and Laura died in 1947.[99]

See Trip 21 (Tony Ranch from Pinto Creek) from the Pinto Creek Trailhead for more history about the area.

TONY RANCH FROM FR287A

This trip follows the north end of Haunted Canyon Trail from FR287A to Tony Ranch. The trail takes you to the grassy ridge near Government Hill and down through the Arizona cypress trees to Haunted Canyon where you find Tony Ranch Spring and Tony Ranch cabin. Tony Ranch is situated in a wide, flat valley under towering sycamore trees.

ITINERARY

From the parking area on FR287A follow Haunted Canyon Trail (203) south to Grapevine Spring. Continue up and over the ridge near Government Hill. Descend into Haunted Canyon where Tony Ranch is located. Return the same way or make a loop or shuttle connection at Miles Ranch Trailhead.

DIFFICULTY

Moderate hike and horse ride. Elevation change is +900 and -1,100 feet one way.

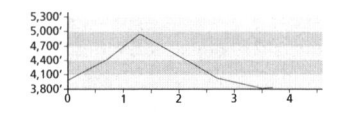

LENGTH and TIME

3.7 miles, 2.5 hours one way.

MAPS

Arizona USGS topo map NAD27: Haunted Canyon. Superstition Wilderness Beartooth map, grids Q13 to Q15. Map 23.

FINDING THE TRAIL

Trailhead map is on page 188. From the small parking area [23-G] (N33° 25' 33.0", W111° 03' 17.3") on the north side of FR287A, cross the road to the south, and locate the signed Haunted Canyon Trail (203). A small wooden corral sits next to the road and trail.

THE TRIP

Start on Map 23 on page 190. From the Haunted Canyon Trailhead [23-G, 0], head southwest on the Haunted Canyon Trail. The trail is well defined and easy to follow as it crisscrosses the ravine many times. You will find sycamore, cypress, and walnut trees along the normally dry ravine. The first landmark is

Grapevine Spring [23-X, 0.9] (N33° 24' 58", W111° 03' 43"), which usually has water in an oval metal trough. You can water horses here, but you won't find much room to maneuver on the narrow trail.

Coming up to the top of the grade, the tall canopy of riparian trees in the ravine is replaced by grasses and scattered juniper trees. Tall grasses sometimes block the large rock cairns that mark the route, but you can locate the Haunted Canyon Trail easily on the ridge as it goes through a gate [23-YY, 1.3] in the barbed wire fence. The hill to the west is named Government Hill. From the gate, the trail begins to descend, and your next landmark is a dirt water tank [23-W, 1.5] (N33° 24' 36", W111° 03' 53"). The trail crosses the berm of the water tank and meets the Paradise Trail (271) on the west side of the tank. On our trips, we have always seen water in the tank, and when the water is clear, it makes a fine photo that reflects the surrounding mountains on the liquid surface. The Paradise Trail goes over the hill to FR287A near Miles Trailhead and can be used in a loop trip. The Paradise Trail also takes you back up to the ridge where you can make a cross-country trek over Government Hill to connect with the Bull Basin Trail (270) [23-N].

From the Paradise Trail junction, continue downhill on Trail 203, which is fairly easy to follow. As you drop down in elevation, the juniper trees are replaced by pinyon pines and scrub oak. A set of switchbacks in the trail ends the descent in a canyon that we call Government Hill Wash where the signed Bull Basin Trail (270) [23-R, 2.7] comes in on the right (west). The Bull Basin Trail can be used in a loop trip that will take you 5.4 miles to Miles Trailhead [23-Z]. Because the Bull Basin Trail is not used very much, you may encounter more catclaw along the trail than you might like.

Haunted Canyon Trail now goes southeast through a relatively flat area with wide benches along the ravine. You can find many fine camping areas here and all the way down to Haunted Canyon Creek. The trees with the peeling bark are Arizona cypress trees. Along this stretch of trail, we have seen claw marks six feet high on the trunks of the trees where bears have used the trees as a scratching post.

Not long after passing a wooden corral on the right (west), you come to a camp area [23-PP, 3.3] near Haunted Canyon Creek, which is lined with sycamore trees. You are now on the 1922 homestead of William Toney. The 78 acres along the creek are private property, so please be respectful of the owner's rights. Go upstream, south, as the trail crosses the normally dry creek, to Tony Ranch Spring [23-QQ, 3.5] (N33° 23' 23", W111° 03' 11"). You can identify the spring by spotting the corrugated sheet metal that covers the spring box. The spring has always had water when we visited.

Tony Ranch cabin [23-T, 3.7] (N33° 23' 14", W111° 03' 15") is a little farther to the south on the west side of the grassy meadow. This is a pretty place, and in the fall the large orange sycamore leaves add a splash of color to the landscape. The cabin is constructed of logs with a corrugated sheet metal roof. The trip ends at Tony Ranch cabin. Return the same way, or continue on Haunted Canyon Trail to Pinto Creek Trailhead in 5.5 miles, which is not recommended for horses.

Horse riders and the former ranch owners often rode to Tony Ranch from the headwaters of Haunted Canyon on an unnamed trail from FR342. They started on FR650 and connected with FR342, which is always considered a four-wheel drive access. We have not traveled on this unnamed trail.

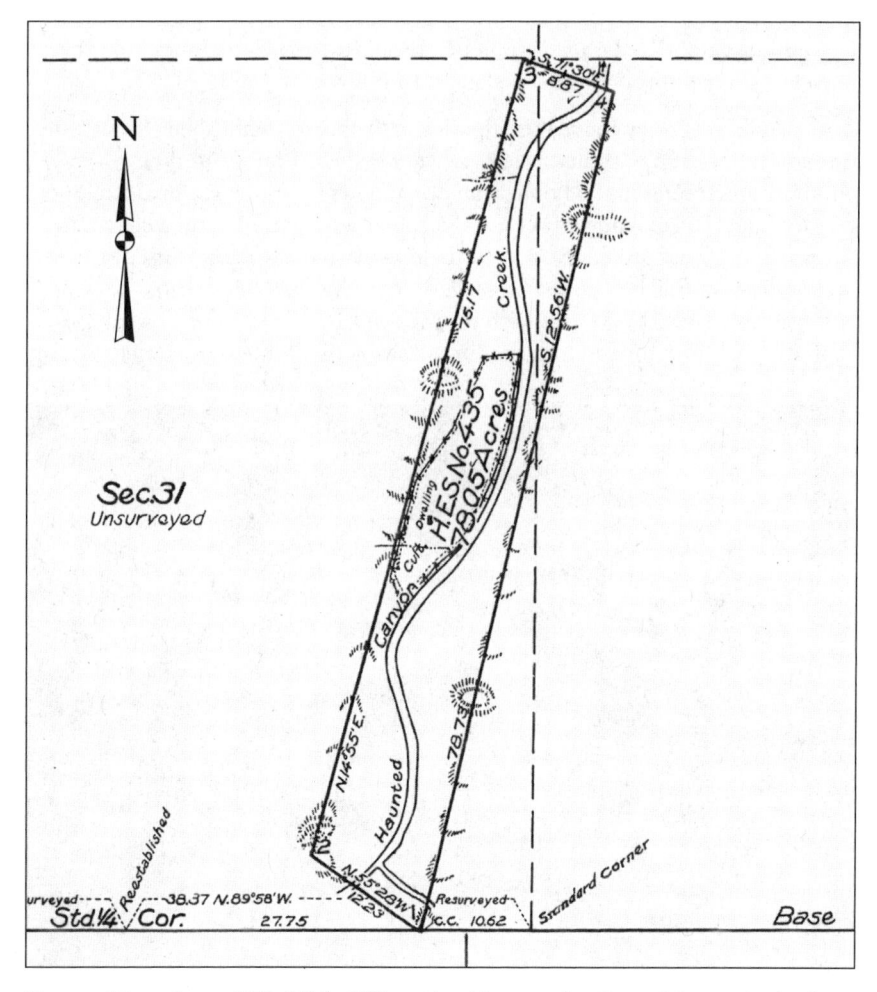

Homestead Entry Survey (HES 435) for William Toney's homestead on Haunted Canyon Creek. The survey was completed on June 7, 1920. Toney received the land patent on January 4, 1922. Map from BLM, Phoenix Office.

HISTORY AND LEGENDS

William Tolliver Toney applied for his Haunted Canyon homestead in 1915 and received the patent for 78 acres in 1922. The map makers left the "e" out of Toney, and the property has been known as the Tony Ranch since the 1940s.

William Toney was born in Scotts Valley, California, on September 26, 1873, and was raised in a ranching family near Silver City, New Mexico. He was ranching at the mouth of Skeleton Canyon, Cochise County, Arizona, in 1908 with his father, Seth T. Toney. Their ranch was less than one-half mile downstream from the place in Skeleton Canyon where Apache leader Geronimo surrendered on September 6, 1886. In 1915, Seth Toney sold the Skeleton Canyon property to Ross Sloan and moved to California.[100]

William Toney moved to Superior, Arizona, to established the Haunted Canyon homestead with his wife, Ella Mary Wilson Toney, and their seven children. According to the homestead documents from the National Archives, he tore down the existing structures—a cabin, a thatch hut, and a corral. In August 1913, he replaced them with the present-day log cabin with a corrugated iron roof.[101] The 12-foot-by-30-foot log cabin had two-rooms, but was enlarged to 12-feet-by-34-feet with three-rooms by 1921. Toney ran a 1600-foot one-inch iron pipe to a spring for domestic use. Since Tony Ranch Spring

Tony Cabin was built by William Toney in 1913. The collapsing hay barn on the left was added at a later date. Toney received the homestead rights in 1922. The cabin and homestead property are now owned by the Superstition Area Land Trust. Photo was taken in March 2001.

(named Hill Spring in the homestead surveys) is only 1000-feet from the cabin, he may have used another spring.

Homesteaders were expected to cultivate the property and Toney had some difficulty complying with the rules, due to the rocky soil and the drought conditions in 1919 and 1920. He eventually applied for a reduction in the required area of cultivation. Water only surfaced in Haunted Canyon on the lower half of the homestead, and he channeled that water for irrigation using ditches and 300-feet of 3-inch pipe. The first crop was planted in 1914—three acres of wheat—and the next year he planted six-hundred apple trees. In later years, beans, corn, potatoes, sorghum, alfalfa and garden truck were planted. By 1919, only one-hundred forty-six of the apple trees were living, but they were beginning to bear fruit.

Wedding photo of Ella Mary Wilson and William Tolliver Toney in Silver City, New Mexico, November 26, 1894. Courtesy of Betty Porter Gilbert, granddaughter of William and Ella Mary Toney.

Forest Ranger Henry Taylor said that "Mr. Toney is a cowman of the old type, and farming is naturally a side issue with him. ...he would not want the place unless he could get a permit to run hogs or cattle on the Forest."[102] In 1915, Toney had 120 chickens, 25 turkeys, 4 horses and a herd of cattle. Later he added milk cows and hogs. In 1921, he had 234 cattle on the nearby range. You can see his *Lazy W Bar T* brand on the inside wall of the Tony cabin.[103]

In 1924, Toney sold his homestead and cattle to George Taylor. After the sale, he was involved in prospecting and mining in Arivaca, Arizona. Toney died on October 1, 1953, and is buried in the Desert Lawn Memorial

Park Cemetery, Yuma, Arizona. Two of the Toney children, Boyd and Ophie Toney Hunter, are also buried there. Ella Mary died on December 11, 1920 and is buried in the Fairview Cemetery, Superior, Arizona. See page 45 for a photo of Ella Mary and five of the eight Toney children. The Toney's son, Ellis, worked for Reavis Ranch, EK Ranch, Bohme Ranch, and other ranches around Superior, Miami, and Globe. Descendants of the Toney family still live in the towns of Globe, Apache Junction, and Silver City.

George Taylor ran the TU Ranch south of Superior and the Tony Ranch in Haunted Canyon. After he died in 1949, his wife Ann hired Jim Herron to manage the TU Ranch and Tony Ranch. When Ann Taylor died in 1989, Jim Herron inherited part of the TU Ranch and a life estate in the Tony Ranch with John Daer, Ben Taylor, and Milford Taylor.[104] Herron died in 2004. The Superstition Area Land Trust purchased the Toney homestead property including the cabin in August 2008 from the Ann Curtis Taylor Trust.

Jim Herron told us that he packed hay, grain, and salt on mules from their Happy Camp corrals on FR650 into the Tony cabin barn for cattle roundups. He said the mules could carry more weight than the horses. They wrapped the hay in canvas to keep the brush from damaging it. He stored the hay in the small barn attached to the south end of the cabin. The barn has mostly collapsed now, but you can still see where the barn was attached to the log cabin. Herron said they later decided not to use that grazing allotment because of problems with mountain lions and bears.[105]

The winter gets very cold in the high country, so we asked Jim Herron if he ever wore earmuffs in the cold weather or just wore his western hat. He said, "No, just the hat." He commented that when a catclaw bush caught his ear in the cold weather, it felt like his ear was going to break off.

Jim Herron also told us of the unexpected death of John T. Oldham in 1959. Seventy year old Oldham (aka Charley Hart) was working for Herron. Earlier in the day, Jim had told John that he did not look very good and maybe he should not ride with them. John insisted he wanted to go. Above the Rock Spring Corral at the head of Haunted Canyon near FR342, John felt hot, so Jim sent a man down to the spring to get a cup of water for Oldham. Jim said, "He was sitting next to me, took a drink of water, then he fell over in my lap"—died of a heart attack. Milford Taylor helped pack Oldham out of the mountains with the body tied over Oldham's horse. They had to retie him to the horse three times while going down the steep hills to Cottonwood Camp. John Oldham is buried in the Fairview Cemetery in Superior, Arizona. He is mentioned in *Fifty Years on the Owl Hoot Trail*, the book about Jim Herron's grandfather.[106]

Paradise Trail Loop

This trip takes you to the high country near Government Hill where the native grasses grow tall on the open hillsides. A pond of water at the Paradise Trail junction reflects the surrounding hills and wildflowers in this normally dry desert country. Although Paradise Spring is usually dry, the trip down through the forested area of Paradise Canyon makes an enjoyable outing.

ITINERARY

From the Haunted Canyon Trailhead on FR287A, follow the Haunted Canyon Trail (203) uphill to the junction with Paradise Trail (271). Follow Paradise Trail down to FR287A, and head back to your vehicle on FR287A.

DIFFICULTY

Moderate hike. Difficult horse ride. Elevation change is ±1,650 feet.

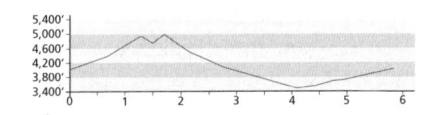

LENGTH and TIME

5.8 miles, 4 hours round trip.

MAPS

Arizona USGS topo maps NAD27: Haunted Canyon. Superstition Wilderness Beartooth map, grids Q13 and Q14. Map 24.

FINDING THE TRAIL

Trailhead map is on page 188. The west end of Haunted Canyon Trail (203) starts at Haunted Canyon Trailhead on FR287A not far from Miles Trailhead. From the small parking area [24-G] (N33° 25' 33.0", W111° 03' 17.3") on the north side of FR287A, cross the road to the south, and locate the signed Haunted Canyon Trail 203. A small wooden corral sits next to the road and trail.

THE TRIP

Start on Map 24 on page 201. From the Haunted Canyon Trailhead [24-G, 0], on dirt FR287A, look for the trail sign marking the start of the Haunted Canyon Trail. Follow the trail southwest along a small ravine. The trail is well-worn, easy to follow, and marked by rock cairns. A gradual ascent takes you up to Grapevine Spring [24-X, 0.9], which usually provides water in an overflowing metal trough. The water trough is right on the trail, so you can't miss it.

Toward the top of the hill, the trail leaves the ravine and goes up the grassy hillside and eventually passes through a gate [24-YY, 1.3] in the barbed wire fence. The tall grass sometimes obscures the Haunted Canyon Trail and the large rock cairns, so look carefully for the trail as it tends to head right (west) and then turns left (south) into a south running ravine. The trail follows the left (east) bank of the ravine a short distance to a dirt dam that backs up a pond of water. The Paradise Trail (271) junction [24-W, 1.5], on the west side of the dirt dam, is marked by a wooden trail sign on the gate post. From the dam, you can take a side trip another 2.2 miles to Tony Ranch if you continue downhill on the Haunted Canyon Trail. But, this trip, Trip 23, goes through the Paradise Trail gate and heads uphill.

Follow Paradise Trail uphill to a saddle [24-U, 1.7] northeast of Government Hill. The Paradise Trail is sometimes difficult to find here, so look closely for the trail heading to the northwest. Although not part of this trip, a route (not a trail) goes southwest up the ridge to Government Hill. That 1.3-mile route makes use of some abandoned cowboy trails and fence line trails that take you over the top of Government Hill (Benchmark 5445) to the Bull Basin Trail at a pass and gate [24-N] on the ridge.

Continuing on the Paradise Trail, follow the path on the west bank of a small ravine, which is the headwaters of Paradise Canyon. As you descend, the bed of the trail becomes less rocky and padded with leaves from the overhanging trees. We have not seen any water developments at Paradise Spring [24-K, 3.4], and the ravine has always been dry when we were here. The remains of a wooden corral are located on the west side of the trail just north of Paradise Spring.

The Paradise Trail skirts the east side of a small waterfall [24-J, 3.8] at the 3,600-foot elevation, and a little farther downhill the trail ends on dirt road FR287A, [24-H, 4.1] (N33° 26' 09.1", W111° 03' 46.3"). A wooden sign along the road marks the junction, but the sign only reads *Trail 271*. Turn right (southeast) and return to your vehicle at the Haunted Canyon Trailhead [24-G, 5.8]. On one trip, we took a shortcut to bypass the switchbacks on FR287A by hiking up the canyon that comes into FR287A at Benchmark 3690, but the easy trail soon became a boulder-strewn canyon, and we had to scramble up the side of the steep canyon to get back on FR287A.

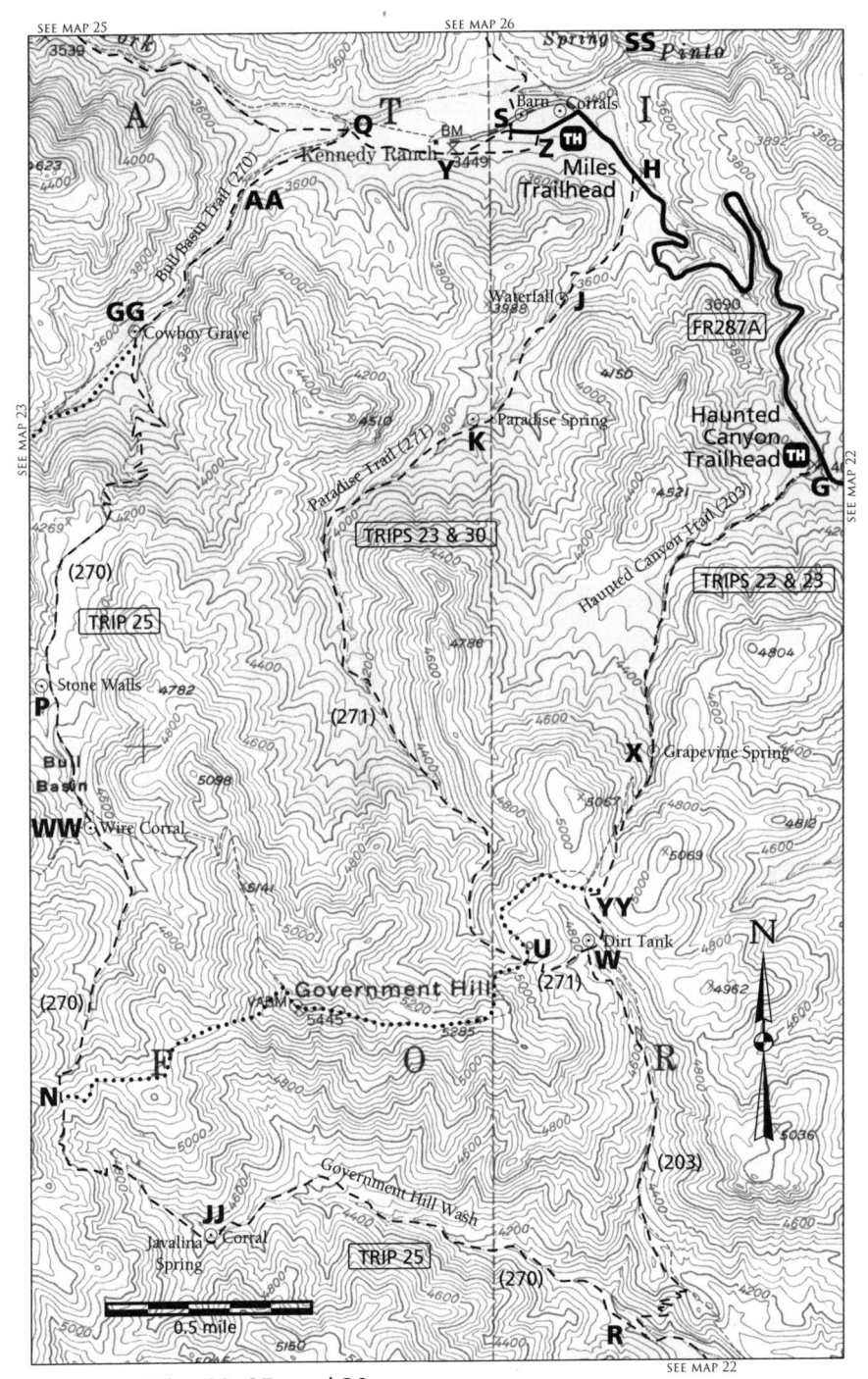

Map 24 – Trips 23, 25, and 30.

Miles Trailhead

From Apache Junction at Idaho Road, on US60, drive 29 miles to Superior. Continue east toward Miami and Globe on US60 for 12 more miles. One mile east of the Pinto Creek highway bridge, turn left (north) on FR287 (Pinto Valley Mine Road) between mileposts 239 and 240. Follow FR287 and FR287A to the trailhead. If you are coming from Miami, drive 4 miles west on US60 to the Pinto Valley Mine Road.

FINDING THE TRAILHEAD

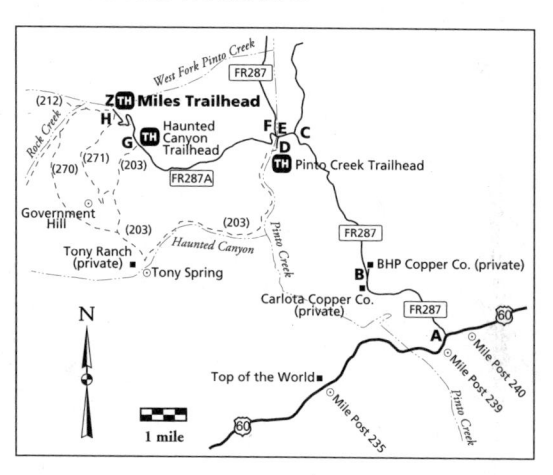

Pinto Valley Mine Road is paved for 2.8 miles to the BHP Copper Company entrance. When you approach the guard station, bear left on the dirt road at the signed intersection—*Public Access Road, JH6 Ranch Road, 287*. Following these signs and the *Haunted Canyon* sign will keep you on the correct road, which is Forest Road 287 (FR287).

FR287 takes you across the facilities of the BHP Copper Company, which include several large, mine-tailing ponds. Do not drive on any roads marked *Active Mining Area*. The route of the public access road may change to accommodate mine operations, so you need to pay close attention to the road signs and speed limit.

From US60 [A, 0], drive north on paved FR287 for 2.8 miles to the BHP entrance [B, 2.8], and bear left where FR287 turns into a dirt road. Continue on dirt FR287 through the BHP property. Turn left at the cattle guard and locked gate [C, 6.7] for JH6 Ranch. Continue on FR287 to the Iron Bridge at Pinto Creek [E, 7.2].

Pinto Creek Trailhead is down the road to your left just before you cross the Iron Bridge. You are headed for Miles Trailhead, so drive across the Iron Bridge. At the signed intersection with FR287A [F, 7.3], turn left on FR287A. FR287A is narrow, so look ahead to make room for oncoming vehicles. You pass Haunted Canyon Trailhead [G, 11.1], Paradise Trail [H, 12.8], and come to the end of FR287A at the *Trail 212* sign with an arrow pointing left. Turn left and drive along the corral to the Miles Trailhead [Z, 13.0] (N33° 26' 14.3", W111° 04' 01.9"). Park or set up camp wherever you like. A medium-clearance vehicle is required. Allow extra driving time for getting lost on the first section of the road [B, 2.8 to C, 6.7].

FACILITIES

The Miles Trailhead has corrals, a barn, plenty of room for parking, and space for group camping under the tall sycamore trees. Bring your own water.

THE TRAILS

From the large *Miles Trailhead* sign, look ahead to the hiker logo sign, walk to the left, and you will see the Superstition Wilderness sign for the start of the West Pinto Trail (212) (N33° 26' 14.3", W111° 04' 01.9") [25-Z]. The beginning of the trail is a bit steep and narrow, so horse riders might want to start their trip at the white metal gate with the B4 brand (N33° 26' 15.0", W111° 04' 04.7"). The gate is locked, so horse riders will want to go through the adjacent barbed wire gate. Stay on the left (south) side of the barbed wire fence, and the old road will connect you with the West Pinto Trail in a few hundred yards.

The Tonto National Forest purchased the western portion of the Miles Ranch property in 1986—the large meadow area—which now has a Wilderness designation. In 1997, Tonto National Forest purchased the eastern end of the ranch. Now used as the trailhead area, you will find plenty of room for parking cars and horse trailers here. The large sycamore and Emory oak trees make this a nice place to car camp and prepare for day trips. The West Pinto Trail (212) and the first part of the Bull Basin Trail (270) on Rock Creek provide easy hiking and horse riding along the seasonal creeks. Many other trails branch off the West Pinto Trail to provide superb hiking and riding possibilities.

Backtracking 0.2 mile on FR287A from the Miles Trailhead, you come to the junction with the Paradise Trail [25-H], which is identified only by the *Trail 271* sign.

Backtracking 1.9 miles on FR287A from the Miles Trailhead, you come to the Haunted Canyon Trailhead (N33° 25' 33.0", W111° 03' 17.3") [25-G] where the Haunted Canyon Trail (203) takes you over to Haunted Canyon and Tony Ranch (private) [22-T] on a well-marked trail. The east end of the Haunted Canyon Trail terminates near the Iron Bridge on Pinto Creek [22-D].

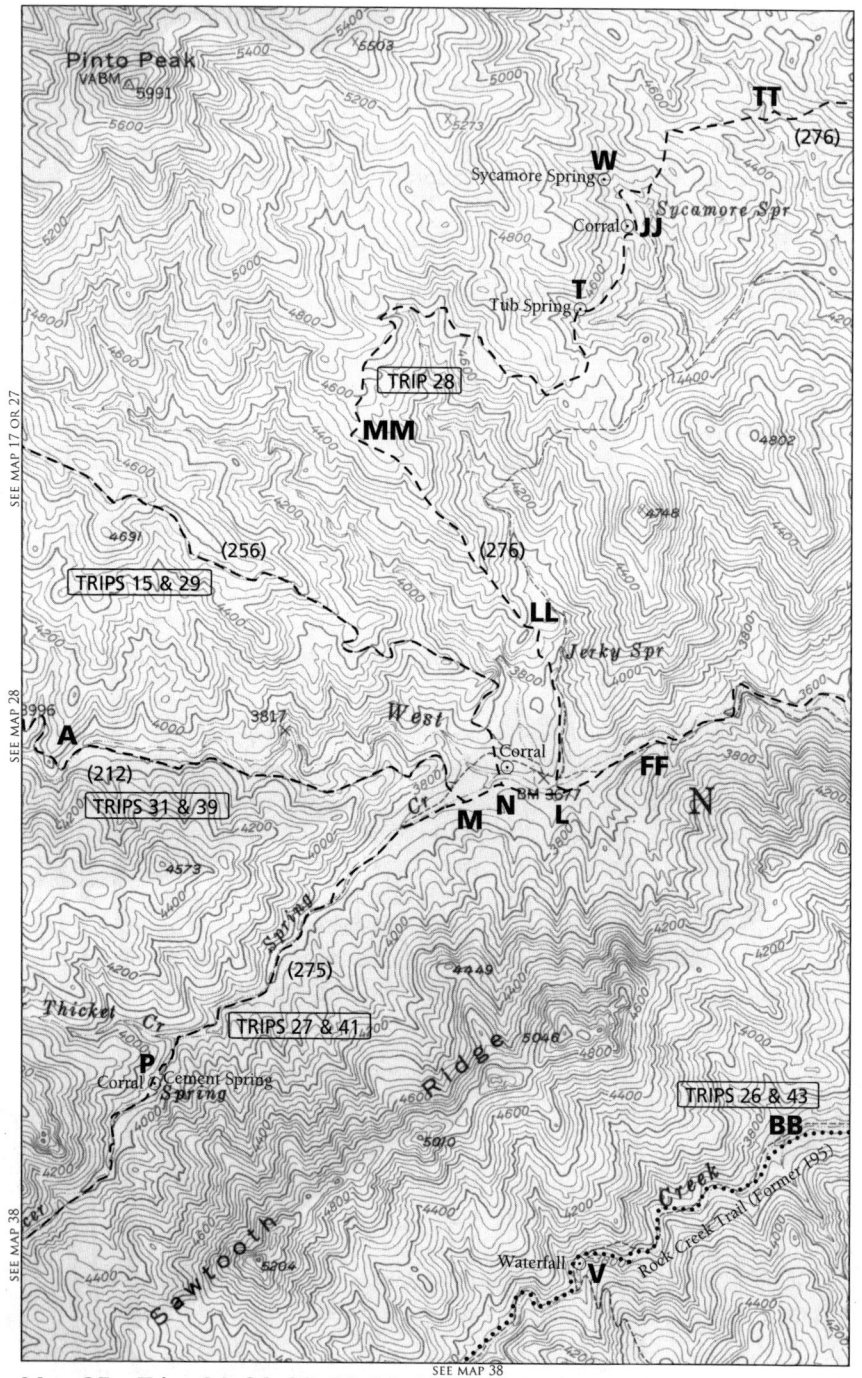

Map 25 – Trips 24, 26, 27, 28, 31, 32 and 43.

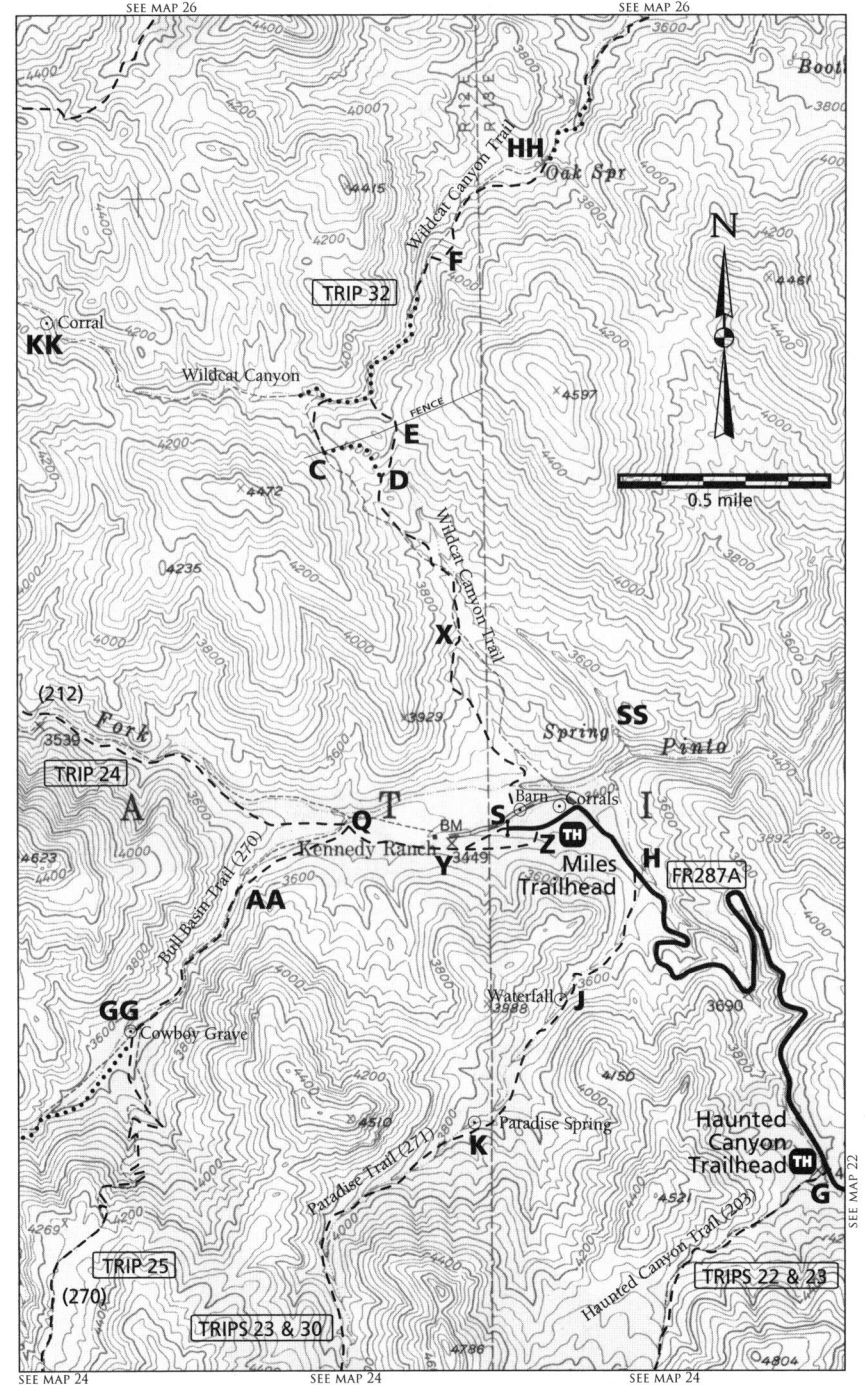

Map 25 continued – Trips 24, 26, 27, 28, 31, 32 and 43.

MILES TRAILHEAD 205

HISTORY AND LEGENDS

John Bourke, who was General George Crook's aide-de-camp, kept a diary and sketched maps of the U.S. Army's campaign in pursuit of the Apache in Arizona. On several of Bourke's maps, for the marches of December 1872 through March 1873 in the Superstition Mountains, he names the West Fork Pinto Creek, Pinto Butte (now Pinto Peak), Cañon Creek (now Fish Creek), and Pinto Creek.[107]

Bourke describes their March 1, 1873, march starting at old Camp Pinal in Mason's Valley (now Top of the World) that took them 7 miles north along Pinto Creek where they probably camped near the Iron Bridge. The next day they continued north, crossing West Fork Pinto Creek up canyon from its junction with Pinto Creek. After a 7.5 mile trek, they probably made their March 2 camp in the upper reaches of Horrell Creek possibly near Musk Hog Spring. He noted that the site of an Apache rancheria they attacked on January 15 was over the ridge to the west. On March 3, they headed west and south, probably using the alignment of the Cuff Button Trail to take them to Oak Flat where they made camp.

After leaving Oak Flat on March 4, the command headed southwest up the mountain between Spencer Spring Creek and West Fork Pinto Creek, but the route is not as apparent because he did not draw a map for the next few days. They came down into their January 11, 1873, camp, which might have been in the Rogers Trough area. On March 5, they went through a pass, maybe Tortilla Pass, and headed downhill and might have camped in the Tortilla Ranch area after a march of 13 miles. On March 6, Bourke and a small mounted party rode over a pass and down into Cañon Creek (now named Fish Creek). They rode upstream 1 mile below high cliffs, then they returned and rode 1 mile downstream until they were blocked by "huge boulders." After this short exploration, they rejoined the main command and continued west, retracing their January trail back to Fort McDowell.

Although Bourke gives mileage and compass directions for the marches, he rarely mentions place names in his diary, so tracing his routes through the mountains is not easy. Our estimates of his camps are only guesses based on mileage, terrain, and his maps, but they give you a general idea of where the army searched. See Trip 27 (Spencer Spring Creek) for the Army's activity in that area. See Tule Trailhead for a description of the march from the Salt River and Pinto Creek to the battle at Skull Cave.

About 1909, Cliff Edwards referred to the Miles Ranch as the Bowman Ranch, but we have not found any Bowman ownership documents. R. Lewis Bowman does not think his family ranched on West Fork Pinto Creek.[108]

Interest in homesteading the Miles Trailhead property officially began on May 20, 1912, when W. L. Greer applied for the HES 554 listing. Rae Clark

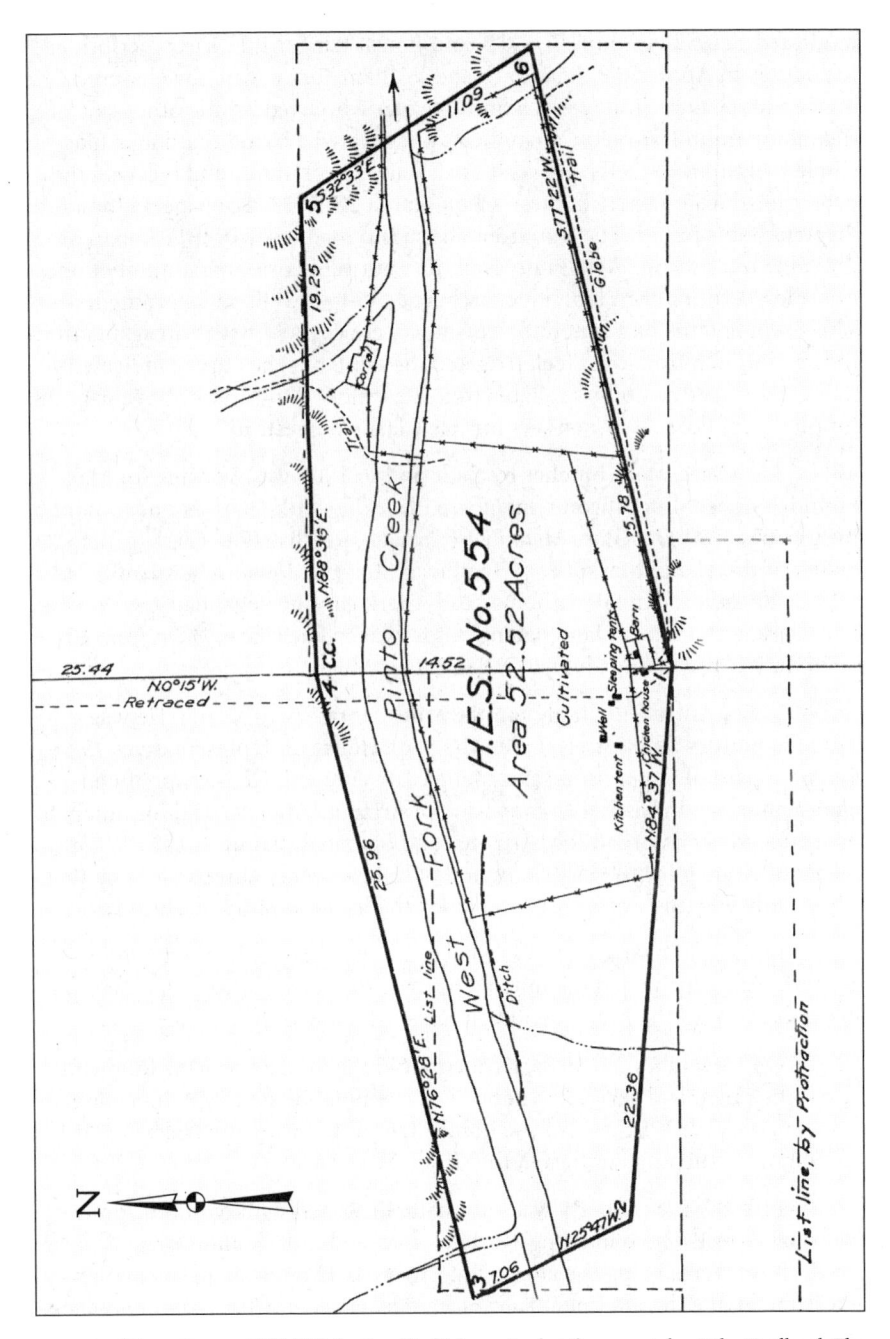

Homestead Entry Survey (HES 554) for Rae Clark's homestead at the present day Miles Trailhead. The survey was completed on April 28, 1919. Clark received the land patent on March 28, 1921. Sleeping tents and kitchen tent are identified on the map near Corner No. 1. Map from BLM, Phoenix Office.

requested a survey on June 7, 1915, and Forest Ranger F. L. Kirby performed the survey in April 1919. Rae Clark and William Toney were the chainmen on the survey crew. Toney was a homesteader who lived on the other side of the mountain in Haunted Canyon. Clark registered a brand that looks like Circle L Slash in 1915 for his West Fork Pinto Creek range and received the patent for the 52.52 acre homestead on March 28, 1921. See page 33 for a diagram of his brand. The trail from Globe (no road until 1938) came in on the same track as the West Pinto Trail. Just north of corner post number one was a log barn, kitchen tent, chicken house, 35-foot well, and sleeping tents. The sleeping tents had concrete floors and were covered with corrugated iron roofing. A ditch from the creek irrigated the field, but the survey indicated that creek water was only available from December 1 to June 1.[109] See page 28 for photos of the survey markers for Rae Clark's homestead.

Rae Clark was a butcher by trade and in 1908 was working for Max Bonn in Globe. Slim Ellison remembered working with Clark at one of Bonn's meat markets.[110] The *Globe Miami Directory* of 1925 lists Rae Clark as the owner of the Miami Market at 603 Sullivan Street in downtown Miami.[111] In a 1923 affidavit for the Periz homestead, Clark gave his legal name as George Rae Clark, although his land patent was issued as Rae Clark.[112] On June 10, 1924, Rae Clark sold his homestead to J. Ney Miles.[113]

J. Ney Miles and family ran the Miles Mortuary in Miami. He was active in politics and was elected to the State House of Representatives, Gila County Board of Supervisors, and Miami City Council. He was appointed chairman of the Industrial Commission of Arizona. After he sold his ranch, he opened a grocery store in Ray, Arizona, and operated that until 1951.[114] Miles owned the ranch for the longest period of time—twenty-three years—so that is probably why the Forest Service named the location Miles Trailhead.

Miles sold his ranch to Vernon (Jack) and Frances Kennedy on June 2, 1947. Kennedy owned the ranch when the Haunted Canyon topo map was made in 1948, so the Kennedy Ranch name was added to that map.

On November 24, 1958, Kennedy sold the ranch. Over the following years, the ranch had several owners, but most notably the Fay Bohme family from 1970 to 1982. In-laws of the Bohme family, Johnson and Hale, are also well-known ranching families in the Globe-Miami area.

In 1986, the property was split with 42.52 acres going to the Tonto National Forest. The remaining 10 acres were sold to Jack and Doris Reeder—ten acres being the amount of private land required to satisfy the government grazing allotment rules. Jack Reeder died in 1991, and his estate sold the land to Linda Policky. Eventually the Tonto National Forest acquired title to those remaining 10 acres of private land on March 27, 1997, from the Deseret Trust.

Trip 24

WEST PINTO TRAIL TO OAK FLAT

If this is your first visit to West Fork Pinto Creek, the trip up West Pinto Trail to Oak Flat is a good choice. The trail is well defined, and the gentle grade has only a few up and down sections. All the major trails in the area branch from this segment of the West Pinto Trail. Seasonal water in West Fork Pinto Creek supports a hardy forest of sycamore, cottonwood, cypress, and Emory oak trees.

ITINERARY

From the Miles Trailhead, follow the West Pinto Trail (212) to Oak Flat. Return the same way.

DIFFICULTY

Moderate hike. Moderate horse ride. Elevation change is +270 and -40 feet one way.

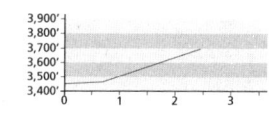

LENGTH and TIME

2.4 miles, 1.5 hours one way.

MAPS

Arizona USGS topo map NAD27: Haunted Canyon. Superstition Wilderness Beartooth map, grids Q13 to P13. Map 25.

FINDING THE TRAIL

Trailhead map is on page 202. The West Pinto Trail starts at Miles Trailhead [25-Z] at the Superstition Wilderness sign (N33° 26' 14.3", W111° 04' 01.9"). Horse riders can start at the white metal gate with the B4 brand (N33° 26' 15.0", W111° 04' 04.7").

THE TRIP

Start on Map 25 on page 205. From the Superstition Wilderness sign, begin on the West Pinto Trail [25-Z, 0]. At the first clearing along the trail, you may see a brass survey marker [25-Y, 0.2] on the left (south) side of the trail. This is the 1919 HES 554 homestead survey corner post number one.

View to the west of the barn at Miles Trailhead in March 2001. The Wilderness boundary fence is on the west side of the barn. West Fork Pinto Creek is off the right side of the photo.

After skirting the left (south) side of the former ranch property and just before crossing Rock Creek, the West Pinto Trail meets the Bull Basin Trail (270) at a wooden sign [25-Q, 0.5]. Some older maps may still show this as an intersection with the former Rock Creek Trail (195). Trip 24 continues west as the West Pinto Trail crosses Rock Creek and heads up the left (south) bench of West Fork Pinto Creek.

The trail, marked by rock cairns, meanders as it crosses West Fork Pinto Creek several times to avoid cliff outcrops and to take advantage of flat benches on either side of the canyon. On the south bench, the trail bypasses a narrow section of canyon and a pool of water (when there is water) by going over a low ridge and through a log fence at an open gate [25-FF, 1.9].

The West Pinto Trail is on the left (south) side of West Fork Pinto Creek when it reaches Oak Flat. Trip 24 stays on the West Pinto Trail as it passes the three trail intersections that we describe below.

The first landmark you will see in Oak Flat is the wooden trail sign [25-L, 2.1] for the Cuff Button Trail (276), which branches off to the right (north). The Cuff Button Trail immediately crosses the normally dry creek near the sign and heads up the left (west) side of the ravine going to Jerky

Spring. We have never seen water at Jerky Spring. Trip 28 takes you another 4.2 miles from Oak Flat to Cuff Button Spring [26-R], which has a small seep of water. The Cuff Button Trail has sections of significant uphill and downhill.

Trip 24, however, continues west on the West Pinto Trail, where the next landmark is the wooden sign [25-N, 2.3] at the intersection with the Campaign Trail (256). Campaign Trail crosses to the right (north) side of the creek where the trail goes close to the wooden-pole corral (N33° 26' 20", W111° 06' 09") that you will see on your right (east). The round corral is still in good repair, and horse riders can use the corral on day or overnight trips, although no permanent water is nearby and the creek is often dry. From Oak Flat, the Campaign Trail goes up and over the Pinto Divide [17-K] into Campaign Creek and ends at Campaign Trailhead [14-A] in 9.7 miles. See Trip 29 if you want to make the trek from Oak Flat up to Pinto Divide on the Campaign Trail.

A little farther west, the last intersection with the West Pinto Trail is marked by the Spencer Spring Trail (275) wooden sign [25-M, 2.4]. From Oak Flat, Trip 27 follows Spencer Spring Trail going left (southwest) and ends on FR650 [36-C] in 3.7 miles.

West Pinto Trail goes across Spencer Spring Creek (normally dry) and continues on the left (south) side of West Fork Pinto Creek. From Oak Flat, Trip 31 takes you on the West Pinto Trail to Rogers Trough Trailhead in another 6.4 miles.

Spencer Spring Creek marks the west end of Oak Flat and the end of this trip (Trip 24) on the West Pinto Trail. Return the same way, or continue on another trail.

HISTORY AND LEGENDS

At Oak Flat, the trail intersections were changed after a flood washed out the trails in the 1990s. The USGS topo map shows the trails in Oak Flat meeting on the north side of West Fork Pinto Creek whereas they now intersect on the south side. The new trail alignment makes a lot of sense for recreational hikers and horse riders, but in the former days of ranching, we can see how the cowboys would have wanted to head straight for the round corral at Oak Flat. On a cattle drive, the animals don't understand how to make a left or right turn at a wooden trail sign.

South of the West Pinto Trail and Campaign Trail sign is an outline of rocks that could be a building foundation. We have heard that this may have been the location of a sheep herder camp.[115] A log structure—three logs high and about 12-feet square—is located on the right side of the West Pinto Trail just after crossing Spencer Creek. These logs could have been the walls for a tent building that had a canvas top.

Stone walls and cattle feeder [24-P] along the Bull Basin Trail (270). Photo taken in December 2007.

In 2001, the Tonto National Forest renamed several trails that connect with West Pinto Trail (212). The Pinto Peak Trail (213) was renamed the Campaign Trail (256), and the portion of the Pinto Peak Trail in the Horrell Creek drainage was abandoned. The Rock Creek Trail (195) was renamed the Bull Basin Trail (270), and the trail in the upper reaches of Rock Creek was abandoned. Some older maps show the former trail names. The abandoned trails are still open for use, but they are not maintained by the Forest Service.[116]

The U.S. Army camped at Oak Flat on January 14 and March 3, 1873 during their campaign against the Apache. See the History and Legends section of the Miles Trailhead for John Bourke's 1872 and 1873 military marches near West Fork Pinto Creek. Also see Trip 27 (Spencer Spring Creek) for more of the story and one of Bourke's map.

Trip 25

BULL BASIN LOOP

The seldom-used Bull Basin Trail is an alternate route to Tony Ranch with a return on the Paradise Trail. The trip takes you from the tree-lined Rock Creek, over the grassy ridge of Government Hill, and down into Haunted Canyon. The mileage is a little longer than using the Haunted Canyon Trail, but the Bull Basin Trail offers travelers some new scenery.

ITINERARY

From the Miles Trailhead, follow the West Pinto Trail (212), Bull Basin Trail (270), and Haunted Canyon Trail (203). Make an optional side trip to Tony Ranch. Return on the Haunted Canyon Trail, Paradise Trail, and a short distance on FR287A.

DIFFICULTY

Moderate day hike or two-day trip. Difficult horse ride due to narrow and steep trails. Elevation change is ±2,670 feet.

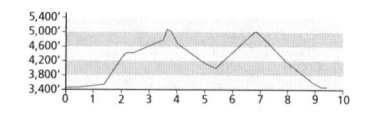

LENGTH and TIME

9.4 miles, 7 hours round trip.

MAPS

Arizona USGS topo map NAD27: Haunted Canyon. Superstition Wilderness Beartooth map, grids Q13, P14, and Q14. Map 24.

FINDING THE TRAIL

Trailhead map is on page 202. The West Pinto Trail starts at Miles Trailhead [24-Z] at the Superstition Wilderness sign (N33° 26' 14.3", W111° 04' 01.9"). Horse riders can start at the white metal gate with the B4 brand (N33° 26' 15.0", W111° 04' 04.7").

THE TRIP

Start on Map 24 on page 201. From the Superstition Wilderness sign at the Miles Trailhead [24-Z], go west on the West Pinto Trail (212). After a short distance on the trail, the large meadow and barbed wire fence will be on your right (north).

At the wooden trail sign [24-Q, 0.5], just before you cross Rock Creek, turn left (southwest) onto the Bull Basin Trail (270). Note that some older maps may still show this as the former Rock Creek Trail (195).

The Bull Basin Trail starts out as dirt road and makes pleasant walking or riding. If you only have a short time for this visit, you might consider turning around at the first creek crossing [24-AA, 0.8]. If there is water in the creek, we are sure you will enjoy your trip here. Another turnaround point is 0.4 mile up the creek at the unknown cowboy grave [24-GG, 1.2].

After the first creek crossing [24-AA, 0.8], the trail disappears in the creek bed. Follow the rock cairns through the washed-out section of road in the normally dry creek, and they will guide you to the left (south) bench where the trail and old road continue.

Shortly before the Bull Basin Trail makes a turn to the left (south), look to the right side of the trail for a pile of rocks under a cypress tree [24-GG, 1.2] (N33° 25' 48.3", W111° 05' 01.4"). This is the grave of an unknown cowboy. From here [24-GG], the old road turns into a trail. Going straight takes you on the former Rock Trail (see Trip 26, Rock Creek from Bull Basin Trail), but this trip goes left and begins the climb up to Bull Basin.

The Bull Basin Trail heads up a series of switchbacks on a well-maintained trail. Some sections of the trail here are steep and may be difficult for some horse riders. When the trail tops out at about the 2 mile mark, you have a gentle downhill grade with open views to Sawtooth Ridge in the west. The trail then turns more to the south and parallels Bull Basin Wash as the trail resumes the uphill course.

Wide piles of rocks on either side of the trail alert you to the stone walls on the right (west) side of the trail [24-P, 2.5] (N33° 25' 07.5", W111° 05' 14.3").[117] Some of these walls look like they might have been built to form a corral that was never completed. We speculate that the rocks may have been recycled from a prehistoric ruin at this site. A wooden hay feeder is still located inside the enclosure. If Bull Basin Wash has flowing water, you can see a small waterfall up canyon from this area.

The post and wire corral in Bull Basin lies on the right (west) side of the trail [24-WW, 2.8] (N33° 24' 50.6", W111° 05' 08.5"). Sherry Spring is shown on some maps on the west side of Bull Basin Wash, but we have not looked for it. Beyond the wire corral, the trail follows Bull Basin Wash for a while, then strikes a course directly up to the pass and gate [24-N, 3.6, 5100] on the west arm of Government Hill. Always leave gates as you find them (open or closed) unless they are signed otherwise.

We have taken an off-trail route across the top of Government Hill by following the fence to the left (east) and connecting with the Paradise Trail. This is one of those shortcuts that is harder and takes more time than you might expect.

Continuing on the Bull Basin Trail, a steep section of trail takes you down to the former water improvements and corral at Javelina Spring [24-JJ, 4.2]. Do not rely on the spring for water, although you might find water here in Government Hill Wash near the spring. From the spring, the trail heads east and follows the bed of the wash where you may encounter catclaw on the trail. The trail soon meets the Haunted Canyon Trail (203) at a signed intersection [24-R, 5.4]. Going straight onto the Haunted Canyon Trail takes you to Tony Ranch Spring [23-QQ] in 0.8 mile. Tony Ranch Spring (N33° 23' 23", W111° 03' 11") normally has water. See Trip 22 (Tony Ranch from FR287A) for the Tony Ranch history. Our trip heads left (north) at the wooden trail sign, taking the switchbacks uphill on the Haunted Canyon Trail.

At a dirt tank, which is often full of water, a wooden trail sign marks the start of the Paradise Trail (271) [24-W, 6.6]. Going right, across the dirt dam on the Haunted Canyon Trail, takes you to FR287A at the Upper Haunted Canyon Trailhead [24-G] in 1.5 miles. This trip picks up the

Snow covers the Bull Basin Trail (270) at the gate [24-N] on Government Hill ridge. View to the south. Photo was taken in December 2007.

Paradise Trail at the dirt tank, goes left, and continues uphill to a saddle [24-U, 6.8] on the eastern ridge of Government Hill. The trail at the saddle is sometimes difficult to see, so look closely for a trail heading down the left (west) side of a ravine, which is the start of Paradise Canyon. Trip 22 (Tony Ranch from FR287A) will give you another perspective on this section of the mountains.

Paradise Spring [24-K, 8.5], which is located south of a historic wooden corral, has always been dry when we have visited. At the 3,600-foot elevation, the trail passes the east edge of a small waterfall [24-J, 8.9] and shortly meets dirt road FR287A [24-H, 9.2]. The junction with FR287A is only marked with a sign that reads *Trail*. Turn left (north) on FR287A, and follow the road to your starting point at Miles Trailhead [24-Z, 9.4] where the trip ends.

HISTORY AND LEGENDS

When the Bull Basin Trail leaves Rock Creek, the trail makes a few switchbacks as it climbs the hill. Rancher Jimmy Herron told us that he once helped his neighbors at the Miles Ranch drive their cattle down this trail and over to the headquarters. They got the cattle started on the trail in Bull Basin and headed downhill, but the cattle would not zigzag down the switchbacks on the Bull Basin Trail. They just walked straight off the end of the hill into the brush. The cowboys found the cattle at the bottom of the hill in Rock Creek, gathered them, and drove them back to the headquarters. It was not an easy day.[118]

Benny Miles said the grave [24-GG] on Rock Creek by the cypress tree is that of an unknown cowboy. He said that Ed Horrell and his cowboys found the dead man and buried him right where he died. The dead man had no identification on him, and no one knows who he was.[119]

The Bull Basin Trail along Rock Creek follows the bed of a former mining road that was used to access magnetite-hematite iron and chrysotile asbestos deposits in the area. Some of the mines were claimed at different times by Jack Kennedy and William Bohme, former owners of Miles Ranch. In 1953, Jack Kennedy's claims were named the K. & S. Asbestos Group, Last Time Group, and Mystery of Mountain Group.[120]

Trip 26

ROCK CREEK FROM BULL BASIN TRAIL

The Rock Creek trip follows the former alignment of the Rock Creek Trail. The abandoned Rock Creek Trail takes you up a pretty tree-lined canyon to its headwaters. The creek is often dry, but when the creek has water, this makes an ideal place for a day trip in the mountains.

ITINERARY

From the Miles Trailhead, take the West Pinto Trail (212) to Bull Basin Trail (270). Follow Bull Basin Trail until the trail leaves Rock Creek, then continue up Rock Creek to the end at FR650. Return the same way or link up with other trails off of FR650.

DIFFICULTY

Moderate hike. Very difficult and maybe impossible horse ride due to fallen trees after the trip leaves the Bull Basin Trail. Elevation change is +1,150 and -60 feet one way.

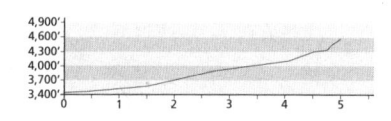

LENGTH and TIME

5.0 miles, 5 hours one way.

MAPS

Arizona USGS topo map NAD27: Haunted Canyon. Superstition Wilderness Beartooth map, grids Q13 to O14. Maps 25 and 38.

FINDING THE TRAIL

Trailhead map is on page 202. The West Pinto Trail starts at Miles Trailhead [25-Z] at the Superstition Wilderness sign (N33° 26' 14.3", W111° 04' 01.9"). Horse riders can start at the white metal gate with the B4 brand (N33° 26' 15.0", W111° 04' 04.7").

THE TRIP

Start on Map 25 on page 205. From the Miles Trailhead [25-Z, 0], start at the Wilderness sign and follow the West Pinto Trail (212). At the signed junction [25-Q, 0.5] with the Bull Basin Trail (270), turn left (southwest) and take the

Bull Basin Trail, which starts out on the left (south) bench of Rock Creek. Note that some older maps still show this part of the Bull Basin Trail as the former Rock Creek Trail (195)—abandoned by the Forest Service.

The Bull Basin Trail follows an old roadbed, so the trail is easy to find until it crosses Rock Creek for the first time. Watch for rock cairns to get you through the washed-out section of road as it zigzags across the creek. The trail soon returns to a wide road when it resumes on the left (south) bench again. This is one of the most pleasant sections of trail in the Wilderness with a canopy of Emory oak, cypress, and sycamore trees overhanging large flat areas.

When the Bull Basin Trail [25-GG, 1.2] leaves the flat bench and heads left (south), uphill, you want to continue straight on the flat bench. At this intersection you might notice a pile of rocks by a cypress tree (N33° 25' 48.3", W111° 05' 01.4"), which is the grave of an unidentified cowboy.[121]

The former Rock Trail (195) crosses the creek many times and may be difficult to follow since the trail is not maintained, although the trail is marked with rock cairns throughout. Horse riders will have difficulty with

The Bull Basin Trail (270) follows the old road at the first crossing on Rock Creek. After rains and in the cooler months, Rock Creek often has water. Photo was taken in March 2001.

the many fallen trees on the trail, and hikers will often have to search for the trail after maneuvering around the deadfall. Only a few sections of trail are covered with catclaw, but those are the portions of trail you will probably remember the most.

Bull Basin Wash, a large ravine with a cairned trail, comes in from the left (south). That trail will take you on an unwanted detour uphill in Bull Basin Wash, so you have to be alert to stay on the Rock Creek Trail here.[122] The Rock Creek Trail crosses Bull Basin Wash at its mouth [25-BB, 1.8] (N33° 25' 36.0", W111° 05' 27.8") and stays on the left (south) side of Rock Creek here.

A small waterfall [25-V, 2.4] (N33° 25' 22.6", W111° 05' 57.0") on the left (south) side of the trail provides a picturesque spot to photograph. The waterfall is only about 20 feet high, but water shooting over the lip of the wide falls into the pool below is impressive. The top of the waterfall is flat, and you can walk out on the smooth rocks.

On the left (east) side of the creek is the one-hundred year-old Y Bar B Corral [38-M, 3.2] (N33° 24' 56.2", W111° 06' 24.0"), which is probably the corral that Cliff Edwards wrote about (see page 221). This is one of the few remaining post and rail corrals in the Wilderness. The ladder-like slats on one of the posts were used to support the rails that formed the gate. The wooden feed box was used to hold hay.

Near the 4,160-foot elevation, the trail may become even harder to follow as it heads right (west) up a tributary arm, goes south, climbs up a ridge, and meets the dirt road FR650 [38-I, 5.0] (N33° 24' 00.8", W111° 07' 22.6") at an unidentifiable location—you just pop out of the bushes onto the road. This is the end of the trip. Return the same way, or use FR650 to connect with another trail. There is no room to park a vehicle near here on FR650. Your options are:

The trail sign shows the former name and number of the Rock Creek section of the Bull Basin Trail (270). All of the former Rock Creek Trail signs have been replaced with Bull Basin Trail signs. Photo was taken in March 2001.

(1) From the end of the Rock Creek Trail, going right (west) on FR650, the distance is 1.9 miles to the signed Spencer Spring Trail junction

(N33° 24' 23.0", W111° 08' 26.6") [38-C]. Following Spencer Spring Trail and West Pinto Trail back to Miles Trailhead makes a total loop mileage of 13.0 miles.

(2) From Rock Creek Trail junction on FR650, going west, the distance is 3.0 miles on FR650 to Reavis Canyon Trail (509) (N33° 24' 19.6", W111° 09' 22.3") [36-M] near Montana Mountain. From Reavis Canyon Trail (509) [36-M] if you continue northwest on FR650 and north on FR172A, the distance is another 2.4 miles to Rogers Trough Trailhead [36-U]. Using the Old Reevis Trail shortcut [36-A] (N33° 25' 02.6", W111° 10' 07.2") to [36-U] will save you 0.6 miles.

(3) From Rock Creek Trail, going left (south) on FR650, the distance is about 5.3 miles to the Arizona Trail and Reavis Trail Canyon Trailhead [37-K] (N33° 21' 09.9", W111° 07' 53.1") at the bottom of Montana Mountain.

HISTORY AND LEGENDS

When we first mapped the Rock Creek Trail in April 1997, the trail was easy to follow and the creek had intermittent stretches of water. See page 34 for a photo of Rock Creek flowing with seasonal water. In 2001, the Forest Service renamed the north end of Rock Creek Trail (195) as the Bull Basin Trail (270), and the portion of the Rock Creek Trail up canyon (south) from the unidentified grave [25-GG] was abandoned. Our last field check of the trail in December 2007 found the trail in poor shape due to fallen trees. A few sections of trail are filled with catclaw, while other parts of the trail are perfectly clear and make pleasant walking.

At one time, the Rock Creek Trail must have been well maintained as evidenced by the trail construction through the canyon and around obstacles. The old trail is marked by blazed trees, which are two vertical marks in the bark of a tree. The blazes are on both sides of the tree and most creek crossings are identified by a blazed tree on both sides of the creek. The blazes are old and sometimes indistinct, so they are not that useful for trail finding. The pinyon pine trees with their thick bark hold the blazes better than the thin-bark sycamore trees. Former trail maintenance is apparent from the many rock water bars across the trail. With a little trail work, the Rock Creek Trail could be restored.

In 1951, Jim and Phyllis Herron took their honeymoon trip into the Superstition Mountains. They had been married the year before and just had the chance to take a break from the work at their ranch on Queen Creek. At the Herron Ranch, they saddled up Tony, Brownie, and packhorse Chapo and rode north to Haunted Canyon. The first night they stayed at the Tony Ranch cabin. Phyllis said they camped and cooked outside because of all the mice and little critters inside the cabin. The next day they rode over to Bull Basin where they met Forest Ranger Bill Baldwin, then continued over to Jack and Frances Kennedy's place, which is now the Miles Trailhead.[123]

In 1938, Jim worked at the ranch when J. Ney Miles owned it. Rita Miles, J. Ney's wife, was the third cousin of Jim's dad. As Jim said, they were "shirt-tail" relations.[124] Jim and Phyllis visited with the Kennedys, and the next morning they headed back home taking the trail up Rock Creek. It was a long ride over the divide, down FR650, and past their Cottonwood Camp. Getting a little saddle sore, they debated which was closer, the Herron Ranch on Queen Creek or their place in Superior. They opted to ride to Superior, which they later determined was the longer route!

Cliff Edwards in his book *Horseback and Airborne* told the story of rounding up wild burros on Rock Creek sometime around 1909. He refers to a corral about two miles up Rock Creek from the Bowman Ranch, which is probably the corral with the Y Bar B brand on the cement water trough [38-M]. See pages 30 and 31 for photos of the Y Bar B corral and brand. The Bowman Ranch was located at the Miles Trailhead. Edwards and four other cowboys repaired the old trigger gate, which would let animals in the corral, but not let them out. When an animal came through the trigger gate to lick

A small waterfall [25-V] along the abandoned Rock Creek Trail. When the seasonal water flows, this trek described in Trip 26 can make a pleasant outing. A similar waterfall [25-J] is located along the Paradise Trail. Photo was taken in December 2007.

Cement Spring [25-P] water troughs and feed crib along Spencer Spring Creek. The water improvements are out of service, but you may find a seep of water in the creek near the spring box. Photo was taken in March 1997.

---

the salt block, the animal would be trapped in the corral. Many of the corrals in the Superstition Mountains are called traps for this reason.

Edwards and five friends planned to ride the county and push the wild horses into the Red Mountain (Pinto Peak) and Haunted Canyon area, hoping that some of them would water at their trap on Rock Creek. After the first day, they trapped twenty-six wild burros and some deer. Several days later, they counted thirty-four head of horses in the corral. They brought some of the horses, a Jack burro, and wild cattle back to the Bowman Ranch on West Fork Pinto Creek where they spent a day breaking the horses and burro before leading them back to Miami.[125]

Tom Kollenborn wrote an article about Bill Cage who was looking for Fool's Canyon, which contained a Mexican gold mine. In his article, Kollenborn describes the clues to the location of the mine that led Bill Cage's searches in the early 1900s to Rock Creek and the Sawtooth Ridge area. Cage never located the two *tinajas* that were key to the mine location.[126]

Trip 27

SPENCER SPRING CREEK

Spencer Spring Trail makes a nice day trip on trails that have mostly gentle grades except for the climb to Spencer Spring at the end of the trail. The terrain varies between tree-lined canyons with seasonal water to open desert hills. Multi-day trippers can link this seldom used trail to dirt road FR650 and connect with the Arizona Trail, the Reavis Ranch Trail, or the Rock Creek Trail.

ITINERARY

From the Miles Trailhead, take West Pinto Trail (212) to Oak Flat. Connect with Spencer Spring Trail (275), and follow the trail to FR650. Return the same way or use FR650 to link up with the Arizona Trail, the Reavis Canyon Trail (509), the Reavis Ranch Trail (109), or the former Rock Creek Trail.

DIFFICULTY

Moderate hike. Difficult horse ride. Elevation change is +1,690 and -250 feet one way.

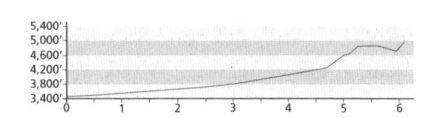

LENGTH and TIME

6.1 miles, 4 hours one way trip.

MAPS

Arizona USGS topo maps NAD27: Haunted Canyon, Iron Mountain. Superstition Wilderness Beartooth map, grids Q13 to N14. Maps 25 and 36.

FINDING THE TRAIL

Trailhead map is on page 202. The West Pinto Trail starts at Miles Trailhead [25-Z] at the Superstition Wilderness sign (N33° 26' 14.3", W111° 04' 01.9"). Horse riders can start at the white metal gate with the B4 brand (N33° 26' 15.0", W111° 04' 04.7").

THE TRIP

Start on Map 25 on page 205. From the Miles Trailhead [25-Z, 0], take West Pinto Trail to Oak Flat using the Trip 24 (West Pinto Trail to Oak Flat) directions. From the West Pinto Trail, just before you cross Spencer Spring Creek, bear left (southwest) onto the Spencer Spring Trail at the wooden trail sign [25-M, 2.4]. The Spencer Spring Trail is marked by rock cairns, and the trail meanders from either side of the normally dry creek.

Cement Spring [25-P, 3.5] comes in on the left (east) side of the creek near a corral and water troughs. It was not apparent how you could obtain water from the spring box, and since we found plenty of pothole water in the creek bed, we have not determined if this spring is a reliable water source. The water improvement has not been maintained for some time.

To avoid a rough section of canyon and waterfall, the trail crosses to the west side of the creek [36-H, 4.7], heads uphill, and meets Spencer Spring [36-N, 5.9] at a water trough near the bed of the creek. J. Ney Miles owned the YY brand that is inscribed as Y Lazy Y on the cement trough. The out-of-service water trough is dated 6-21-36. The spring box is a little way up the creek from the water trough at the end of the pipe where you might find some water. Nearby Pope Spring may have water, but it is difficult to approach. The Spencer Spring Trail ends after a steep climb up the hill to the south where it meets FR650 [36-C, 6.1] (N33° 24' 23.0", W111° 08' 26.6").

OPTIONAL LOOP OR CONTINUING TRIPS

(1) From the end of Spencer Spring Trail [36-C], go right (west) on FR650 1.1 miles to connect with the Reavis Canyon Trail (509) (Arizona Trail) (N33° 24' 19.6", W111° 09' 22.3") [36-M] on Montana Mountain.

(2) From the end of Spencer Spring Trail [36-C], you can connect with the Reavis Ranch Trail (109) (Arizona Trail) at Rogers Trough Trailhead [36-U] by taking FR650 and FR172A for 3.5 miles. Using the Old Reevis Trail shortcut [36-A] to [36-U] will save you 0.6 miles.

(3) From the end of Spencer Spring Trail [36-C], going left (east) on FR650 takes you downhill to the unmarked junction [38-I] (N33° 24' 00.8", W111° 07' 22.6") with the former Rock Creek Trail in 1.9 miles. Rock Creek Trail, Bull Basin Trail, and West Pinto Trail take you back to Miles Trailhead for a total loop mileage of 13.0 miles.

(4) From Rock Creek Trail junction [38-I] on FR650, going downhill another 5.3 miles, you can link up with the Arizona Trail at the bottom of Montana Mountain in Reavis Trail Canyon where Reavis Canyon Trail 509 meets FR650 [37-K] (N33° 21' 09.9", W111° 07' 53.1").

(5) From the Spencer Spring water trough [36-N], walk up Spencer Spring Creek bed for 0.8 mile to the top of the smooth-rock pour-off section of creek. Head northwest for 100 yards along an unnamed small wash to the Spencer Canyon Road (N33° 24' 43.6", W111° 09' 36.8"). Going west on the Spencer Canyon Road will take you to FR650 [36-B] in another 0.4 mile.

HISTORY AND LEGENDS

Major Brown took his troops down Spencer Spring Creek on January 14, 1873, and camped in the area of Oak Flat. Second Lieutenant John G. Bourke, A.D.C., wrote in his diary that they were rationed for a 20 day march out of Camp McDowell, which they left on January 6. Archie McIntosh was one of the guides. The command included 30 Apache scouts, but Bourke did not give the total number of troops and pack animals. The command must have been large, because he noted that the time for all the troops to pass a single point took 46 minutes.[127] See map on page 226.

On January 15 at Oak Flat, Bourke wrote that Captain Adams of the 5th Cavalry took all the riding and pack horses downstream about 2 miles on West Fork Pinto Creek to make camp, which was probably in the Miles Trailhead area. The rest of the command went on foot to the north, up the mountain east of Pinto Peak. At dawn, they arrived at an Apache Rancheria, which could have been on Campaign Creek, and made their attack. Bourke's diary reads, "We captured thirteen women and children and killed three. We also captured the old chief of the band. These people are very poor..." Bourke and the rest of the command regrouped with Captain Adams and the pack train for the January 16 camp near Miles Trailhead.

In the following days, Major Brown's command continued the march to Pinto Creek, Masons Valley, and Mineral Creek. Bourke wrote that on January 19, four companies left the main force and proceeded to a new camp at Mount Graham. Major Brown arrived at Camp Grant on January 22, 1873, where they made preparations for a new march to Sulfur Springs. The purpose of that trip was to ask Agent Jeffords for a meeting with Cochise.

Trip 42 describes an 1891 road survey through the Superstition Mountains. One possible route for that survey might have been down Spencer Spring Canyon. A more probable route ended in Deer Spring Canyon—the next canyon to the west. A trail across the ridges is shown on the 1902 (reprinted 1912) edition of the Florence, Arizona, USGS 15 minute topographic map. See Trip 42 (1891 Road Survey Route) for more about this proposed road.

Rancher Jim Herron said at one time his cattle on the Superior grazing allotment, branded with the TU, had access to the Spencer Spring troughs. The steep trail from FR650 to the troughs created a dangerous condition for the cattle, so they fenced off the troughs at the top of the hill on FR650.[128]

Jim Herron worked for Ney Miles in 1938. Lum Martin from Tonto Basin and Jim lived at the Miles Ranch then. Jim said they branded the Y Bar, but the brand conflicted with someone up north, so they had to change the brand to Y Lazy Y. They referred to the new brand as YY, but Jim said you could also call the brand Y Lazy Y.[129]

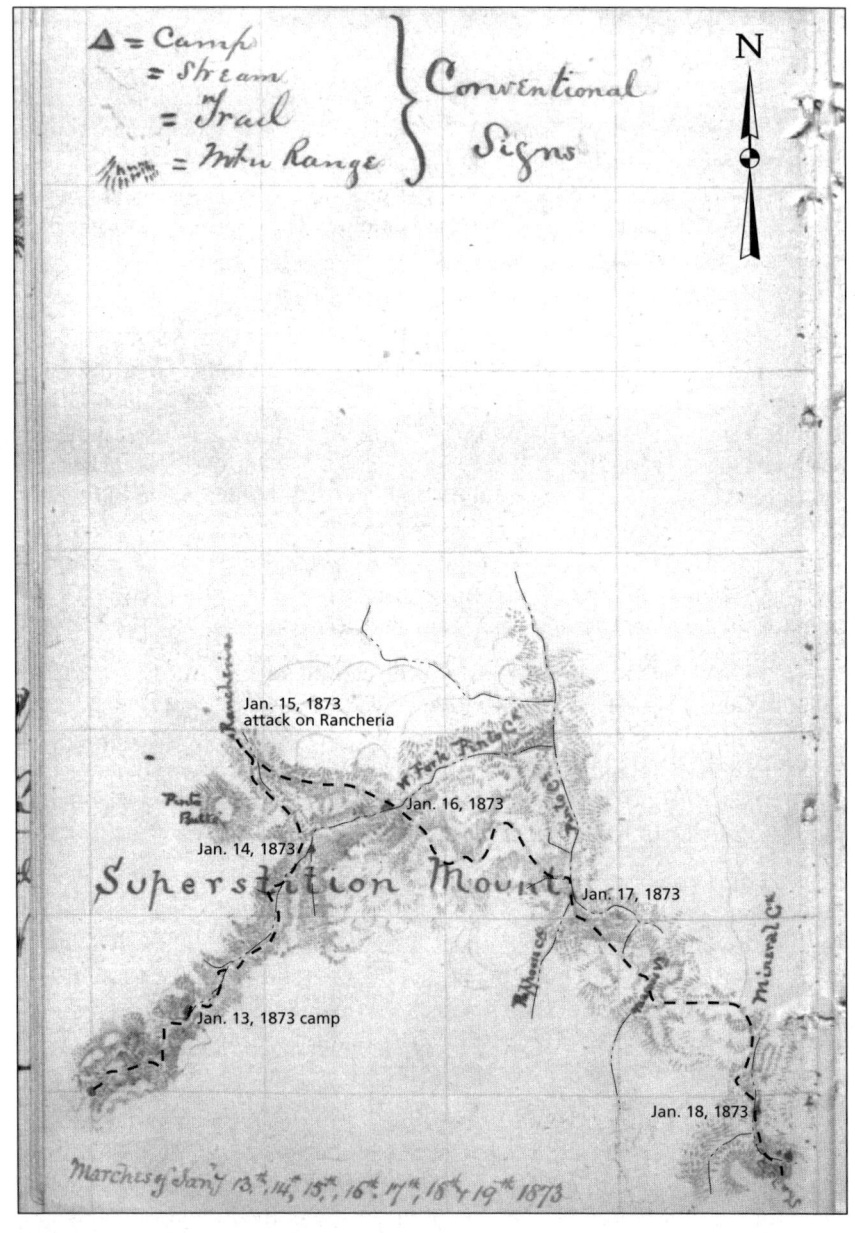

Page from John G. Bourke's diary showing the Army's marches from January 13 to 19, 1873. Several place names are familiar: Pinto Creek, West Fork Pinto Creek, Pinto Butte, Masons Valley, and Mineral Creek. We overlaid dashed lines for the trail and streams. We also added typeset dates for his camps and the north arrow. Jan. 13 Camp was on Spencer Spring Creek, Jan. 14 Camp was at Oak Flat, Jan. 16 Camp was near Miles Trailhead, and Jan. 17 Camp was on Pinto Creek. The Jan. 15 attack on the Rancheria may have been on Campaign Creek. Map from USMA Library, West Point, NY.

Trip 28

CUFF BUTTON TRAIL

Much of the Cuff Button Trail was a former ranch road for access to a series of springs in the rugged mountains. Time has returned the road to a trail that is well suited for horses, although the trail can be overgrown in places. A photogenic wooden corral and a small seep of water at Cuff Button Spring make this a fine destination.

ITINERARY

From the Miles Trailhead, follow the West Pinto Trail (212) to Oak Flat where the Cuff Button Trail (276) begins. Follow Cuff Button Trail to Cuff Button Corral and Spring. Return the same way or make a loop on a cross-country route described in Trip 32 (Wildcat Canyon to Cuff Button Spring).

DIFFICULTY

Difficult hike. Difficult horse ride. Elevation change is +1,590 and -1,570 feet one way.

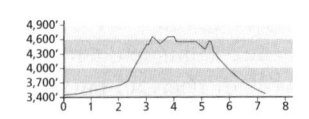

LENGTH and TIME

6.3 miles to Cuff Button Corral, 4 hours one way. Add another 1.0 mile to reach the end of the Cuff Button Trail.

MAPS

Arizona USGS topo maps NAD27: Haunted Canyon. Superstition Wilderness Beartooth map, grids Q13, P13, P12, and Q12. Map 26.

FINDING THE TRAIL

Trailhead map is on page 202. The West Pinto Trail starts at Miles Trailhead [26-Z] at the Superstition Wilderness sign (N33° 26' 14.3", W111° 04' 01.9"). Horse riders can start at the white metal gate with the B4 brand (N33° 26' 15.0", W111° 04' 04.7").

THE TRIP

Start on Map 26 on page 231. From the Miles Trailhead [26-Z, 0], Trip 24 (West Pinto Trail to Oak Flat) will take you to Oak Flat using the West Pinto Trail (212). At Oak Flat, the Cuff Button Trail begins at the wooden trail sign, [26-L, 2.1] (N33° 26' 18", W111° 06' 00"). Turn right (north) here and cross West Fork Pinto Creek, which is normally dry. The trail follows the west bench of Jerky Spring Wash (normally dry) and passes under some very large diameter Emory oak trees. As you continue up the ravine, the trail gets steeper and the vegetation becomes denser. At one point, while in the dense vegetation, you make a 90-degree turn to the left (west), so watch for rock cairns and be aware that overhanging bushes may obscure the tread of the trail until you reach the open ridge [26-LL, 2.5]. On the open ridge, a faint trail going north (right) can be identified by a few wooden water bars embedded in the dirt.

If you plan to return on the Cuff Button Trail, take note of the trail alignment as you come out of the scrub oak bushes onto the open ridge [26-LL]. These bushes grow fast, and keeping the trail clear is a problem, since the bushes tend to snap back and cover up the trail. On your return trip, remember to look left (east) into the bushes at the end of the ridge for the turn in the trail.

Once on the open ridge, the trail is easier to follow, although the trail is easier to see going down than up. Following the rock cairns will keep you on track until the trail intersects the former roadbed [26-MM, 3.2] (N33° 27' 00", W111° 06' 31") at a flat area that might make a good, but dry camp. Going left here takes you to Iron Trough Spring, which we have not visited. The Cuff Button Trail goes right and continues uphill. The trail and old road pass through the rock outline of several prehistoric ruins. Do not disturb anything at the site. As you go higher, West Fork Pinto Creek and the surrounding mountains come into view, and you begin to appreciate the tough uphill climb you have just made.

The trail continues up and downhill passing several former water improvements at the springs. Do not rely on these springs for water. You pass Tub Spring [26-T, 4.2], a CCC-built water tank [26-JJ, 4.5], Sycamore Spring [26-W, 4.6], Wildcat Canyon Wash [26-TT, 5.1], and finally arrive at Cuff Button Corral [26-P, 6.3]. If you lose the trail in this rough country due to the overhanging manzanita, scrub oak, and laurel bushes, the best strategy is to always backtrack and locate the tread of the trail and former road.

The water trough at Cuff Button Corral has not been working, so to find water, you need to follow the underground pipe 0.2 mile back to the ravine where Cuff Button Spring [26-R] originates. Note that the Haunted Canyon USGS topo map incorrectly locates Cuff Button Spring at nearby Thicket Spring, which is normally dry.

From Cuff Button Corral [26-P, 6.3], continue down canyon on the Cuff Button Trail. A wooden feeder box [26-B, 6.5] marks the Thicket Spring Wash, which is normally dry. The trail follows the former road, which crosses

Cuff Button Spring Corral near the east end of the Cuff Button Trail (276). This post and rail corral is in better shape than most of the historic corrals in the Wilderness. Photo was taken in January 2004.

the wash many times. We end the trail description at the junction with Wildcat Canyon [26-O, 7.3].

Return the same way, or see Trip 32 (Wildcat Canyon to Cuff Button Spring) for a mostly cross-country loop return to Miles Trailhead in another 2.7 miles.

HISTORY AND LEGENDS

Howard Horinek, former manager of the JH6 Ranch, worked on the springs along the Cuff Button Trail and had them all in service at one time during the 1980s. The CCC installed the tank near Sycamore Spring on the JH6 pasture in the 1930s. Other CCC water improvements were made at Mountain Spring and on top of JK Mountain. Horinek said the location of the Sycamore Spring CCC cement water tank was never an ideal installation due to the elevation of the tank above the source of water at Sycamore Spring.[130]

The Cuff Button Trail was established as a road by rancher Louie Horrell to improve access to his springs.[131] The Cuff Button Trail does not appear on the 1948 USGS Haunted Canyon topographic map. The 1969 Superstition Wilderness Forest Service map is the first map that we found to show the Cuff Button Trail, but it was not named or numbered. After 1982, the Forest Service maps generally identify the Cuff Button Trail as Forest Service Trail 276.

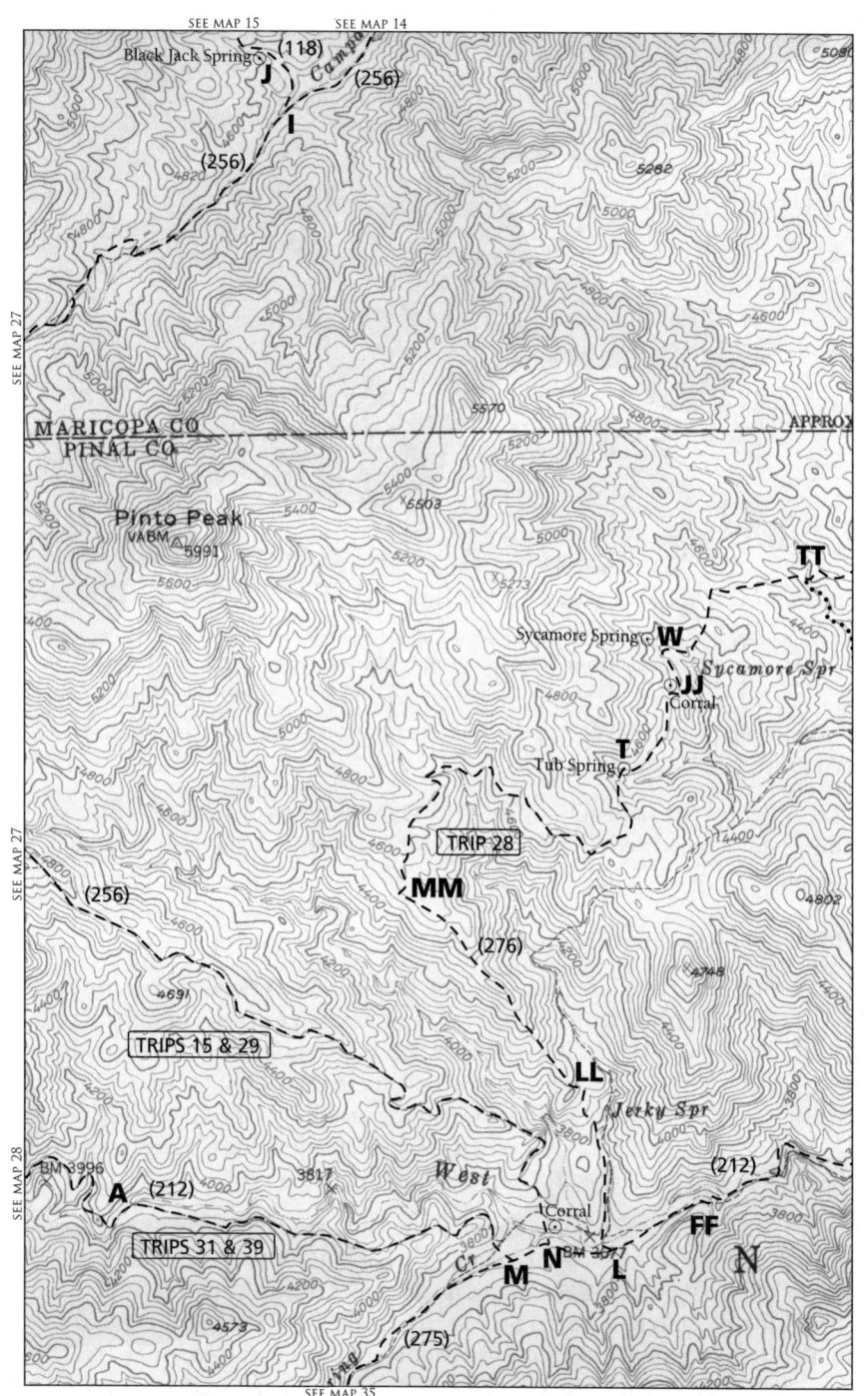

Map 26 – Trips 24, 28, 29, 31, and 32.

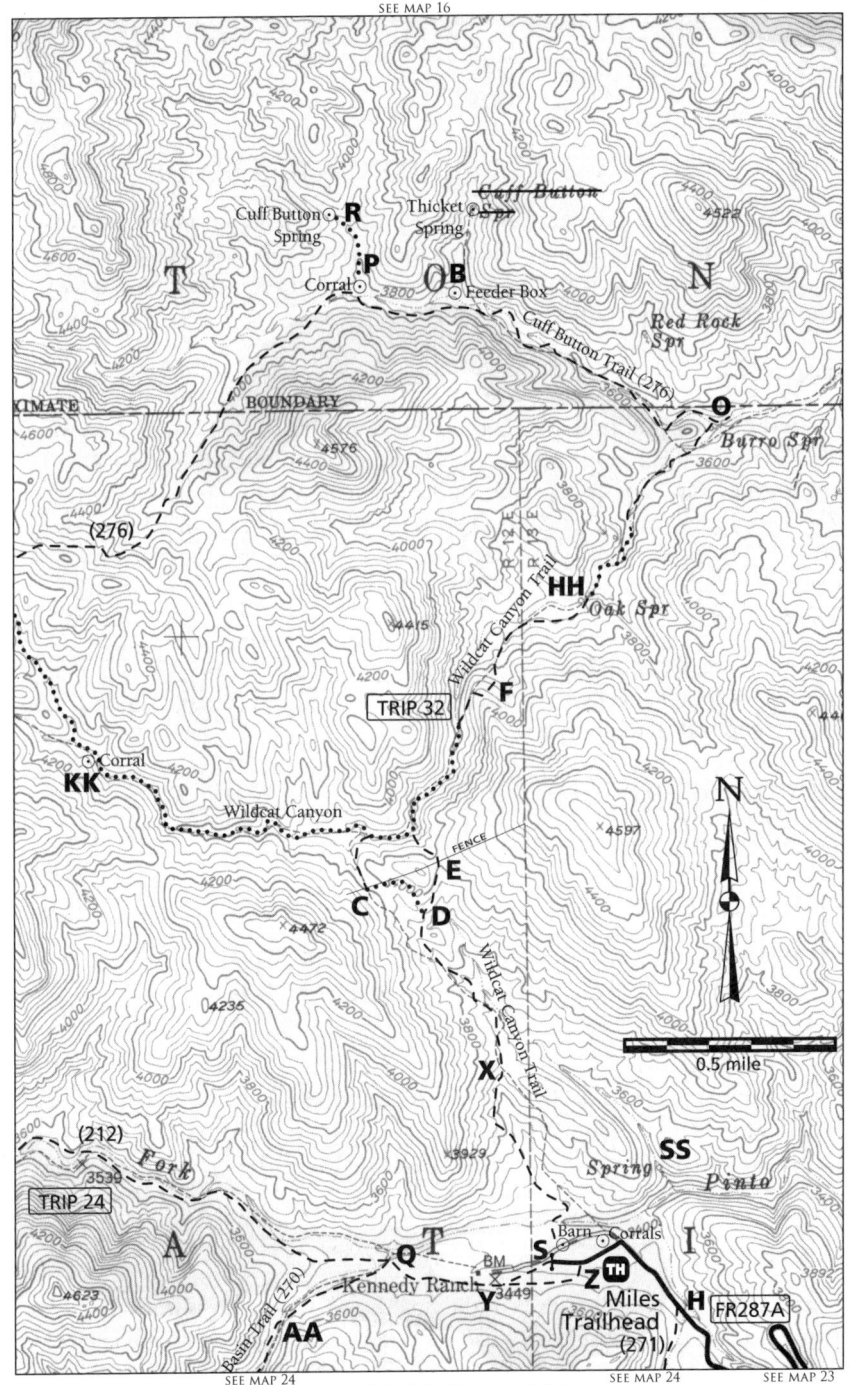

Map 26 continued – Trips 24, 28, 29, 31, and 32.

MILES TRAILHEAD—TRIP 28. CUFF BUTTON TRAIL 231

Trip 29

CAMPAIGN TRAIL TO PINTO DIVIDE

The Campaign Trail connects West Fork Pinto Creek with Campaign Creek. The trail takes you up in the higher country where you have a perspective of the canyons below. Early day pioneer, U.S. Army, and Apache travelers may have used this same route.

ITINERARY

From the Miles Trailhead, follow the West Pinto Trail (212) to Oak Flat where the Campaign Trail (256) begins. Follow Campaign Trail to the Pinto Divide. Return the same way, or continue on the Campaign Trail into Campaign Creek for longer treks that connect with the Fire Line (118) or Reavis Gap Trails (117) (See Campaign Trailhead).

DIFFICULTY

Difficult hike. Difficult horse ride. Elevation change is +1,910 and -60 feet one way.

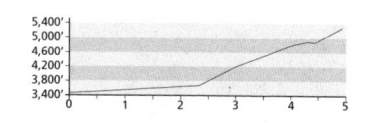

LENGTH and TIME

4.9 miles, 3 hours one way.

MAPS

Arizona USGS topo map NAD27: Haunted Canyon. Superstition Wilderness Beartooth map, grids Q13, O13, and O12. Maps 26 and 27.

FINDING THE TRAIL

Trailhead map is on page 202. The West Pinto Trail starts at Miles Trailhead [26-Z] at the Superstition Wilderness sign (N33° 26' 14.3", W111° 04' 01.9"). Horse riders can start at the white metal gate with the B4 brand (N33° 26' 15.0", W111° 04' 04.7").

THE TRIP

Start on Map 26 on page 231. For the first segment of the trip from the Miles Trailhead [26-Z, 0], Trip 24 (West Pinto Trail to Oak Flat) will take you to Oak Flat on the West Pinto Trail. At Oak Flat, the Campaign Trail begins at the wooden trail sign, [27-N, 2.3] (N33° 26' 19", W111° 06' 09"). Turn right

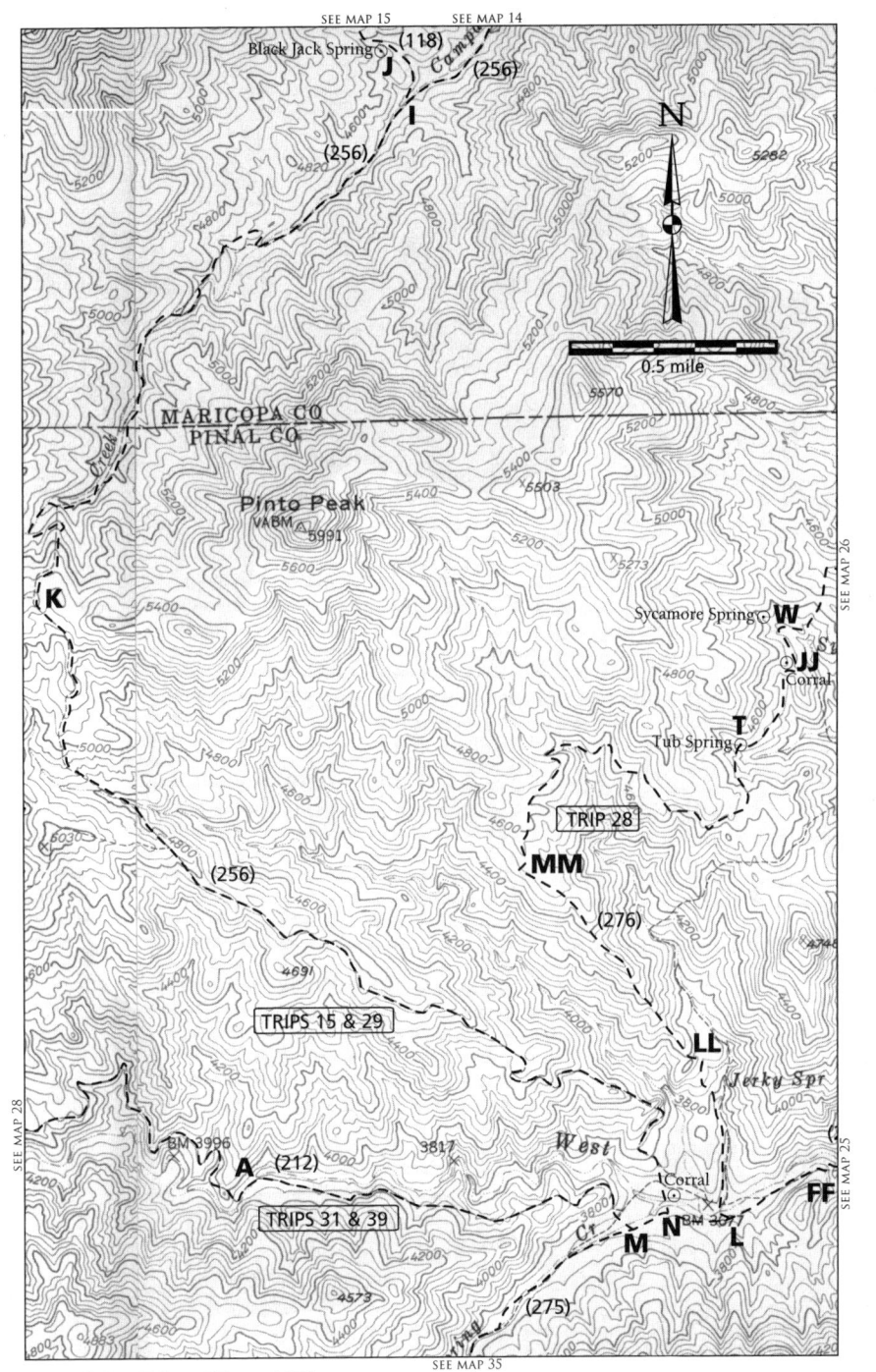

Map 27 – Trips 15 and 29.

Miles Trailhead—Trip 29. Campaign Trail to Pinto Divide

Wooden corral at Oak Flat on West Fork Pinto Creek. Note the horizontal metal cable around the outside of the wooden posts holding the corral together. Photo was taken in March 1997.

(north) here and cross the normally dry West Fork Pinto Creek. The round wooden corral will be on your right after you cross the creek.

Travel is mostly uphill on the Campaign Trail, so take your time, and stop to enjoy the views. Once above the canopy of trees along West Fork Pinto Creek, the terrain is open and you will feel the warmth of the sun—no shade. The hillside is covered with mountain mahogany, scrub oak, and sugar sumac. Near the top, the grass grows tall, and as you approach the divide [27-K, 4.9], some alligator juniper and Emory oak trees appear.

Return the same way, or continue into the normally dry Campaign Creek drainage. Water in Campaign Creek can usually be found at Brushy Spring [15-H] and the stretch of creek at the Reavis Gap Trail junction [15-D]. Black Jack Spring [15-J] on the Fire Line Trail usually has water.

HISTORY AND LEGENDS

The section of Campaign Trail from West Fork Pinto Creek to the Pinto Divide next to Pinto Peak was probably a prehistoric route as evidenced by occasional potsherds on the trail and a nearby rock wall. Enjoy the history and prehistory of the area, but don't remove anything—removing artifacts is neither ethical nor lawful.

See History and Legends on pages 206, 225, and 226 for John Bourke's 1872 and 1873 military marches, which may have gone near Pinto Divide. Some of Bourke's maps show Pinto Butte (now Pinto Peak) and the military campaign through the region. The military was looking for an Apache rancheria just north of Pinto Peak and probably found the rancheria in nearby Campaign Creek on January 15, 1873.

Newspaper articles in 1891 mention a road survey near Masten's Peak. The peak was named for Col. C. S. Masten, superintendent of the Maricopa and Phoenix Railroad. The Masten's Peak reference is probably for Pinto Peak since one article said that local people called the peak Red Mountain, which may be a description of the red cliffs on the east side of Pinto Peak.[132] See History and Legends in Trip 42 (1891 Road Survey Route) for more about the Mesa to Globe Road survey.

See History and Legends in Trip 15 (Campaign Trail to West Fork Pinto Creek) for the story of the former Campaign-Pinto Creek Divide sign that was located at the pass—Pinto Divide.

Elizabeth Stewart at Pinto Divide [27-K] on the Campaign Trail (256). The sign, shown in both photos above, was donated by the Tonto National Forest to the Superstition Mountain Museum. Photos were taken in February 1997.

Trip 30

PARADISE TRAIL

The Paradise Trail is often used in longer loop hikes up and over Government Hill, but more leisurely trips can be made from its lower end starting from dirt road FR287A. The tree-lined trail takes you uphill starting on a gentle grade, past a low waterfall, by the Paradise Corral and normally dry Paradise Spring to the east ridge of Government Hill.

ITINERARY

From FR287A near Miles Trailhead, follow the Paradise Trail (271) to its terminus with Haunted Canyon Trail (203). Return the same way or connect with other trails to make a loop trip.

DIFFICULTY

Moderate hike. Difficult horse ride. Elevation change is +1,510 and -200 feet one way.

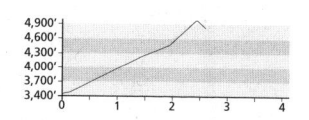

LENGTH and TIME

2.6 miles, 2 hours one way.

MAPS

Arizona USGS topo map NAD27: Haunted Canyon. Superstition Wilderness Beartooth map, grids Q13 and Q14. Map 24.

FINDING THE TRAIL

Trailhead map is on page 202. Backtrack on FR287A from Miles Trailhead [24-Z] about 0.2 mile and look for a wooden sign that reads *Trail 271*. The sign is on the north side of FR287A, and the Paradise Trail begins on the south side, [24-H, 0] (N33° 26' 09.1", W111° 03' 46.3").

THE TRIP

Start on Map 24 on page 201. From FR287A [24-H, 0], the Paradise Trail begins in a wide clearing and soon narrows to what looks like an old road. Shortly, the trail becomes more defined and is marked by rock cairns as it meanders across the ravine. At about the 3,600-foot elevation, you pass a small waterfall [24-J, 0.3] (N33° 25' 54", W111° 03' 58") that may have seasonal flows. The waterfall would be a good turnaround if you had less than an hour for your trip.

Historic wooden corrals [24-K, 0.7] near the normally dry Paradise Spring stand on your right as you pass through the last open area before the gradient of the trail begins to increase. Leaving the tree-lined path behind, the trail becomes steeper, and you finally reach the pass [24-U, 2.4] on the east ridge of Government Hill. The terrain up here is mostly treeless with wide expanses of tall native grasses. This pass makes a good turnaround point.

If you want to go to the end of the Paradise Trail, continue south and east as the Paradise Trail heads downhill a short distance where it meets the Haunted Canyon Trail at a dirt water tank [24-W, 2.6]. The trail junction is marked by a wooden trail sign. This is the end of the trip. Return the same way, or see Trips 22 (Tony Ranch from FR287A) and Trip 25 (Bull Basin Loop) for the history of the area and ideas for making loop trips using Haunted Canyon Trail or cross-country routes on Government Hill.

Some trip options from the end of the Paradise Trail [24-W] are: (1) Tony Ranch Spring [23-QQ] in 2.0 miles, (2) Haunted Canyon Trailhead [24-G] on FR172A in 1.5 miles, (3) cross-country over Government Hill to Bull Basin Trail [24-N], Bull Basin Trail, and West Pinto Trail to Miles Trailhead [24-Z] in 5.1 miles.

Remains of the wooden corral [24-K] near Paradise Spring. Photo was taken in February 2004.

Trip 31

WEST PINTO TRAIL TO ROGERS TROUGH

The West Pinto Trail connects Miles Trailhead to Rogers Trough Trailhead. Backpackers and horse riders making loop trips in the eastern Superstition Mountains can use West Pinto Trail to connect the Campaign and Reavis Ranch Trails. Day trippers will enjoy the tree-lined canyon, which has seasonal water.

ITINERARY

From the Miles Trailhead, follow the West Pinto Trail (212) to Reavis Ranch Trail (109) near Rogers Trough Trailhead. Return the same way, or connect with Reavis Ranch Trail for an extended trip.

DIFFICULTY

Difficult hike. Difficult horse ride. Elevation change is +2,520 and -1,160 feet one way.

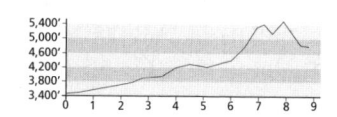

LENGTH and TIME

8.8 miles, 6 hours one way.

MAPS

Arizona USGS topo maps NAD27: Haunted Canyon, Iron Mountain. Superstition Wilderness Beartooth map, grids Q13 to M14. Maps 25, 28, and 34.

FINDING THE TRAIL

Trailhead map is on page 202. The West Pinto Trail starts at Miles Trailhead [25-Z] at the Superstition Wilderness sign (N33° 26' 14.3", W111° 04' 01.9"). Horse riders can start at the white metal gate with the B4 brand (N33° 26' 15.0", W111° 04' 04.7").

THE TRIP

Start on Map 25 on page 205. From the Miles Trailhead [25-Z, 0], take West Pinto Trail, and follow the directions for Trip 24 (West Pinto Trail to Oak Flat). From the west end of Oak Flat at the junction with Spencer Spring Trail [28-M, 2.4], bear right on the West Pinto Trail, crossing Spencer Spring Creek

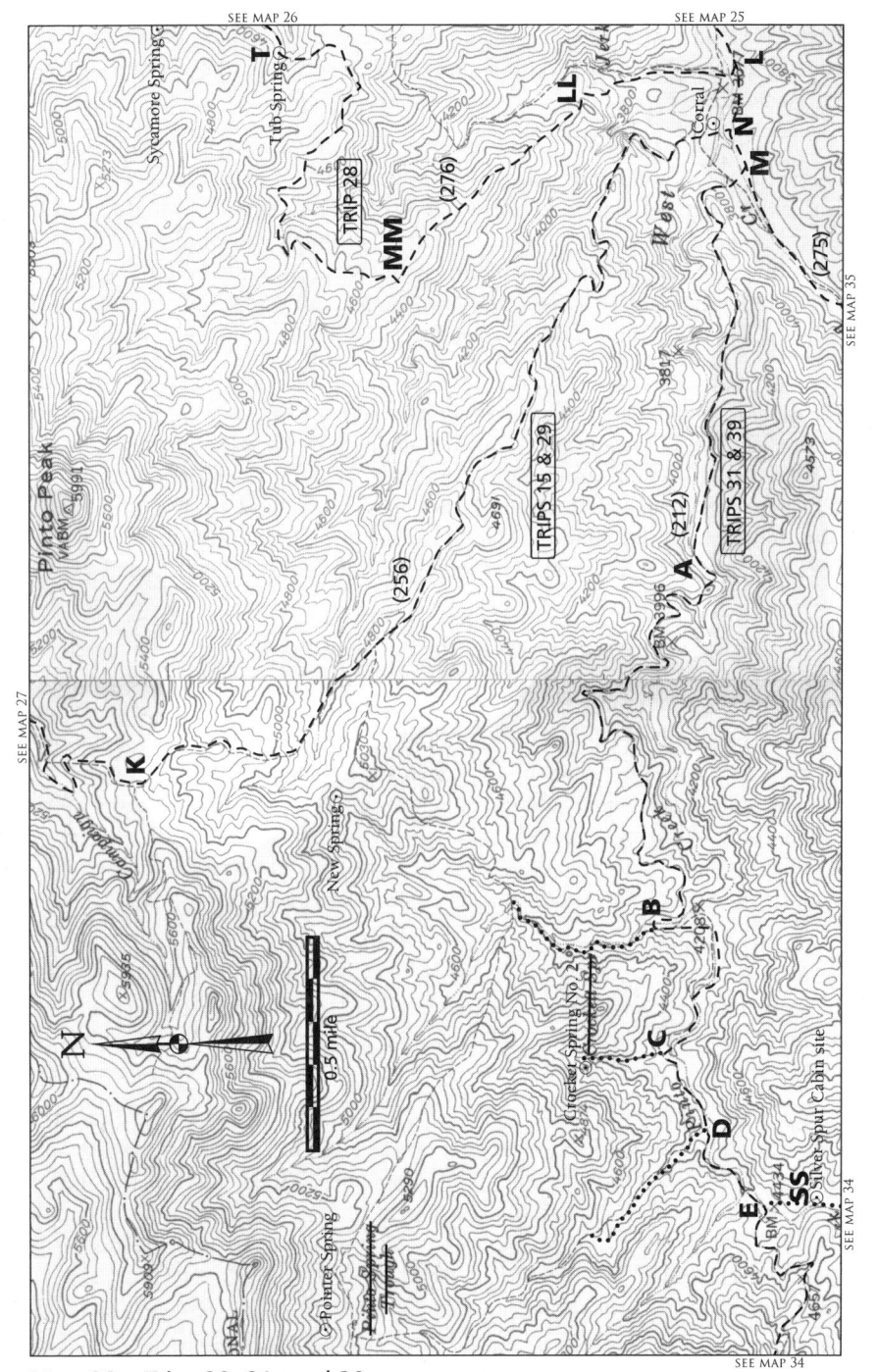

Map 28 – Trips 29, 31, and 39.

Miles Trailhead—Trip 31. West Pinto Trail to Rogers Trough

to the west side. After crossing the normally dry creek, look to your right (north) about 50 feet for a 12-foot square log structure. The deteriorating logs are stacked three high.

The West Pinto Trail stays on the left bench and quickly climbs high above the rocky and winding bed of West Fork Pinto Creek. We haven't walked through these narrows in the creek bed, but a detour through the narrows might make an interesting side trip, although you would have to walk through water if the normally dry creek was running. The trail crosses to the right (north) side [28-A, 3.4] of the creek and again climbs up on the hillside. This crossing would be a good turnaround for a shorter day trip.

The trail continues on the right (north) hillside and meets an old trail [28-B, 5.0], which goes toward New Spring. On our last visit, we left the West Pinto Trail and followed the unnamed trail going north in New Spring Wash. Within about 0.4 mile, around the 4,400-foot elevation, we came to a seep of water where the Iron Mountain USGS map shows an east-west connecting trail, but we could not find the trail in the dense vegetation. We have not checked New Spring, which is farther up canyon near the 4,800-foot elevation.

Back on the West Pinto Trail, the trail continues up canyon at creek bed level. The Crocket Spring No. 2 Wash [28-C, 5.5] comes in on the right (north) side of the creek. We looked for the trail to Crocket Spring No. 2, but had to bushwhack up the ravine about 0.2 mile where we found a good seep of water at the spring. Some differences in spring names exist between the Iron Mountain USGS map and the Superstition Wilderness map. On the 2006 Superstition Wilderness map, Crocket Spring No. 2 is only identified as *Spr*. Crocket Spring is shown in the middle of West Fork Pinto Creek, but we did not see any water improvements in the creek or any indication of a spring.

Continuing on the West Pinto Trail, the next drainage on the right (north) is Pointer Spring Wash [28-D, 5.7]. We followed an intermittent trail in Pointer Spring Wash to the northwest, where we found a small seep at about the 4,500-foot elevation. The thick vegetation and rough terrain dampened our enthusiasm for going farther up canyon. Pointer Spring is named Pinto Spring on the Iron Mountain USGS map.

From Pointer Spring Wash, the West Pinto Trail continues up canyon a short distance to the place where the West Pinto Trail leaves the creek and heads uphill [28-E, 6.0] at an unsigned location that is marked well with rock cairns. Before you take the trail uphill, check out a few things in the area. On the left (south) bank, the 4,434-foot benchmark is mounted on a rock near the creek bed.

From the 4,434-foot benchmark, go about 0.2 mile south in West Fork Pinto Creek to the site of the Silver Spur Cabin [34-SS] (N33° 26' 06.9",

W111° 08' 45.4") on the left (east) bench. The cabin burned, but you can still see the corral and abandoned water trough at the site. We named the wash heading southwest from the Silver Spur Cabin site, Deer Spring Canyon. You can explore Deer Spring Canyon up to about the 4,800-foot elevation before the box canyon makes travel difficult. Deer Spring Canyon is normally dry, but seasonal water collects in the bedrock potholes.

Back on the West Pinto Trail, the trail leaves the creek bed [34-E, 6.0] at the rock cairns and starts uphill. The first part of the uphill section of trail is not well defined, so look closely for the small rock cairns that mark the trail. As the trail gains a little elevation on the ridge, the tread of the trail is more defined. Thick vegetation tends to hang over the trail, so you may have to push through some bushes if the trail has not had recent maintenance.

The West Pinto Trail goes about 200 feet higher on the ridge than you might expect, then heads south and down to Iron Mountain Spring and corral [34-G, 7.6]. The old corral was designed as a trap, and you might recognize the parts of a swivel gate that let animals in, but not out. A short distance up the trail is the concrete water trough, which is out of service. Cattle brands and maybe cowboy initials are inscribed in the concrete, such as Y Lazy Y, JH, RE, X Bar P, but we have not seen a date inscription. The only brand we recognized was the Y Lazy Y belonging to rancher J. Ney Miles. Water for the concrete trough came from a seep uphill where the trail crosses the ravine. If you were in desperate need of water, you could dig a small basin to capture the water.

Continuing uphill toward the saddle, the West Pinto Trail makes a short climb where the trail hugs the hillside below the cliffs. From the saddle and open gate [34-PP, 7.9] on the ridge of Iron Mountain, the trek is downhill for the last leg of the trip. Rogers Spring [34-P] is off the trail a few hundred yards. To get your water, follow the pipes down to the water trough where Benchmark 4883 is cemented into the top of the trough. Billy Martin said this is the best spring on his ranch. Don't disconnect any of the pipes. Cattle, horses, wildlife, and people depend on the trough for water.

The trip ends at the signed junction [34-T, 8.7] with the Reavis Ranch Trail (109), which is also called the Arizona Trail here. Going left (south) takes you to Rogers Trough Trailhead parking [34-U] at the end of FR172A in 0.1 mile. Going right (north) takes you to Reavis Ranch [3-I] in 6.4 miles or Rogers Canyon Cliff Dwellings [29-G] in 3.8 miles.

HISTORY AND LEGENDS

Silver Spur cabin [34-SS] was built by Jack Kennedy, but we don't know the exact date.[133] Jack Kennedy bought the ranch from J. Ney Miles in 1947, so the cabin was built sometime after that. A Forest Service archaeology report

Elizabeth Stewart in Wildcat Canyon at the pour-off and water hole [26-F] where the horse trail heads up the hill on the right (east) side of the canyon. Photo was taken in April 1997.

was made on the historical aspects of the burned site in 1991, which gives us a time frame when the cabin was used.[134] See History and Legends on pages 282 and 283 for more stories about the cabin.

Rancher Billy Martin said the water for the Silver Spur water improvements was carried through one mile of pipe, which was probably from Deer Spring.[135] We have not been able to locate Deer Spring in the rough overgrown country.

At first, we thought that continued interest from the 1890s for a road alignment in West Fork Pinto Creek might be the reason for the seven elevation surveys in West Fork Pinto Creek, but a better guess at the purpose might be that they were used in the preparation of the 1948 edition of the topo maps. We located the benchmark, dated 1946, at elevation 4,434 feet, that is shown on the Iron Mountain topo map, but we have not found the others identified on the Haunted Canyon topo map.

See History and Legends on pages 248 and 249 for the history around the Rogers Trough Trailhead area.

Trip 32

WILDCAT CANYON TO CUFF BUTTON SPRING

Former ranch trails and cross-country trekking take you through seldom traveled country. The seasoned traveler will enjoy the remoteness and the challenge in making the trip to one of the few historic wooden corrals in the Superstition Wilderness.

ITINERARY

From the Miles Trailhead, follow a former trail (193) north to Wildcat Canyon. Go down canyon to South Fork Horrell Creek. Go up South Fork Horrell Creek to Cuff Button Spring. Return the same way, or return on Cuff Button Trail (276) and West Pinto Trail (212).

DIFFICULTY

Difficult hike. Very difficult horse ride due to cross-country travel. Elevation change is +950 and -640 feet one way.

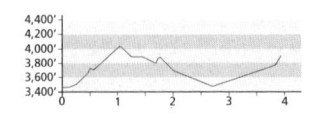

LENGTH and TIME

3.9 miles, 3.5 hours one way.

MAPS

Arizona USGS topo map NAD27: Haunted Canyon. Superstition Wilderness Beartooth map, grids Q13 to P12. Map 26.

FINDING THE TRAIL

Trailhead map is on page 202. The trail starts near the Miles Trailhead [near 26-S] at the open gate along West Fork Pinto Creek (N33° 26' 18.5", W111° 04' 05.2"). The open gate is near the northwest corner of the barn.

THE TRIP

Start on Map 26 on page 231. You will need good route-finding skills on this trip. The former Trail 193 is overgrown and often seems to disappear. The rounded impression of the track under the vegetation is sometimes the only sign of the trail. We have seen horse tracks on the route, but overhanging tree branches may divert riders from the benches and into the washes.

From the Miles Trailhead [26-Z, 0], head to the northwest corner of the barn, go north through the open gate, cross West Fork Pinto Creek to the north side, and bear right (east) on the flat bench. Do not take the ravine on the left (west) that looks like a trail when you first climb up on the bench, but look for some rock cairns on the northeast side of the open area. Rock cairns mark the start of the trail and define the route until you find the deeply eroded track of the former Trail 193.

At the ridge [26-X, 0.5], the trail passes between a pinyon pine tree on the right and a juniper tree on the left. This would be a good turnaround for a casual walk or ride away from the trailhead.

From the ridge, the trail becomes more difficult to follow as it winds its way through the scrub oak, down into a ravine, and then up to a grassy hill where we usually lose the trail [26-D]. Your objective is to find one of two gates in the barbed wire fence to the north where the trail is well-defined on the north side of the fence. We usually go through the west gate at [26-C, 1.2] (N33° 27' 00", W111° 04' 32"). The east gate at [26-E] (N33° 27' 02", W111° 04' 22") leads to a steeper and rougher trail. The best strategy for finding the gate is to head north when the trail disappears and locate the fence. Pick a route that avoids the dense manzanita forest. Follow the fence going east or west until you come to the gate.

Both gates will put you on trails that lead to the bed of Wildcat Canyon[136] where you can avoid the overgrown trail on the bench by traveling in the normally dry wash. Horse riders will have to decide for themselves if this wash is doable—amid sand, boulders, and slick rock.

In about 0.3 mile, a horse trail [26-F, 1.7] on the right (east) bypasses a pour-off in the bed of the slick rock canyon. See photo on page 242. This is a pretty area where the rocks are smooth and have a reddish hue. Hikers can climb down the pour-off and stay in the bed of the creek, or take the horse trail over the hill. The horse trail starts out as a faint track across a shale-strewn hillside and then becomes more defined as the trail continues uphill. On the downhill portion, vegetation encroaches on the trail, but the rounded tread of the trail is still obvious. When the horse trail drops down to creek level again, you will pass a large rock cairn. This rock cairn will be the landmark for finding the horse trail on the return trip, so take note of the rock cairn and the surrounding terrain.

The trail follows the right bench under a canopy of sycamore, juniper, Emory oak, and pinyon pine trees. As you near Oak Spring [26-HH, 2.2], water may appear in the bed of the wash. The remains of former water improvements at Oak Spring are the only sign that this is the site of the spring. Down canyon from Oak Spring, the trail meanders in and out of the wash, which may have intermittent water, and makes use of the benches on either side of the canyon. Several flat benches in this section of canyon provide possible camping areas. Just beyond a large cottonwood tree and its tangled root system, you will come to the Wilderness boundary fence and a gate that is supported by a rock basket [26-O, 2.7]. See photo below.

From the Wilderness gate, our trip continues across the South Fork Horrell Creek and takes the former road (FR305) and now Cuff Button Trail (276) up canyon on the north bench. This road does not look like it has been used recently, and some of the maps show the road as the Cuff Button Trail (276). The old road narrows to a trail in several places as it makes use of the benches on both sides of the wash. A carsonite signpost at mile 3.2 marks the trail as it enters the Wilderness again. The Haunted Canyon USGS topo map incorrectly identifies Thicket Spring as Cuff Button Spring. You can identify Thicket Spring wash by the cattle feeder box [26-B, 3.5], which is on the flat below Thicket Spring. Thicket Spring has always been dry whenever we checked it.

You finally reach the Cuff Button Corral on the right bench [26-P, 3.7], which is one of the few remaining wooden corrals in the Wilderness (photo on page 229). The water trough at the corral has been dry due to broken pipes, so you have to follow the buried pipeline to the north where you can find a trickle of water in the ravine at Cuff Button Spring [26-R, 3.9]. Return the same way, or take one of the optional routes described on the next page.

Wilderness gate [26-O] at the mouth of Wildcat Canyon where it meets Cuff Button Trail (276). The rock basket braces the gate post and eliminates the need for a concrete footing. Howard Horinek built the rock basket when he managed the JH6 Ranch from 1985 to 1992. Photo taken in January 2004.

OPTIONAL ROUTES

From Cuff Button Corral [26-P, 3.7] you can continue southwest and uphill on the Cuff Button Trail (276) to Oak Flat [26-L, 7.9] connecting with the West Pinto Trail (212) for a return to Miles Trailhead [26-Z, 10.0]. The Cuff Button Trail has a lot of ups and downs and may require some trail scouting, so make sure you have enough time to complete the loop. At the least, you need to get to Oak Flat and on the West Pinto Trail before dark.

You can inspect the remains of a wooden corral that we call Double Corral [26-KK] in Wildcat Canyon by entering Wildcat Canyon from the Cuff Button Trail [26-TT] crossing or entering down canyon from where this trip (Trip 32) first intersects the canyon. The old trail in Wildcat Canyon is overgrown, so you will need to travel in the wash of Wildcat Canyon. Horse riders will have problems in a few narrow and rocky spots, but hikers can scramble through the wash. Look for Double Corral [26-KK] on the south side of Wildcat Canyon at about the 4,080-foot elevation level (N33° 27' 16", W111° 05' 13"). Howard Horinek calls the seasonal seep near the corral Viejo Potrero Spring.

HISTORY AND LEGENDS

Howard Horinek, former ranch manager for the JH6 Ranch from 1985 to 1992, built the large rock baskets along the Cuff Button Trail and in the surrounding area to make secure anchors for the gates and fences. Horinek added a metal lever to some of the barbed wire gates to make them easier to close. The levers are made of rebar. If you can figure out how to position the lever on the gate post, the lever will make the job of stretching the barbed wire gate easier so you can pull the wire bail over the post.[137]

In the 1980s, Horinek maintained all the springs along the Cuff Button Trail and added improvements to them while he managed the JH6 Ranch, but most have since fallen into disrepair. Daily work on the water improvements required cleaning silt and leaves out of the spring boxes, removing fallen trees, and repairing broken pipes due to freezing temperatures.

Howard Horinek heard from Bob Hale that the name the cowboys used for Oak Spring was Wildcat Spring. That maybe the origin for the Wildcat Canyon name. Hale worked for rancher Louie Horrell during World War II.[138]

Wildcat Canyon may have been the main access to this part of the country in the 1940s since a trail in the canyon is shown on the 1948 Haunted Canyon USGS topographic map. The 1969 Tonto Forest map shows Trail 193 going up Horrell Creek from Pinto Creek, up Wildcat Canyon, across the ridge, and ending at Miles Ranch, so Trail 193 covers the first part of our Trip 32 from [26-Z] to [26-O]. After 1970, the maps do not show Trail 193, so it was apparently abandoned. We do not know the name of Trail 193.

Rogers Trough Trailhead

From Apache Junction at Idaho Road, go east 15 miles on US60 to Florence Junction. Two miles east of Florence Junction on US60, between mileposts 214 and 215, turn north on Queen Valley Road for 1.8 miles to FR357 (Hewitt Station Road). Go right 3 miles to FR172. If you are coming from Superior on US60, go past the Arboretum. Between mileposts 222 and 223, take FR357 for 5 miles to FR172. Go north on FR172 for 9 miles to the junction of FR172A, and go right 4 miles on four-wheel-drive FR172A to the end of the road. A high-clearance vehicle is required on FR172 and four-wheel-drive on FR172A.

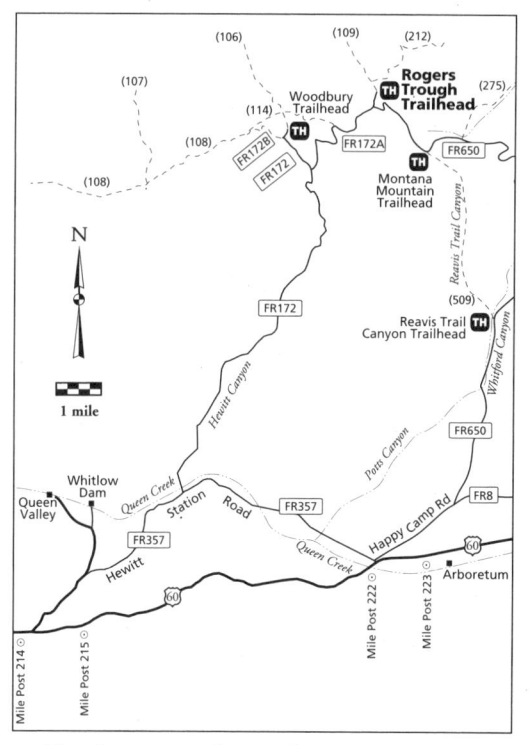

FINDING THE TRAILHEAD

Nine miles on FR172 brings you to the junction of FR172A where you go right (east) for 4 miles to Rogers Trough Trailhead. After heavy rains, FR172A sometimes requires four-wheel-drive. If you can't drive up the steep grades of FR172A, you can use the Woodbury Trailhead as an alternate parking area, but you will have to use the Coffee Flat Trail and FR172A to walk or ride horseback 3.7 miles to the Rogers Trough Trailhead.

FACILITIES

Rogers Trough Trailhead has a large parking lot and hitching posts for stock. Bring your own water. Horse riders may find seasonal water for their stock in the bed of Rogers Creek or at a water trough 0.25 mile east on the West Pinto Trail, but the trough is not always maintained when cattle are not in this pasture.

THE TRAILS

Reavis Ranch Trail (109) (N33° 25' 19.9", W111° 10' 21.7") goes north from the Rogers Trough parking lot to Reavis Valley. A short distance from the Rogers Trough parking lot, the West Pinto Trail (212) branches off to the northeast and ends at Miles Trailhead.

HISTORY AND LEGENDS

Rogers Canyon is named for James Rogers. He was born about 1848 and was married to Maria Selma Beyer in the early 1880s. They owned property in the town of Pinal and had many mining claims in the area. Maria was the sister of Rosalie Beyer who married J. D. Reymert. See History and Legends for Trip 36 (Rogers Ridge) for a description of the mines. In 1889, James Rogers and his partners sold their claims to J. D. Reymert, and that is the last transaction we have found for James Rogers. He died in 1917 at Pinal County Hospital and is buried in the Florence Cemetery, Florence, Arizona, although we have not been able to locate his grave.[139]

Charles Ceslinger, born in 1851, was a partner of James Rogers on the earliest mining claims in 1876. After the mining claims were sold to Reymert, an October 12, 1889, newspaper article noted that Ceslinger was "employed…in developing a group of six mines belonging to Judge J. D. Reymert."[140]

In 1883, Donahue-Hutchinson & Co. built a three-ton-per-day adobe smelter in Rogers Canyon for the mines. The first design with a horse-powered blower did not work, so it was replaced with a small steam engine to run the blower and rock breaker. The woodcutters, probably Binkley and Bennett, were extending the wagon road from Happy Camp to Mount Cachimba (Montana Mountain) at that time.[141]

James Rogers and his partners owned the Silver Chief Mine in the late 1800s. Ron Feldman describes a trip he made to the Silver Chief Mine in Chapter 18 of his book *Deep Fault*. Although Feldman does not name all of the landmarks, we believe he traveled down Rogers Canyon and turned up Silver Chief Canyon to reach the Silver Chief Mine near the top of Rogers Ridge. The shaft of the Silver Chief Mine has collapsed, the ladders are gone, and the mine is no longer accessible. See Chapter 9 of Jesse Feldman's book, *Jacob's Trail*, for more history of the Silver Chief Mine.

About 300 yards down the Reavis Ranch Trail from the Rogers Trough Trailhead look for a small hill to the right (east). The site of the old Rogers Mill—an early 1900s mine operated by the Woodbury family—was on the side of this hill. The old boiler still stood here in the 1950s, and two cyanide tanks were observed in 1964, but nothing remains except for the concrete foundation and a few scraps of metal.[142]

Rogers Trough Trailhead in April 2008 at the start of the Reavis Ranch Trail (109). Iron Mountain is on the left horizon. West Pinto Trail (212) goes through the notch on the right horizon.

You'll find Rogers Spring to the east up a small drainage along the West Pinto Trail. Rogers Spring was named Cane (Can or Kane) Spring in the 1880s, and the *Pinal Drill* newspaper often mentioned the Cane Spring cabin. "The camp of Frank Broerman, Charley Ceslinger, and James Rogers is on the hillside near a constant spring. They have a garden luxuriant with vegetables and flowers. Young fruit trees are giving future promise."[143]

In the early 1900s, the Woodbury family owned many Rogers Canyon mining claims. Later, in 1957, Quentin "Ted" Cox and his partners filed their claims in the Rogers Canyon and Randolph Basin areas. A few of those claims had fanciful names such as the *Lost Peralta Mine of Death*.[144] Ted Cox was a prolific writer and documented his unpublished explorations and mining efforts with detailed notes and drawings.

The 750-mile Arizona Trail, extending from Mexico to Utah, passes through Rogers Trough Trailhead. Coming from the south, the Arizona Trail climbs Montana Mountain on Reavis Canyon Trail (509), meets FR650, and enters the Superstition Wilderness at Rogers Trough Trailhead on FR172A. In the Wilderness, the Arizona Trail follows the Reavis Ranch Trail (109), Reavis Gap Trail (117), and Two Bar Ridge Trail (119). The Arizona Trail exits the Wilderness at FR83 and continues on Cottonwood Trail (120) and Thompson Trail (121) to Roosevelt Lake Bridge.[145]

Trip 33

ROGERS CANYON CLIFF DWELLINGS

This trip leads you through beautiful Rogers Canyon along the shortest trail to the cliff dwellings near Angel Basin. You will enjoy the wide variety of trees and the seasonal pools of water in this scenic canyon. Angel Basin offers excellent camping.

ITINERARY

From Rogers Trough parking lot, follow Reavis Ranch Trail (109) northeast to the junction with Rogers Canyon Trail (110). Follow Rogers Canyon Trail to the cliff dwellings. Return the same way, or return to the Woodbury Trailhead via Tortilla Pass on JF Trail (106).

DIFFICULTY

Moderate hike. Not recommended for horses due to a dangerous slick rock section of trail [29-NN] just south of the cliff dwellings. Elevation change is -1,050 feet one way.

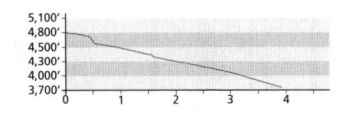

LENGTH and TIME

3.9 miles, 2.5 hours one way. Add 0.3 mile to reach Angel Basin.

MAPS

Arizona USGS topo map NAD27: Iron Mountain. Superstition Wilderness Beartooth map, grids M13 to L12. Map 29.

FINDING THE TRAIL

Trailhead map is on page 247. Reavis Ranch Trail (109) starts at the north side of the Rogers Trough parking lot at the end of FR172A (N33° 25' 19.9", W111° 10' 21.7").

THE TRIP

Start on Map 29 on page 253 where the trip begins on Reavis Ranch Trail (109) at the Rogers Trough Trailhead [29-U, 0]. The trail crosses Rogers Creek a few yards from the parking lot. Although you may find water here, the water may not be potable due to cattle and people. Within a 0.1 mile,

West Pinto Trail (212) comes in from the east [29-T, 0.1]. Trip 39 describes the 8.7 mile trek from the Reavis Ranch Trail [29-T] to the Miles Ranch Trailhead [25-Z] on West Pinto Trail (212).

The Reavis Ranch Trail continues down Rogers Canyon making many stream crossings. This part of Rogers Canyon has seasonal water, and the canyon supports a few Arizona sycamore and juniper trees. At the signed junction with Rogers Canyon Trail (110) [29-S, 1.6], the Reavis Ranch Trail is heading northeast toward Reavis Ranch. This trip goes left (west) on the Rogers Canyon Trail and continues down Rogers Canyon toward the cliff dwellings. Rogers Canyon has seasonal water although the water may be intermittent. The cement water trough at Rogers Canyon Spring [29-RR, 2.8] (N33° 27' 04.7", W111° 11' 47.5") is out of service, but you may find water in the bed of the creek there. The remains of the Rogers Canyon Spring corral and trap are on the nearby flat bench (photo on page 254). The thick canopy of Arizona sycamore, Emory oak, netleaf hackberry, Arizona walnut, and Fremont cottonwoods make this a pleasant section of the trail.

Just south of the cliff dwellings, slick rock [29-NN, 3.5] (N33° 27' 39.9", W111° 12' 05.2") on the trail, high above the creek bed, makes about 200 feet of trail hazardous for horses. Experienced riders have lost a horse here when the horse slipped and fell off the 100-foot-high cliff into the creek bed. Closer to the cliff dwellings, the trail weaves over and around large boulders that may be difficult for many horses to negotiate. Most outfitters do not use this part of the Rogers Canyon Trail due to this hazard.

The cliff dwellings [29-G, 3.9] (N33° 27' 49.3", W111° 12' 19.9") are located on the north side of Rogers Canyon just after the canyon makes a gradual bend to the west. Located in a cave about 100 feet above the canyon floor, the cliff dwellings are easy to see from the trail. At the ruins, the trail is on the south side of the canyon. From below the ruins, walk up a rough, steep trail to the lower ruin. A Forest Service sign, a few feet from the lower cliff dwelling, provides some important information for visitors. These ruins were occupied by the Salado around A.D. 1300. Don't take anything. Don't camp here. Don't do anything to degrade the ruins. Climbing on the walls and roof can cause them to crumble, and building a fire may cause a hidden roof structure to burn.

The trip description ends at the cliff dwellings. Return the same way to Rogers Trough Trailhead [29-U, 7.8], or if you came here to camp, you will find large campsites 0.3 mile down the canyon at Angel Basin [29-F].

HISTORY AND LEGENDS

The Rogers Canyon cliff dwellings were built and occupied by the Salado around A.D. 1300. Archaeologists have two theories about the Salado. Harold

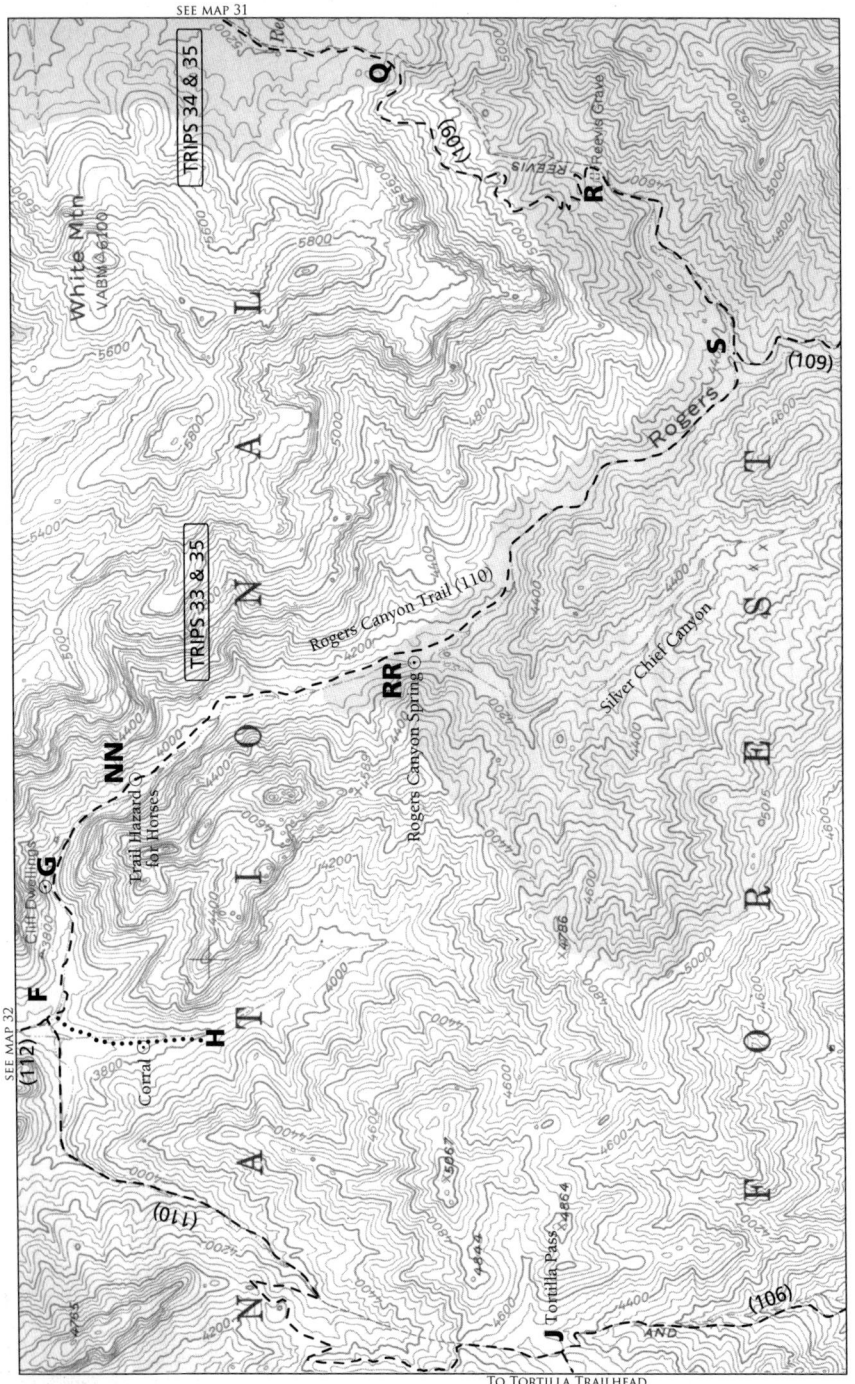

Map 29 – Trips 33, 34, 35, and 36.

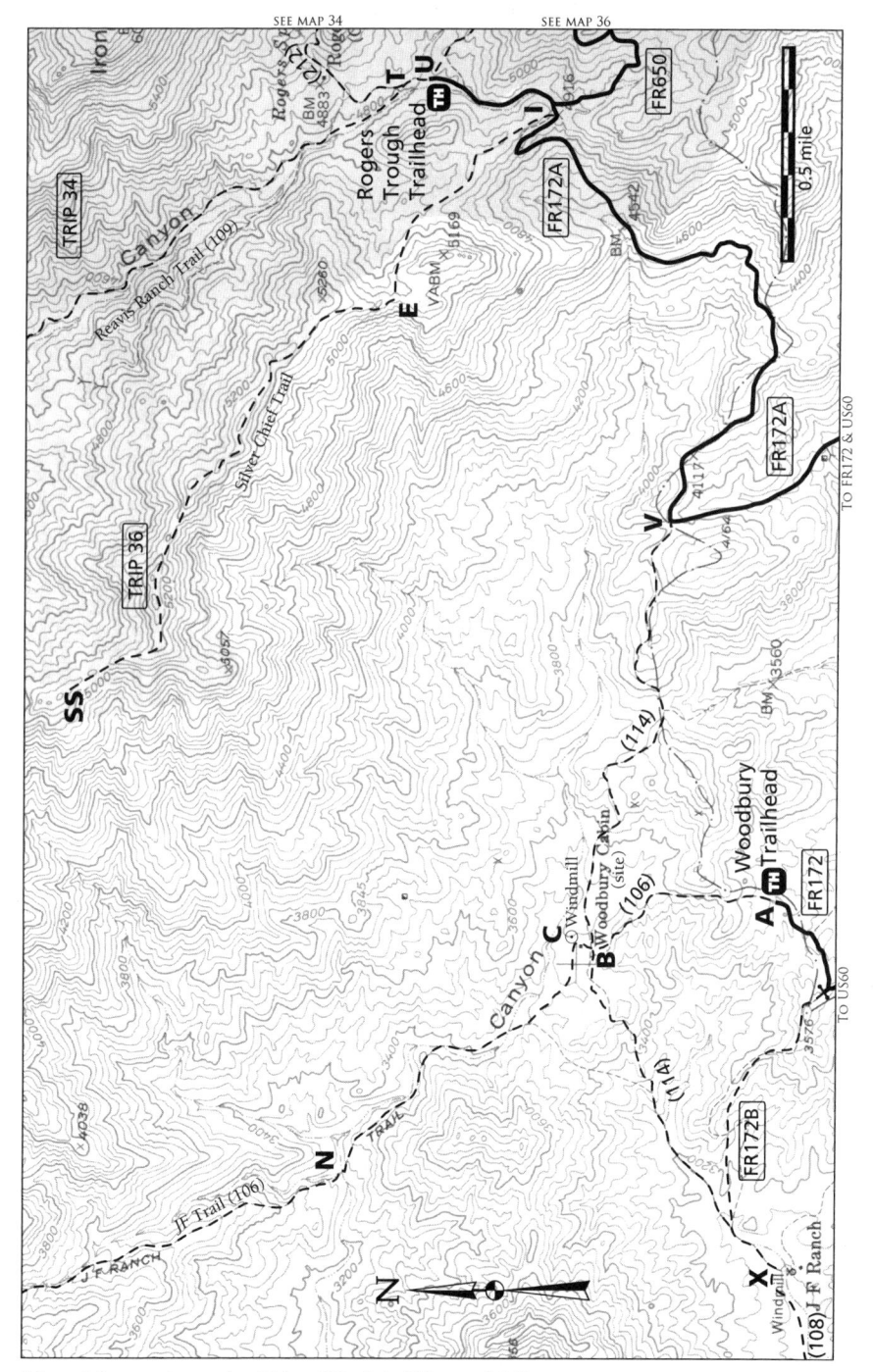

Map 29 continued – Trips 33, 34, 35, and 36.

Rogers Canyon Spring Corral Trap [near 29-RR] in May 1999. The photo shows one side of one the few remaining gates on a trap corral. Animals pushed their way through the V-shaped gate, but once in the corral, a spring closed the gate and the pointed ends of the gate poles prevented the animals from leaving. The gate rotated on a metal spike in the base of the wooden post.

Gladwin, noted archaeologist from the 1920s through the 1940s, proposed that the Salado migrated from the north near the Little Colorado and were mingling with the Hohokam about A.D. 1300. At that time, the Hohokam were located in the Salt River and Gila River basins, and contact with the Salado seemed to be a friendly and peaceful cultural exchange. Another theory suggests that the Salado evolved from within the Hohokam culture by adopting cultural traits from the surrounding communities.[146]

The thick-wall, multi-story architecture of the Salado is evident in Hohokam construction. The Hohokam, before the Salado influence, built single-story, thin-wall houses. Some of the other well-known structures built or influenced by the Salado are the Great House at Casa Grande National Monument, Besh-Ba-Gowah Pueblo at Globe, and the cliff dwellings at Tonto National Monument. By A.D. 1450 both the Hohokam and Salado people left the area. Archaeologist Brett Hill theorized that flooding damage to the canal system and the degradation of the soil by intensive irrigation may have reduced the potential of the farmland. A shortage of food may have led to a decrease in population, which resulted in a scarcity of labor to maintain the Hohokam canal system in the Salt River Valley.[147]

Since some of the Rogers Canyon buildings were constructed in a cave, they have survived the elements rather well. The wood and mud roof is still in good shape on part of one structure. The area is devoid of the usual graffiti seen at many other prehistoric sites. We hope everyone continues to preserve these unique structures.

Rogers Canyon cliff dwellings have been the destination of many hikers and trail riders since the late 1890s. Four men from Phoenix reportedly made the ride to the ruins in January 1899. After a stop at the Bark and Criswell Ranch (now the Quarter Circle U Ranch), they proceeded to the ruins. The newspaper article did not give the complete itinerary of their hunting trip but reported that they rode over to Reavis Ranch, after leaving the ruins, to visit with rancher Jack Fraser.[148]

Down the canyon from the ruins about 0.3 mile is a large, flat grassy area locally called Angel Basin. At this location the Rogers Canyon Trail meets the Frog Tanks Trail. The tall trees, netleaf hackberry, Arizona sycamore, and Arizona walnut in Angel Basin are silhouetted against the surrounding sheer, buff-colored cliffs. This is a fine place to camp with room for large groups.

Greg Davis is standing next to the prehistoric house in the cave at Rogers Canyon cliff dwelling. Photo was taken in May 1999.

Jack Carlson (left) and Greg Davis (right) at Angel Spring Corral [near 29-H] not far from Angel Basin. The cement water trough is inscribed with "Bacon & Upton, Aug. 27, 1948, Mage, Duane, Mrs. Gladys Bacon." Photo was taken in May 1999.

The intermittent pool of water in Rogers Canyon in front of the cliff dwellings is often called Angel Spring by present day visitors. The early ranchers probably used the Angel Spring name for the corral and water trough to the south of Angel Basin. That spring and corral are now in disrepair and not useful as a water source. Ranchers Bacon and Upton inscribed the Angel Spring cement trough with their names and dated the trough August 27, 1948.

Southwestern artist Ettore "Ted" DeGrazia is well known for his paintings of the land and people he loved. DeGrazia made many treks into the Superstition Mountains, and several of his trail rides were well publicized. In protest of Federal estate taxes on artwork to be left to his heirs, DeGrazia burned a collection of his paintings valued at more than one million dollars in Angel Basin on January 27, 1976.[149] The March 1983 issue of *Arizona Highways* shows a photograph of his paintings engulfed in the bonfire on the grassy flat at Angel Basin.[150] Ted DeGrazia died in Tucson at the age of seventy-three on September 17, 1982.

Trip 34

ROGERS TROUGH TO REAVIS RANCH

The trip to Reavis Ranch is a popular hike and trail ride for many apple lovers each fall. Reavis Ranch has more to offer than the apple orchards and expansive meadows. Worthwhile side trips to Circlestone ruin, Pine Creek, and Reavis Grave make this an outstanding trip. Reavis Valley normally has some water, and the large stands of Arizona walnut, Arizona sycamore, alligator juniper, and ponderosa pine make this area a special destination.

ITINERARY

From Rogers Trough Trailhead follow Reavis Ranch Trail (109) to Reavis Ranch. A side trip to Circlestone ruin uses the Fire Line Trail (118) and the Allen Blackman Trail. Return the same way.

DIFFICULTY

Moderate 2 or 3 day backpack or difficult horse pack trip. The steep and narrow trail in Rogers Canyon at the start of the trip may be a problem for some horses. Elevation change is +1,170 and -920 feet one way.

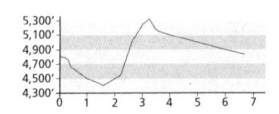

LENGTH and TIME

6.5 miles, 4.5 hours one way.

MAPS

Arizona USGS topo maps NAD27: Iron Mountain, Pinyon Mountain. Superstition Wilderness Beartooth map, grids M13 to N11. Maps 30 and 31.

FINDING THE TRAIL

Trailhead map is on page 247. Reavis Ranch Trail (109) starts at the north side of the Rogers Trough parking area at the end of FR172A (N33° 25' 19.9", W111° 10' 21.7").

THE TRIP

Start on Map 30 on page 259. The trip begins on Reavis Ranch Trail (109) at the Rogers Trough Trailhead [30-U, 0] and immediately crosses the upper arm of Rogers Creek. West Pinto Trail (212) enters from the east [30-T, 0.1] and heads 8.7 miles over to the Miles Ranch Trailhead [25-Z]. The Reavis Ranch Trail continues down Rogers Canyon making many stream crossings, where horse riders may have difficulty with the steep and narrow trail. Seasonal water flows in the canyon and fills the potholes. The water course is dotted with netleaf hackberry, Arizona sycamore, and juniper trees.

At the signed junction with Rogers Canyon Trail (110) [30-S, 1.6], the Reavis Ranch Trail heads northeast toward Reavis Ranch. Just north of the junction [30-S], the trail follows the Grave Canyon drainage through some large stands of manzanita. Sycamore trees dot the ravine.

The Reavis Ranch Trail wanders back and forth across the water course in Grave Canyon until the trail passes the unsigned spur trail to Reavis Grave [30-R, 2.2] (N33° 26' 42", W111° 10' 37"). The last time we were there, a tall rock cairn marked the spur trail up the hill to the west. You can take a rest here and then walk the few yards up to the small flat, grassy area where you will find the grave site marked by a rectangular mound of rocks. See page 263 for a photo of Reavis Grave. A good way to find the spur trail is to note that the Reavis Ranch Trail leaves the rocky wash and goes up a set of switchbacks about 200 feet north of the Reavis Grave spur trail.

After visiting the grave site, continue on Reavis Ranch Trail, which follows the switchbacks up the left (west) side of the ravine. With an elevation gain of 700 feet, the trail tops out at Reavis Saddle [30-Q, 3.2], and you get your first glimpse of the inviting forest on the north side of the ridge. You will find some flat, grassy campsites at the pass, but be aware that the pass can get very windy in stormy weather. From Reavis Saddle, you have an easy and enjoyable downhill walk or ride through the pine forest all the way to Reavis Ranch. You may find water at the seasonal Honeycutt Spring [31-P, 4.1], which is up a wide ravine to the (left) west. Many nice campsites lie along Reavis Ranch Trail, and the forest of Emory oak, alligator juniper, and ponderosa pine makes this stretch of the trip one of the most pleasant experiences of the trek. The trail crosses Reavis Creek many times and then favors the west bank for most of the remainder of the trek.

Evidence of the May 1966 Iron Mountain burn is still present, but detracts little from the beauty of the area. Greg Hansen of the Forest Service said the tall lovegrass was planted to stop erosion after the fire, but the non-native lovegrass stifled the indigenous grasses and shrubs. The forest here has a feeling of openness with the grassy undercover being broken only by scattered ponderosa pine trees. A large alligator juniper tree [31-N, 5.3] along the trail is often measured by travelers to determine its circumference. It takes about five people holding hands to span the girth of this ancient tree.

The trail continues north and soon drops down near the water course of Reavis Creek. You may find intermittent water here. At this point, the trail

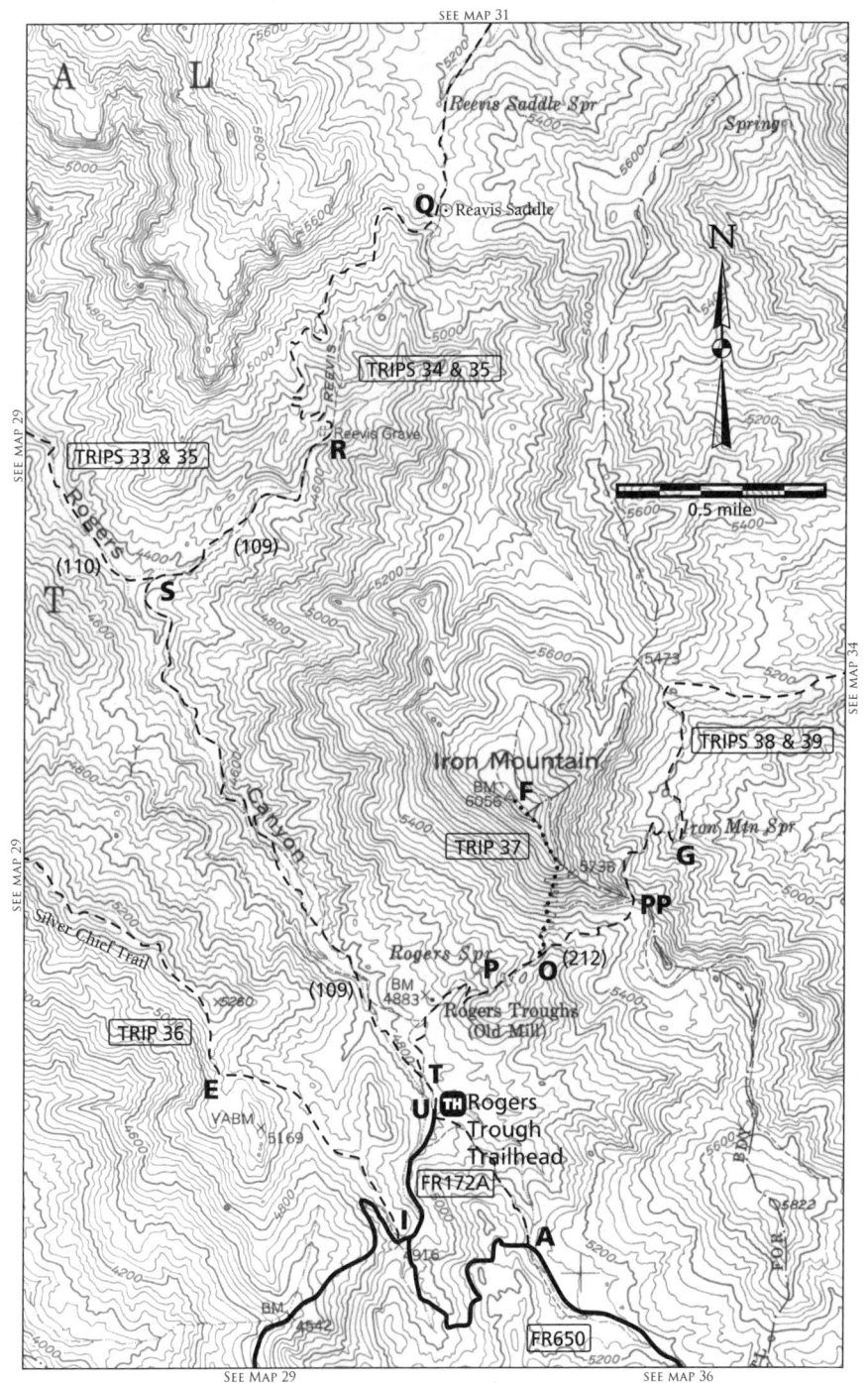

Map 30 – Trips 33, 34, 35, 36, 37, 38, and 39.

crosses to the east side of the creek and closely follows the water course, then returns to the west bank. About fifteen minutes farther downstream, the trail crosses again to the east bank, which should alert you to watch for the junction with the Fire Line Trail (118) [31-J, 6.2]. This would be a good place to filter water for your water bottles.

The Fire Line Trail is the beginning of the 2.5-mile side trip to Circlestone ruin [18-O]. See Trip 1 for the Circlestone trail description. Reavis Ranch Trail continues north as it crosses to the west bank and cuts through the ranch area. A small apple orchard stands to the east just before you reach the site of the ranch house. The Reavis Ranch house site [18-I, 6.5] is on the west side of the trail. The ranch house burned in November 1991, and only the cement floor remains now. A few feet to the south, you can still see the depression in the earth where the pond was located. The trip description ends here. Return the same way.

Review Trip 1 for the optional day trips from Reavis Ranch. Since Reavis Valley can be reached by several other trails, you should read the descriptions and history for the following trips—Trip 1 (Reavis Ranch from

Elisha Reavis at his farm on Reavis Creek. Courtesy of Gregory Davis, Superstition Mountain Historical Society, Mrs. Dudley Craig Collection. Date and photographer unknown.

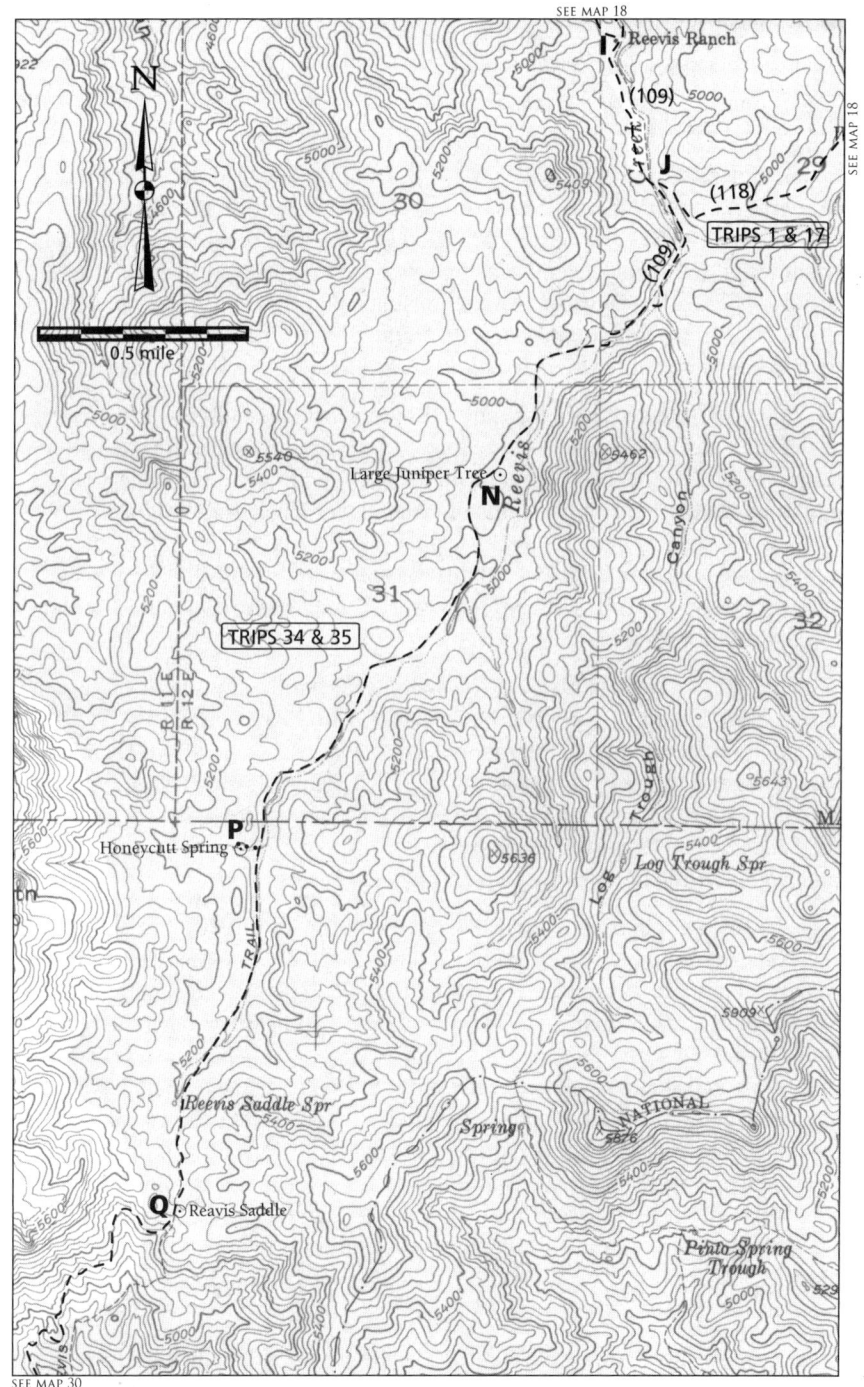

Map 31 – Trips 34 and 35.

Reavis Trailhead); Trip 17 (Campaign Trail to Reavis Ranch Loop), and Trip 18 (Reavis Gap Trail to Reavis Ranch) both starting from Campaign Trailhead.

HISTORY AND LEGENDS

Elisha M. Reavis was born in Beardstown, Illinois about 1827. In 1867, he married Maria Sexton in San Gabriel, California. They had a daughter, Louisa Maria Reavis, the next year. When Reavis came to Arizona, his family remained in California. Louisa married Richard Ratcliff, and they had three children. Elisha Reavis was a distant cousin of James Addison Reavis, the Baron of Arizona, who perpetrated the Peralta Land Grand fraud. They were both descendants of brothers born to Edward Reavis, Sr. (1680-1751).[151]

In 1876, Reavis sold his ranch that was located about five miles north of the Fort McDowell post, and we guess that he came over to Reavis Valley shortly after that to establish his farm. He was well known for his vegetables, which he sold in the nearby towns of Pinal, Silver King, and Florence.[152] He was a newsworthy character. A newspaper labeled him the Hermit of the Superstitions, although his personality was far from hermit-like. Reavis was a friendly sort of person with contemporary friends using nicknames such as Jim and Bill for him.[153]

Matt Cavaness, who built the board house at the present day Quarter Circle U Ranch, and a party of friends visited with Reavis on August 30, 1883. They rode horseback from the town of Pinal, where they lived, up Montana Mountain and followed the present day Reavis Ranch Trail to the Reavis farm. Reavis was the perfect host and even guided the group down Pine Creek to the Salt River the next day. He shot a deer for them and camped at the river that night, telling more stories to entertain his guests.[154]

Most people think Reavis lived alone in the mountains, but several accounts tell a different story. In 1883, James Reymert and Charles Ceslinger rode up the mountain to visit Reavis, and, while Reavis was not there, host Mr. Wilmott treated them to a dinner of venison and garden vegetables. They were impressed with the six acres of potatoes and a large plot of onions that Reavis planted. In 1896, A. J. Henderson said that a Mexican woman was in charge of his cabin when Reavis left the farm just before his death. According to the probate records, Henderson had several men working with him at the Reavis farm, and Reavis owed him for plowing seven acres of land, work on the dam and ditch, irrigating, and fence work. Henderson was a rancher, branding the Bar S L, on the range near the community of Salt River. Pedro Madrid, also working for Reavis, submitted a claim for his previous month's labor at the farm.[155]

Prospector James Delabaugh, expecting Reavis to come into town, went to check on him and found his body on May 5, 1896. Reavis had appar-

Elizabeth Stewart at Reavis Grave [30-R] in February 1999. The inscription (inset photo) was added later and photographed in January 2004. Elisha Reavis died about April 21, 1896 and he is buried in Grave Canyon on a bench above the Reavis Ranch Trail (109). The inscription should read 1827-1896.

ently not been feeling well and had set up camp on the trail in what is now known as Grave Canyon. Delabaugh continued on to the Reavis cabin and then down to Salt River where he alerted the community. John Narron, A. J. Henderson, and F. M. Cooper came up to the Reavis farm and continued up the trail where they located the body of Reavis. They buried him on the site of a prehistoric ruin where his grave remains today. Narron removed $36.60 from the body before Reavis was buried, and, in what was probably an embarrassing situation, was summoned by the probate court to return the money to the estate, which he did.[156]

The probate court estimated that Reavis died about April 21, 1896. Most newspapers and the court indicated that Reavis died of natural causes and no foul play was involved. Jack Fraser and James Delabaugh were hired as the estate appraisers and made a detailed list of all the food, tools, and equipment at the farm, which included twenty burros, two horses, nine pigs, three turkeys, farming equipment, and a wagon. We have not found a document supporting the transaction, but we understand that Fraser obtained the possessory right and expanded his JF cattle operation to the Reavis farm.[157]

See History and Legends in Trip 1 (Reavis Ranch from Reavis Trailhead) for the stories of early ranchers—Fraser, Knight, Clemans, Bacon, Upton, and Stone. We pick up the history of the Reavis Ranch in 1946 when the Clemans Cattle Company was selling the ranch, which comprised three ranches—the Reavis, the JF, and the Tortilla. William H. Martin, Sr., foreman for Clemans, bought a portion of the JF that was referred to as the desert range on Queen Creek. Bacon and Upton bought the rest of the ranches. When Bacon and Upton sold in 1952, Martin, Sr., acquired the JF and Tortilla Ranches, while Floyd Stone got the Reavis Ranch in 1955. Martin then sold the Tortilla to the Stones. Stone traded the Reavis Ranch with the Forest Service in exchange for the IV Ranch in 1966, and that ended the ranching era for the Reavis.[158]

Bill Martin, Sr., hired on at the Reavis in 1913 and moved up to foreman in 1915. He married Lenora Olson in 1922, who had two sons—John and Rollie. John Olson helped his stepfather on the Reavis and later, in 1938, received the homestead patent for the 640 acres of Elephant Butte property.[159]

Billy Martin, Jr., was born in 1925 and grew up on the ranches that his father managed. He said the cowboys had to rebuild the dam across Reavis Creek, upstream from the Fire Line Trail crossing, each year because high water would wash the dam away. The dam diverted water into the ditch that fed the pond next to the Reavis Ranch house. Billy said the dam was always in place by the time he got up to the ranch after school let out for the summer.

Billy Martin, Jr., married Helen "Teta" Gillette in 1943, and they had one son, George Martin, who was born in 1952. They bought the JF Ranch and Millsite allotment from Martin, Sr. in 1958. Billy Martin, Jr., in 1990 received the Chester A. Reynolds Award at the Cowboy Hall of Fame for his contributions to the heritage of the American West.[160] In 2008, George Martin bought the ranch from his parents.

The Martin Ranch brands are the J Slash A, 2 E, Lazy E Spear, and more recently they acquired the original JF brand that Jack Fraser recorded in the 1800s. The cattle are still worked on horseback in the tradition of Martin, Sr., but modern methods such as solar water pumps and pasture rotation have been incorporated into the operation.

Trip 35

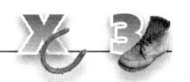

Rogers Trough to Reavis Ranch Loop

This trip takes you through the high country where a ponderosa pine and alligator juniper forest, near Reavis Ranch, provides a setting ideal for camping and relaxation. The weather is usually cooler here, and in the winter months of December and January you might see snow. This trek takes you to the Rogers Canyon cliff dwellings, upper Fish Creek, Reavis Ranch, Reavis apple orchards, Circlestone ruin, and Reavis Grave. This is a popular November destination for many apple lovers.

ITINERARY

From Rogers Trough Trailhead, follow Reavis Ranch Trail (109) and Rogers Canyon Trail (110) to Angel Basin. Continue on Frog Tanks Trail (112) and Reavis Ranch Trail (109) to Reavis Ranch. Return on Reavis Ranch Trail (109) to Rogers Trough Trailhead.

DIFFICULTY

Difficult 3 to 5 day backpack trip. Not recommended for horses due to dangerous section of Roger Canyon Trail. Elevation change is ±3,100 feet.

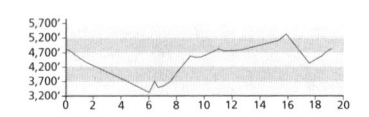

LENGTH and TIME

19.1 miles, 3 days round trip.

MAPS

Arizona USGS topo maps NAD27: Iron Mountain, Pinyon Mountain. Superstition Wilderness Beartooth map, grids M13 to L12, L12 to N11, and N11 to M13. Maps 29, 32, 4, 18, and 31.

FINDING THE TRAIL

Trailhead map is on page 247. Reavis Ranch Trail (109) starts at the north side of the Rogers Trough parking lot at the end of FR172A (N33° 25' 19.9", W111° 10' 21.7").

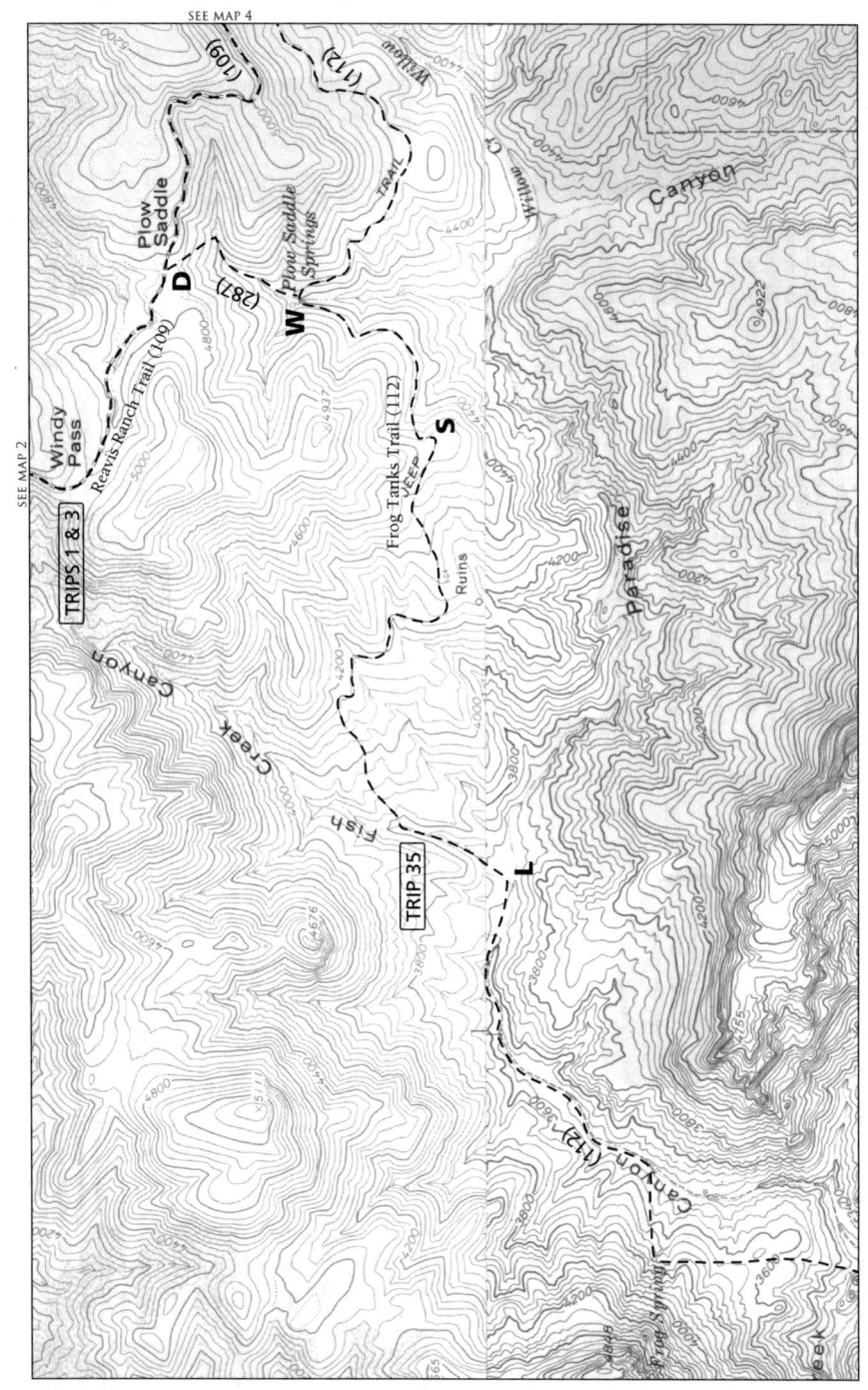

Map 32 – Trips 1 and 35.

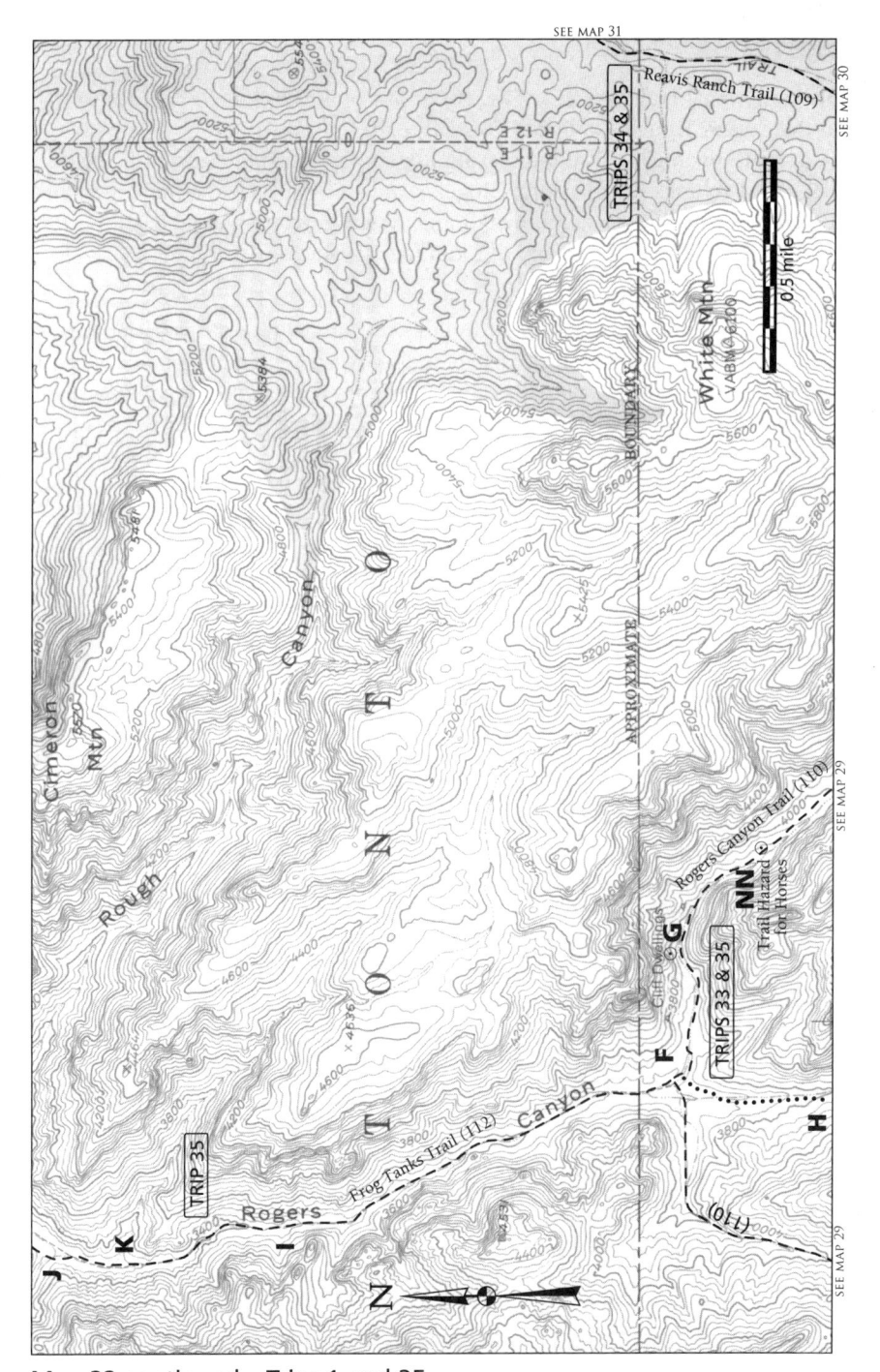

Map 32 continued – Trips 1 and 35.

THE TRIP

Start on Map 29 on page 253. The trip begins on Reavis Ranch Trail (109) at the Rogers Trough Trailhead. For the first leg of this trip, follow Trip 33 (Rogers Canyon Cliff Dwellings) from Rogers Trough Trailhead [29-U, 0] to the cliff dwellings [29-G, 3.9] in Rogers Canyon. After viewing the Rogers Canyon cliff dwellings, continue 0.3 mile down canyon to Angel Basin [29-F, 4.2] where you will find plenty of room for camping.

The trip continues down Rogers Canyon on the Frog Tanks Trail (112). Frog Tanks Trail is difficult to follow when the trail drops in and out of the normally dry creek bed. Depending on recent trail maintenance, part of the trail may be overgrown with catclaw mimosa (cougar claw), and you may find walking in the bed of the canyon easier. Good sections of trail exist on either side of the water course, but the many crossings, and sometimes lack of any trail, can make the Frog Tanks Trail a tiring trek. For hike planning, use an estimated 0.5 mile per hour hiking speed—it is slow going. A nice canopy of sycamore and oak trees shades the canyon. You may find water where some reeds grow [near 32-I, 5.3] in the bed of the canyon. The Superstition Wilderness Forest Service map shows Hole Spring 0.2 mile up canyon (south) from where we found water in the streambed. Intermittent seasonal water

Camp along the Reavis Ranch Trail (109) south of Reavis Ranch. The open meadows and ponderosa pine trees have recovered from the earlier forest fires. Photo was taken in October 2000.

may be found from Hole Spring [32-I] down to the junction with Fish Creek. Verify the water conditions with the Forest Service before you go. Near Fish Creek, the trail on the east side of Rogers Canyon crosses an unnamed ravine [32-K, 5.7] entering from the east. This ravine is spanned by a barbed wire fence that seems to hang in the air and makes a good landmark signaling the entrance of Fish Creek only five minutes downstream.

Rogers Canyon ends when the small drainage of Fish Creek enters from the east [32-J, 5.8]. This junction is easy to miss. Fish Creek is a very pretty area, and you may find seasonal running water north of here. The Frog Tanks Trail (112) goes to Frog Spring, but finding the trail at the Rogers Canyon and Fish Creek junction is difficult. Look for some rock cairns on the north side of Fish Creek, 100 yards or less from where Fish Creek enters from the east. Follow any sign of a trail, and be persistent until you break through the bushes onto a well-defined horse trail. The trail parallels a fence that runs north, so you might see the fence first. The trail is on the west side of the fence. The uphill climb to Frog Spring is steep. The spring may be dry even when Fish Creek has water. To the east, enjoy the good views of Cimeron Mountain and Rough Canyon before the trail drops back into Fish Creek. As the trail heads east, it passes the cement cow troughs at Frog Tank where the catclaw mimosa (cougar claw) grows in nearby patches. Catclaw mimosa (mimosa biuncifera) is also called *wait-a-minute bush*, but some local people appropriately refer to it as cougar claw. After seasonal rains, this section of Fish Creek may have water.

At a sharp bend in the creek [32-L, 7.5], the trail leaves Fish Creek, passes an abandoned corral, and heads uphill on a well-defined path. The terrain changes to open, grassy areas with clumps of sugar sumac, mesquite, prickly pear, and juniper. At the saddle [32-S, 8.9] a prehistoric ruin is just a few yards to the right (south) of the trail. Only the outline of the rock structure remains. As the trail continues east, it crosses a ravine [32-W, 9.5], which may have seasonal water flowing from the direction of Plow Saddle. Some tall Fremont cottonwood and Arizona sycamore trees grow in the ravine, and thick grass covers the banks. Two former Reavis Ranch owners carved their names in the cement cow tank here—*Bacon & Upton 12-2-48*. If you want to check out Plow Saddle Springs, which may contain seasonal water, take Trail 287 to the north for about 0.3 mile. This trip continues east on Frog Tanks Trail where the trail ends at a junction [4-E, 11.0] with Reavis Ranch Trail (109). Bear right (east) onto the Reavis Ranch Trail. Within 0.2 mile the trail turns south as it enters Reavis Valley.

We briefly describe Reavis Ranch and Circlestone in this section, but we suggest you read Trip 1 (Reavis Ranch from Reavis Trailhead) for a full description of the Reavis Valley. The Reavis Ranch Trail follows the old road south as it passes a large group camping area [4-F, 11.6].

The wooden sign at the Reavis Gap Trail [4-G, 12.2] will help you orient yourself. Reavis Valley has plenty of good campsites. You can usually find water in Reavis Creek at the Reavis Gap Trail crossing where access to the creek is easy for watering stock animals. The main apple orchard [4-H] is southeast of the Reavis Gap Trail sign. Continuing south on the Reavis Ranch Trail a short distance, the Reavis Ranch house site [4-I, 12.6] is on the high bench to the west. Only the cement floor of the house remains today. The debris from the November 1991 fire was removed in 1993, and the ranch house walls were taken down in January 1994.

From Reavis Ranch house site, continue south on Reavis Ranch Trail past another apple orchard. The trail crosses the creek to the east side near the signed junction [18-J, 12.9] with the Fire Line Trail (118). You can usually find water in the creek here, and access to the creek is easy for your stock.

For a 2.5-mile (one way) side trip to Circlestone ruin [18-O] from [18-J], take the Fire Line Trail east, up and over the pass [18-K], then connect with the unsigned Allen Blackman Trail [18-L] heading south across the ridge line. Circlestone [18-O] is on the small knoll (elevation 6,010 feet) just northeast of Mound Mountain. The climb to the ruin is an 1,160 foot elevation gain, so allow at least three hours for the round trip to Circlestone.

From the junction with the Fire Line Trail [31-J, 12.9], the trip continues on the east side of Reavis Creek for a short distance before crossing to the west side. Then the trail is diverted through the creek bed for a short stretch. In the dry season, the creek water becomes intermittent and this is often the last place to find water as you go upstream (south) along Reavis Creek. The trail resumes on the west side of the creek and goes up on a high bench where a nice stand of ponderosa pine and alligator juniper trees are growing. Some signs of the May 1966 Iron Mountain burn are visible but do not detract from the beauty of the forest. We enjoy this section of the trail because the trail is well defined, the forest is pleasant, and the uphill grade is very gradual all the way to Reavis Saddle.

An old alligator juniper tree [31-N, 13.8] next to the trail is somewhat of a tourist attraction because of its size. Near ground level, the large tree is about seven feet in diameter. The tall lovegrass that covers the ground in this area was planted after the forest fire to prevent erosion. The grass is so dense in some areas that the grass covers the trail. Here you have to follow the trail by feeling the worn track under the tangles of grass with your feet. Depending on the season, you might see wildflowers.

Honeycutt Spring [31-P, 15.0] and the former corral and trap rest in a wide drainage to the west of the trail. The unimproved spring has seasonal water. Reavis Creek might have a few small puddles of water near here, but the terrain is much dryer, and Reavis Creek changes to a dry wash and seasonal water course.

At Reavis Saddle [31-Q, 15.9], you will find some flat camping places and several shade trees. A few yards down from Reavis Saddle, the terrain quickly changes to a dry desert where you see redberry buckthorn, catclaw mimosa (cougar claw), sugar sumac, manzanita, and scrub oak. Iron Mountain is directly to the south. The switchback trail is hot and dry along the south slope of Reavis Saddle compared to the cool pine forest on the north side of Reavis Saddle.

At the bottom of the switchbacks, the trail enters and heads down Grave Canyon wash. Look for the spur trail to Reavis Grave [29-R, 16.9] about 200 feet south of where the switchback trail enters the rocky wash. The spur trail, marked by a tall cairn, goes up the bank (west) for a few yards to the Reavis Grave. Reavis Grave rests on a small, flat grassy bench above the wash. The gravestone is not there anymore, but a rectangular mound of rocks marks the grave site. Elisha Reavis was buried here in April of 1896. See pages 262 and 263 for more about Reavis and a photo of his grave.

The Reavis Ranch Trail continues down Grave Canyon, which is lined with sycamore trees, makes several ravine crossings, and arrives at the signed junction [29-S, 17.5] with the Rogers Canyon Trail (110). From the wooden trail sign, bear left and retrace the beginning of the trip on the Reavis Ranch Trail. When you just want to get back to the parking lot, the trail going up Rogers Canyon seems to go up and down more than most people prefer. After the trail passes through a closed barbed wire gate, the terrain becomes open and flatter. The West Pinto Trail (212) [29-T, 19.0] comes in from the east, and the parking lot can be seen a few hundred yards to the south. The Reavis Ranch Trail and this trip end at the Rogers Trough Trailhead parking lot [29-U, 19.1].

Trip 36

ROGERS RIDGE

The west ridge of Rogers Canyon was probably the route to several of the mines claimed by James Rogers and his partners in the 1870s. We named the old road and trail across the west ridge after the Silver Chief Mine, which produced gold and silver. The ridge provides good views into Randolph Basin and Rogers Canyon.

ITINERARY

From FR172A near Rogers Trough Trailhead, take an abandoned road up to the west ridge of Rogers Canyon. Follow the ridge north for about 2 miles and return the same way.

DIFFICULTY

Moderate hike. Difficult horse ride for the first section of the trip on the old road. The overgrown trail on the ridge may be too difficult for most horses. Elevation change is +630 and -420 feet one way.

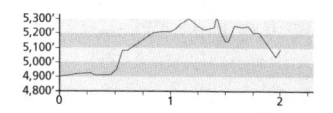

LENGTH and TIME

2.1 miles, 3 hours one way.

MAPS

Arizona USGS topo map NAD27: Iron Mountain. Superstition Wilderness Beartooth map, grid M13. Map 29.

FINDING THE TRAIL

Trailhead map is on page 247. The unsigned Silver Chief Trail starts on FR172A near Rogers Trough Trailhead where the map on page 253 shows elevation 4,916 at [29-I] (N33° 25' 03.9", W111° 10' 26.4"). This is the high point on FR172A just west of the junction with FR650. On the south side of the road, you'll find a small pull-off for two four-wheel-drive vehicles. Vehicles without four-wheel-drive can park near the intersection of FR172A and FR650.

THE TRIP

Start on Map 29 on page 253. From the small parking area [29-I, 0, 4916] on the south side of FR172A, cross the road to the north and follow the closed and abandoned road winding its way up the grade to the west ridge of Rogers Canyon. The road ends when you reach the top of the ridge [29-E, 0.7, 5060]. Look for a large rock cairn that marks the approximate start of a trail of use heading north along the top of the ridge. You will have to search for the trail a little, but once you are on it, you will find that it stays mostly near the top of the ridge with a lot of uphill and downhill stretches of trail. The bushes

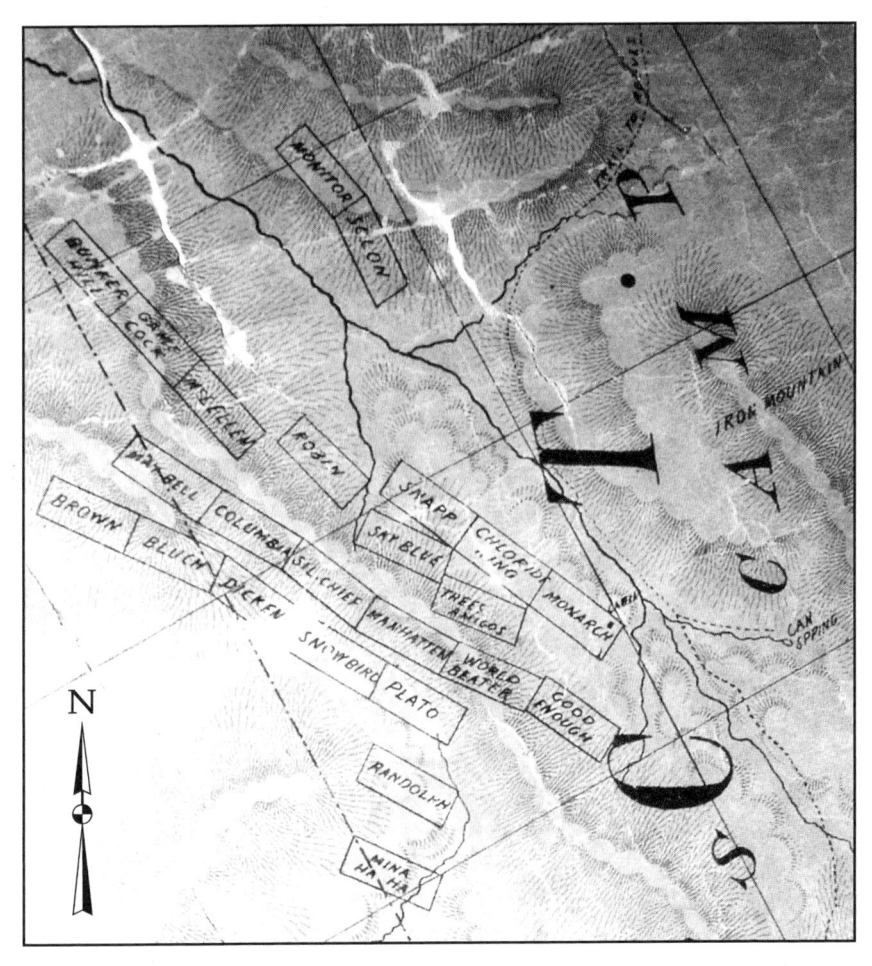

Rogers Camp portion of Topographical Map of Pioneer Mining District and Adjacent Country by Gustavus Cox, 1882. Can Spring is now Rogers Spring. The trail to Reevis Ranch is shown going down Rogers Canyon and up the present-day Grave Canyon. The Silver Chief (Sil Chief) and World Beater claims are on the west ridge of Rogers Canyon. Courtesy of Arizona Historical Society, Tucson.

have closed in over the top of the trail, but you can sometimes follow the trail by the track on the ground. The trail on the ridge disappears after 2.1 miles when the trail reaches the headwaters of Silver Chief Canyon [29-SS, 2.1, 5070]. At your turnaround point, be sure to look for Weavers Needle, below the horizon, among the peaks and mountains to the west. Return the same way.

Just west of the high point on the trip, you can make a short but strenuous detour, downhill, to a point marked as elevation 5,057 on the Iron Mountain topo map. We expected to find an elevation marker here, but we did not find one. This is the exact elevation as Peak 5,057 on Superstition Mountain, which you can see on the horizon many miles to the west.

HISTORY AND LEGENDS

The Rogers Camp portion of the Pioneer Mining District 1882 map (see page 273) shows several mining claims on Rogers Ridge. Going from south to north across the ridge are the following claims: Good Enough, World Beater, Manhatten, Silver Chief, Columbia, and Maybell.[161]

Hugh Hewitt, an early pioneer and rancher, recorded the Yellow Bird Mine in 1877, which was the northwest extension of the Silver Chief Mine. The Yellow Bird claim was renamed the Columbia on the 1882 map. Hewitt was born in Ireland about 1857 and became a U.S. citizen in 1890. Hewitt Station, where he lived, and Hewitt Canyon are named for him.[162]

Silver and gold mines were first recorded on the west ridge of Rogers Canyon in March 1877 by Fleming and Ceslinger, although *The Pinal Drill* newspaper credits James Rogers with discovering the mineral ledge and locating the Silver Chief mine two years earlier in 1875.[163] Charles Ceslinger, Charles Fleming, and Frank Broerman were mining partners with James Rogers. Of the nineteen mining claims on the west ridge of Rogers Canyon, the Silver Chief and World Beater mines were the biggest producers. The *Arizona Weekly Enterprise* reported that "…while the ledges are not large, the ore is a rich carbonate…"[164]

Production from the Rogers District is sketchy, but *The Pinal Drill* newspaper occasionally gave a detailed account of the mines. In 1881, the Silver Chief mine shipped seven tons of ore to San Francisco at $250 per ton. With freight at $44 and expenses at $16, the net profit was $190 per ton. The ore was described as "…carbonate ore showing native silver…free gold…" The total shaft and tunnel work was about 400 feet. Assays for the ore ranged from $120 to $9,500 per ton.[165]

The same newspaper article reported that in 1881 the World Beater mine shipped five tons of ore to San Francisco at $250 per ton. In 1882, the World Beater was described as "a 60 foot shaft and a 75 foot tunnel…the

The Silver Chief Trail on Rogers Ridge is brushy and sometimes a bushwhack, but the views are fantastic. Hikers left to right are, Trent Barber, Dick Walp, Jack San Felice, and Clint Rowley. The photo, taken in April 2008, shows Four Peaks on the right side of the horizon.

ledge is seven feet wide of chloride ore, assaying from $90 to $4000. Native silver is found throughout. There are now on the dump about 40 tons of $120 ore." In 1883, *The Pinal Drill* reports were encouraging, "...taking out at the rate of one ton of ore per day to each man, some ore running from $400 to $1600 per ton. Each man cleans at least $150 per day." Newspaper reports were optimistic near year's end, "Work was started this month (September) on a new shaft at the top of the hill. It is now down 16-feet, disclosing a four-foot vein, with a pay streak twelve-inches wide, of very good ore." Optimism continued in October, "...the owners are determined to sink a shaft on the World Beater to the depth of 100 feet. This is the most promising mine in the district..."[166]

On July 17, 1889, James Rogers, Charles Ceslinger, and Tom Peterson, all of Pinal City, sold their mines in the Rogers District to James DeNoon Reymert. Reymert was a lawyer, an owner of *The Pinal Drill* newspaper, and a miner. The former towns and mines of DeNoon and Reymert, west of Picket Post Mountain, were named for him. Charles Ceslinger, a former mine owner, and other miners were employed by Reymert to develop the Rogers District mines under the supervision of Mr. Atchison from California.[167]

Iron Mountain from the southeast in December 1999. The steep route to the top of Iron Mountain follows the ridge line on the left side of the mountain all the way to the top. The West Pinto Trail (212) traverses a pass below the cliff in the center of the photo and goes right toward West Fork Pinto Creek.

Trip 37

IRON MOUNTAIN

Iron Mountain is the high point near Rogers Trough Trailhead. A trek up the abandoned trail to the top of Iron Mountain is rewarded with fine views of Superstition Mountain and Weavers Needle toward the west. To the east you look down into the West Fork Pinto Creek drainage where Pinto Peak is the prominent landmark.

ITINERARY

From Rogers Trough Trailhead, take the Reavis Ranch Trail, West Pinto Trail and a cross-country route up the abandoned Iron Mountain Trail to the top of Iron Mountain. Return the same way.

DIFFICULTY

Difficult hike. Elevation change is +1,230 feet one way. Not recommended for horses due to the steepness of the route, loose rocks, and no trail.

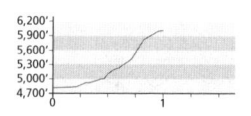

LENGTH and TIME

1.0 mile, 3 hours one way.

MAPS

Arizona USGS topo map NAD27: Iron Mountain. Superstition Wilderness Beartooth map, grid M13. Map 30.

FINDING THE TRAIL

Trailhead map is on page 247. Reavis Ranch Trail (109) starts at the north side of the Rogers Trough parking lot at the end of FR172A (N33° 25' 19.9", W111° 10' 21.7").

THE TRIP

Start on Map 30 on page 259. From Rogers Trough Trailhead parking lot [30-U, 0, 4840], go north on the Reavis Ranch Trail (109) to the intersection with the West Pinto Trail (212) [30-T, 0.1]. Take the West Pinto Trail, going easterly, up the hill. Just before you pass through a gate, you may find water in the concrete water trough to your left (north) within 200 feet. A brass marker on the concrete tank shows the 4,883-foot elevation. The trough may only have water when the rancher has cattle in this pasture, so you should not rely on this water source. Carry your own water or filter water from the wash just up the trail from here.

Continue up the West Pinto Trail to the first ridge [30-O, 0.6, 5230]. From here you leave the West Pinto Trail and go uphill on a mostly cross-country route, following the abandoned horse trail we named Iron Mountain Trail.

From the ridge on West Pinto Trail, [30-O, 0.6] you head uphill toward a yellow colored rock outcrop. A trail of use goes around either side of the rock outcrop. Look for rock cairns and signs of the abandoned trail that is still shown on the 1948 Iron Mountain USGS topo map. The old trail used short switchbacks to negotiate the steep hill. Unfortunately, the whitetail deer in the area have cut across the switchbacks making their own steep trails. The deer, erosion, and new vegetation have taken their toll on the trail, so you will find yourself on and off the old trail as you link the course of the trail and the deer paths together. We usually see some of these whitetail deer when traveling in this area near the West Pinto Trail.

View of Iron Mountain from FR650 in December 2007. The Iron Mountain route goes up the ridge in the center of the photo. The West Pinto Trail (212) goes through the notch on the right of the photo.

As you approach the top, you reach a ridge (N33° 25' 49.7", W111° 10' 4.2") where the route on the ground diverges from the trail on the Iron Mountain topo map. Your route now follows the crest of the ridge on a well-defined, but brushy trail, all the way to the top of the mountain [30-F, 1.0, 6066].

Two brass markers are located at the top of Iron Mountain. The Forest Service marker is dated 1938, and the Geologic Survey marker, about 30 feet away, is dated 1946. The top of the mountain is a flat grassy area dotted with alligator juniper trees. As the mountain slopes downward to the north, the open landscape exposes a fine view of White Mountain on the horizon. The rare hedgehog cactus, *Echinocereus Triglochidiatus Arizonicus*, is abundant up here and grows in large clumps in rocky outcrops with a deep scarlet flower blooming in May.

Return the same way. Use the yellow rock outcrop that you passed on the way up as your visual guide to stay on course as you descend to the West Pinto Trail.

HISTORY AND LEGENDS

Rancher Billy Martin said Rogers Spring [30-P] has been the best spring on the Martin Ranch. Early maps and records from the 1870s and 1880s show that this spring was called Kane Spring, with various spellings such as Can Spring and Cane Spring. Earlier prospectors had several names for this site—Millsite Claim, Kane Spring, and the Tunnel Site Claim.[168]

In 2004, Ron Feldman and the Historical Exploration and Treasures, L.L.C. (HEAT) obtained the first Treasure Trove Permit ever issued by the Tonto National Forest. The permit allowed them to excavate Rogers Spring [30-P] to look for evidence of pre-Anglo mining. The HEAT team's mining plans were based on reports written by prospector and treasure hunter Ted Cox. Since no wheeled vehicles are allowed in the Wilderness, the timbers for the head frame and all the mining equipment had to be carried about 0.4 mile from the Rogers Trough Trailhead to Rogers Spring. HEAT members reopened Cox's 1958 shaft, which had collapsed, and entered the tunnel from the top of Rogers Spring. As they dug out the eighteen-foot shaft and twenty-five-foot adit, they installed new supports and bracing. No precious metal was found, but the 2005 archaeology report by Erik Steinbach and Glen Rice concluded that mining took place in Rogers Canyon before 1860—the Mexican era.[169] After the project was complete, the head frame was disassembled, the site was restored to a natural appearance, and all the equipment and materials were carried out of the Wilderness. A photograph of the head frame is on page 36.

Jesse Feldman's book, *Jacob's Trail*, describes the HEAT project at Rogers Spring in great detail. See Chapter 2 of his book.

Trip 38

SILVER SPUR CABIN SITE

The West Pinto Trail takes you over the south ridge of Iron Mountain and into the West Fork Pinto Creek drainage. From the trail, you have good views of the surrounding mountains. The site of the Silver Spur cabin is a short distance off the trail where the remains of the cabin and corral can be found.

ITINERARY

From the Rogers Trough Trailhead, follow the Reavis Ranch Trail (109) to West Pinto Trail (212). Take West Pinto Trail over to West Fork Pinto Creek near the site of the former cabin. Return the same way.

DIFFICULTY

Moderate hike. Difficult horse ride. Elevation change is +990 and -1,590 feet one way.

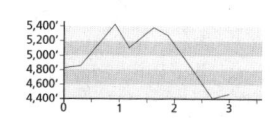

LENGTH and TIME

3.0 miles, 2 hours one way.

MAPS

Arizona USGS topo map NAD27: Iron Mountain. Superstition Wilderness Beartooth map, grids M13 to N13. Maps 33 and 34.

FINDING THE TRAIL

Trailhead map is on page 247. The Reavis Ranch Trail starts at the north end of the Rogers Trough parking lot (N33° 25' 19.9", W111° 10' 21.7").

THE TRIP

Start on Map 33 on page 281. From the Rogers Trough Trailhead [33-U, 0], take the Reavis Ranch Trail to the signed junction with the West Pinto Trail [33-T, 0.1]. The water trough at benchmark 4883 or the gully along the trail may have water. Be sure to purify all water before drinking. Do not disturb or uncouple the piping from Rogers Spring, since you may damage the pipe and not be able to repair it. The Martin Ranch relies on the spring water for horses, cattle, and wildlife.

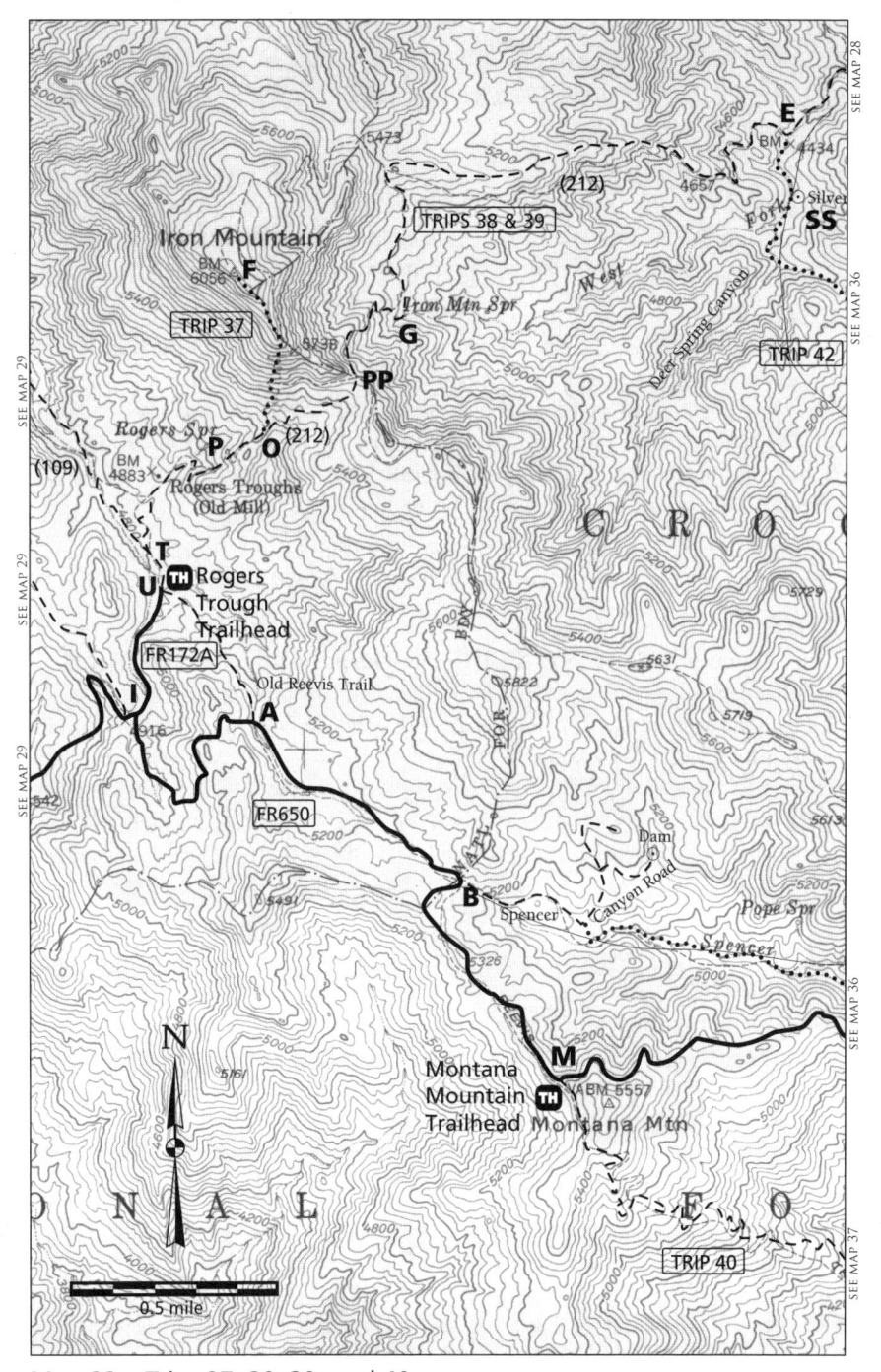

Map 33 – Trips 37, 38, 39, and 40.

As you climb toward the pass [33-PP, 0.9], watch for whitetail deer. We almost always see one or two deer around this area. In the early morning and evening, the deer come down Iron Mountain to get a drink at the spring or in Rogers Canyon.

At the pass and open gate [33-PP, 0.9], you leave the Globe Ranger District and enter the Tonto Basin Ranger District. This ridge is the divide for the Gila and Salt River watersheds. Water on the west side of the pass [33-PP] drains into the Gila River basin, and water on the east side drains into the Salt River basin.

The West Pinto Trail leads downhill from the pass [33-PP] to Iron Mountain Spring. The concrete water trough [33-G, 1.2] is out of service, so don't count on the spring for water. Some cattle brands and possibly cowboy initials are inscribed in the concrete such as Y Lazy Y, JH, RE, X Bar P, but we have not seen a date inscription. The only brand we recognized was the Y Lazy Y belonging to rancher J. Ney Miles.

The trap corral, which let cattle in, but not out, is a short distance on the trail beyond the spring. You may still be able to see part of the swinging gate that was closed with a coil spring.

From the corral [33-G, 1.2], the trail turns uphill for a short stretch. As disconcerting as this uphill turn might seem, it is best to stay on the trail rather than to bushwhack down the hillside. Jack took the ravine from Iron Mountain Spring, which is the headwaters of West Fork Pinto Creek, as a shortcut to the bottom of the hill. No obstacles stopped him, but ducking under the tree branches and scrambling on the leaf-covered ground made it a tiring shortcut. He has not repeated that trek and now sticks to the trail.

When the West Pinto Trail meets the bed of West Fork Pinto Creek [34-E, 2.8], the trail goes east (left) on the left bench of the normally dry creek. Our trip leaves the trail here and goes into the dry creek bed and heads up canyon (right). The benchmark—elevation 4,434 feet, dated 1946—on the south side of the creek bed is fairly easy to find. Continue up canyon about 0.2 mile to the corral and site of the Silver Spur cabin [34-SS, 3.0] (N33° 26' 6.9", W111° 08' 45.4"), which will be on a grassy bench to your left (east). Flat camping places nearby make this a good area for lunch or a longer stay, but there is no permanent water. Return the same way, or continue down canyon using the directions for Trip 39 (West Pinto Trail).

HISTORY AND LEGENDS

In 1991, the Forest Service surveyed the remains of the fire that consumed the one-room Silver Spur cabin. We don't have a date for the fire. Notable items found during the survey were a Franklin style wood stove and cans in the dump that dated through the 1950s. The surveyors measured the concrete

The wooden corral and stone water trough at the Silver Spur Cabin site [34-SS] in October 1999.

and stone cabin floor at 20 by 30 feet and observed that the building was wood framed with a corrugated steel roof and walls. They found wiring and insulators and speculated that an electric generator had been used there. The round corral, which survived the fire, was built in a double-post style with rail inserts and included a concrete and stone water trough.[170]

Jack Kennedy built the Silver Spur cabin, putting the construction date between 1947 and 1958 when Kennedy owned the ranch.[171] They piped water, probably from Deer Spring, one mile down Deer Spring Canyon from the south to the cabin and corral.[172]

Billy Martin said that Jack Kennedy spent a lot of time at the cabin. On a lion hunt, Billy and Teta Martin spent several nights there. They said the cabin had a steep tin-covered roof with tin on the sides of the building. Inside the cabin, the walls and ceiling were covered with tongue and groove wooden boards. Rats would get between the tin roof and the board ceiling and make a thumping sound that was kind of eerie. Teta said, "We could hear the rats running back and forth." Kennedy packed the refrigerator to the cabin on a mule coming up the West Pinto Trail from the Kennedy Ranch headquarters. When the Martins stayed at the cabin, it did not have electricity, so the refrigerator must have run on gas. Billy Martin said the cabin burned sometime after Kennedy sold the ranch in 1958.[173]

WEST PINTO TRAIL

West Pinto Trail follows the West Fork Pinto Creek from Iron Mountain downhill to Miles Trailhead. The creek is normally dry, but seasonal rains fill the rock potholes and support a nice canopy of sycamore, cottonwood, cypress, and Emory oak trees along its course. Three of the four connecting trails offer loop trip possibilities.

ITINERARY

From the Rogers Trough Trailhead, follow the Reavis Ranch Trail (109) a short distance to the West Pinto Trail (212). Follow West Pinto Trail to Miles Trailhead. Return the same way, or make a loop using Spencer Spring Trail (275); or Rock Creek Trail; or Campaign (256), Fire Line (118), and Reavis Ranch Trails.

DIFFICULTY

Moderate hike. Difficult horse ride. Elevation change is +1,160 and -2,520 feet one way.

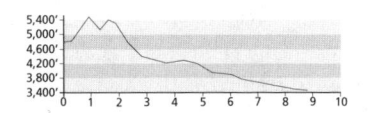

LENGTH and TIME

8.8 miles, 5.5 hours one way.

MAPS

Arizona USGS topo maps NAD27: Iron Mountain, Haunted Canyon. Superstition Wilderness Beartooth map, grids M13 to Q13. Maps 34, 28, and 25.

FINDING THE TRAIL

Trailhead map is on page 247. The Reavis Ranch Trail starts at the north end of the Rogers Trough parking lot (N33° 25' 19.9", W111° 10' 21.7").

THE HIKE

Start on Map 34 on page 285. From the Rogers Trough Trailhead [34-U, 0], follow the directions in Trip 38 (Silver Spur Cabin Site), for the first part of the trip. The cabin site and corral, which are only a short detour off the West Pinto Trail will be a worthwhile stop on your trip.

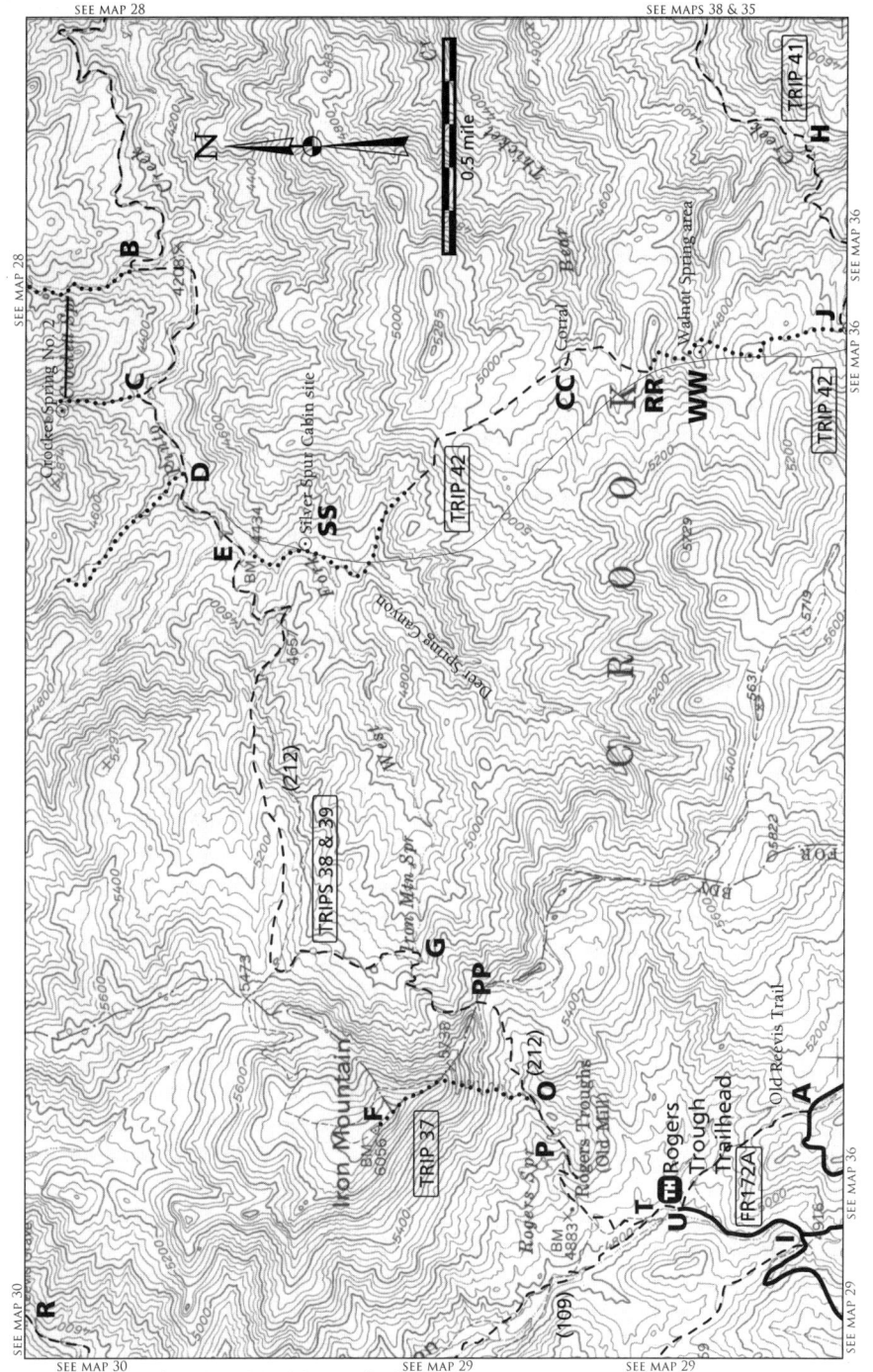

Map 34 – Trips 37, 38, 39, and 42.

No permanent water is available at the cabin site or nearby springs that are marked on the map. Be sure to carry enough water if the rains have not replenished the seasonal pothole water in the normally dry West Fork Pinto Creek.

After coming down the hill from Iron Mountain, the West Pinto Trail [34-E, 2.8] continues on the left bench of West Fork Pinto Creek—marked by rock cairns. Down canyon a short distance [34-D, 3.1], we took a side trip about 0.5 mile going north up the drainage that heads to Pinto Spring Trough (Pointer Spring). We found a small seep of water at our half-mile turnaround point. The bushwhacking was rough going, so we decided not to explore the old overgrown trail any farther.

The next drainage [28-C, 3.3] coming in from the north goes to Crocket Spring No. 2 where we found a good seep of water. This old trail was also overgrown. Some maps add a number to the Crocket Spring name, so we don't know for sure the correct name for the spring. We did not find evidence of the Crocket Spring, farther down canyon, that is shown on some maps in the bed of West Fork Pinto Creek.

The West Pinto Trail continues to meander down canyon, and just before reaching the 4,208 elevation benchmark, the trail turns left (north) and goes up a drainage [28-B, 3.8] that we call New Spring Wash. We followed an old trail up the drainage, finding water along the way and at our turnaround point where the trail disappeared in about 0.4 mile.

The West Pinto Trail, which has now left the creek bed, contours around the hills on the north side of West Fork Pinto Creek. Bushes may crowd the trail along here, making it hard to follow, although the tread of the trail is well-defined.

The trail crosses to the south side of West Fork Pinto Creek [28-A, 5.4] and moves up on the hillside to avoid the narrows. Just before reaching Spencer Spring Creek, the trail drops back to creek level, crosses normally dry Spencer Spring Creek, and meets the Spencer Spring Trail (275) at a wooden trail sign [25-M, 6.4] in an area called Oak Flat. Trailwise, a lot is going on here at Oak Flat with four trails coming into the flat. Nice campsites abound, and a large corral is available for stock animals, but there is no permanent source of water. See Trip 24 (West Pinto Trail to Oak Flat) for the details on the Oak Flat area.

At Oak Flat, the West Pinto Trail stays on the south side of the normally dry creek. Continuing east across the flat, you pass the wooden signs for the Campaign Trail (256) [25-N, 6.5] and the Cuff Button Trail (276) [25-L, 6.7]. Some older maps still show the former Pinto Peak Trail (213) coming into Oak Flat, but that name has been dropped, and the trail is now called the Campaign Trail (256).

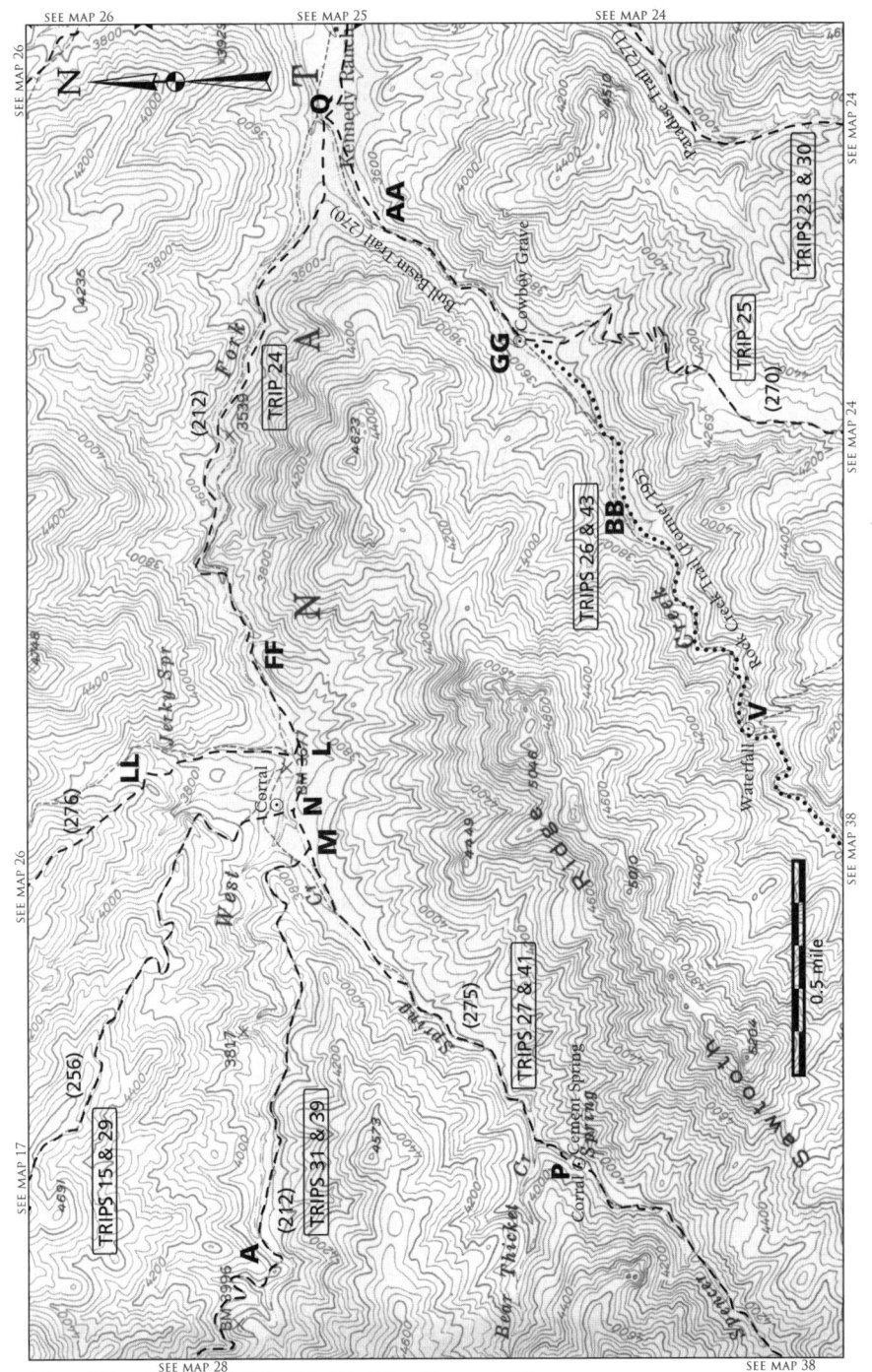

Map 35 – Trips 24, 26, 27, 31, 39, 41, and 43.

Rogers Trough Trailhead—Trip 39. West Pinto Trail

Former trail sign at the junction of Rock Creek and West Fork Pinto Creek reflects the old trail names. The Pinto Peak Trail (213) is now named the Campaign Trail (256). Spencer Peak Trail should have read Spencer Spring Trail (275). The mileages, rounded to the nearest mile, are correct. Photo was taken in April 1997.

Beyond Oak Flat, the trail meanders from bench to bench and reaches the normally dry Rock Creek at the junction with the Bull Basin Trail (270), which is marked with a wooden trail sign [25-Q, 8.3]. Note that the former Rock Creek Trail (195) has been re-named the Bull Basin Trail at this junction. The West Pinto Trail continues east, skirting the meadow on the right (south) side and ending at the Miles Trailhead sign [25-Z, 8.8], not far from the barn. Return the same way. Consider a loop trip from West Pinto Trail.

LOOP TRIPS

(1) From Miles Trailhead [25-Z, 8.8] take Bull Basin Trail (270) and Rock Creek Trail to FR650 [38-I, 13.8] and return to Rogers Trough Trailhead [36-U] on FR650 and FR172A for a total loop trip of 19.2 miles.

(2) From Oak Flat [25-M, 6.4], take Spencer Spring Trail (275) to FR650 [36-C, 10.1] and return to Rogers Trough Trailhead [36-U] on FR650 and FR172A for a total loop trip of 13.6 miles.

(3) From Oak Flat [25-M, 6.4], take Campaign Trail (256), Fire Line Trail (118) [17-I, 10.8], and Reavis Ranch Trail (109) [18-J, 14.1] to Rogers Trough Trailhead [30-U] for a total loop trip of 20.3 miles.

Montana Mountain Trailhead

From US60 at Idaho Road in Apache Junction, go east for 15 miles on US60 to Florence Junction. Two miles east of Florence Junction on US60, between mileposts 214 and 215, turn north on Queen Valley Road for 1.8 miles to FR357 (Hewitt Station Road), go right 3 miles to FR172. If you are coming from Superior, pick up FR357 just west of the Arboretum between mileposts 222 and 223 and take FR357 for 5 miles to FR172. Go north 9 miles on FR172 to the junction with FR172A. Go right about 3.6 miles on four-wheel-drive FR172A to the signed junction with FR650. Take FR650 for 2 miles to the Montana Mountain Trailhead. A high-clearance vehicle is required on FR172 and FR172A. Wet weather conditions may dictate four-wheel-drive on FR172A. FR650 is always four-wheel-drive.

FINDING THE TRAILHEAD

Montana Mountain Trailhead is about 2.4 miles southeast of Rogers Trough Trailhead on FR172A and FR650. Sharp turns and a steep grade require four-wheel-drive on FR650. In the winter at higher elevations, shady sections of FR650 may have ice and snow. Heavy rains sometimes wash out FR172A, and conditions may require four-wheel-drive until the road is repaired. Montana Mountain Trailhead (N33° 24' 19.6", W111° 09' 22.3") is marked by a fallen down trail sign that reads *Trail 509*.

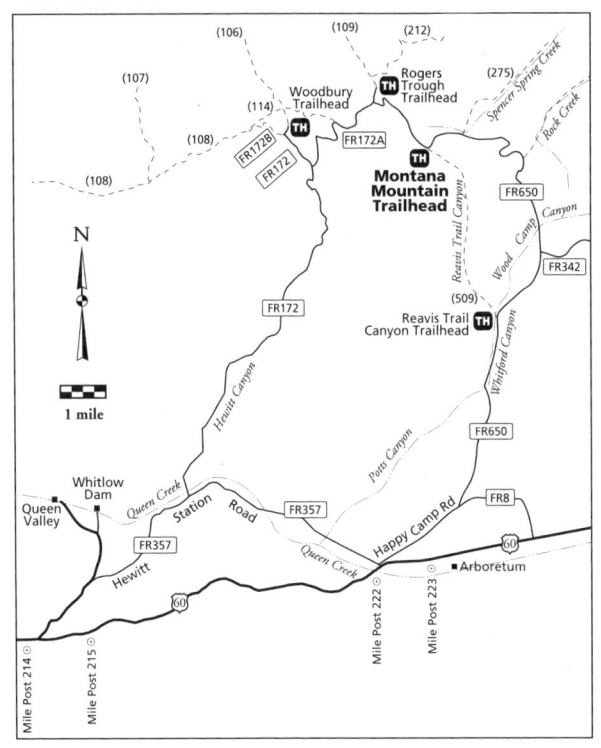

A small rock cairn marks the Reavis Canyon Trail (509) heading to the right. Although FR650 is fairly flat and in good shape here, other sections are steep and require four-wheel-drive. The view is to the east with the top of Montana Mountain on the horizon. Photo was taken in November 2007.

FACILITIES

Montana Mountain Trailhead does not have any facilities. Bring your own water.

THE TRAILS

Several trails start from FR650, and we have grouped them all under the Montana Mountain Trailhead. Reavis Canyon Trail (509) heads southeast from the Montana Mountain Trailhead, two other trails begin several miles to the east on FR650, and a trip using Spencer Canyon Road starts a short distance to the west.

From the vehicle pullout [36-M, 0] at the Montana Mountain Trailhead, Trip 40, Reavis Canyon Trail, takes you 5.1 miles down the mountain to Reavis Trail Canyon Trailhead [37-K] where the Reavis Canyon Trail meets FR650 again. This is part of the Arizona Trail.

The signed junction on FR650 for the Spencer Spring Trail (275) (N33° 24' 23.0", W111° 08' 26.6") [36-C] is 1.1 miles east on FR650 from the

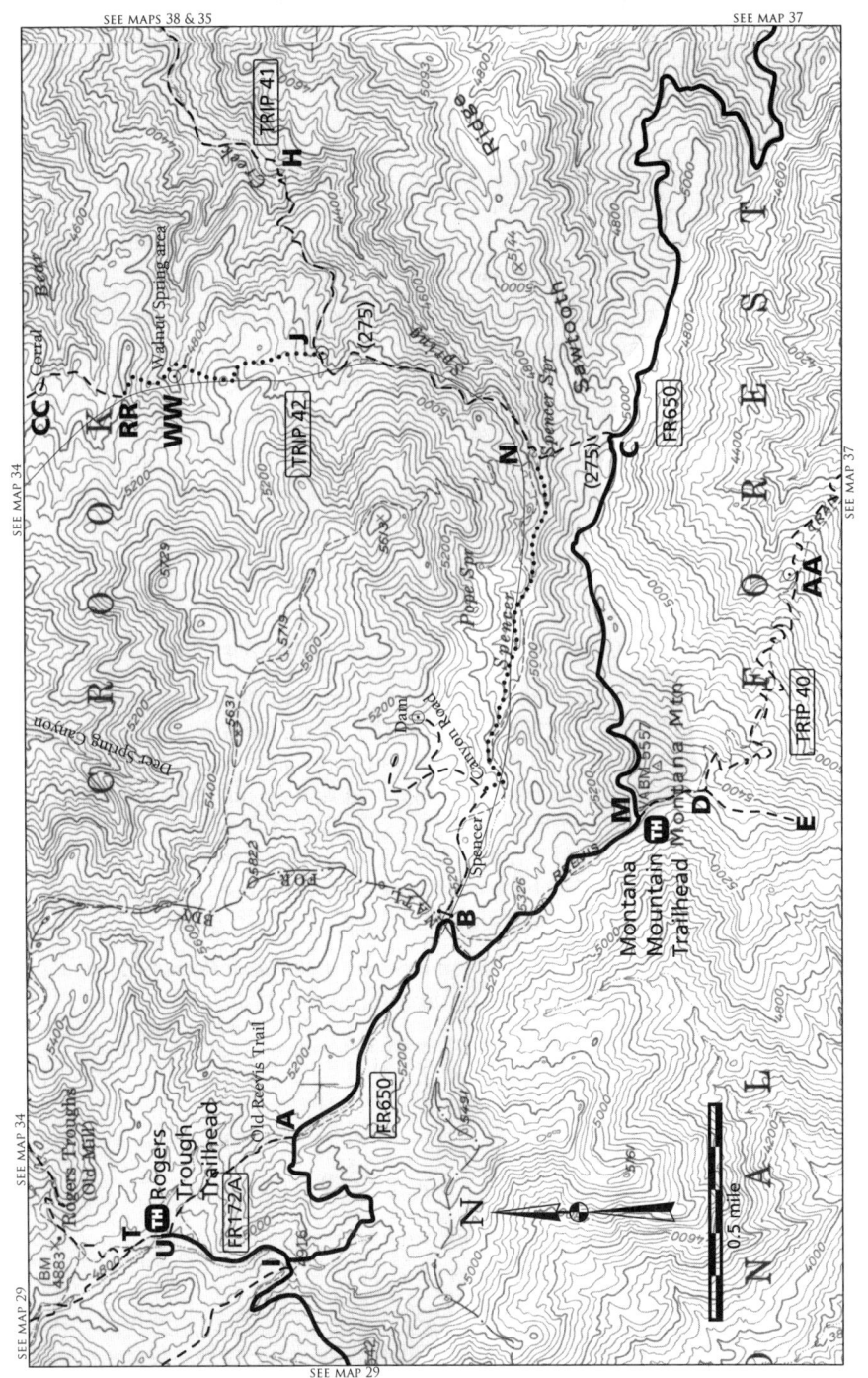

Map 36 – Trips 40, 41, and 42.

Montana Mountain Trailhead. Trip 41, Spencer Spring Trail, takes you from FR650 to Oak Flat [25-M] where Spencer Spring Trail meets West Fork Pinto Creek.

The unsigned junction with the Spencer Canyon Road (N33° 24' 43.6", W111° 09' 36.8") [36-B] is 0.7 mile west of the Montana Mountain Trailhead on FR650. The Spencer Canyon Road is closed to vehicles. Trip 42 (1891 Road Survey Route) takes you from the Spencer Canyon Road [36-B] over to West Fork Pinto Creek below Iron Mountain [34-E].

The unsigned junction for the Rock Creek Trail (N33° 24' 00.8", W111° 07' 22.6") [38-I] is 3.0 miles east of the Montana Mountain Trailhead on FR650. Trip 43 (Rock Creek from FR650) takes you to Miles Trailhead [25-Z] on the Rock Creek Trail, Bull Basin Trail, and West Pinto Trail.

You can use the segment of the Old Reevis Trail from FR650 [36-A] to Rogers Trough Trailhead [36-U] to shorten your trips between trailheads. Look for the shortcut trail at a ravine crossing on FR650 (N33° 25' 02.6", W111° 10' 07.2") [36-A] and uphill (N33° 25' 17.9", W111° 10' 19.2") from the hitching post at Rogers Trough Trailhead near [36-U].

HISTORY AND LEGENDS

The 750-mile Arizona Trail, extending from Mexico to Utah, passes through the Superstition Wilderness. Coming from the south, the Arizona Trail climbs Montana Mountain on Reavis Canyon Trail (509), meets FR650, and enters the Superstition Wilderness at Rogers Trough Trailhead from FR172A. In the Wilderness, the Arizona Trail follows the Reavis Ranch Trail (109), Reavis Gap Trail (117), and Two Bar Ridge Trail (119). The Arizona Trail exits the Wilderness on FR83 and continues on Cottonwood Trail (120) and Thompson Trail (121) to Roosevelt Lake Bridge.

The following list will help you link our trip descriptions with each segment of the Arizona Trail through the Superstition Wilderness.

Reavis Canyon Trail (509)	Trip 40 in reverse
Reavis Ranch Trail (109)	Trip 34
Reavis Gap Trail (117)	The last part of Trip 18 in reverse
Two Bar Ridge Trail (119)	Trip 20
Cottonwood Trail (120)	Trip 11 in reverse
Thompson Trail (121)	Trip 10

REAVIS CANYON TRAIL

Great views to the south at the beginning of this trip near the top of Montana Mountain make this an exhilarating trip on part of the Arizona Trail. The trail traces the 1880s pioneers' route during the prosperous days of the Rogers Camp mines.

ITINERARY

From FR650 at the top of the mountain, take Reavis Canyon Trail (509) downhill to FR650 at the bottom of the mountain. Return the same way or make a vehicle shuttle on four-wheel-drive FR650. An optional trip starts at the bottom of Montana Mountain and follows the creek for about 3 miles.

DIFFICULTY

Moderate hike and difficult horse ride. Trail is obscure in some places. Elevation change is +70 and -2,560 feet one way. The optional trip along the creek is rated easy for hikers, and rated moderate for riders.

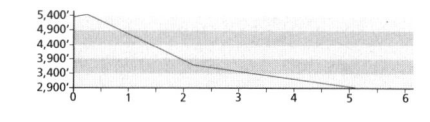

LENGTH and TIME

5.1 miles, 4 hours one way.

MAPS

Arizona USGS topo maps NAD27: Iron Mountain, Picketpost Mountain. Superstition Wilderness Beartooth map, grids N14 to N16. Map 37.

FINDING THE TRAIL

Trailhead map is on page 289. Start on FR650 at the Montana Mountain Trailhead [37-M] (N33° 24' 19.6", W111° 09' 22.3"), just west of the top of Montana Mountain, which is about 2.4 miles southeast of Rogers Trough Trailhead [36-U] on FR172A and FR650. A broken sign, *Trail 509*, east of the trail junction on FR650 and a small rock cairn on the south side of FR650 may help you find the Reavis Canyon Trail (509). About 100 yards, going south, on Trail (509), a wooden sign reads, *Reavis Can. Tr. 580, Road 650 5*. This is Trail (509) even though the sign reads (580).

THE TRIP

Start on Map 37 on page 296. This trip is not inside the Superstition Wilderness, but we included Trip 40 since it is a worthwhile trek, physically the same mountain range, and part of the Arizona Trail. Begin on FR650 at the rock cairn [37-M, 0], marking the start of Reavis Canyon Trail. The trail goes around the west side of Montana Mountain just below its peak. At the saddle [37-D, 0.2], a spur trail goes about 0.1 mile out on the point [37-E] where you get good views across the southern range of the Superstition Mountains. You can find flat camping spots among the trees along the spur trail, but the camps do not have water.

From the saddle [37-D, 0.2], you can see the gate in the fence where the switchback trail begins its downhill course into Reavis Trail Canyon, which is the western arm of Whitford Canyon. The trail traverses a steep ridge with switchbacks. Down the hill, three tall posts mark the location of a former gate [37-AA, 1.1] in a fence on the left side of the trail.

Near the bottom of Montana Mountain, the trail enters the bed of the canyon at a smooth rock crossing [37-G, 1.9]. Farther along the trail, look for four prehistoric bedrock grind holes in a boulder on the left (northeast) side of the trail [37-H, 2.2]. Continuing south, the trail closely follows the flat benches along the normally dry watercourse of the canyon.

Two riparian areas along the trail at 3.1 and 3.3 miles offer a shady place to stop on a hot day. At about the 3.6 mile mark, you start to see signs of the old road, and by mile 4.4, when you pass through a green metal gate, the road is well-defined.

A large stone corral on the east side of the creek may have been an 1880s woodcutters camp [37-J, 4.8]. A short distance farther south, Wood Camp Canyon comes in from the left and combines with Reavis Trail Canyon to form Whitford Canyon. The large metal *Arizona Trail* sign signals the end of this trip at the Reavis Trail Canyon Trailhead [37-K, 5.1]. Return the same way, make a loop trip, or use a shuttle vehicle on FR650. Sections of FR650 require four-wheel-drive.

OPTIONAL TRIP FROM THE BOTTOM OF MONTANA MOUNTAIN

You can make an easy trip on the Reavis Canyon Trail (509) by starting at the bottom of Montana Mountain. This is the last part of the trip described above—done in the reverse direction.

See page 289 for the trailhead map. The best way to get to the start of the optional trip is to take FR357 from US60 between mileposts 222 and 223 and continue on FR8 (Happy Camp Road) and FR650 to the metal *Arizona Trail* sign [37-K, 0] (N33° 21' 09.9", W111° 07' 53.1"). A high clearance vehicle—and sometimes four-wheel-drive—is required for a rough section of road in the creek bed just north of Cottonwood Camp and Corral on FR650.

The trip mileages going in the northerly direction are: *Arizona Trail* sign [37-K, 0], stone corral [37-J, 0.3], green gate [0.7], riparian areas [1.8 and 2.0], bedrock grind holes [37-H, 2.9], and slick rock crossing [37-G, 3.2] at the turnaround place. Return the same way.

HISTORY AND LEGENDS

A portion of the 1882 mining claims map by Gustavus Cox is shown on page 273. In the Rogers Canyon area, he labels the Reavis Ranch Trail as *Trail to Reeves Ranch*. Although not shown on the map on page 273, Cox identifies the trail in Reavis Trail Canyon as *Trail from Pinal*. The Florence USGS topo map, surveyed in 1900, shows an unnamed trail where we estimate Trail 509 to be located and labels the canyon as *Reevis Trail Canyon*.[174]

The 1948 edition of the Iron Mountain USGS topo map names Reavis Canyon Trail (109) as *Reevis Trail*. The *Reevis Trail* noted on the map continues northwest from the Montana Mountain area, follows the approximate course of FR650 to [36-A], takes the Old Reevis Trail to Rogers Trough [36-U], and then parallels the present day Reavis Ranch Trail (109) to Reavis Valley. FR650 is not shown on the 1948 map.

The 1948 edition of the Picketpost Mountain USGS topo map shows Reavis Trail Canyon, but the trail is unnamed. The stone corral [37-J] is located at the junction of Reavis Trail Canyon and Wood Camp Canyon where Whitford Canyon begins. Wood Camp Canyon, shown on the map, might have received its name from a woodcutter's camp and stone building about two miles upstream from this junction. The wood was used to run the Silver King smelter at Pinal City in the late 1800s.

We found two examples of early pioneers using the Montana Mountain route to reach Rogers Canyon. Both of those groups, which continued to Reavis Ranch, probably climbed Montana Mountain through Reavis Trail Canyon on the course of Trail 509.[175]

In 1883, J. D. Reymert, editor of *The Pinal Drill* newspaper, described his trip to Reavis Ranch. His group traveled from Pinal City through Happy Camp and on to the wood station, where the packers loaded burros with wood for the smelter in Pinal City. Wood station may have been the location of the present day stone corral [37-J]. The wagon road from Happy Camp to the wood station had been completed sometime during the year before Reymert made this trip.

From the wood station, which was the end of the road in 1883, Reymert's party started the climb on a trail up Mount Cachimba (Montana

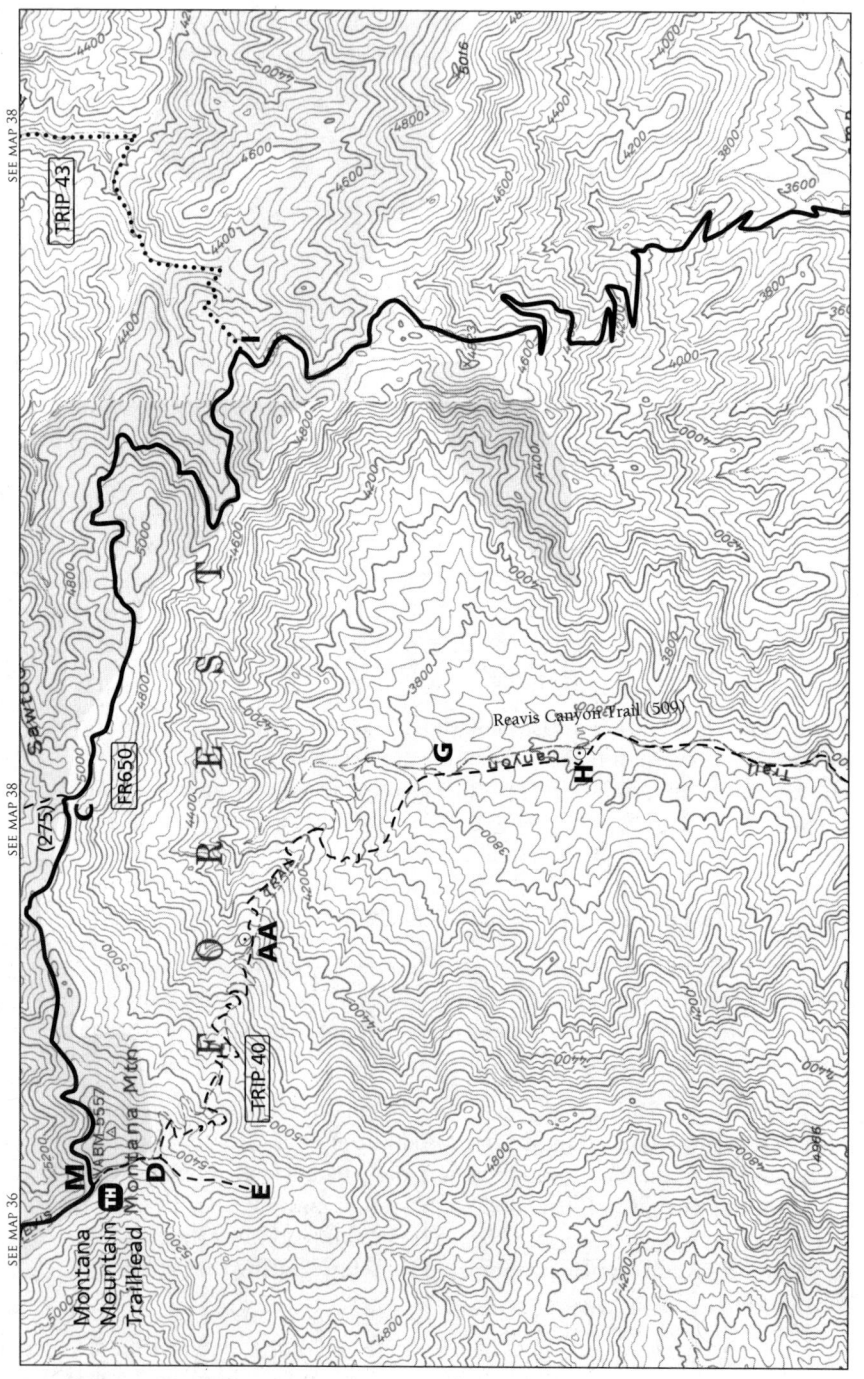

Map 37 – Trips 40 and 43.

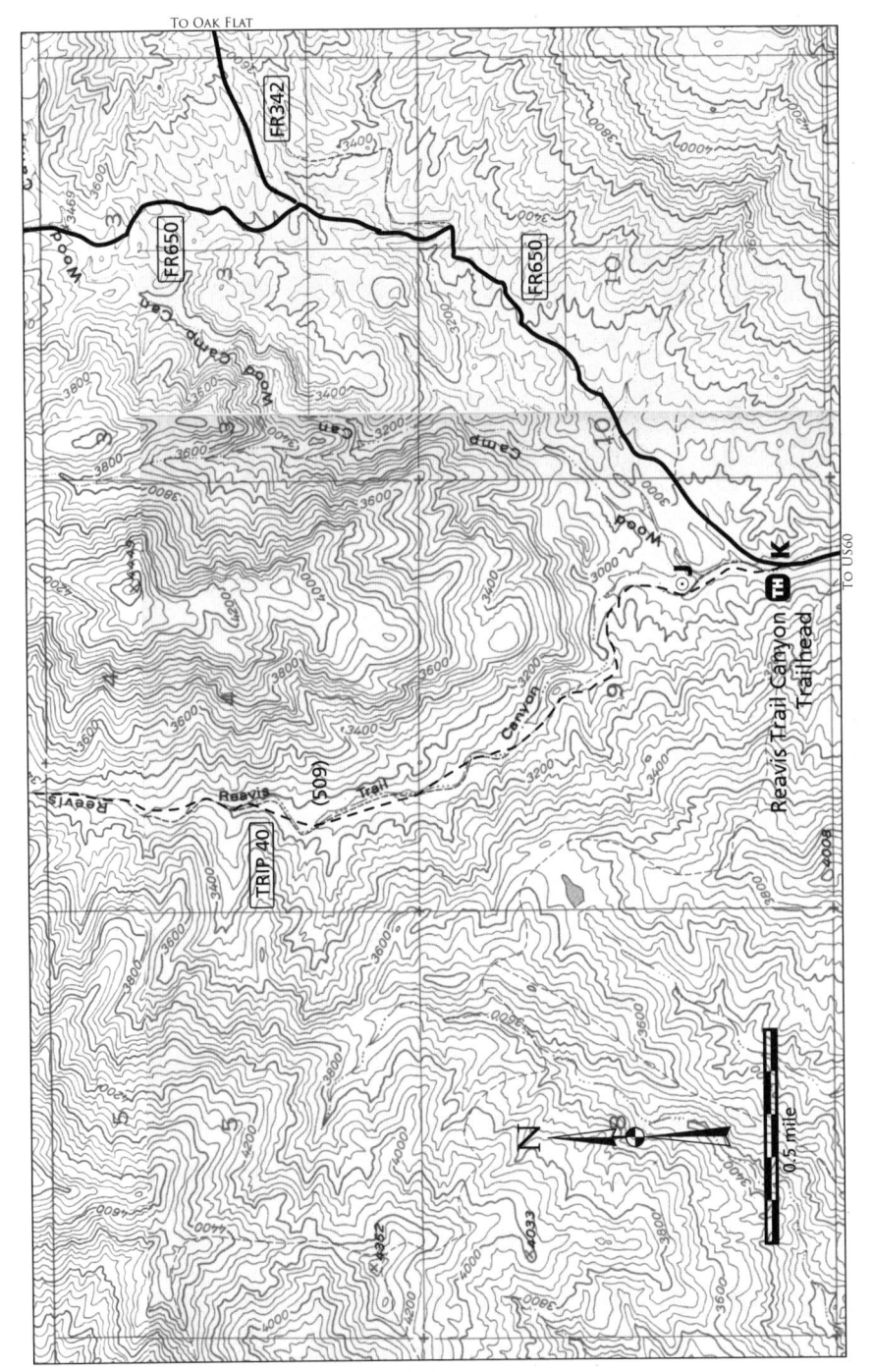

Map 37 continued – Trips 40 and 43.

The Reavis Canyon Trail passes through this stone corral [37-J] in Whitford Canyon, which could be the location of the wood station that J. D. Reymert wrote about in his 1883 newspaper story. Photo was taken in December 2007.

Mountain). Picket Post Mountain was named Tordillo Peak then, which they could see from the high places on their ride. From Rogers Camp (present day Rogers Trough Trailhead area), they continued on the Reavis Ranch Trail to Reavis Valley for their visit with Elisha Reavis.

Matt Cavaness and a party of men and women made a similar trip over Reymert's route after Elisha Reavis invited them to visit his ranch. Matt Cavaness, in his memoirs, and *The Pinal Drill* articles indicate that they left Pinal City early in the morning on August 30, 1883, traveled by horse and mule, and arrived at the Reavis place about 2 p.m. the same day. See Trip 34 (Rogers Trough to Reavis Ranch) for more stories about the Cavaness party's visit with Elisha Reavis.

Trail 509, which is outside the Superstition Wilderness, is open to mountain bike riders. In 2003, Mark Trainor documented one of his mountain bike trips and suggested that a loop ride is best made by riding up FR650 from Reavis Trail Canyon Trailhead to the top of Montana Mountain and then taking Trail 509 down the mountain. He also made a longer loop bike ride from Picket Post Trailhead on the Arizona Trail by coming up Hewitt Canyon on FR172, FR172A, and FR650 to the top of Montana Mountain. Neither of those bike rides are for the faint-hearted.[176]

Trip 41

SPENCER SPRING TRAIL

The Spencer Spring Trail takes you downhill to Oak Flat and the West Fork Pinto Creek. This seldom used trail links FR650 with the more widely used trails from Miles Trailhead. The upper end of Spencer Spring Creek features seasonal waterfalls while the lower end near Oak Flat is characterized by a thick canopy of sycamore, cypress, and oak trees.

ITINERARY

From the Montana Mountain Trailhead, continue east on FR650 to the signed junction with Spencer Spring Trail (275). Follow Spencer Spring Trail to West Pinto Trail at Oak Flat. Return the same way, or make a loop trip through Miles Trailhead or Rogers Trough Trailhead.

DIFFICULTY

Moderate for hikers and difficult for horse riders. Elevation change is +110 and -1,410 feet one way.

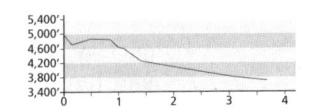

LENGTH and TIME

3.7 miles, 2.5 hours one way.

MAPS

Arizona USGS topo maps NAD27: Iron Mountain, Haunted Canyon. Superstition Wilderness Beartooth map, grids N14 to P13. Maps 36 and 25.

FINDING THE TRAIL

Trailhead map is on page 289. The trip starts 1.1 miles east of Montana Mountain on FR650 [36-C] at the Spencer Spring Trail (275) (N33° 24' 23.0", W111° 08' 26.6") leading to Spencer Spring. Driving east on FR650, you will see the *Trail 275* sign a few yards east of the trail junction.

THE TRIP

Start on Map 36 on page 291. Begin on FR650 [36-C, 0] on the signed Spencer Spring Trail (275). Go north, down the hill, to the Spencer Spring cement water-trough [36-N, 0.2]. The water trough has not been maintained, so don't count on it for water. You might find water at the spring, which is about 75 yards up canyon just beyond a large sycamore tree. From the Y Lazy Y inscribed cement trough, pass through the two wooden fence posts and follow the Spencer Spring Trail northeast. The trail soon drops down to creek level [36-H, 1.4] after bypassing some waterfall sections of the creek.

The trail meanders across the course of the creek as the trip heads north. Cement Spring [25-P, 2.6] and a corral on the right (east) side of the trail were in disrepair when we visited, and it did not look like it would be easy to get water out of the spring box.

The Spencer Spring Trail ends when the trail meets the West Pinto Trail (212) at Oak Flat [25-M, 3.7]. See Trip 24 (West Pinto Trail to Oak Flat) for things to look for in the Oak Flat area. Trip 27 (Spencer Spring Creek) describes the above trip from Miles Trailhead. Return the same way, or you have two choices for a loop trip as described below:

(1) From Oak Flat [25-M], you can travel 2.4 miles going right (east) on West Pinto Trail (212) to Miles Trailhead [25-Z]. For a tough loop trip, you could take the Bull Basin Trail (270) and the abandoned Rock Creek Trail going up Rock Creek and ending at FR650 [38-I]. The trip up Rock Creek adds 6.4 miles to the trip. The walk on FR650 from Rock Creek Trail [38-I] to Spencer Spring Trail [36-C] is another 1.9 miles to complete the loop.

(2) From Oak Flat [25-M], you can travel 6.4 miles going left (west) to Rogers Trough Trailhead [34-U] on the West Pinto Trail (212) and Reavis Ranch Trail (109). A shuttle vehicle (truck or mountain bike) can be used to complete the loop from Rogers Trough Trailhead [34-U] to the starting place on FR650 [36-C] in another 3.5 miles.

Spencer Spring cement water trough [36-N]. The ranchers pronounced the brand as YY, but it was drawn as Y Lazy Y. The date inscribed on the trough is 6-21-36. Photo was taken in March 1997.

Trip 42

1891 ROAD SURVEY ROUTE

This trip traces a section of the 1891 Mesa to Globe Road survey. The trek covers wild and little visited country without a fixed route. Modern day explorers will revel in the thought of finding evidence of this survey.

ITINERARY

This is a loop trip. Start on FR650 and follow the Spencer Canyon Road downhill. When the road heads uphill, follow the small wash going right (southeast) to Spencer Spring Creek. Follow the creek to Spencer Spring cement troughs. Pick up the Spencer Spring Trail, and then go cross-country to connect with West Fork Pinto Creek near Silver Spur Cabin site. Return on the West Pinto Trail (212) to Rogers Trough Trailhead. Take the Old Reevis Trail and FR650 back to the Spencer Canyon Road.

DIFFICULTY

Very difficult for hikers. Probably not doable for riders. Mostly no trail. For seasoned hikers with a passion for exploration. Elevation change is ±2530 feet.

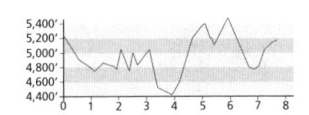

LENGTH and TIME

7.7 miles, 11 hours loop trip.

MAPS

Arizona USGS topo map NAD27: Iron Mountain. Superstition Wilderness Beartooth map, grids N14, N13, M13, and M14. Maps 34 and 36.

FINDING THE ROUTE

Trailhead map is on page 289. The trip starts 0.7 mile northwest of Montana Mountain Trailhead on FR650 [36-B] at the Spencer Canyon Road (N33° 24' 43.6", W111° 09' 36.8"). The Spencer Canyon Road is closed to vehicles, but the steep and eroded road is open to foot and stock traffic.

THE TRIP

Start on Map 36 on page 291. The object of this trip is to trace the route of the 1891 Mesa to Globe Road survey in the region southeast of Iron

Mountain. The History and Legends section, on the following pages, will give you the background information for this trek.

From FR650 [36-B, 0], go down the Spencer Canyon Road. When the road heads uphill (N33° 24' 39.1", W111° 09' 17.7"), take the small wash to the right (southeast) to Spencer Spring Creek. Follow the bed of the creek (no trail) to the abandoned water troughs [36-N, 1.2] where you will intersect the unsigned Spencer Spring Trail (275). You can shorten the trip by beginning on FR650 [36-C] at the signed Spencer Spring Trail (275). See Trip 41 for those details.

Spencer Spring has not been maintained, so don't count on the trough for water. If you follow the water pipe up canyon, you might find water at

The trail shown on this map is part of our Trip 42 (1891 Road Survey Route). The trail comes from the west (A), turns north near Spencer Spring (B), curves into West Fork Pinto Creek (C), and continues east. Fraser's Ranch on the left is present-day JF Ranch. Fraser's Ranch at the top is now Reavis Ranch. USGS topographic map, Florence, Arizona, surveyed 1900, March 1902 edition, reprinted 1917. We added the north arrow and letters A, B, and C. Courtesy of Arizona State Archives, Map Room.

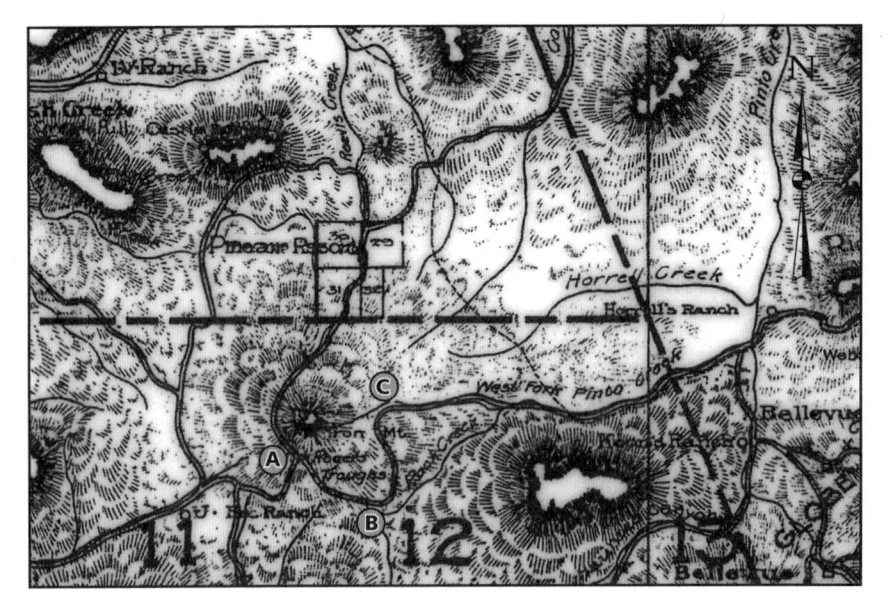

The road shown on this map is part of our Trip 42 (1891 Road Survey Route). The road goes through Rogers Trough (A), heads southeast, turns north before reaching Rock Creek (B), drops into West Fork Pinto Creek (C), and follows the creek east. Pineair Resort was near Reavis Ranch. Horrell's Ranch (JH6) was on Pinto Creek. Map of Central Arizona by F. N. Holmquist, 1916. We added the north arrow and letters A, B, and C. Courtesy of Arizona State Archives, Map Room.

the spring box. From the YY inscribed cement water trough, Trail 275 goes between the two large wooden posts and then heads uphill to the northeast.

At the ruins of a wood and sheet metal stock feeder, [36-J, 1.9] (N33° 25' 00.1", W111° 08' 14.4") this trip continues north going cross-country. The cross-country portion of the trip tries to follow a trail drawn on the Florence, Arizona, USGS topographical map that was surveyed in 1900 (opposite page). It is rough traveling (no trail) because of the thick vegetation. We show a dashed line on the map where we found the overgrown trail, otherwise the trip is shown as a dotted line (cross-country route). We represent the trail from the Florence USGS map as a thin solid-line on Maps 33, 34, and 36.

The route passes the Walnut Spring area [34-WW, 2.3], which we did not locate, but we placed the spring on the map according to the position on the Superstition Wilderness map by the Tonto National Forest. From the top of a ridge [34-RR, 2.5], we located an overgrown horse trail and followed the faint trail to a wood and wire corral [34-CC, 2.8] (N33° 25' 34.4", W111° 08' 19.7").

The route drops into an upper arm of West Fork Pinto Creek, which we named Deer Spring Canyon. Water collects in the potholes after a rain, but you will not find permanent water here. The Silver Spur Cabin site is a short distance down canyon on the right (east) bench [34-SS, 3.8] (N33° 26' 6.9", W111° 08' 45.4"). Connect with the West Pinto Trail (212) in West Fork Pinto Creek [34-E, 3.9] (N33° 26' 13.6", W111° 08' 47.1"), which is normally dry. See Trip 38 (Silver Spur Cabin Site) for a description of the cabin site.

From the junction with West Pinto Trail [34-E, 3.9], take West Pinto Trail to Reavis Ranch Trail (109) and Rogers Trough Trailhead [34-U, 6.7]. The remaining leg of the trip leaves Rogers Trough Trailhead on Old Reevis Trail (N33° 25' 17.9", W111° 10' 19.2"), connects with FR650 [36-A, 7.1] (N33° 25' 02.6", W111° 10' 07.2"), and ends at the beginning [36-B, 7.7].

HISTORY AND LEGENDS

Historian Tom Kollenborn found the first mention of the Mesa to Globe wagon road in the July 17, 1880, *Pinal Drill* newspaper. A group of men attempted to build a toll road that passed by the Marlow Ranch and went up Fraser Canyon. Lack of funds ended that project.[177] A decade later, newspaper stories from October through December 1891 describe another attempt at the Mesa to Globe Road.[178]

On horse rides out of the Quarter Circle U Ranch on the Old Coffee Flat Trail, Jack Carlson and Howard Horinek noticed circles of rocks that were probably remnants of the markers from the 1891 survey. The newspaper reported that the road was chained and staked every 200 feet.

The 1891 survey started at Desert Wells, went by Marlow Ranch, Little Cottonwood Gulch (Reeds Water), Fraser Ranch, Iron Mountain, Masten's Peak (Pinto Peak), Campaign Creek, and Narron Ranch (Reevis Mountain School). Leaving Campaign Creek 4 miles below Narron Ranch, the survey route crossed the mesas by the William Gann Ranch (Spring Creek Ranch), crossed Pinto Creek one-half mile below the Pinto Creek Box, and connected with the Salt River to Globe road 19 miles from Globe. A variation of this route went from Masten's Peak (Pinto Peak), continued east of Campaign Creek, and intersected the lower route at William Gann's Ranch (Spring Creek Ranch). That second route might have used West Fork Pinto Creek.

Holmquist's 1916 map on page 303 shows a broad line for the route of the Mesa to Globe Road, but his map is only useful as a general guide since the landmarks are not accurately placed. The Florence Quadrangle, Arizona, USGS map on page 302, surveyed in 1900, on the other hand, shows a trail winding from Spencer Spring, to the Silver Spur Cabin site, and into West Fork Pinto Creek.[179] This is the route we overlaid on the Iron Mountain USGS map (thin solid line on maps 34, 36, and 38) and the route we picked for this trip. Considering the rough terrain on our Trip 42 route, we speculate that the 1891 survey party did no more than ride the existing trails here and propose a general plan for the Mesa to Globe Road.

Trip 43

Rock Creek from FR650

The old Rock Creek Trail follows Rock Creek from FR650 to the former Miles Ranch. Although a major ranch trail for more than one hundred years, the trail has fallen into disrepair. Great views of Sawtooth Ridge, an old corral, and a seasonal waterfall along the tree-lined canyon—featuring cypress, oak, and sycamore—make this a worthwhile trip.

ITINERARY

From FR650, 3 miles east of Montana Mountain Trailhead, take the Rock Creek Trail northeast. Connect with Bull Basin and West Pinto Trails and end at Miles Trailhead. Return the same way, or make a loop trip or shuttle.

DIFFICULTY

Moderate hike. Not recommended for horse riders due to the fallen trees and a few rough creek crossings. Elevation change is +60 and -1,150 feet one way.

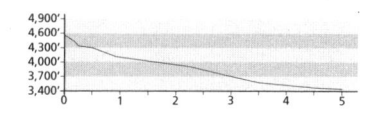

LENGTH and TIME

5.0 miles, 5 hours one way.

MAPS

Arizona USGS topo maps NAD27: Haunted Canyon, Iron Mountain. Superstition Wilderness Beartooth map, grids O14 to P13. Maps 38 and 25.

FINDING THE TRAIL

Trailhead map is on page 289. Start on FR650 at the unsigned south end of Rock Creek Trail (N33° 24' 00.8", W111° 07' 22.6"), which is marked by a small rock cairn. This trail junction [38-I] is about 3 miles east of Montana Mountain Trailhead [37-M] on FR650. You can park a vehicle about 0.4 mile east of the Rock Creek Trail or 0.3 mile west on FR650—no room to leave a vehicle where the Rock Creek Trail meets FR650.

THE TRIP

Approaching Rock Creek from FR650 might not be practical for many people, but we included the directions for those who want to explore the edge of the Wilderness from FR650. These GPS coordinates and the connecting trip descriptions will make your planning easier for the loop trips from the Miles Trailhead or the Rogers Trough Trailhead that use FR650.

Start on Map 38 on page 307. Begin on FR650 at the rock cairn [38-I, 0] marking the south end of the Rock Creek Trail. The trail follows a ridge down to Rock Creek and then stays fairly close to the seasonal creek. The Tonto Forest has abandoned the trail (former trail number 195) and no longer performs trail maintenance on it. As a result, fallen trees and encroaching vegetation make the traveling difficult—so plan for a slower trip and enjoy what is left of this historic trail.

Here are your Rock Creek Trail waypoints starting from FR650:

Rock cairn on FR650	[38-I, 0]	(N33° 24' 00.8", W111° 07' 22.6")
Y Bar B Corral	[38-M, 1.8]	(N33° 24' 56.2", W111° 06' 24.0")
Waterfall	[38-V, 2.6]	(N33° 25' 22.6", W111° 05' 57.0")
Bull Basin Trail	[25-GG, 3.8]	(N33° 25' 48.3", W111° 05' 01.4")
West Pinto Trail	[25-Q, 4.5]	(N33° 26' 14.5", W111° 04' 29.8")
Miles Trailhead	[25-Z, 5.0]	(N33° 26' 14.3", W111° 04' 01.9")

Rock Creek Trail comes up the hill from the right and meets FR650 on a narrow turn in the road. Vehicles can be parked at some small pullouts in either direction on FR650—about 15 minutes away. From left to right are Jack San Felice, Dick Walp, and Greg Davis. Photo was taken in December 2007.

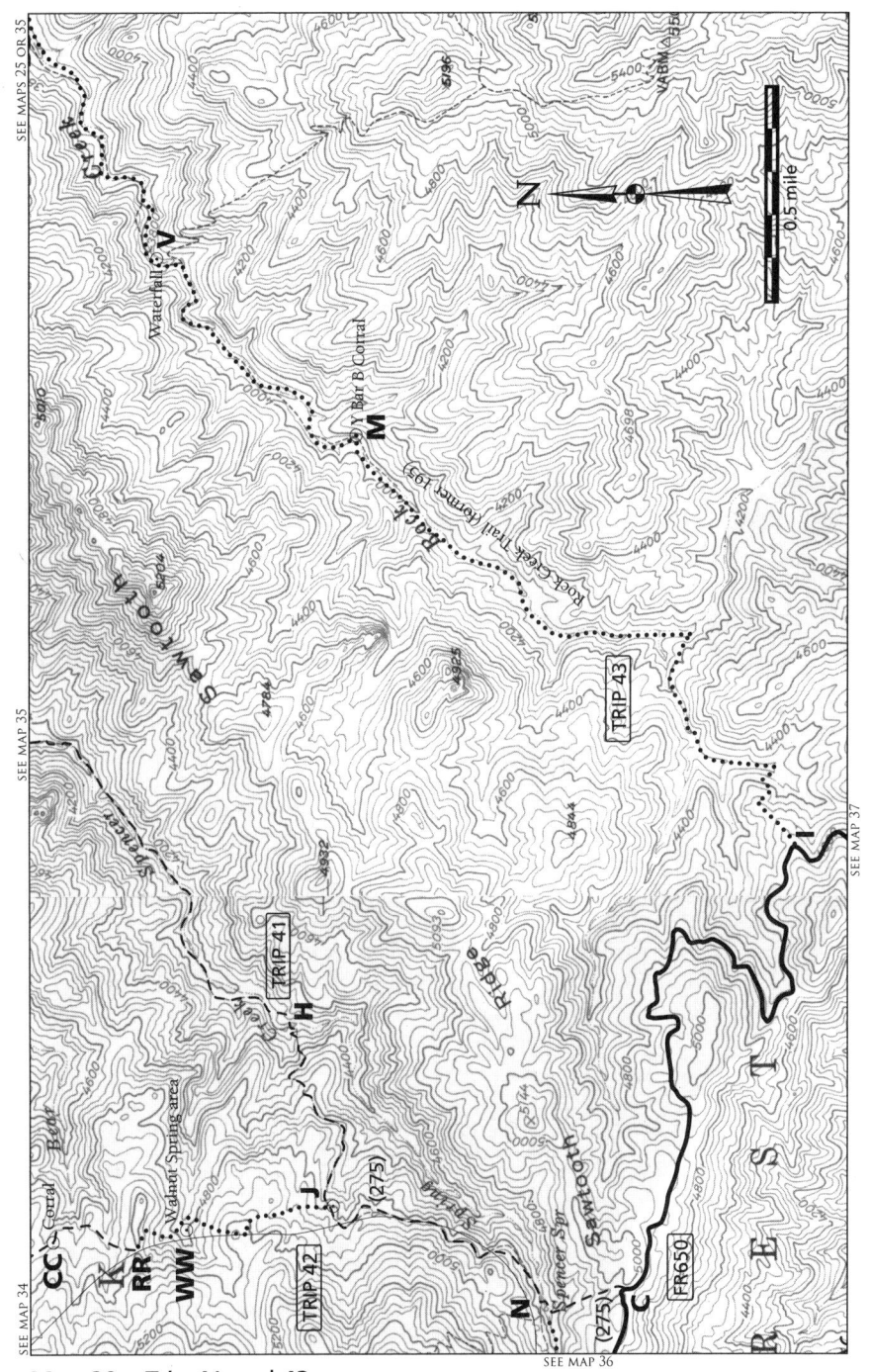

Map 38 – Trip 41 and 43.

View from FR650 near the junction with the Rock Creek Trail toward Sawtooth Ridge. Rock Creek is on the right side (east) of Sawtooth Ridge. Photo was taken in December 2007.

The vegetation encroaching on the trail is mostly friendly—no stickers—but be prepared for several hundred yards of trail between the corral [38-M] and the waterfall [38-V] that is overgrown with catclaw.

If you just want to make a leisurely outing, beginning the Rock Creek Trail from the Miles Trailhead [25-Z] will be more appealing than this remote access [38-I] from FR650. See the Trip 26 (Rock Creek from Bull Basin Trail) description and history for the complete story of Rock Creek.

WOODBURY TRAILHEAD

From Apache Junction, go east 15 miles on US60 to Florence Junction. Two more miles east on US60, between mileposts 214 and 215, turn north on Queen Valley Road for 1.8 miles to FR357 (Hewitt Station Road); go right 3 miles to FR172. If you come from Superior on US60, go past the Arboretum, then between mileposts 222 and 223, take FR357 for 5 miles to FR172. Go north on FR172 for 10.4 miles to end of road. Turn right at the locked gate to FR172B and the JF Ranch Headquarters. A high-clearance vehicle is required.

FINDING THE TRAILHEAD

The Woodbury Trailhead parking lot is at (N33° 24' 33.8", W111° 12' 19.5").

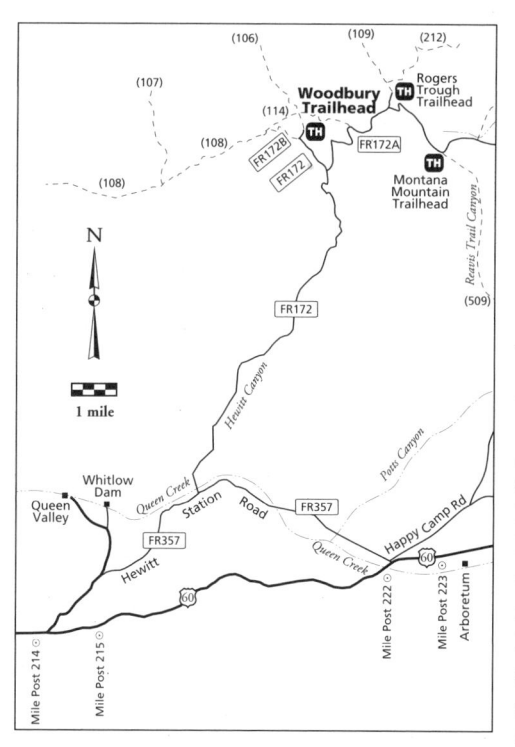

FACILITIES

No facilities are here except for a hitching post. Bring your own water.

THE TRAILS

Take the JF Trail (106) north out of the trailhead parking lot, which connects to Woodbury Trail (114). JF Trail goes straight (north) toward the windmill. Woodbury Trail goes east 1.3 miles to FR172A and west 1.0 mile to JF Ranch Headquarters and the Coffee Flat Trail (108). The signed Coffee Flat Trail starts on the north side of the large corral. Rogers Canyon cliff dwellings are 5.5 miles on JF Trail (106) and Rogers Canyon Trail (110). Also, see Trip 33 for the trail to the ruins from Rogers Trough Trailhead.

Complete trip descriptions, maps, and history for Woodbury Trailhead are in our companion book, *Superstition Wilderness Trails West*.

Peralta Trailhead

From US60 and Idaho Road in Apache Junction, go 8 miles east on US60. Turn left, north, between mileposts 204 and 205 onto Peralta Road (also named Peralta Trail and FR77). Peralta Trailhead is 7.2 miles at the end of Peralta Road.

FINDING THE TRAILHEAD

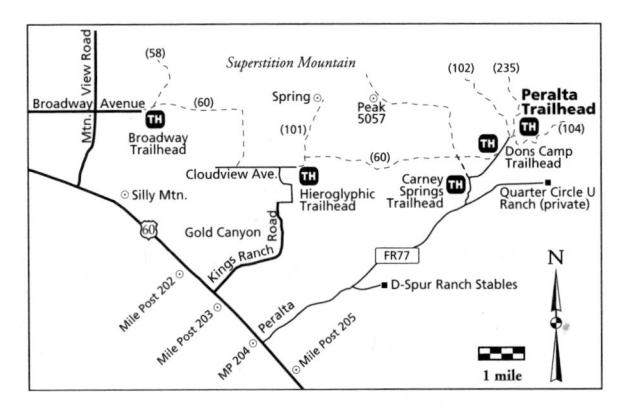

Trailhead parking is at the end of Peralta Road (N33° 23' 51.2", W111° 20' 49.6").

FACILITIES

Pit toilets with accessibility are located at the main parking lot. Bring your own water.

THE TRAILS

Three trails start from the northeast side of the Peralta Trailhead parking lot. Peralta Trail (102) goes left (north) up Peralta Canyon to Fremont Saddle in 2.1 miles where you have a great view of Weavers Needle. Peralta Trail ends in East Boulder Canyon (5.9 miles) not far from Aylor's former camp.

The Dutchman's Trail (104) goes right (east) and immediately crosses Peralta Canyon creek bed. Fifty yards up the path, Bluff Spring Trail (235) branches off to the left (north), goes to Bluff Spring in 3.4 miles, and in another 2.1 miles on the Dutchman's Trail takes you to La Barge Canyon.

The Dutchman's Trail goes right (east) and over Miners Summit to the junction with Bluff Spring Trail in 5.4 miles, Charlebois Spring in 8.9 miles, and ends at First Water Trailhead, 17.4 miles later.

Complete trip descriptions, maps, and history for Peralta Trailhead are in our companion book, *Superstition Wilderness Trails West*.

DONS CAMP TRAILHEAD

From US60 and Idaho Road in Apache Junction, go 8 miles east on US60. Turn left (north) between mileposts 204 and 205 onto Peralta Road (also signed as Peralta Trail and FR77). Follow FR77 for 7.0 miles to the unmarked Dons Camp Road. From FR77 turn left (west) into the large parking area and look for the Lost Goldmine Trail kiosk. This trailhead is also named Peralta Road Trailhead.

FINDING THE TRAILHEAD

The Dons Camp Trailhead for the Lost Goldmine Trail is located at the kiosk in the parking area south of the Dons Camp entrance gate. If you missed the turnoff for the Dons Camp, you can backtrack on Peralta Road about 0.2 mile, going south, from the cattle guard and Tonto National Forest boundary.

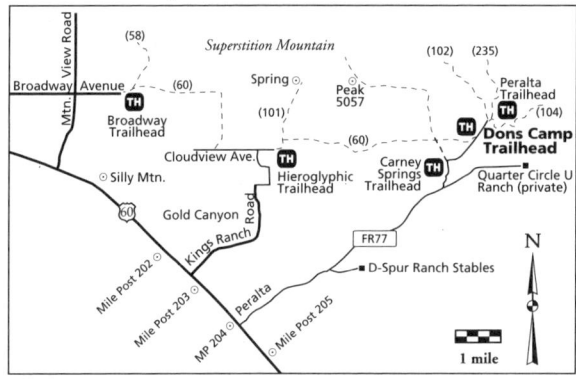

FACILITIES

No facilities are available except for a stone bench. Bring your own water. Nearby Peralta Trailhead has toilets.

THE TRAIL

From the Dons Camp Trailhead (N33° 23' 32.3", W111° 21' 12.0"), Lost Goldmine Trail (60) goes east and west mostly following the southern boundary of the Superstition Wilderness. Going 0.2 mile northeast from Dons Camp Trailhead, Lost Goldmine Trail ends at the cattle guard on Peralta Road (Peralta Road Access). Heading west from Dons Camp Trailhead, the Lost Goldmine Trail leads to West Boulder Trail gate in 1.2 miles, Hieroglyphic Trailhead in 5.7 miles, and ends near Broadway Trailhead in 10.2 miles.

Complete trip descriptions, maps, and history for the Dons Camp Trailhead are in our companion book, *Superstition Wilderness Trails West*.

CARNEY SPRINGS TRAILHEAD

From US60 and Idaho Road in Apache Junction, go 8 miles east on US60. Turn left (north) between mileposts 204 and 205 onto Peralta Road (also named Peralta Trail and FR77). Continue 6.2 miles on Peralta Road to an unsigned parking area on the left (west) side of Peralta Road. Carney Springs Trailhead is at the cable barricade on the former Carney Springs Road.

FINDING THE TRAILHEAD

The Carney Springs Trailhead (N33° 23' 8.7", W111° 21' 44.7") is about 1 mile south on FR77 from the cattle guard near Peralta Trailhead parking lot.

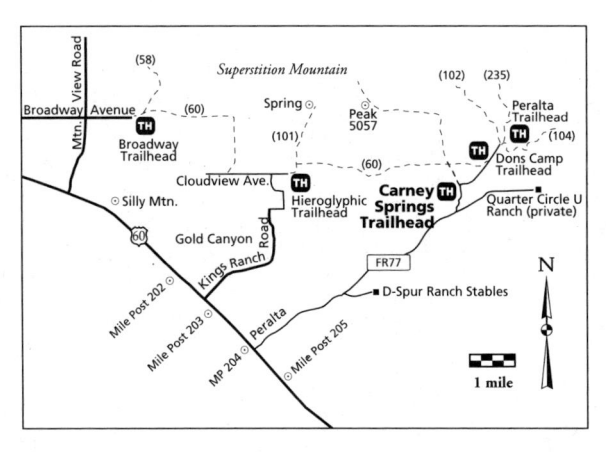

FACILITIES

No facilities are here. Bring your own water.

THE TRAILS

From the Carney Springs Trailhead, the unsigned Carney Trail begins at the open gate in the cable barrier on the west side of the parking area.

Go northwest on the Carney Trail for 0.6 mile, following the south side of the old roadbed, to the Superstition Wilderness boundary fence and gate. The West Boulder Trail begins at the gate in the barbed wire fence, heads northwest toward the mountain, and reaches West Boulder Saddle in 1.7 miles. Continuing on the Superstition Mountain Ridge Line Trail takes you to Lost Dutchman State Park for a total of 10.5 miles.

The Lost Goldmine Trail (60) follows the south side of the Wilderness fence, from the West Boulder Trail gate, heading east to Dons Camp Trailhead in 1.2 miles, and heading west to Hieroglyphic Trailhead in 4.5 miles.

Complete trip descriptions, maps, and history for the Carney Springs Trailhead are in our companion book, *Superstition Wilderness Trails West*.

Hieroglyphic Trailhead

From US60 and Idaho Road in Apache Junction, go east on US60 about 6 miles to Gold Canyon. Between mileposts 202 and 203, turn left (northeast) onto Kings Ranch Road, go 2.8 miles to Broadway Avenue, take local roads 1.2 miles to Cloudview Avenue and the parking area—also named Cloudview Trailhead and Kings Trailhead.

FINDING THE TRAILHEAD

The GPS for the trailhead is (N33° 23' 23.2", W111° 25' 26.0"). From the cattle guard at Kings Ranch Road and Baseline Avenue, turn right on Baseline Avenue and drive 0.25 mile. Go left (north) on Mohican Road for 0.3 mile, then left (west) on Valleyview Road. Valleyview Road meanders north northwest, connecting with Whitetail Road, which meets Cloudview Avenue. Go right (east) on Cloudview Avenue to the parking lot and kiosk at the end of the road.

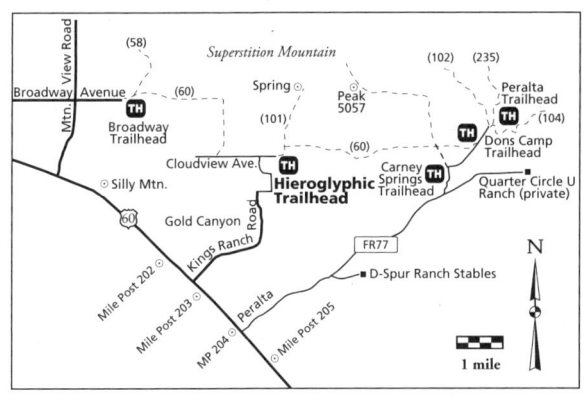

FACILITIES

No facilities are here. Bring your own water.

THE TRAILS

The Lost Goldmine Trail (60) runs east and west through Hieroglyphic Trailhead. Going east, the Lost Goldmine Trail connects with a trail leading north to Hieroglyphic Canyon and Hieroglyphic Trail (101) within 0.1 mile, which takes you to the petroglyphs in 1.4 miles. Continuing east on the Lost Goldmine Trail brings you to the Dons Camp Trailhead in 4.5 miles.

Heading west, Lost Goldmine Trail follows Cloudview Avenue, meanders on easements across private property and Arizona State Trust land, and ends at the Jacobs Crosscut Trail (58) near Broadway Trailhead in 4.5 miles.

Trip descriptions, maps, and history for Hieroglyphic Canyon Trailhead are in our companion book, *Superstition Wilderness Trails West*.

Broadway Trailhead

From US60 and Idaho Road in Apache Junction, go 3 miles east on US60 toward Gold Canyon. At the end of the Superstition Freeway, between mileposts 199 and 200, turn left (north) onto paved Mountain View Road. Follow Mountain View Road north 1.6 miles, turn right (east) on Broadway Avenue, and go 1 mile until the road curves into South Broadway Lane. Park on the left (north) in a small parking area facing the fence.

FINDING THE TRAILHEAD

Parking spaces are marked by cement tire stops for six vehicles in the unsigned gravel parking area. The signed Jacob's Crosscut Trail (N33° 24' 28", W111° 28' 34") begins at the west end of the parking area and connects with the Lost Goldmine Trail in 0.5 mile. Please obey all *No Trespassing* and *No Parking* signs.

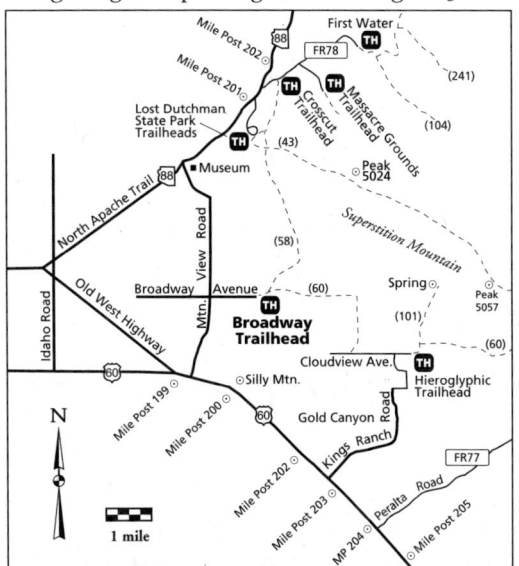

FACILITIES

No facilities are here. Bring your own water.

THE TRAILS

The Jacob's Crosscut Trail (58) begins at Broadway Trailhead, intersects the Lost Goldmine Trail (60) in 0.5 mile, intersects the Cave Trail in 1.1 miles, reaches the Lost Dutchman State Park in about 3.8 miles, and ends at Crosscut Trailhead in 5.7 miles. From Broadway Trailhead, the cave on the hill to the north is 1.8 miles. From the junction with the Jacob's Crosscut Trail, the Lost Goldmine Trail goes 3.9 miles east to Hieroglyphic Trailhead. These trails are outside the Superstition Wilderness, so bicyclists, as well as hikers and horse riders, are allowed to use the trails.

Complete trip descriptions, maps, and history for Broadway Trailhead are in our companion book, *Superstition Wilderness Trails West*.

LOST DUTCHMAN STATE PARK TRAILHEADS

The Lost Dutchman State Park Trailheads are located about 5 miles north of Apache Junction on SR88 (between mileposts 201 and 202). From SR88 turn right (east) on the paved road and drive into the State Park. SR88 is the famous Apache Trail, now designated as a National Forest Scenic Byway.

FINDING THE TRAILHEADS

The Siphon Draw Trail begins from the Siphon Draw Trailhead (N33° 27' 33.2", W111° 28' 45.4") inside the State Park. After entering the park, follow the road signs for Siphon Draw Trailhead.

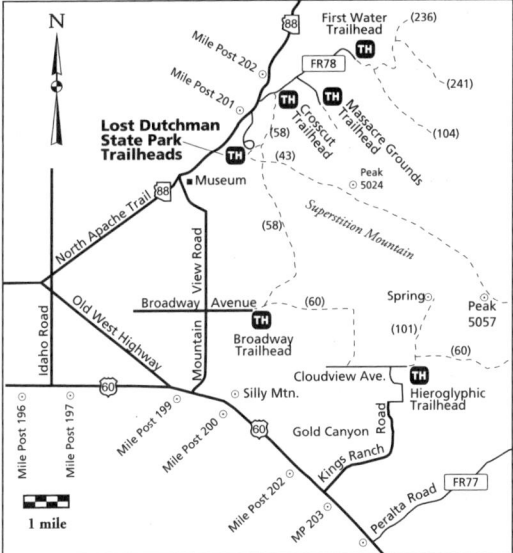

FACILITIES

The State Park has picnic tables, single and group ramadas, rest rooms, showers, drinking water, telephone, developed campsites, RV hookups, and a dump station. The State Park charges a daily fee for parking and use of the picnic facilities. See www.azstateparks.com for the overnight camping and daily fees.

THE TRAILS

From the Siphon Draw Trailhead, the Siphon Draw Trail (53) intersects the Jacob's Crosscut Trail (58) in 0.8 miles, continues to the Basin at the base of Superstition Mountain in 1.9 miles, reaches the Flat Iron on top of Superstition Mountain in 2.4 miles, and crosses the Superstition Mountain Ridge to Carney Springs Trailhead in 10.5 miles.

Two other parking areas inside the park serve as the Treasure Loop trailheads. Complete trip descriptions, maps, and history for the State Park trailheads are in our companion book, *Superstition Wilderness Trails West*.

CROSSCUT TRAILHEAD

Crosscut Trailhead is located on FR78. From Apache Junction, drive about 5 miles northeast on SR88 to the First Water Road (FR78), which is between mileposts 201 and 202. From SR88 turn right (east) onto dirt FR78 and continue 0.6 mile to the signed Crosscut Trailhead parking lot.

FINDING THE TRAILHEAD

FR78 is about 0.2 mile north of Lost Dutchman State Park on SR88. The signed Crosscut Trailhead (N33° 28' 16", W111° 28' 08") is on the right (south) side of FR78. Look for the large trailhead sign to distinguish this parking area from the many small pullouts along the road.

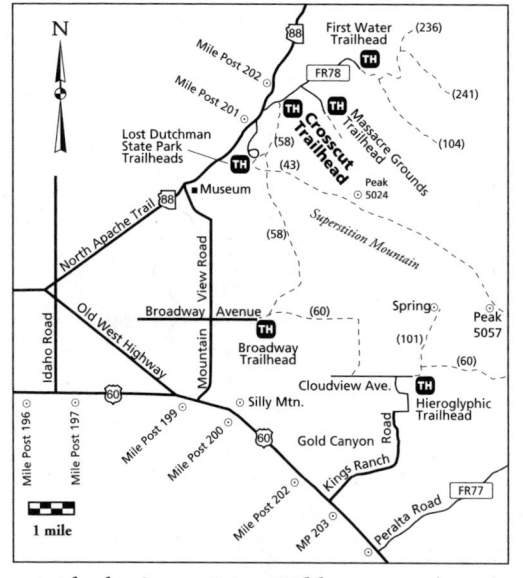

FACILITIES

No facilities are here. Bring your own water.

THE TRAIL

Only one trail, the Jacob's Crosscut Trail, starts from this trailhead. This trail is outside the Superstition Wilderness, so bicyclists, as well as hikers and horse riders, are allowed to use the trail.

The Jacob's Crosscut Trail (58) begins at the southwest corner of the Crosscut Trailhead parking lot near the information billboard sign. From the Crosscut Trailhead using the Jacob's Crosscut Trail (58), the mileages are, 1.0 mile to the Treasure Loop Trail (56) near Lost Dutchman State Park, 1.8 miles to the Siphon Draw Trail (53), and 5.7 miles to the Broadway Trailhead. The Lost Dutchman State Park has drinking water, rest rooms, telephone, and many other facilities, but the park does not provide access for horses.

Complete trip descriptions, maps, and history for Crosscut Trailhead are in our companion book, *Superstition Wilderness Trails West*.

MASSACRE GROUNDS TRAILHEAD

Massacre Grounds Trailhead is located off FR78 between Crosscut Trailhead and First Water Trailhead. From Apache Junction, drive about 5 miles northeast on SR88 to First Water Road (FR78), which is between mileposts 201 and 202. From SR88 turn right (east) onto dirt FR78 and continue 1.0 mile to the unsigned FR28 dirt road where you turn right (southeast). Continue on FR28 (Massacre Grounds Road) for 0.7 mile where the road ends in a small unsigned parking lot at the wire fence.

FINDING THE TRAILHEAD

From FR78, turn right (east) on the Massacre Grounds Road, which is identified by a large metal sign, *Congested Area, Target Shooting Prohibited.* Massacre Grounds Road is rocky near the end, but we have seen low clearance cars here. Drive cautiously, and watch your oil pan. You will know you are at the right trailhead when you see an earthen cow tank across from the barbed wire boundary fence just south of the parking area (N33° 28' 02.2", W111° 27' 23.5").

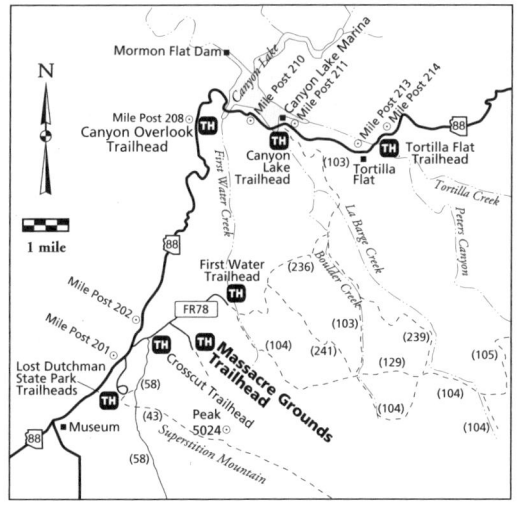

FACILITIES

No facilities or trailhead signs are at the Massacre Grounds Trailhead. Be sure to bring drinking water.

THE TRAIL

The unsigned Massacre Grounds Trail starts from the south side of the parking area. It begins as a wide dirt road at the barbed wire boundary fence gate, goes south toward Superstition Mountain, and ends in 1.5 miles near a seasonal waterfall.

Complete trip descriptions, maps, and history for Massacre Grounds Trailhead are in our companion book, *Superstition Wilderness Trails West.*

First Water Trailhead

First Water Road (FR78) is about 5 miles north of Apache Junction on SR88 between mileposts 201 and 202. The First Water Road turnoff is just 0.2 mile north of the Lost Dutchman State Park entrance. From SR88, turn right (east) on dirt FR78, and continue 2.6 miles to the First Water Trailhead parking lot at the end of dirt road FR78.

FINDING THE TRAILHEAD

The horse trailer parking area is on the left at mile 2.1 and the main parking lot is at mile 2.6 at the end of FR78 (N33° 28' 47.7", W111° 26' 32.1"). If the main lot is full, you can drive back on FR78 about 0.5 mile and park in the larger area where the outfitters saddle up for their pack trips.

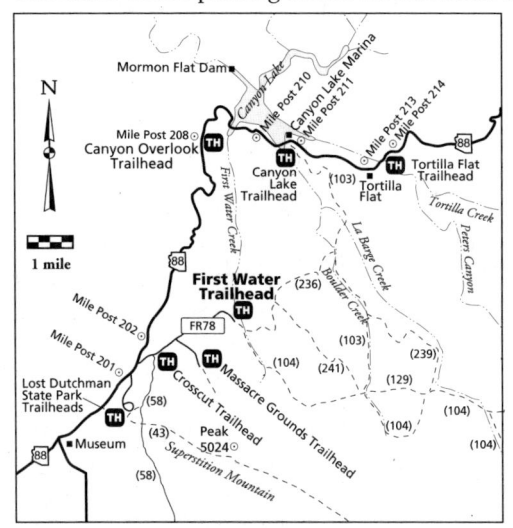

FACILITIES

Both parking areas have toilet facilities, but no drinking water. Theft and vandalism are common at this trailhead, so don't leave valuables in your vehicle.

THE TRAILS

The Dutchman's Trail (104) leaves the east side of the main parking lot and heads east, down a rough dirt road. In about 0.3 mile, the Dutchman's Trail meets the Second Water Trail, continues to Parker Pass in 2.5 miles, Aylors Camp in 4.4 miles, Charlebois Spring in 8.5 miles, Bluff Spring in 12 miles, and ends at Peralta Trailhead in 17.4 miles. The Second Water Trail (236) goes east crossing Garden Valley in 1.8 miles, passes Second Water Spring in 3.3 miles, and ends at Boulder Canyon Trail (103) in Boulder Canyon in 3.5 miles.

Complete trip descriptions, maps, and history for First Water Trailhead are in our companion book, *Superstition Wilderness Trails West*.

Canyon Overlook Trailhead

The Canyon Lake Trailhead is two different vehicle pullouts on SR88, about 12 miles northeast of Apache Junction between mileposts 207 and 208.

FINDING THE TRAILHEAD AND THE TRAILS

The first pullout (N33° 31' 59.7", W111° 27' 13.7") for this trailhead is for the First Water Creek Overlook Trail. The trailhead is about halfway between mileposts 207 and 208 at a metal electric tower on the east side of SR88. The metal electric tower can be identified by the painted number "#174" on the tower. From the vehicle pullout by the tower, follow the well-worn trail that heads south into the wash. The unsigned trail ends at an overlook above First Water Creek within 0.4 mile.

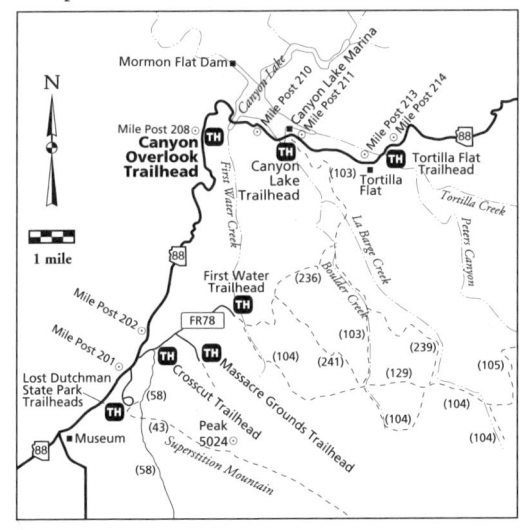

The second vehicle pullout is farther north on SR88 at the milepost 208 sign. Locate the nearby wooden power pole (N33° 32' 14.9", W111° 27' 11.1") and stand next to the pole with milepost 208 behind you. Look straight ahead for a steep trail that heads southeast into the wash. Go toward the bottom of the wash and follow the wash beyond a barbed wire fence to the bed of First Water Creek within 0.5 mile. Turn left (north) and follow the normally dry creek to Canyon Lake or explore upstream as far as you like.

FACILITIES

The trailhead does not have any facilities. Bring your own water.

Complete trip descriptions, maps, and history for Canyon Overlook Trailhead are in our companion book, *Superstition Wilderness Trails West*.

Canyon Lake Trailhead

The Canyon Lake Trailhead is on SR88, about 14 miles northeast of Apache Junction between mileposts 210 and 211. The distance is 28 miles southwest on SR88 from Roosevelt Lake Dam.

FINDING THE TRAILHEAD

Coming from Apache Junction, you will cross two single-lane bridges along the stretch of road at Canyon Lake. After crossing the second bridge, the trailhead is on the right (south) side of SR88. Free trailhead parking is provided inside the fenced area at the Canyon Lake Marina complex.

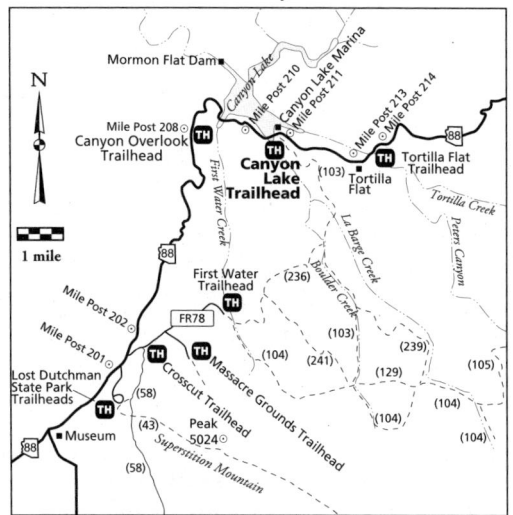

FACILITIES

Canyon Lake Marina has a restaurant, marina, beach area, and free fenced parking. You can also use the USFS picnic area (fee required) and paved parking on the southwest side of the bridge where you can park your vehicle. Ramadas, picnic tables, and toilets are available, but no water. Bring your own drinking water.

THE TRAIL

The Boulder Canyon Trail starts from the paved road, SR88, on the marina side of the bridge at a big sign reading *Boulder Canyon Trail 103* (N33° 32' 02", W111° 25' 20"). Heading south and uphill on Boulder Canyon Trail, the distance is 0.6 mile to the viewpoint at the Wilderness sign, 3.0 miles to La Barge Creek, 3.3 miles to Indian Paint Mine, 3.8 miles to the junction with Second Water Trail (235) and 7.3 miles to First Water Trailhead.

Complete trip descriptions, maps, and history for Canyon Lake Trailhead are in our companion book, *Superstition Wilderness Trails West*.

TORTILLA FLAT TRAILHEAD

The Tortilla Flat Trailhead is on SR88, about 16 miles northeast of Apache Junction between mileposts 213 and 214.

FINDING THE TRAILHEAD

Tortilla Flat Trailhead is located at one of the vehicle pullouts about a half mile east of Tortilla Flat. We often park next to the power pole near milepost 214 (N33° 31' 50.6", W111° 22' 51.5") along the road east of Tortilla Flat.

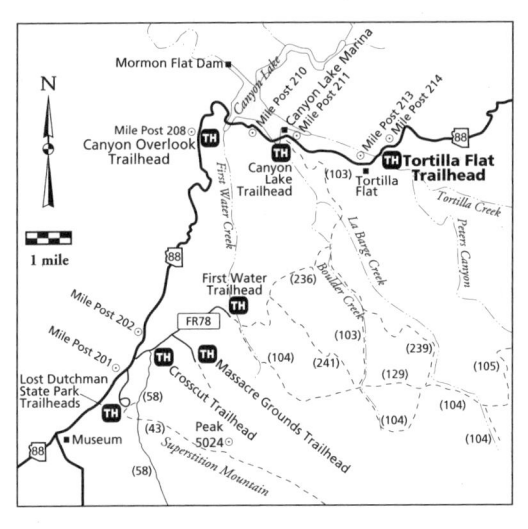

FACILITIES

The town of Tortilla Flat has a general store, restaurant, bar, ice cream shop, and gift shop. Rest rooms are available when the stores are open. Bring your own water. The parking area at Tortilla Flat is posted, *No Overnight Parking*. For overnight and day-hike vehicle parking, talk to the friendly owners in the restaurant who are accommodating and may make special arrangements for you. Do not park here without permission. From October through May, you can reserve a campsite at the nearby Tortilla Campground. They have rest rooms and running water.

THE ROUTE (NO TRAIL)

From milepost 214, walk down the slope to Tortilla Creek. Go upstream (south) in Tortilla Creek. At the junction with Peters Canyon in 1.6 miles, go right (south) into Peters Canyon to the bedrock potholes at 1.9 miles, or continue upstream to the cave at 2.6 miles.

Complete trip descriptions, maps, and history for Tortilla Flat Trailhead are in our companion book, *Superstition Wilderness Trails West*.

Tortilla Trailhead

From Apache Junction, go 22 miles northeast on SR88 to milepost 221 and turn south into the signed Tortilla Trailhead parking area. If you have four-wheel-drive, you can continue 3.3 miles on FR213 to Tortilla Well. From Roosevelt Lake Dam, the distance is 20 miles southwest on SR88 to FR213.

FINDING THE TRAILHEAD

Leave your vehicle at the parking lot on SR88 if four-wheel-drive FR213 is too rugged—the first 0.1 mile is the roughest. From SR88 to the decommissioned Tortilla Well and water tank at the end of FR213 (N33° 29' 33.2", W111° 17' 41.2"), the 1.25 hour walk or horse ride (3.3 miles) is easy.

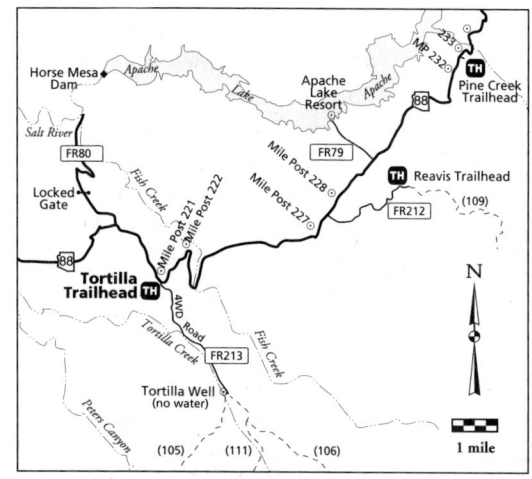

FACILITIES

No facilities. Bring your own water. Theft and vandalism are common, so don't leave valuables in your vehicle.

THE TRAILS

Three trails start near the south end of FR213. Signed Peters Trail (105) begins at the Tortilla Well windmill and water tank. Peters Trail heads southwest up the bed of Tortilla Creek, follows Peters Canyon, goes over Peters Mesa, and ends near Charlebois Spring in 7.4 miles.

The unsigned JF Trail (106), 0.1 mile east of Tortilla Well windmill, goes southeast, up the hill, across the ridge to Tortilla Pass in 6.3 miles, and ends at Woodbury Trailhead in 9.4 miles.

The Hoolie Bacon Trail (111) branches off the JF Trail at the top of the first hill. The Hoolie Bacon Trail proceeds 5.2 miles south through Cedar Basin and Horse Camp Basin to La Barge Canyon where it connects with the Red Tanks Trail (107).

Complete trip descriptions, maps, and history for Tortilla Trailhead are in our companion book, *Superstition Wilderness Trails West*.

Trans-Wilderness Trips

We selected several long hikes and horse rides that connect one trailhead to another. More possibilities exist. All the trips can be traveled in either direction. You can enhance the quality of the treks by including side trips. Shuttle distance is rounded to the nearest mile. Roads are suitable for passenger cars, except as noted. The individual trip descriptions note trail hazards that may block your stock animals. Portions of trips marked with an asterisk (*) are described in our companion book, *Superstition Wilderness Trails West*.

Trip 44. Reavis Trailhead to Peralta Trailhead*

From Reavis Trailhead, follow Reavis Ranch Trail (109) to Reavis Ranch, then continue to Rogers Canyon where you connect with Rogers Canyon Trail (110). At Tortilla Pass, pick up the JF Trail (106) and go south. Take Woodbury Trail (114), Coffee Flat Trail (108), and Dutchman's Trail (104) to end at Peralta Trailhead. See Reavis Trailhead and Peralta Trailhead. See Trip 33 (Rogers Canyon Cliff Dwellings), Trip 34 (Rogers Trough to Reavis Ranch), and Trip 1 (Reavis Ranch from Reavis Trailhead). The trail distance is 31.9 miles. Vehicle shuttle distance is 45 miles. Trip 33 describes a section of Rogers Canyon Trail that is dangerous for horses.

Trip 45. Reavis Trailhead to First Water Trailhead*

This is the reverse itinerary for Tom Kollenborn's well-known *Ride Through Time*. From Reavis Trailhead, take Reavis Ranch Trail (109) to Reavis Ranch. Continue on Reavis Ranch Trail to Rogers Canyon. Follow Rogers Canyon Trail (110) and JF Trail (106) to Tortilla Ranch. Take Peters Trail (105) to Charlebois Spring and connect with Dutchman's Trail (104), which goes over Black Top Mesa Pass, and ends at First Water Trailhead. See Reavis Trailhead and First Water Trailhead. See Trip 33 (Rogers Canyon Cliff Dwellings), Trip 34 (Rogers Trough to Reavis Ranch), and Trip 1 (Reavis Ranch from Reavis Trailhead). The trail distance is 36.9 miles. Vehicle shuttle distance is 29 miles. A section of Rogers Canyon Trail is dangerous for horses—see Trip 33.

Trip 46. Miles Trailhead to First Water Trailhead*

Hikers from www.hikearizona.com first made this trek in November 2007. Follow West Pinto Trail (212) to Oak Flat. Take Campaign Trail (256) to Fire Line Trail (118). Side trip to Circlestone adds 1.6 miles. Camp in Reavis Valley. Take Reavis Ranch Trail (109) north, Frog Tanks Trail (112) west, Rogers Canyon Trail (110) south, JF Trail (106) south to Woodbury Trailhead for camp and water cache. Take Coffee Flat Trail (108) southwest, Red Tanks Trail (107) north and west, and camp at La Barge Spring. Take Dutchman's Trail (104) to First Water Trailhead ending the 47-mile trek. Vehicle shuttle distance is 64 miles. See Miles Trailhead, Woodbury Trailhead, and First Water Trailhead. See Trip 24 (West Pinto Trail to Oak Flat), Trip 29 (Campaign Trail to Pinto Divide), Trip 17 (Campaign Trail to Reavis Ranch Loop), Trip 1 (Reavis Ranch from Reavis Trailhead), and Trip 35 (Rogers Trough to Reavis Ranch Loop).

Trip 47. Arizona Trail. Rogers Trough Trailhead to Frazier Trailhead

Traveling from south to north, start at the Rogers Trough Trailhead and follow Reavis Ranch Trail (109) to Reavis Valley. Take Reavis Gap Trail (117) and Two Bar Ridge Trail (119), which connects with FR83. Continue on Cottonwood Trail (120) to Frazier Trailhead and the Frazier Equestrian Campground. See Rogers Trough Trailhead and Frazier Trailhead. See Trip 34 (Rogers Trough to Reavis Ranch), Trip 18 (Reavis Gap Trail to Reavis Ranch), Trip 20 (Two Bar Ridge Trail), and Trip 11 (Cottonwood Trail to FR83). The trail distance is 24.9 miles. Vehicle shuttle distance is 68 miles.

Trip 48. Tule Trailhead to Frazier Trailhead

From Tule Trailhead, take Tule Trail (122) as described in Trip 12 to Two Bar Ridge Trail (119). Go north on Trail (119) to FR83 and connect with Cottonwood Trail (110), which ends at Frazier Trailhead for a total of 15.4 miles. Vehicle shuttle distance is 9 miles.

Trip 49. Campaign Trailhead to Reavis Trailhead

From Campaign Trailhead, take Campaign Trail (256) and Reavis Gap Trail (117) to Reavis Valley. Continue on Reavis Ranch Trail (109) to Reavis Trailhead for a total of 15.7 miles. See Trip 18 and Trip 1. Vehicle shuttle distance is 32 miles.

Trip 50. Peralta Trailhead to First Water Trailhead*

Follow Peralta Trail (102) to Fremont Saddle, connect with Dutchman's Trail (104) in East Boulder Canyon, and go over Parker Pass to First Water Trailhead. See Peralta Trailhead and First Water Trailhead. The trail distance is 10.9 miles. Vehicle shuttle distance is 25 miles.

Trip 51. Peralta Trailhead to Canyon Lake Trailhead*

Follow Peralta Trail (102) to Fremont Saddle, connect with Dutchman's Trail (104) in East Boulder Canyon, and go down Boulder Canyon taking

Boulder Canyon Trail (103) to Canyon Lake Trailhead. See Peralta Trailhead and Canyon Lake Trailhead. The trail distance is 12.7 miles. Vehicle shuttle distance is 31 miles.

Trip 52. Peralta Trailhead to Tortilla Trailhead*

Follow Dutchman's Trail (104) to Bluff Spring, La Barge Spring, and Charlebois Spring. Take Peters Trail (105) to Tortilla Trailhead. See Peralta Trailhead and Tortilla Trailhead. The trail distance is 15.4 miles. Vehicle shuttle distance is 42 miles. Four-wheel drive is required for Tortilla Trailhead, or add 3.3 miles to trail distance.

Trip 53. Carney Springs Trailhead to Lost Dutchman State Park*

Take the Carney Springs Trail and West Boulder Trail to Boulder Saddle. Take Superstition Mountain Ridge Line Trail across Superstition Mountain to Siphon Draw. Follow Siphon Draw Trail (53) to Siphon Draw Trailhead inside the Lost Dutchman State Park. See Carney Springs Trailhead and Lost Dutchman State Park Trailheads. The distance, mostly cross-country, is 10.5 miles. Vehicle shuttle distance is 21 miles. Not doable for horses.

Trip 54. First Water Trailhead to Canyon Lake Trailhead*

Follow Dutchman's Trail (104) and Second Water Trail (236) to Boulder Canyon. Connect with Boulder Canyon Trail (103), which ends at Canyon Lake Trailhead. See First Water Trailhead and Canyon Lake Trailhead. The trail distance is 7.1 miles. Vehicle shuttle distance is 12 miles.

Trip 55. Tortilla Trailhead to Woodbury Trailhead*

Take FR213 to Tortilla Trailhead. Pick up the JF Trail (106), and follow the trail to Woodbury Trailhead. See Tortilla Trailhead and Woodbury Trailhead. The trail distance is 9.2 miles. Vehicle shuttle distance is 57 miles. A four-wheel-drive vehicle is required if you drive to the Tortilla Trailhead at the end of FR213. Add 3.3 miles to trail distance if you cannot drive on FR213.

Trip 56. Woodbury Trailhead to Rogers Trough Trailhead*

Follow JF Trail (106) to Tortilla Pass. Continue on Rogers Canyon Trail (110) and Reavis Ranch Trail (109) to Rogers Trough Trailhead. See Woodbury Trailhead and Rogers Trough Trailhead. See Trip 33 (Rogers Canyon Cliff Dwellings). The trail distance is 9.4 miles. Vehicle shuttle distance is 5.3 miles. A four-wheel-drive is sometimes required for Rogers Trough Trailhead on FR172A. If you cannot drive on FR172A, add 3.7 miles to the trail distance to make a loop back to the start at Woodbury Trailhead using FR172A, Woodbury Trail (114), and JF Trail (106).

REFERENCE NOTES

1. Earline Horrell Tidwell, interviews in Globe on November 14 and 27, 2006.
2. Roscoe G. Willson, *Pioneer Cattlemen of Arizona* (Phoenix, Arizona: The Valley National Bank, 1951), vol. 1, p. 45; Donna Anderson, *History of Globe Arizona*, (Seattle, Washington: Classic Day Publishing, 2007), pp. 149-151; Earline Horrell Tidwell, interviews in Globe on November 14 and 27, 2006.
3. John S. Goff, *Arizona Biographical Series, Volume 1, King S. Woolsey* (Cave Creek, Arizona: Black Mountain Press), 1981, pp. 40-47.
4. James Swanson, Thomas Kollenborn, *Circlestone, A Superstition Mountain Mystery* (Apache Junction, Arizona: Goldfield Press, 1986), pp. 67-77.
5. Michael Sullivan, communication on April 7, 1994.
6. Jack San Felice, conversation on July 6, 2007; Robert Rogers, "Bill Martin, Half A Century In The Superstitions," *Arizona Cattlelog*, January 1967, pp. 30-38, continued in February 1967, pp. 25-32; Pinal County Recorder, Marks and Brands Book 1, p. 154; Pinal County Recorder Book of Deeds #6, p. 428.
7. Ann Knight Rose, *Emigrant Knight of Cornwall* (private printing 1991), pp. 7-24, 28-35.
8. Robert Rogers, "Bill Martin, Half A Century In The Superstitions," *Arizona Cattlelog*, January 1967, pp. 30-38, continued in February 1967, pp. 25-32.
9. *Arizona Daily Gazette*, January 26, 1899, p. 5, col. 2, reprinted in *Early Newspaper Articles of The Superstition Mountains and The Lost Dutchman Gold Mine* by Gregory Davis (Apache Junction, Arizona: Superstition Mountain Historical Society 1992), pp. 44-45.
10. Tom Kollenborn, Pineair entries in *Chronological History of the Superstition Wilderness*, (Apache Junction: private printing, 1988, rev. 2000); Tom Kollenborn, "Pineair: A Mountain Wilderness Resort," *Arizona Territorial Newspaper*, January 12, 1998, pp. 1, 4, 8, 9; "Pineair Road Included in Forest Fund," *Arizona Republic*, January 22, 1924, p. 8, col. 1.
11. Richard G. Schaus, "William Hardin (sic) Martin, 1891," *Arizona Cattlelog*, March 1966, back cover.
12. BLM homestead records for HES 412. Copies from Gregory Davis. Original papers at the National Archives, RG 49, Serial Patent #659550, January 16, 1919.
13. Ann Knight Rose, *Emigrant Knight of Cornwall* (private printing 1991), pp. 36-61; Ann Knight Rose, "Ranch Life on the JF and Reavis Ranches," *Superstition Mountain Journal*, vol. 14, 1996, pp. 13-31.
14. Robert Rogers, "Bill Martin, Half A Century In The Superstitions," *Arizona Cattlelog*, January 1967, pp. 30-38, continued in February 1967, pp. 25-32.
15. Ibid.
16. Mary Leonhard, "Reavis Ranch Closed, Historic Superstition Homestead Returning to Wilderness," *Arizona Republic*, July 11, 1967; Patent 02-67-0035 for IV Ranch, BLM records, Phoenix, January 23, 1967.
17. Nyle Leatham, "Secluded waterfall enhances wonderment of the Superstitions," *The Arizona Republic*, May 1, 1983, p. G4, cols. 1-6; Tom Kollenborn, "Reavis Falls," *Superstition Gold*, vol. 7 (Fountain Hills, Arizona: Orion Publishing Co., Jan. 1986), p. 67; Linda Barnett, "Trekking To Reavis Falls," *The News*, Apache Junction, Arizona, June 4 - June 10, 2001, p. A-3, cols. 3-4; Stan Smith, David Elms, "The Mystery Falls of the Superstitions," *Arizona Highways*, November 1993, pp. 38-44.
18. Stan Smith, *Arizona Highways*, November 1993, pp. 38-44.
19. Charles Liu, *60 Hikes within 60 Miles, Phoenix, including Tempe, Scottsdale, and Glendale* (Birmingham, Alabama: Menasha Ridge Press, 2006 and 2007), p. 135, 2009, p. 175.
20. Kenneth R. Nelssen, interview in Camp Verde, Arizona on June 10, 2002.
21. Chuck Backus, Bill Smith, and others, conversations in 2005, 2006, and 2008.
22. John G. Bourke, *Field Notes, Scouts in Arizona Territory, Nov. 18th 1872 to April 8th 1873*, p. 34. Courtesy of Susan Lintelmann, USMA Library, Special Collections and Archives, Department of the Army, United States Military Academy, West Point, NY.
23. Bruce Grubbs, "Lower Pine Creek Trip" in *Hiking Arizona's Superstition and Mazatzal Country* (Helena, Montana: Falcon Publishing, Inc., 2000), pp. 56-58.
24. Dwight Cooper, conversation at the GCCG Calf Sale on April 17, 2002.
25. Bob Wallauer, "Danny Boy, the Lead Horse," *The Museum Messenger* (Apache Junction, Arizona: Superstition Mountain Museum,

April-June 2004), vol. 21-2, pp. 6-7.
26. Barry Storm, *Thunder God's Gold* (Apache Junction, Arizona: Schoose Publishing, reprint, 1986), p. 28.
27. Sources used in this section include: John and Lillian Theobald, *Arizona Territory Post Offices and Postmasters* (Phoenix, Arizona: Arizona Historical Foundation, 1961); Alan Patera, John Gallagher, *Arizona Post Offices* (Lake Grove, Oregon: The Depot, 1988); *1882-1907, School Census, Gila County, Arizona* (Payson, Arizona: Northern Gila County Genealogical Society, Inc.); Dorothy C. Morris, editor, *Globe Arizona Cemetery Inscriptions* (Globe, Arizona: Ladies of the Cemetery Committee,1989 and 2000); Homestead surveys and patents from BLM records in Phoenix, Arizona; Jeffery Clark, *Tracking Prehistoric Migrations, Pueblo Settlers among the Tonto Basin Hohokam* (Tucson, Arizona: The University of Arizona Press, 2001); also see Notes 146 and 147 for more about the Salado.
28. *Map of the Territory of Arizona* (Department of the Interior, General Land Office, November 1, 1869), map copied from BLM, Phoenix Office; John S. Goff, *King S. Woolsey* (Cave Creek, Arizona: Black Mountain Press, 1981), pp. 44-45; *Arizona Place Names* by Will Barnes (1935) locates Grapevine Spring 6 miles north of Old Camp Reno on Tonto Creek. Byrd Granger corrects that entry in the revised printing (1960) to indicate that Grapevine Spring is on the Salt River east of the confluence with Tonto Creek, which agrees with Woolsey's 1864 trip report.
29. Donna Anderson, *History of Globe Arizona* (Seattle, Washington: Classic Day Publishing, 2007), pp. 85-89; Roscoe G. Willson, *Pioneer Cattlemen of Arizona* (Phoenix, Arizona: The Valley National Bank, 1951), vol. 1, p. 37; Henry Armer BLM records Nos. 232 and 345 from Phoenix Office.
30. Homestead file No. 44, Archie McIntosh, June 20, 1884 and November 9, 1891, Tucson Land Office, RG49, National Archives, Washington, DC.
31. Juana Fraser Lyon, "An Apache Branch of Clan Mackintosh," *Clan Chattan, (Journal of the Clan Chattan Association)*, vol. IV, No. 2., 1960, pp. 15-18, listed under Indians of North America-Apache-McIntosh ephemera files at AHS, Tucson, Arizona; Dan L. Thrapp, "Archie McIntosh, Scout, A Very Human Hero," typed manuscript in MS887, Box 8, S2, F93 at AHS, Tucson; Sim Plex, "Correspondence, Fort Apache Letter," *The Argus*, Holbrook, Arizona, April 9 and 23, 1896; Gila County Recorder, Marks and Brands Book 1, p. 10, April 10, 1882.
32. *Honor the Past...Mold the Future, Gila Centennials 1976* (Globe, Arizona: Gila Centennials, Inc., 1976), pp. 72-73.
33. Pat H. Stein, *Homesteading in Arizona, 1870-1942* (Phoenix, Arizona: Arizona State Parks, August 1990); *Suggestions to Homesteaders and Persons Desiring to Make Homestead Entries*, Circular No. 541, Department of the Interior, Jan. 16, 1922.
34. Plat maps for the Roosevelt Lake area, BLM Phoenix, Office; Nancy C. Dallett, *At the Confluence of Change, a History of Tonto National Monument* (Tucson, Arizona: Western National Parks Association, 2008), pp. 40-41. In Note 10, Dallett includes a list from the Richard Schaus Collection, Arizona Historical Foundation, MSS-6 box 1, folder 9, which shows a list of 37 land owners that sold to the U.S. government.
35. National Archives, Washington, Alma Kirby homestead, RG49, Serial Patent 364831.
36. BLM records for HES 70 homestead; Dorothy C. Morris, editor, *Globe Arizona Cemetery Inscriptions* (Globe, Arizona: Ladies of the Cemetery Committee,1989 and 2000); Will C. Barnes, revised by Byrd H. Granger, *Arizona Place Names* (Tucson, Arizona: University of Arizona Press, 1982), p. 107; Alan Patera, John Gallagher, *Arizona Post Offices* (Lake Grove, Oregon: The Depot, 1988), pp. 69-70; Birth and Death Certificates for the Kerby (Kirby) family, Arizona Bureau of Vital Statistics, Arizona State Archives and Library, and http://genealogy.az.gov.
37. "Gila County Cattleman Dies Near Globe," *Arizona Republic*, September 8, 1944, p. 6, col. 2; *Honor the Past...Mold the Future, Gila Centennials 1976* (Globe, Arizona: Gila Centennials, Inc., 1976), pp. 132-133.
38. Earline Horrell Tidwell, interviews in Globe on November 14 and 27, 2006.
39. Birth Certificate, Marion E. Jackson, March 24, 1914, Livingstone, Arizona, parents are Luther and Anna Henderson Jackson, Arizona Bureau of Vital Statistics; Gila County Marriage Affidavits, April 11, 1904; David Introcaso, *Roosevelt Power Canal and Diversion Dam*, HAER No. AZ-4 (Phoenix, Arizona: Salt River Project Research Archives, 1984), courtesy of Shelly Dudley, Salt River Project Research Archives.
40. *Roosevelt Cemetery: Reminiscing A Lost Era* (pamphlet by Tonto National Forest, printed 9-2000); Lu DuBois, "Historic Roosevelt Cemetery," *Copper Country News*, June 19, 2001, p. 11.
41. Bill Ahrens, "Desert tomb," *The Arizona Republic*, April 5, 1981, pp. B1 cols. 1-5 and B2 cols. 1-5. Newspaper reference from *Northern Gila County, Arizona, Cemetery Inscriptions*, by Margaret A. Furtkamp, Payson, Arizona, 1998, pp. 111-114.
42. "Triumph And Tragedy Recalled At Roosevelt Dam Project," *The Phoenix Gazette*, April 7,

REFERENCE NOTES

1966, p. 16, Section A; Tonto Forest Special Use Permit, 1945, from SMHS Frazier file, courtesy of Gregory Davis; Vince Taylor, "Mrs. Stella Frazier, 82, strove to save family place in Tonto Forest," *The Arizona Republic*, Nov. 23, 1969, p. B-21.

43. Post Office Department, letter to Mrs. Stella Frazier, July 21, 1916, appointment to postmaster, courtesy Gregory Davis, SMHS Frazier file; *The Arizona Republic*, "Stella Frazier resort owner at Roosevelt," March 24, 1971, p. 46, col. 1; E. H. Cook, *Map of Gila County, Arizona Territory, 1889*, copy of map from Susan Clardy.

44. Robert Mason, "Ft. McDowell Patrols," *Tonto Basin News*, February. 6, 2006, pp. 5-6.

45. Dwight Cooper, conversation at Gila County Cattle Growers Auction on April 17, 2002.

46. *Arizona Trail News*, "Reports from the Field" (Phoenix, Arizona: Arizona Trail Association, date unknown), p. 4.

47. Helen Schulze, interview on March 14, 2001; Ed Bacon, conversation on July 2, 1999.

48. E. A. Eckhoff and P. Riecker, *Official Map of the Territory of Arizona, 1880*, copy from Arizona State Library and Archives; Unnamed 1881 map, original from AHS, Tucson, Case 2, Dr. 4, #2687, 1881, also at Arizona State Library and Archives.

49. Al LeCount, *The History of Tonto* (Punkin Center, Arizona: Bicentennial Project by the Punkin Center Homemakers 1976), pp. 37-38.

50. Helen Schulze, interview at the Schulze Ranch near Miami on March 14, 2001.

51. John Schulze, conversation at Gila County Museum on July 28, 2000.

52. John G. Bourke, *Field Notes, Scouts in Arizona Territory, Nov. 18th 1872 to April 8th 1873*. Sketches and maps on pp. 34, 36 and 54. Microfilm copied from Arizona State University, Hayden Library, Special Collections; John G. Bourke, *The Diaries of John Gregory Bourke, Volume One, November 20, 1872 – July 28, 1876*, ed. Charles M. Robinson III (Denton, Texas: University of North Texas Press, 2003), pp. 34-54.

53. John G. Bourke, *Field Notes, Scouts in Arizona Territory, Nov. 18th 1872 to April 8th 1873*. Map on p. 54. Color copy of map made for us by Susan Lintelmann, USMA Library, Special Collections and Archives, Department of the Army, United States Military Academy, West Point, NY.

54. Susan Clardy, *Sometimes the Blues: The Letters and Diaries of Frank Hammon, A Lonely Frontiersman in Globe and Phoenix* (Tucson, Arizona: The Arizona Historical Society, 2007), pp. 122-125; E. H. Cook, *Map of Gila County, Arizona Territory, 1889*, copy of map from Susan Clardy.

55. *The Webb Story*, compiled stories of the Webb family, excerpts from the *Arizona Cattlelog*, vol. III, no. 1, September 1947 and others.

56. *1882-1907, School Census, Gila County, Arizona* (Payson, Arizona: Northern Gila County Genealogical Society, Inc.), pp. 34, 45.

57. Territorial Brand Book of Arizona, June 10, 1897, Narron, p. 195, Arizona State Library and Archives, Film 3.2.4; Gila County Recorder, Marks and Brands, Book 1, p. 98, Gann, October 29, 1888; Gila County Recorder, Bill of Sale, Book 1, p. 110, Gann to Narron, October 24, 1892.

58. Lillie Narron and Charles Chilson, Affidavit of Applicant for Marriage License, Gila County, Arizona State Library and Archives, Box 1, D2-6-1, 1900, film 69.10.2; E-mail from Denise Cortelyou, April 11, 2008; *A Cultural History of The Pioneer Women of Gila County, Arizona and their Descendants* (Payson, Arizona: Daughters of the Gila County Pioneers, 2007), pp. 66-67.

59. Jess G. Hayes, *Sheriff Thompson's Day*, (Tucson, Arizona: The University of Arizona Press, 1968), pp. 31-33; *Honor the Past...Mold the Future, Gila Centennials 1976* (Globe, Arizona: Gila Centennials, Inc., 1976), p. 36; Earline Horrell Tidwell, interviews in Globe on November 14 and 27, 2006.

60. *1882-1907, School Census, Gila County, Arizona* (Payson, Arizona: Northern Gila County Genealogical Society, Inc.), p. 61.

61. Earline Horrell Tidwell, interviews in Globe on November 14 and 27, 2006; Peter Busnack heard another version of the story that attributed Ida May Gann's death to a scorpion bite.

62. Gila County Recorder, Marriages, Book 1, p. 4, Emily Knudson, William Gann, September 19, 1881.

63. *The Arizona Silver Belt*, May 21, 1892.

64. Gila County Recorder, Bill of Sale, Book 1, p. 186, W. T. Gann to T. E. Gann, June 8, 1897; E-mails from Denise Cortelyou on February 14 and April 11, 2008.

65. Al LeCount, *The History of Tonto* (Punkin Center, Arizona: Bicentennial Project by the

66. Punkin Center Homemakers, 1976), pp. 37.
66. Homestead survey for the Upper Horrell Place HES 448, BLM records.
67. Homestead patent for the Upper Horrell Place HES 448, BLM records.
68. Earline Horrell Tidwell, interviews in Globe on November 14 and 27, 2006.
69. Ibid.
70. John "Fritzski" Fritz, "Campaign Trail to Pinto Divide," www.hikearizona.com, 2002.
71. Bruce Grubbs, *Backpacking Arizona* (Berkeley, Calif.: Wilderness Press, 2003), pp. 194-199.
72. Jack Carlson and Elizabeth Stewart, "Mystery of K.R.N. Trail," *The Museum Messenger* (Apache Junction, Arizona: Superstition Mountain Museum, July-October 2002); Kenneth Nelssen, interview in Camp Verde, Arizona on June 10, 2002.
73. Howard Horinek (former manager of the JH6 Ranch) interview at the Quarter Circle U Ranch, Arizona on January 17, 2001.
74. Howard Horinek, conversation and clarification about the old road on December 14, 2008 at the Quarter Circle U Ranch, Arizona; F. N. Holmquist, *Map of Central Arizona, 1916.* Copy of map obtained from the Arizona State Library and Archives Map Department, Phoenix, with the help of Julie Hoff.
75. Bruce Grubbs, *Backpacking Arizona* (Berkeley, Calif.: Wilderness Press, 2003), pp. 194-199. *Hiking Arizona's Superstition and Mazatzal Country* (Helena, Montana: Falcon Publishing, Inc., 2000), pp. 61-65.
76. "A Ghastly Find," *The Arizona Silver Belt*, Globe, Arizona, May 14, 1896.
77. Kelly Tighe and Susan Moran, *On the Arizona Trail* (Boulder, Colorado: Pruett Publishing, 1998), pp. 167-170.
78. Bruce Grubbs, *Hiking Arizona's Superstition and Mazatzal Country* (Helena, Montana: Falcon Publishing, Inc., 2000), pp. 56-58.
79. John G. Bourke, *Field Notes, Scouts in Arizona Territory, Nov. 18th 1872 to April 8th 1873.* Sketches and maps on pp. 28, 102, 122, and 124. Microfilm copied from Arizona State University, Hayden Library, Special Collections; John G. Bourke, *The Diaries of John Gregory Bourke, Volume One, November 20, 1872 – July 28, 1876*, ed. Charles M. Robinson III (Denton, Texas: University of North Texas Press, 2003), p. 91.
80. Maricopa County Recorder, Mining Claims Book 2, pp. 56-57 (Mazatzal Mountains); Gila County Recorder, Record of Mines Book 6, p. 20 (Pinto Creek); Gila County Recorder, Mining Deed dated July 20, 1901, sale from Sieber to Shanley.
81. Tom Kollenborn, "Waltz in Pinto Creek," Kollenborn's Chronicles, *The News*, Apache Junction, Arizona, September 6-12, 2004, p. A4; John D. Mitchell, *Lost Mines & Buried Treasures Along the Old Frontier* (1953; reprint, Glorieta, New Mexico: Rio Grande Press, Inc., 1982) pp.171-172.
82. Susan Clardy, *Sometimes the Blues: The Letters and Diaries of Frank Hammon, A Lonely Frontiersman in Globe and Phoenix, 1882–1889* (Tucson, Arizona: Arizona Historical Society, 2007), p. 212.
83. John Wilburn, conversations at the Blue Bird Mine and Gift Shop on the Apache Trail on January 13, 1999 and SMHS Museum on November 3, 2007.
84. Ibid.
85. Gila County Recorder, Book 1, p. 25 (brands); Territorial Brand Book of Arizona, p. 24, Arizona State Library and Archives, film 3.2.4, Phoenix, Arizona; Livestock Sanitary Board of Arizona, Bill of Sale Book #2, p. 24, copied from Arizona State Library and Archives, Phoenix, Arizona.
86. Gila County Recorder, Book 1, p. 5 (brands), October 4, 1881; Earline Horrell Tidwell, interviews in Globe on November 14 and 27, 2006; *Honor the Past…Mold the Future, Gila Centennials 1976* (Globe, Arizona: Gila Centennials, Inc., 1976), pp. 100-101; Donna Anderson, *History of Globe Arizona* (Seattle, Washington: Classic Day Publishing, 2007), pp. 149-151.
87. Land patent, Marion L. Horrell, patent number 396764, BLM serial number AZPHX 0016271, issue date April 7, 1914; Land Patent, Susan Harrell (sic), BLM serial number AZAZAA 023051, issue date November 16, 1901. Records at www.glorecords.blm.gov.
88. "Ed Horrell Wins Steer-Tying Contest," *Phoenix Daily Enterprise*, December 18, 1899, p. 1, col. 4; Clara Woody files, MS887, box 15, S4, F40, Arizona Historical Society, Tucson; Land Patent, Ed Horrell, patent number 697413, BLM serial number AZPHX 000026659, issue date July 10, 1919. Records at www.glorecords.blm.gov.
89. Winnie Horrell, "Tripping," *Arizona Cattlelog*, September 1949, pp. 22-26; October 1949, pp. 38-45; November 1949, pp. 30-38; Winnie Horrell, "Christmas in Chichicastenango," *Arizona Cattlelog*, December 1951, pp. 4-8; Abbie Keith, "Tripping–On Air," *Arizona Cattlelog*, January 1951, pp. 68-71; Earline Horrell Tidwell, interviews in Globe on November 14 and 27, 2006; Donna Anderson, *History of Globe Arizona* (Seattle, Washington: Classic Day Publishing, 2007), pp. 149-151.
90. Homestead Entry Survey records, HES 164, and other records from the Bureau of Land Management, Phoenix, Arizona; National Archives, Washington, DC, Jose Periz, RG49, Serial Patent 912808.
91. Ibid.
92. Arizona Department of Heath Services, Periz, May 24, 1913 and July 20, 1927, Gila County; National Archives, Washington,

REFERENCE NOTES

DC, Jose Periz, RG49, Serial Patent 912808.
93. Howard Horinek, interviews at the Quarter Circle U Ranch on January 17, 2001 and August 1, 2002. Horinek said Bob Hale and Fidalis Rocha told him the story about Frenchy.
94. Gila County Assessor and Recorder, April 16, 1969, Docket 258, pp. 596-598.
95. Tom Kollenborn, "Hoax or History," *Superstition Gold Magazine* (Fountain Hills, Arizona: Orion Publishing Company, January 1986), pp. 50-51; Tom Kollenborn, "The Ghost of the Dutchman's Gold Refuses to Die," *AJ News*, December 12-18, 2000 and December 19-25, 2000; Tom Kollenborn, "The Secret of Haunted Canyon," *AJ News*, August 18-24, 1998. The original references for the newspaper stories are:
    Pete Moraga story, "Lost Dutchman is Investigated," *Arizona Daily Silver Belt*, November 8, 1913; "The Legend of Pete Moraga's Diggings," *Arizona Republic, Arizona Magazine*, January 17, 1982.
    Sidow and Moraga story, "Lost Dutchman Mine May Be Found," *Gazette*, November 29, 1913.
    Jose Perez story, "Lost Dutchman Ghost is Seen Once More," *Arizona Gazette Daily*, July 22 and 23, 1916; "Ghost of the Lost Dutchman," *Arizona Daily Silver Belt*, July 27, 1916.
    Joe Modock story, "Claims Diamond Mine Discovery," *Mesa Journal Tribune*, March 22, 1935.
96. Homestead Entry Survey records, HES 431, Serial Patent 699299 and other records from the Bureau of Land Management, Phoenix.
97. Geraldine Craig, manuscript collection, MS193, at the Arizona Historical Society Library, Tucson, Arizona, no date. She was the wife of Dudley Craig and related to the Irion family that owned Pinal Ranch. For the history of Pinal Ranch, see *Within Adobe Walls, 1877-1973* by Helen Baldock Craig (Phoenix, Arizona: Art-Press Printers, 1975); Byrd Howell Granger, *Arizona's Names, X Marks the Place* (Tucson, Arizona: The Falconer Publishing Company, 1983), p. 293; *Arizona Enterprise*, August 8, 1891, p. 3; Nyle Leatham, "Haunted Canyon makes perfect spot for portrait," *The Arizona Republic*, March 30, 1986, p. T2, col. 1-6.
98. Gila County Recorder, Marriages Book 1, p. 20, E. P. "Pete" Gann and Laura Horrell, July 17, 1883; Gila County Recorder, Marks and Brands, Book 1, p. 78, "GAN" brand recorded for W. "Walter" P. Gann at request of E. P. Gann on January 21, 1887. Also, in Book 1, p. 53, E. P. Gann recorded the "Club" brand on July 21, 1885.
99. Denise Cortelyou, E-mail on February 11, 2007, Paso Robles, California. Pete and Laura Gann are her great-grandparents and Hilda Gann is her grandmother.
100. Tony Ranch patent 861707, May 4, 1922 from BLM records; Betty Porter Gilbert of Arizona and Marion Williams of New Mexico provided information and photographs for the William Toney family history; Ross Sloan patent 706114, September 22, 1919, BLM records; Territorial Brand Book of Arizona, (Slash W brand), p. 1392, August 17, 1908, (Y Cross 7 brand), p. 1406, October 5, 1908.
101. National Archives, Washington, DC, William Toney, RG49, Serial Patent 861707.
102. Ibid.
103. Territorial Brand Book of Arizona, (Lazy W Bar T brand), p. 2372, June 7, 1915.
104. Jim, Phyllis, and Frank Herron, interviews at the Herron Ranch on June 14, 1998 and October. 14, 1999; Pinal County Recorder, Docket 1639, p. 990-991, life estate papers for HES 435.
105. Jim, Phyllis, and Frank Herron, interview at the Herron Ranch on June 14, 1998.
106. Jim, Phyllis, and Frank Herron, interview at the Herron Ranch on June 14, 1998; Harry E. Chrisman, *Fifty Years on the Owl Hoot Trail* (Chicago: Sage Books, 1969), pp. 265 and 329n4.
107. John G. Bourke, *Field Notes, Scouts in Arizona Territory, Nov. 18th 1872 to April 8th 1873*. Maps on pp. 102, 122 and 124. Microfilm copied from Arizona State University, Hayden Library, Special Collections. Color copy of maps made for us by Susan Lintelmann, USMA Library, Special Collections and Archives, Department of the Army, United States Military Academy, West Point, NY; John G. Bourke, *The Diaries of John Gregory Bourke, Volume One, November 20, 1872 – July 28, 1876*, ed. Charles M. Robinson III (Denton, Texas: University of North Texas Press, 2003), pp. 55-70.
108. Cliff Edwards, *Horseback and Airborne, The Life and Times of Cliff "Tailspin" Edwards* (Coolidge, Arizona: Cliff Edwards, 1995), pp. 20, 32-33; R. Lewis Bowman, conversa-

tion at the Arizona History Convention, Hon-Dah Resort, Pinetop, Arizona on April 27, 2001. Mr. Bowman is the author of the two books describing the ranching and rodeo history of the Bowman family, *Bumfuzzled* (Bisbee, Arizona: Copper Queen Publishing, Inc., 1995) and *Bumfuzzled Too* (Bisbee, Arizona: Copper Queen Publishing, Inc., 2000).
109. Field Notes of Homestead Entry Survey No. 554 (Crook National Forest: U.S. Department of Agriculture, Forest Service, 1920).
110. Slim Ellison, *More Tales from Slim Ellison* (Tucson, Arizona: The University of Arizona Press, 1981), pp. 107-108, (date on page 92); Howard Horinek, conversation on February 24, 2002. Howard said Lloyd (Barney) McClain told him that Clark was a butcher in Globe, Arizona.
111. *Globe and Miami City Directory, 1925* (Long Beach California: Western Directory Company, 1925). The directory is from the Gila County Historical Society Library, Globe, Arizona. Handwritten on the directory's cover is "Mine Rescue Station."
112. National Archives, Washington, DC, RG49, Jose Periz, Serial Patent 912808.
113. Pinal County Recorder, Florence, Arizona, Warranty Deed, Book 39, pp. 244-245.
114. "Miles Again Named to Industrial Board," *The Arizona Republic*, December 7, 1955 p. 2, cols. 6-7; "Your Lawmakers, J. Ney Miles Operates Ray Grocery," *Arizona Republic*, February 14, 1951, page unknown (from Arizona State Library and Archives, Special Collections).
115. Conversation with the Tonto National Forest rangers. Date not recorded.
116. Pete Weinel, telephone conversation on September 25, 2001, Tonto National Forest, Phoenix Office.
117. We first learned of this stone corral from Tim's (screen name) December 26, 2005 trip report on www.hikearizona.com.
118. Jim, Phyllis, and Frank Herron, interview at the Herron Ranch on June 14, 1998.
119. Howard Horinek, interviews on June 4, 2001 and February 21, 2002. Story told to Horinek by Dutch Ortega who heard the story from Benny Miles; Dutch Ortega, conversation at the Gila County Cattle Growers Auction on May 13, 2009.
120. Jimmie E. Jinks, *Mineral Investigation of the Superstition Wilderness...*, USGS Open-File Report 83-885, MLA 136-82, 1982, pp. 22-23; L. A. Stewart, *Chrysoltile-Asbestos Deposits of Arizona*, U.S. Department of Interior, Bureau of Mines, Information Circular 7706, January 1955, pp. 110-113.
121. See note 119.
122. We thought this was John Fritz's "Trick in the Trail" in his www.hikearizona.com trip description "Bull Basin Loop," but we later determined that his canyon was located downstream from the Y Bar B Corral. In 1997, we did not see either of these cairned routes.
123. Jim, Phyllis, and Frank Herron, interview at the Herron Ranch on June 14, 1998.
124. Jim, Phyllis, and Frank Herron, interview at the Herron Ranch on October 14, 1999.
125. Cliff Edwards, *Horseback and Airborne, The Life and Times of Cliff "Tailspin" Edwards* (Coolidge, Arizona: Cliff Edwards, 1995), pp. 20, 32-33.
126. Tom Kollenborn, "Fool's Canyon Gold," *Arizona Territorial Newspaper*, February 2, 1998, p. 13, cols. 1-6.
127. John G. Bourke, *Field Notes, Scouts in Arizona Territory, Nov. 18th 1872 to April 8th 1873*. Map on p. 102. Microfilm copied from Arizona State University, Hayden Library, Special Collections. Color copy of map on page 226 was made for us by Susan Lintelmann, USMA Library, Special Collections and Archives, Department of the Army, United States Military Academy, West Point, NY; John G. Bourke, *The Diaries of John Gregory Bourke, Volume One, November 20, 1872 – July 28, 1876*, ed. Charles M. Robinson III (Denton, Texas: University of North Texas Press, 2003), pp. 55-70.
128. Jim, Phyllis, and Frank Herron, interviews at the Herron Ranch on June 14, 1998 and October 14, 1999.
129. Arizona Livestock Sanitary Board, Brand Book Supplement for 1935, p. 37, row 23. The 1943 brand book also lists J. Ney Miles as the owner of the Y Lazy Y brand, p. 130, row 9. The 1953 brand book lists V. H. and Frances Kennedy as the owners of the Y Lazy Y brand, p. 145, row 14.
130. Howard Horinek, interview at the Quarter Circle U Ranch on January 17, 2001.
131. Howard Horinek, interview at the Quarter Circle U Ranch on January 17, 2001 and telephone conversation on May 12, 2008. Bob Hale told Horinek about the Cuff Button Road.
132. "A Road to Globe," *Arizona Daily Star*, October 20, 1891, p. 3, col. 2; F. P. Trott, "Grade of the Globe Road," *Phoenix Herald*, December 1, 1891, p. 1, col. 2; F. P. Trott, "That Globe Road," *Phoenix Daily Herald*, December 19, 1891, p. 2, col. 3.
133. Jim, Phyllis, and Frank Herron, interview at the Herron Ranch, October 14, 1999.
134. Tonto National Forest Cultural Resources Inventory, Silver Spur Cabin, Site No. AR-03-12-02-991, project no. 91-127, June 8, 1991, by Kevin Craig and E. Zamora.
135. Billy Martin, conversation at the Martin Ranch on Queen Creek. Date not recorded.
136. Howard Horinek, interview at the Quarter Circle U Ranch on January 17, 2001.

Reference Notes

Howard said they called this canyon "Wildcat Canyon" when he was the ranch manager for the JH6 Ranch between 1985 and 1992.

137. Howard Horinek, interview at the Quarter Circle U Ranch on January 17, 2001.
138. Howard Horinek, interview at the Quarter Circle U Ranch on January 17, 2001 and conversation at the Quarter Circle U Ranch on April 20, 2007.
139. Pinal County District Court, Florence, Arizona Territory, Civil Case #431, April 5, 1884; Pinal County Clerk of the Court, Florence, Arizona Territory, Marriages, Book 1, February 1, 1885; Pinal County Recorder, Florence, Arizona, Book of Deeds #12, July 22, 1889, p. 25; Certificate of Death, Index No. 317, Pinal County, Florence, Arizona, James Rogers, July 24, 1917.
140. Maricopa County Recorder, Mining Claims Book 1, p. 54, November 21, 1876; "Good Mines," *Arizona Weekly Enterprise* newspaper, October 12, 1889, p. 3 col. 3.
141. "Rogers District," *The Pinal Drill*, June 16, 1883; "Our Mines," *The Pinal Drill*, July 28, 1883; "Arizona Mines," *The Pinal Drill*, September 1, 1883.
142. Gregory Davis, communication on April 12, 1994; Bernice McGee, "The Other World of the Superstitions," *Old West*, Winter 1964, p. 15.
143. "Rogers District," *The Pinal Drill*, June 16, 1883.
144. Pinal County Recorder, Florence, Arizona, Location Notice, Lode Mining Claim, Docket 184, p. 150, July 31, 1957.
145. Tom Lorang Jones, *Arizona Trail: The Official Guide* (Englewood, Colorado: Westcliffe Publishers, 2005), pp. 156-165.
146. Scott Wood, Martin McAllister, Michael Sullivan, *11,000 Years on Tonto National Forest* (Albuquerque, New Mexico: Southwest Natural and Cultural Heritage Association), pp. 12-30; Jeffery Dean, *Salado* (Albuquerque, University of New Mexico Press); H. Wormington, *Prehistoric Indians of the Southwest* (Denver, Colorado, The Denver Museum of Natural History, 1947-1968), pp. 118-147; Robert Bigando, *Besh-Ba-Gowah Archaeological Park Interpretive Guide* (Globe, Arizona: City of Globe, 1987), pp. 1-40; Jeffery Clark, Patrick Lyons, J. Brett Hill, Anna Neuzil, William Doelle, "Immigrants and Population Collapse in the Southern Southwest," *Archaeology Southwest*, Fall 2008, vol. 22, no. 4, pp.1-15; also see Notes 27 and 147 for more about the Salado.
147. J. Brett Hill, "Hohokam Population Collapse in Salt River Valley," *Archaeology Southwest*, Fall 2007, vol. 21, no. 4, pp.15-16; also see Notes 27 and 146 for more about the Salado.
148. *Arizona Daily Gazette*, January 26, 1899, p. 5, col. 2, reprinted in *Early Newspaper Articles of The Superstition Mountains and The Lost Dutchman Gold Mine* by Gregory Davis (Apache Junction, Arizona: Superstition Mountain Historical Society 1992), pp. 44-45; Dave Wilson, *Hiking Ruins Seldom Seen* (Helena, Montana: Falcon Publishing) pp. 66-68.
149. Carol Locust, *DeGrazia, The Rest of the Story* (Tucson, Arizona: U.S. Press and Graphics, 2004); John Dahlmann, *A Tiny Bit of God's Creation* (Tempe, Arizona: Reliable Reproductions, 1979), p. 144. Swanson, *Superstition Mountain*, p. 193.
150. Maggie Wilson, *Arizona Highways*, March 1983, p. 6.
151. Marie Reavis Hall, *The Reavis Family* (Winston-Salem, N.C.: Smith Printing, 1971), p. 94. Elisha M. Reavis files and Reavis family correspondence from the files of Gregory Davis; Robert Mason, *More Verde Valley Lore* (Phoenix, Arizona: Phoenix Publishing Group, 2004), pp. 10-14.
152. Robert Mason, *The Burning* (Phoenix, Arizona: Phoenix Publishing Group, 2000), pp. 136, 141-149; "Maricopa County, Correspondence of the Arizona Miner, The Indians," *Weekly Arizona Miner*, May 3, 1873, p. 3, col. 2; "A Mountain Ranch," *Arizona Weekly Enterprise*, February 25, 1888, p. 3, col. 3.
153. Lottie C. Devine, *Es Verdad or It is True* (Coolidge, Arizona: Coolidge Shopper Printing and Publishing Co., 1964), p. 67-69; "Old Bill Reavis," *Arizona Enterprise*, August 31, 1893, p. 1, col. 9.
154. "City and County Croppings," *The Pinal Drill*, Sept. 8, 1883; Matt Cavaness, *Memoirs of Matt Cavaness*, typed by Joseph Miller, Arizona State Library and Archives, Phoenix, #58531, manuscript pp. 59-61.
155. "Our Mines, Rogers District, Rieves's (sic) Ranch, the Forest and the Pinery," *The Pinal Drill*, July 7, 1883; "A Ghastly Find," *The Arizona Silver Belt*, Globe, Arizona, May

14, 1896; Pinal County Probate Court, Florence, AT, Cases 160 and 161, Elisha Reavis, Arizona State Library and Archives, Phoenix, Arizona, Film 88.4.20.
156. "A Ghastly Find," *The Arizona Silver Belt*, Globe, Arizona, May 14, 1896; Pinal County Probate Court, Florence, AT, Cases 160 and 161, Elisha Reavis, Arizona State Library and Archives, Phoenix, Film 88.4.20.
157. Probate Court, Florence, AT, Cases 160 and 161, Elisha Reavis, Arizona State Library and Archives, Phoenix, Film 88.4.20.
158. Richard G. Schaus, "William Hardin (sic) Martin, 1891," *Arizona Cattlelog*, March 1966, back cover; Robert Rogers, "Bill Martin, Half A Century In The Superstitions," *Arizona Cattlelog*, January 1967, pp. 30-38, continued in February 1967, pp. 25-32.
159. John W. Olson, interview by Gladys Walker on August 12 and 13, 1989, transcribed by Jack Carlson.
160. Bill and Helen Martin, interviews on October 15, 1999, April 11, 2007, and June 5, 2007.
161. Gustavus Cox, *Topographical Map of Pioneer Mining District and Adjacent Country, Pinal County, Arizona Territory, 1882*, oversize map call number G4331.H1 P5 from Arizona Historical Society, Tucson, Arizona or University of Arizona, Special Collections, Tucson, Arizona.
162. Pinal County Recorder, Record of Mines #1, February 24, 1877, p. 448; B. Salyer, *1890 Great Registers of Arizona* (Mesa, Arizona: Arizona Genealogical Advisory Board, 2001) p. 9. "1896 Pinal County Great Register" from Pinal County Historical Society records, Florence, Arizona.
163. Pinal County Recorder, Florence, Arizona, Record of Mines #1, January 19, 1877, p. 413; "The Rogers District and Camp, Pinal County," *The Pinal Drill*, July 17, 1880, p. 1 cols. 4-5; "What is doing in our Mines, Rogers District," *The Pinal Drill*, March 11, 1882, p. 4 cols. 1-2.
164. *Arizona Weekly Enterprise*, December 29, 1883, p. 2 cols. 1-4.
165. "What is doing in our Mines, Rogers District," *The Pinal Drill*, March 11, 1882, p. 4 cols. 1-2.
166. "Our Mines," *The Pinal Drill*, March 10, 1883. "Rogers District, Worldbeater," *The Pinal Drill*, September 22, 1883; "Our Mines," *The Pinal Drill*, October 13, 1883.
167. Pinal County Recorder, Florence, Arizona, Book of Deeds #12, July 22, 1889, p. 25; "Good Mines," *Arizona Weekly Enterprise*, October 12, 1889, p. 3 col. 3.
168. Pinal County Recorder, Florence, Arizona, Miscellaneous Records, Book 1, August 5, 1879, p. 341 and Record of Mines #37, July 31, 1921, p. 590; Gustavus Cox, *Topographical Map of Pioneer Mining District and Adjacent Country, Pinal County, Arizona Territory, 1882*, call number G4331.H1 P5, oversize map from Arizona Historical Society, Tucson, Arizona or University of Arizona, Special Collections, Tucson, Arizona.
169. Erick Steinbach, Glen E. Rice, "Archaeological Monitoring of Debris Fill…," Rio Salado Archaeology, L.L.C., Technical Report No. 05-12, June 14, 2005, revised September 28, 2005.
170. Tonto National Forest Cultural Resources Inventory, Silver Spur Cabin, Site No. AR-03-12-02-991, project no. 91-127, June 8, 1991, by Kevin Craig and E. Zamora.
171. Jim, Phyllis, and Frank Herron, interview at the Herron Ranch on October 14, 1999.
172. Billy Martin, conversation, no date.
173. Billy and Helen "Teta" Martin, conversation at the Martin Ranch on June 5, 2007.
174. Gustavus Cox, *Topographical Map of Pioneer Mining District and Adjacent Country, Pinal County, Arizona Territory, 1882*, oversize map call number G4331.H1 P5 from Arizona Historical Society, Tucson, Arizona or University of Arizona, Special Collections, Tucson, Arizona; USGS map, Florence, Arizona, edition of March 1902, reprinted October 1912, surveyed in 1900.
175. "Rogers District," *The Pinal Drill*, June 16, 1883; "Our Mines, Rogers District, Rieves's (sic) Ranch, the Forest and the Pinery," *The Pinal Drill*, July 7, 1883; "Our Mines," *The Pinal Drill*, July 28, 1883; "City and County Croppings," *The Pinal Drill*, September 8, 1883; Memoirs of Matt Cavaness, typed by Joseph Miller, Arizona State Library and Archives, Phoenix, Arizona, #58531, manuscript pp. 59-61.
176. Mark Trainor, "Reavis Canyon, A Gem of the Arizona Trail," *Sweat*, November 2003, pp. 14-15.
177. Tom Kollenborn, "Mesa City–Globe Wagon Road, Part 1,"*Apache Junction News*, June 11-17, 2001, p. A4, reference to the July 17, 1880 *Pinal Drill* newspaper article.
178. F. P. Trott, "That Globe Road," *Phoenix Daily Herald*, December 19, 1891, p. 2, col. 3; F. P. Trott, "Grade of the Globe Road," *Phoenix Herald*, December 1, 1891, p. 1, col. 2; "A Road to Globe," *Arizona Daily Star*, October 20, 1891, p. 3, col. 2.
179. F. N. Holmquist, *Map of Central Arizona* (Phoenix, Arizona: F. N. Holmquist, 1916); USGS map, Florence Quadrangle, Arizona, surveyed in 1900, March 1902 edition, reprinted October 1912, 100 foot contour interval, 30 minute topographic map.

Selected Bibliography

Additional research sources can be found in the Reference Notes.
Aitchison, Stewart, and Bruce Grubbs. *The Hiker's Guide to Arizona.* Helena, Montana: Falcon Press, 1987.
Anderson, Donna. *History of Globe, Arizona.* Seattle, Washington: Classic Day Publishing, 2007.
Anderson, Guy, and Donna Anderson (editors). *Honor the Past...Mold the Future.* Globe, Arizona: Gila Centennials, Inc. Celebration Committee, 1976.
Bailey, Lynn R. *Shaft Furnaces and Beehive Kilns.* Tucson, Arizona: Westernlore Press, 2002.
Bigando, Robert. *Besh-Ba-Gowah Archaeological Park Interpretive Guide.* Globe, Arizona: City of Globe, 1987.
Bigando, Robert. *Globe, Arizona, The Life and Times of a Western Mining Town.* Globe, Arizona: Mountain Spirit Press, 1990.
Bourke, John. *The Diaries of John Gregory Bourke, Volume One.* Edited by Charles M. Robinson, III. Denton, Texas: University of North Texas Press, 2003.
Bourke, John. *Field Notes, Scouts in Arizona Territory, Nov. 18th 1872 to April 28th 1873.* Arizona State University, Special Collections, microfilm of diary, 973.8 B567. Color copies of Bourke's maps from United States Military Academy Library, Special Collections, West Point, New York.
Bourke, John. *On the Boarder with Crook.* New York: Charles Scribner's Sons, 1891, 1892.
Brown, Wynne. *Trail Riding Arizona.* Guilford, Connecticut: The Globe Pequot Press, 2006.
Carlson, Jack, and Elizabeth Stewart. *Hiker's Guide to the Superstition Wilderness: With History and Legends of Arizona's Lost Dutchman Gold Mine.* Tempe, Arizona: Clear Creek Publishing, 2002.
Clardy, Susan. *Sometimes the Blues, the Letters and Diaries of Frank Hammon.* Tucson, Arizona: The Arizona Historical Society, 2007.
Clinger, Wade. *GPS Waypoints of Colorado's Fourteeners.* Boulder, Colorado: Pruett Publishing Company, 2000.
Curnow, Alice. *The Journey with Tom, Memories of an Arizona Pioneer Woman.* Prescott, Arizona: HollyBear Press, 2003.
Dallett, Nancy. *At the Confluence of Change: A History of Tonto National Monument.* Tucson, Arizona: Western National Parks Association, 2008.
Daughters of the Gila County Pioneers. *A Cultural History of The Pioneer Women of Gila County, Arizona and Their Descendants, Vols. 1 and 2.* Payson, Arizona: Git A Rope! Publishing, Inc., 2002 and 2005.
Davis, Gregory, E. *Early Newspaper Articles of the Superstition Mountains and the Lost Dutchman Gold Mine.* Apache Junction, Arizona: Superstition Mountain Historical Society, 1992.
Dean, Jeffrey, S. *Salado.* Albuquerque: University of New Mexico Press, 2000.
Edwards, Cliff. *Horseback and Airborne.* Coolidge, Arizona: Cliff Edwards, 1995.
Ellison, Glenn. *Cowboys Under the Mogollon Rim.* Tucson, Arizona: The University of Arizona Press, 1968.
Ellison, Glenn. *More Tales from Slim Ellison.* Tucson, Arizona: The University of Arizona Press, 1981.
Epple, Anne Orth, and Lewis E. Epple. *A Field Guide to the Plants of Arizona.* Mesa, Arizona: LewAnn Publishing Company, 1995.
Farish, Thomas. *History of Arizona.* Vols. 1 and 2. Phoenix, Arizona: Second Legislature of the State of Arizona, 1915.
Feldman, Jesse. *Jacob's Trail: The Legend of Jacob Waltz's Lost Dutchman Gold Mine.* Apache Junction, Arizona: Jesse Feldman, 2009.
Feldman, Ron. *Crooked Mountain.* Apache Junction, Arizona: World Publishing Corp., 2000.
Feldman, Ron. *Deep Fault.* Apache Junction, Arizona: Ron Feldman, 2005.
Furtkamp, Margaret. *Northern Gila County, Arizona, Cemetery Inscriptions.* Payson, Arizona: Margaret Furtkamp, 1998.
Ganci, Dave. *Arizona Day Hikes.* San Francisco, California: Sierra Club Books, 1995.
Garrido, Betty (editor). *Superior, Arizona, 1882-1982 Centennial.* Superior, Arizona: Superior Centennial Celebration Committee, 1982.
Grubbs, Bruce. *Best Hikes Near Phoenix.* Guilford, Connecticut: The Globe Pequot Press, 2008.
Grubbs, Bruce. *Hiking Arizona.* Guilford, Connecticut: The Globe Pequot Press, 2008.
Grubbs, Bruce. *Hiking Arizona's Superstition and Mazatzal Country.* Guilford, Connecticut: The Globe Pequot Press, 2000.
Grubbs, Bruce. *Best Loop Hikes, Arizona.* Seattle, Washington: The Mountaineers Books, 2004.
Grubbs, Bruce, and Stewart Aitchison. *Hiking Arizona.* Guilford, Connecticut: The Globe Pequot Press, 2002.
Haak, William. *Copper Bottom Tales, Historic Sketches from Gila County.* Globe, Arizona: Gila County Historical Society, 1991.

Hancock, Jan. *Horse Trails in Arizona*. Phoenix, Arizona: Golden West Publishers, Inc., 1994.
Hayes, Alden. *A Portal to Paradise*. Tucson, Arizona: The University of Arizona Press, 1999.
Hayes, Jess. *Sheriff Thompson's Day*. Tucson, Arizona: The University of Arizona Press, 1968.
Jones, Tom. *Arizona Trail, The Official Guide*. Englewood, Colorado: Westcliffe Publishers, Inc., 2005.
Joy, Betty E. *Hammer. Angela Hutchinson Hammer: Arizona's Pioneer Newspaperwoman*. Tucson, Arizona: The University of Arizona Press, 2005.
Knight, Ann Rose. *Emigrant Knight of Cornwall*. Arizona: Ann Rose Knight, 1991.
Kollenborn, Thomas. *The Chronological History of the Superstition Wilderness Area, The Lost Dutchman Mine and the Adjacent Central Mountain Region*. Apache Junction, Arizona: Thomas Kollenborn, 1st edition 1988, rev. 2000.
Kollenborn, Tom, and James Swanson. *Superstition Mountain, In the Footsteps of the Dutchman*. Apache Junction, Arizona: Ray's Printing, 2008.
Laine, Don, Barbara Laine, and Lawrence Letham. *Best Short Hikes in Arizona*. Seattle, Washington: The Mountaineers Books, 2005.
Lamb, Samuel. *Woody Plants of the Southwest*. Santa Fe, New Mexico: Sunstone Press, 1989
Lankford, Andrea. *Biking the Arizona Trail: The Complete Guide to Day-Riding and Thru-Biking*. Englewood, Colorado: Westcliffe Publishers, Inc., 2002.
LeCount, Al. *The History of Tonto*. Punkin Center, Arizona: A Bicentennial Project by the Punkin Center Homemakers, 1976.
Liu, Charles. *60 Hikes within 60 Miles, Phoenix: including Tempe, Scottsdale, and Glendale*. Birmingham, Alabama: Menasha Ridge Press, 2006 and 2007.
Live Stock Sanitary Board. *Arizona Brand Book and Supplement, State of Arizona*. Phoenix, Arizona: Live Stock Sanitary Board, 1943, 1953, and 1963.
Locust, Carol. *DeGrazia: The Rest of the Story*. Tucson, Arizona: U.S. Press and Graphics, 2004.
Mason, Robert. *The Burning*. Phoenix, Arizona: Phoenix Publishing Group, 2000.
Mazel, David. *Arizona Trails: 100 Hikes in Canyon and Sierra*. Berkeley, California: Wilderness Press, 1993.
Mitchell, James. *50 Hikes in Arizona*. Baldwin Park, California: Gem Guides Book Co., 1973, 1991.
Mitchell, John. *Lost Mines and Buried Treasures*. Glorieta, New Mexico: Rio Grande Press, 1982.
Nelson, Dick, and Sharon Nelson. *Hiker's Guide to the Superstition Mountains*. Glenwood, New Mexico: Tecolote Press, 1978.
Northern Gila County Genealogical Society. *1882-1907 School Census, Gila County, Arizona*. Payson, Arizona: Northern Gila County Genealogical Society, Inc., no date.
Northern Gila County Historical Society. *Rim Country History*. Payson, Arizona: Rim Country Printery, 1984.
Padegimas, Tony. *Day & Overnight Hikes: Tonto National Forest*. Birmingham, Alabama: Menasha Ridge Press, 2008.
Patera, Alan, and John Gallagher. *Arizona Post Offices*. Lake Grove, Oregon: The Depot, 1988.
Salyer, Barbara. *Arizona 1890 Great Registers*. Mesa, Arizona: Arizona Genealogical Advisory Board, 2001.
San Felice, Jack. *Lost El Dorado of Jacob Waltz*. Mesa, Arizona: Millsite Canyon Publishing, 2007.
San Felice, Jack. *When Silver Was King*. Mesa, Arizona: Millsite Canyon Publishing, 2006.
Sheridan, Michael F. and Jan B. Sheridan. *Recreational Guide to the Superstition Mountains and the Salt River Lakes*. Tempe, Arizona: Impression Makers, 1984.
Storm, Barry. *Thunder God's Gold*. Phoenix, Arizona: Southwest Publishing, 1946.
Superstition Mountain Historical Society. *Superstition Mountain Journal*. Apache Junction, Arizona: Superstition Mountain Historical Society, 1981-2007.
Swanson, James, and Tom Kollenborn. *Circlestone: A Superstition Mountain Mystery*. Apache Junction, Arizona: Goldfield Press, 1986.
Swanson, James, and Tom Kollenborn. *Superstition Mountain: A Ride Through Time*. Phoenix, Arizona: Arrowhead Press, 1981.
Theobald, John, and Lillian Theobald. *Arizona Territory Post Offices and Postmasters*. Phoenix, Arizona: Arizona Historical Foundation, 1961.
Tighe, Kelly, and Susan Moran. *On the Arizona Trail: A Guide for Hikers, Cyclists, and Equestrians*. Boulder, Colorado: Pruett Publishing Company, 1998.
U. S. Forest Service. *Superstition Wilderness, Tonto National Forest*. Phoenix, Arizona: U. S. Forest Service, 1991.
Wachholtz, Florence (editor). *Arizona, the Grand Canyon State: A History of Arizona*. Vols. 1 and 2. Westminister, Colorado: Western States Historical Publishers, Inc., 1975.
Warren, Scott. *100 Hikes in Arizona*. Seattle, Washington: The Mountaineers, 1994.
Waterstrat, Elaine. *Commanders and Chiefs*. Fountain Hills, Arizona: Mount McDowell Press, 1993.
Wilson, Dave. *Hiking Ruins Seldom Seen*. Helena, Montana: Falcon Publishing, 1999.
Wood, Scott, Martin McAllister, and Michael Sullivan. *10,000 Years on Tonto National Forest*. Albuquerque, New Mexico: Southwest Natural and Cultural Heritage Association, no date.
Woody, Clara, and Milton Schwartz. *Globe, Arizona*. Tucson, Arizona: The Arizona Historical Society, 1977.
Zarbin, Earl. *Roosevelt Dam: A History to 1911*. Phoenix, Arizona: Salt River Project, 1984.

USEFUL ADDRESSES

EMERGENCY TELEPHONE NUMBERS

Dial 911 from any telephone for emergency help. For non-emergency problems see the listings under *Government Agencies, Parks*, and the comments below.

Pinal County Sheriff's Department has jurisdiction in the southern part of the Superstition Wilderness. Contact them at 971 North Jason Lopez Circle, Building C., Florence, AZ 85132, (520) 866-5111, 1-800-420-8689, www.pinalcountyaz.gov.

Maricopa County Sheriff's Department has jurisdiction in the northern portion of the Superstition Wilderness. Contact them at 100 W. Washington St., Suite 1900, Phoenix, AZ 85003, (602) 856-1011, Crime Stop Number (602) 262-6151, www.mcso.org.

Gila County Sheriff's Department has jurisdiction on the eastern end of the Superstition Wilderness near Roosevelt Lake. Contact them at 1100 South Street, Globe, AZ 85501, (928) 425-4449, www.co.gila.az.us.

GOVERNMENT AGENCIES

Arizona State Land Department, 1616 W. Adams St., Phoenix, AZ 85007, permits and general information (602) 542-4631, www.land.state.az.us/.

Forest Supervisors Office, Tonto National Forest, 2324 E. McDowell Road, Phoenix, AZ 85006, (602) 225-5200, www.fs.fed.us/r3/tonto.

Globe Ranger District, Tonto National Forest, 7680 S. Six Shooter Canyon Road, Globe, AZ 85501, (928) 402-6200, www.fs.fed.us/r3/tonto.

Mesa Ranger District, Tonto National Forest, 5140 E. Ingram Street, Mesa, AZ 85205, (480) 610-3300, www.fs.fed.us/r3/tonto.

Tonto Basin Ranger District, Tonto National Forest, HC02 Box 4800, Roosevelt, AZ 85545, (928) 467-3200, located at Roosevelt Lake Visitors Center, www.fs.fed.us/r3/tonto.

MUSEUMS AND COLLECTIONS

Blue Bird Mine Gift Shop, 5405 N. Apache Trail, Apache Junction, AZ 85119, (480) 982-2653, 4.5 miles northeast of Apache Junction on State Route 88.

Bob Jones Museum and Superior Historical Society, 300 Main Street, Superior, AZ 85173, (520) 689-0200, www.geocities.com/superiorhs.

Buckboard Restaurant and Museum, 1111 W. Highway 60, Superior, AZ, 85173, museum (520) 208-0634, cafe (520) 689-5800, www.worldssmallestmuseum.com.

Bullion Plaza Cultural Center & Museum, Bullion Plaza, Miami, AZ, (928) 473-3700, www.bullionplazamuseum.org.

Gila County Historical Museum and Society, 1330 N. Broad Street, Globe, AZ 85501, (928) 425-7385, www.globemiamichamber.com.

Goldfield Ghost Town, 4650 N. Mammoth Mine Road, Apache Junction, AZ 85119, (480) 983-0333, www.goldfieldghosttown.com. On Route 88, north of Apache Junction.

Pinal County Historical Museum and Society, 715 S. Main St., Florence, AZ 85132, (520) 868-4382, http://pinalcountyaz.gov/Visitors.

Superstition Mountain Museum and Society, 4087 N. Apache Trail, Apache Junction, AZ 85119, (480) 983-4888, www.superstitionmountainmuseum.org. On State Route 88, northeast of Apache Junction.

Tortilla Flat Restaurant, One Main Street, Tortilla Flat, AZ 85190, (480) 984-1776, www.tortillaflataz.com, 17 miles northeast of Apache Junction on State Route 88.

Roosevelt Lake Visitors Center, (Tonto Basin Ranger Station), HC02 P.O. Box 4800, Roosevelt, AZ 85545, (928) 467-3200, , www.fs.fed.us/r3/tonto.

ORGANIZATIONS

Apache Junction Chamber of Commerce, 567 W. Apache Trail, Apache Junction, AZ 85120, (480) 982-3141, www.apachejunctioncoc.com.

Arizona Mountaineering Club, 4340 E. Indian School Road, Ste. 21-164, Phoenix, AZ 85018, www.amcaz.org.

Arizona Trail Association, P.O. Box 36736, Phoenix, AZ 85067, (602) 252-4794, www.aztrail.org.

The Dons of Arizona, P.O. Box 44740, Phoenix, AZ 85064, (602) 258-6016, www.donsofarizona.com.

Globe-Miami Chamber of Commerce, 1360 North Broad Street (Route 60), Globe, AZ 85501, (928) 425-4495, 1-800-804-5623, www.globemiamichamber.com.

Reevis Mountain School, HC02 Box 1534, Roosevelt, AZ 85545, messages (928) 467-2675, questions (480) 961-0490, www.reevismountain.org.

Superior Chamber of Commerce, P.O. Box 95, Superior, AZ 85173, (520) 689-0200, www.superiorazchamber.net.

Superstition Area Land Trust (SALT), P.O. Box 582, Apache Junction, AZ 85117, (480) 983-2345, www.azsalt.org.

Superstition Mountain Treasure Hunters, 940 W. Apache Trail, Apache Junction, AZ 85117, (480) 983-3484, www.smth-gold.com.

Superstition Search and Rescue, P.O. Box 1123, Apache Junction, AZ 85117, (480) 350-3993, www.superstition-sar.org.

PARKS

Besh-Ba-Gowah Archaeological Park, on Jess Hayes Road, c/o City of Globe, 150 N. Pine Street, Globe, AZ 85501, (928) 425-0320, www.globemiamichamber.com.

Boyce Thompson Arboretum State Park, 37615 U.S. Highway 60, AZ 85173, at milepost 223, (520) 689-2811, (520) 689-2723, http://arboretum.ag.arizona.edu.

Lost Dutchman State Park, 6109 N. Apache Trail, Apache Junction, AZ 85119, on State Route 88 northeast of Apache Junction, (480) 982-4485, www.pr.state.az.us.

Tonto National Monument, HC02 Box 4602, Roosevelt, AZ 85545, (928) 467-2241, on State Route 188 across from Roosevelt Lake, www.nps.gov.

RIDING STABLES

Apache Lake Ranch, P.O. Box 15693, Tortilla Flat, AZ 85190, (928) 467-2822, 2 miles west of Apache Lake at milepost 227 on State Route 88.

Don Donnelly's D-Spur Ranch Stables, 15371 Ojo Road, Gold Canyon, AZ 85118, off of Peralta Road, (602) 810-7029, www.dondonnelly.com.

OK Corral Stables and RV Horse Campground, 2645 E. Whiteley, Apache Junction, AZ 85117, (480) 982-4040, www.okcorrals.com.

INDEX

Bold indicates map or photo caption.

A

Adams, Captain, 225
Alchesay Vista, 92
Allen Blackman Trail, 52, 140, 153, 156, 270
Allen, George, **95**
Allison (Frank Hammon's prospecting partner), 176
Anderson, John, 146
Anderson Ranch, 146, 180
Angel Basin, 255, **256**
Angel Spring, 256
Ann Curtis Taylor Trust, 198
Apache, 54, 93, 111, 117–119, 176, 206, 225, **226**
Apache Junction, Arizona, 21
Apache Lake, 46, 69
Apache Lake Marina and Resort, 46, 69
Apache Lodge, **101**
Apache Trail, 315
apple orchards, 49, **50**, **54**, 57, 58, 158, 159, 162, 197, 270. *See also* orchards
Arivaca, Arizona, 197
Arizona State Trust land, 22, 32
Arizona Trail, **25**, 92, 100, **103**, 110, 113, 249, 292, 298, 324
Armer, Henry, 93, 94, **95**
Armer, Lucinda, 94
Armer, Preston, 94
Armer Post Office, 94
Armer Ranch, 93, 94, **95**, 127
army. *See* military
Atchison (Rogers District mine supervisor), 276
Avendano, Danny, 144

B

B4 brand, 209
Backus, Charles "Chuck," 32, 68
Backus, Judy, 32
Backus, Tony, **66**, 68
Backus Ranch, 32, 68
Bacon, Alice. *See* Bacon, Lucille
Bacon, Earl, 133
Bacon, Earl E., 116, 133
Bacon, Gladys, **256**
Bacon, Grant, 133
Bacon, John "Hoolie," 32, 58, 83, 133, **256**, 264, 269
Bacon, Lucille, 58
Bacon, Ruth (Cooper), 133
Baldwin, Bill, 221
Barber, Trent, **275**
Bark, James, 32
Bark-Criswell Ranch, 32, 255
Barkley Cattle Company, 32
Bark Ranch, 32, 255
barn building, **196**, 198, **210**, 244
Bar SL brand, 262
Bar V Bar brand, 97, **123**
Beanie (pack burro), 172
Beanie Burrito Canyon, 85, 88, 172
Beardstown, Illinois, 262
bears, 167, 194
Bear Spring, 146
Beartooth Maps, 18
Bebeau, Gerard "Cap," 178
Bennett (woodcutter), 248
Beyer, Maria Selma (Rogers), 248
Beyer, Rosalie (Reymert), 248
BHP Copper Company, 175, 188, 202
bicycles, 22, 314
Bigfoot, Peter. *See* Busnack, Peter "Bigfoot"
bikes. *See* bicycles
Binkley (woodcutter), 248
Bixby Ranch, 180
Black Brush Ranch, 113, 116. *See also* Two Bar Ranch
Black Bush Ranch, 116. *See also* Two Bar Ranch
Black Jack Spring, 140, 142, 148, 152, 156, 234
Blackman, Allen, 54, 63. *See also* Allen Blackman Trail
Black Mesquite Spring, 94, 116
Blevins (man who followed Waltz), 89
Blevins Cemetery, 97
Blevins family, 97
Bloomerville, Arizona, 56
Bluff Spring, 38, 310, 318
Bluff Spring Trail, 310
Board House, 32

Bohme, Fay, 208
Bohme, Martha, 186
Bohme, William, 146, 216
Bohme Ranch, 198
Bonn, Max, 208
Bonn's Meat Market, 208
Boulder Canyon Trail, 318, 320
bouldering, 15, 26
Boulder Pass, 159, 162, **168**
Boulder Peak, 162
Bourke, John, 76, 77, 79, 117–120, **121**, 168, 176, 206, 225, **226**, 234
Bourke's Butte, **76, 77, 121**
Bowen, Robert, 56
Bowman, R. Lewis, 206
Bowman Ranch, 206, 221
brands. *See also* ranches
   2E, 264
   2 Lazy H, 97
   B4, 209
   Bar SL, 262
   Bar V Bar, 97, 123
   Circle L Slash, **33**, 208
   Club, 192
   Cross P, 35, 97, 129, 134
   Diamond X, 132
   DO, 94
   Flying H, 127
   GAN, 132, 192
   Half Diamond Cross, 35, 134
   Hat, 132
   Hay Hook, 81, 113
   J Bar B, 134
   JF, 56, 58, 264
   JH, 241, 282
   JH6, 33. *See also* JH6 Ranch
   JK, 33, 178
   J Slash A, 58, 264
   Lazy E Spear, 264
   Lazy W Bar T, 197
   N, 129
   Quarter Circle V, 132, 133
   Rafter Cross, 134
   RE, 241, 282
   TU, 225
   Two Bar, 116
   V, 96
   X Bar P, 241
   Y Bar, 225
   Y Bar B, **30**, 31, 219, 221
   YJ, 129
   Y Lazy Y, 224, 225, 241, 282, **300**, 330n129
   YY, 224, 225, **300**, 303
Broadway Trailhead, 44, 314

Broerman, Frank, 249, 274
Brown, Major, 79, 117, 118, 225
Brownie (horse), 220
Brushy Spring, 137, 140, 156, 234
Buehman, Henry, **180**
Bull Basin, 214, 216
Bull Basin Corral, 214
Bull Basin Trail, 213-217, **218, 219**
Bull Basin Wash, 219
Burns, Captain, 79
Burns, Captain James, 118
Burns, Mike, 118
Busnack, Peter "Bigfoot," 35, 133, 134, **137**, 168

C

Cage, Bill, 222
Campaign Creek. *See* Campaign Trail and Campaign Trailhead
Campaign Trail, 135–142, 147–152, 154, 232–235, 286, **288**
Campaign Trailhead, 40, 128–134, 324
Camp Grant, 117, 118, 225
campgrounds,
   Canyon Lake area, 320
   Lost Dutchman State Park, 315
   Roosevelt Lake area, 90, 91, 92, 93, 104
   Tortilla Flat area, 321
Camp McDowell (Fort), 120, 225, 262
Cane Spring, 249. *See also* springs, Rogers
Canon Creek, 206
Can Spring, 249. *See also* springs, Rogers
Canyon Lake Trailhead, 45, 320, 324, 325
Canyon Overlook Trailhead, 319
Carlisle Indian School, 94
Carlson, Jack, **81, 158, 256**, 304, 351
Carney Mine, 35
Carney Springs Trailhead, 43, 312, 325
Carney Trail, 312
Carter, Blanche (Horrell), 134
Castle Dome, 48, 49, 59, **60**
Catalpa, Arizona, 94
cavalry. *See* military
Cavaness, Alice, 32
Cavaness, Matt, 32, 262, 298
Cavaness Ranch, 32
Cave, Peters Canyon, 321
Cave of a Thousand Eyes, 186
Cave Trail, 314
CCC (Civilian Conservation Corps), 33, 146, 178, 228, 229
Cedar Basin, 83
Cement Spring, **222**, 224, 300

cemeteries,
  Blevins, 97
  Cowboy Grave, 214, 216, 218
  Fairview, 198
  Florence, 248
  Globe, 93, 96
  Reavis Grave, 258, **263**, 271
  Reevis Mountain School, 20, 132
  Roosevelt, 98, 100, 101, 110
Cemetery Trail, 98, 100, 101, 110
Ceslinger, Charley "Charles," 248, 262, 274, 276
Chapo (packhorse), 220
Charlebois, Alfred, 32
Charlebois Ranch, 32
Charlebois Spring, 38, 310, 318
Charlebois Trail, 31
Cherry Creek, 56, 127
Chilson, Charles, 129
Chilson, Emily Jane (Gann), 129
Chilson, John, 129
Chiricahua (Cochise), 225
Cholla Tank, 31
Cimeron Mountain, 269
Circle L Slash brand, **33**, 208
Circlestone ruin, 50, 52, 54, 140, 151, **152**, **153**, 156, 270
Civilian Conservation Corps. *See* CCC
claims. *See* mines and claims
Clark, Frank, 178
Clark, Rae, **28**, **33**, 186, 206, **207**, 208
Clearlake, California, 192
Clemans, Earle, 56
Clemans, Mark Twain, 56, 57
Clemans, William, 56
Clemans, William, Jr., 56
Clemans Cattle Company, 32, 56, 264
cliff dwellings, 56, 250, 251, 254, **255**, 256
Cline, Frank, 94, **95**
Club brand, 192
Clymenson, John. *See* Storm, Barry
Cochise (Chiricahua leader), 225
Coffee Flat Trail, 309
Cohea, W. M., 96
Columbia Mine, **273**, 274
Coon Creek, 127
Coon Spring, 33, 178
Cooper, brothers, 133
Cooper, Chester, 96
Cooper, Dwight, 81, 96, 113, 168
Cooper, F. M., 162, 263
Cooper, Ruth, 133
corrals,
  Angel [near 29-H], **256**
  Bull Basin [24-P], 214

corrals (continued),
  Bull Basin [24-WW], 214
  Campaign Creek [near 14-G], 136
  Cement [25-P], **222**, 224
  Cottonwood Trail [10-E], 113
  Cuff Button [26-P], 146, 228, **229**, 245
  Double Corral [13-D], 122, **123**, 126
  Double Corral [26-KK], 246
  FR665 [6-A], 69
  Government [5-SS], 50, 65, 68
  Happy Camp, (along FR650] 198
  Haunted Canyon [near 23-PP], 194
  Haunted Canyon Trailhead [23-G], 193
  Honeycutt [31-P], 270
  Iron Mountain [34-G], 241, 282
  Klondike [20-KK], 167, 172
  Mormon [14-N], 142, **144**, 146
  Oak Flat [near 25-N], 148, 211, **234**, 286
  Paradise [24-K], 200, 216, **237**
  Pine Creek [7-N], 83
  Pinto Creek [22-V], 176, 184
  Rock [19-U], 167
  Rock Spring (Haunted Canyon), 198
  Rogers Canyon [near 29-RR], 251, **254**
  Silver Spur [33-SS], **283**
  Survey Route [34-WW], 303
  Tule Trail [13-K], 126
  Upper Pine Creek [15-Q], 153, 156, **166**, 167, 168
  Upper Pine Creek [15-X], 167, **168**
  Upper Pine Creek [15-Y], 167
  Whitford Canyon, [37-J], 294, 295, **298**
  Y Bar B [38-M], **30**, 31, 219, 221, 306, 308
  Yellow Jacket [6-G], 81
  Yellow Jacket [6-H], 81
Cortelyou, Denise, **132**, **192**, 330n99
Cottonwood Camp, 198, 295
Cottonwood Canyon, 110, 113
Cottonwood Creek, 104, 111, 113
Cottonwood Day Use Site, 92
Cottonwood Spring (Marlow Ranch), 31
Cottonwood Spring (Trail 120), 113, 116, 173
Cottonwood Trail, 104, 107, 110, 111, 112, 173, 174
Cowboy Grave, 214, 216, 218
Cox, Author, **95**
Cox, Gustavus, **273**, 295
Cox, Quentin "Ted," 249, 279
Craig, Geraldine, 192, 330n97
Criswell Ranch, 32, 255
Crocket Spring, 240, 286
Crocket Spring Wash, 240
Crook, General George, 93, 117, 118, 206
Crosscut Trail. *See* Jacob's Crosscut Trail
Crosscut Trailhead, 44, 316

Cross P brand, 35, 129, 134
Cross P Ranch, 35, 97, 129, 134
Cuff Button Corral, 146, 228, **229**, 245
Cuff Button Spring, 228, **229**, 245
Cuff Button Trail, 227-229, 245, 246

D

Daer, John, 198
Daley, E., 79
Danforth, George, 94, **95**
Danny Boy (horse), 83
Davis, A. P., **78**, 79
Davis, Gregory "Greg," 20, **255**, **256**, **306**
Deer Spring, 242, 283
Deer Spring Canyon, 225, 241, 283, 303
De Grazia, Ettore "Ted," 256
Delabaugh, James, 162, 262–264
Deseret Trust, 208
Desert Wells, 304
Diamond X brand, 132
difficulty ratings, 15, 16
DO brand, 94
Donahue-Hutchinson & Company, 248
Dons Camp Trailhead, 43, 311
Dons Club, 106
Double Corral [13-D], 122, **123**, 126
Double Corral [26-KK], 246
Duey, Jacob, **95**
Duryea, William, **95**
Dutchman, The. *See* Waltz, Jacob
Dutchman's Trail, 310, 318

E

East Fork Pinto Creek, 176
easy trips, 38
Edwards, Cliff, 206, 219, 221, 222
EK Ranch, 198
Elephant Butte, 264
elevation change definition, 17
Ellison, Slim, 208
Elms, David Jr., 63
ethics, Wilderness, 23-26

F

Fairview Cemetery, 198
Feldman, Jesse, **36**, 248, 279
Feldman, Ron, **36**, 37, 279
Fire Line Trail, 152, 153
First Water Ranch, 29, 31, 32
First Water Trailhead, 44, 318, 323–325
Fish Creek, 269
Fleming (Charles Ceslinger's mining partner), 274

Flippen, Joseph, 94, **95**
Florence, Arizona, 162, 262
Florence Cemetery, 248
Flying H brand, 127
Fool's Canyon, 222
Forest Service, 22, 23, 32, 33, 35, 96, 97, 116, 142, 150, 168, 186, 197, 221, **235**, 241
Fort McDowell (Camp), 110, 120, 225, 262
Foster, Winnie (Horrell), 180
Four Peaks Wilderness, 92, **103**
FR77, 310–312
FR78, 316–318
FR83, 112, 113, 126, 173, 174
FR172, 247, 289
FR172A, 247, 289
FR212, 46
FR213, 322
FR287, 175, 178, 188, 202
FR287A, 178, 188, 193, 199, 200, 202
FR305, 144, 245
FR306, 144
FR341, 101, 102, 110, 113
FR342, 195, 198
FR357, 247, 289
FR449, 117, 128
FR449A, 128
FR650, 198, **290**, 195, **306**
FR665, 69, 73, 74
Fraser, John "Jack," 32, 56, 57, 106, 255, 264
Fraser Canyon, 56, 304
Fraser Ranch, **302**, 304
Frazier, Stella (Pemberton), 106
Frazier, Thaddeus "Thad," 106
Frazier Horse Campground, 92, 104, 107
Frazier Recreation Site, 92, 104, 107
Frazier's Store, 97, **106**
Frazier Trailhead, 40, 104–106, 324
Fremont Saddle, 310
Frenchy (nickname for Jose Periz), 186
Fritz, John, 136
Frog Spring, 269
Frog Tank, 269
Frog Tanks Trail, 49, 268, 269

G

GAN brand, 132, 192
Gann, Alice. *See* Gann, Martha Alice
Gann, Andrew, 129
Gann, Emily Jane (Chilson), 129
Gann, Ephraim P. "Pete," 127, 129, **132**, **192**
Gann, Hilda, 192, 330n99
Gann, Ida May, **20**, 132, 328n61
Gann, Isaac, 133
Gann, Laura (Horrell), **192**

Gann, Martha Alice (Narron), 132, 133
Gann, Pete. *See* Gann, Ephraim
Gann, Teddie, 133
Gann, Travis, 132
Gann, Walter, 192
Gann, William T., 34, 127, 129, 132, 133, 192, 304
Gann Ranch, 132–134, 304
Gans Hole Spring, 127
Garden Valley, 31
Geronimo (Apache leader), 196
giardia (water purification), 38
Gila County Mountaineers, 116
Gilbert, Betty Porter, **45**, **189**, **197**
Gillette, Helen "Teta" (Martin), 264
Gladwin, Harold, 251, 254
Globe, Arizona, 21, 132
Globe Cemetery, 93, 96
Globe Ranger District, 23
Goldfield Mines, 35
Gold Gulch, 35, 178
gold ore, 35, 81, 176, 178, 274
gold panning, 37
Good Enough Mine, 274
Goodson, John, 134
Gordon, Elizabeth, 94, **95**
Government Camp, 65
Government Corral, 50, **65**, 68
Government Hill, 194, 200, 215, 237
Government Hill Wash, 194, 215
GPS (use and format), 18, 19
Grapevine, Arizona, 94, 132
Grapevine Bay Campground, 90
Grapevine Group Campground, 90
Grapevine Spring (at Roosevelt Lake), 32, 93, 94, 116, 327n28
Grapevine Spring (on Trail 203), 194, 200
Grave Canyon, 162, 258, **263**, 271, **273**
graves. *See* cemeteries
Greer, W. L., 206
Griffin, Charles, **95**
group size, 22, 23
Grubbs, Bruce, 79, 140, 141, 159, 173

H

Hackberry Spring, 38
Hale, Bob, 246
Hale family, 208
Half Diamond Cross brand, 35, 134
Half Diamond Cross Ranch, 134
Hammon, Frank, 35, 127, 176
Hansen, Greg, 258
Happy Camp, 198, 248, 295
Hargrave, Jemima, **95**

Hart, Charley. *See* Oldham, John
Hat brand, 132
Haunted Canyon, 184, **189**, 192, **195**, 196–198
Haunted Canyon Trail, 176, 181, 193, 194, 195, 199, 200
Haunted Canyon Trailhead, 42, 188, 189
Hay Hook brand, 81, 113
Hay Hook Ranch, 96, **111**, 113
Hazard, James, **95**
HEAT, **36**, 37, 279
heat exhaustion, 29
Henderson, A. J., 97, 162, 262, 263
Henderson, Annie (Jackson), **97**
Henderson, George, 134
Henderson Ranch, 134
Herron, Jim, 32, 216, 220, 221, 225
Herron, Phyllis, 32, 220, 221
Herron Ranch, 33, 220, 221, 225
HES. *See* Surveys, homestead
Hewitt, Hugh, 274
Hewitt Canyon, 274, 298
Hewitt Station, 274
Hieroglyphic Canyon, 313
Hieroglyphic Trail, 313
Hieroglyphic Trailhead, 44, 313
Hill Spring, 197
Hocker, E. A., 134
Hocker, James, 94, **95**
Hohokam, 254, 255
Hole Spring, 268, 269
Holmquist, F. N., **74**, 79, 168, **303**, 304
homesteaders, **28**, 29-35, 93-97, 185–187, **189**, 192, 196–198, 206–208
 Allen, George, **95**
 Armer, Henry, 93, 94, **95**
 Clark, Rae, **28**, 33, 186, 206, **207**, 208
 Cline, Frank, 94, **95**
 Cooper, Chester, 96
 Cox, Author, **95**
 Danforth, George, 94, **95**
 Duey, Jacob, **95**
 Duryea, William, **95**
 Flippen, Joseph, 94, **95**
 Gordon, Elizabeth, 94, **95**
 Griffin, Charles, **95**
 Hargrave, Jemima, **95**
 Hazard, James, **95**
 Hocker, James, 94, **95**
 Horrell, Edwin Elisha "Edward and Ed," 32, 33, 34, 35, **133**, 178, **179**, 180, 192, 216
 Horrell, Marion, 33, **179**, 180
 Horrell, Susan, 178, **180**
 Jackson, Luther, 35, **97**, 123, 134

homesteaders (continued)
　Johnson, Isaac, 96
　Kenton, Edmund, 94, **95**
　Kerby, Alma (Kirby), 96
　Knight, William "Billy," 56, **57**, 58
　Lee, William, 97
　McIntosh, Archie, 32, 93, 94, **95**, 116, 225
　Moraga, Pedro, 186
　Periz, Jose, 30, 33, 184–186, **187**, 208
　Powers, Freeman, **95**
　Robertson, Peter, 94, **95**
　Schell, Robert, **95**
　Tebbs, Charles, **95**
　Tebbs, Quintus, **95**
　Thomson, Louis, **95**
　Toney, William, 32, **45**, **58**, 194, **195**, **196**, **197**, 208
　Vinyard, John, 94, **95**
　Whalley, Robert, 96
　Willey, Julius, **95**
homestead rules, 31, 32, 94, 327n33
homesteads. *For list see* ranches. *For maps see* surveys, homestead.
homestead surveys. *See* surveys, homestead
Honeycutt Spring, 258, 270
Hoolie Bacon Trail, 58, 322
Horinek, Howard, 144, 146, 229, **245**, 246, 304
Horrell, Alice (Wilson), 180
Horrell, Blanche (Carter), 34, 134, **148**
Horrell, Earl Edwin, 34, 35, 134, 142, **148**, 180
Horrell, Earline (Tidwell), 34, 35, 97, 134, **148**, 180
Horrell, Edward and Ed. *See* Horrell, Edwin
Horrell, Edwin Elisha "Edward and Ed," 32, 33, 34, 35, **133**, 178, **179**, 180, 192, 216
Horrell, John W., 33, 178, **180**
Horrell, Laura (Gann), **192**
Horrell, Laverna. *See* Horrell, Martha Laverna
Horrell, Louie, 180, 229, 246
Horrell, Marion, 33, **179**, 180
Horrell, Martha Laverna (Williams), 180
Horrell, Susan, 178, **180**
Horrell, Winnie (Foster), 180
Horrell Creek, 136, 143–146, 178
Horrell Ranch, 129, 132–134, **148**, **303**
Horses, 15, 16, 22, 24, 25
Houston, Barton M., **192**
Hutchinson, Donahue & Co., 248
hypothermia, 29

I
Indians. *See* Apache, Chiricahua, Hohokam, Salado, Yavapai
Inspiration Vista, 92
Iron Bridge, 33, 175, 176, 178, 188, 202
Iron Mountain, **249**, **276**, 277–279
Iron Mountain burn, 258, 270
Iron Mountain Spring, 241, 282
Iron Mountain Spring Corral, 241, 282
Iron Mountain Trail, 277
Iron Trough Spring, 228
IV Ranch, 58, 264

J
Jaca, Spain, 186
Jackson, Annie (Henderson), **97**
Jackson, Luther, 35, **97**, 123, 134
Jacob's Crosscut Trail, 313-316
Javelina Spring, 215
J Bar B brand, 134
J Bar B Ranch, 35, 97, 134
J Bar B Ranch Road. *See* FR449
Jeffords, Thomas (Chiricahua Agent), 225
Jerky Spring, 210, 211, 228
Jerky Spring Wash, 228
JF brand, 56, 58, 264, **302**
JF Ranch, 30, 32, 56–58, 264, **302**
JF Ranch headquarters. *See* JF Ranch
JF Ranch Trailhead. *See* Woodbury Trailhead
JF Trail, 309, 322
JH brand, 241, 282
JH6 brand, 33. *See also* JH6 Ranch
JH6 Ranch, 144, 146, 178, **179**, 180, 186, 229, **245**, 246, **303**
JK brand, 33, 178
JK CCC Camp, 33, 178
JK Mountain, 33, 178, 229
JK Ranch, 33, 178
Johnson, Arkie, **66**, 68
Johnson, Isaac, 96
Johnson family, 208
Jones, J. D., **49**
Jones, Tom Lorang, 92
J Slash A brand, 58, 264

K
Kane Spring, 249, 279. *See also* springs, Rogers
Kennedy, Frances, 208, 221
Kennedy, Vernon "Jack," 208, 216, 221, 241, 283
Kennedy Ranch, 33, 208, 221, 283
Kenton, Edmund, 94, **95**
Kerby, Alma LeCornu, 96

Kerby, Amelia, 96
Kerby, L. A, 96
Kings Ranch Road, 313
Kirby, Alma. *See* Kerby, Alma
Kirby, Arizona, 94, 96
Kirby, F. L. (Forest Ranger), 208
Kirby Station, 96
Klondike Spring, 88, 167, 172
Knight, Eunice (Riggs), 57
Knight, John, 56
Knight, William "Billy," 56, **57**, 58
Knudson, Emily, 132
Kollenborn, Thomas "Tom," 54, 63, 176, 186, 222, 304, 323
Kollenborn Falls, 63
Koons, John, 33, 178
Koons Canyon, 33, 178
Koons Ranch, 30, 33, 178
KRN Trail, 136, 141, 142

L

La Barge Spring, 38
Lake County, California, 192
Lakeview Park (Roosevelt area), 101, **111**
LaMonica, Tom, **36**
Lane, Bud, 63
Layton, L. R., 33, 144, 180
Layton Ranch, 144
Lazy E Spear brand, 264
Lazy W Bar brand, 197
LeBarge, John, 31
LeBarge Ranch, 31
Leatham, Nyle, 63
Lee, William, 97
Lewis and Pranty Creek, 59
Lime Mountain, 60
Little Cottonwood Gulch (Reeds Water area), 30, 304
Livingstone, Arizona, 94, 129
Livingstone, Charles, 94, 96, 129
Los Angeles County, California, 133
Lost Dutchman Mine, 89
Lost Dutchman Spring, 123, 126
Lost Dutchman State Park Trailheads, 44, 315, 325
Lost Goldmine Trail, 311–314
lovegrass, 258
Lower Cottonwood Trail, 104, 110
Lower Ranch (Spring Creek Ranch), 134
Lower Trailhead (Trail 203), 175, 176
Lui, Charles, 63
Lyall, Neil, 116

M

Madrid, Pedro, 262
Mammoth Mine, 35
Manhatten Mine, 274
Maple Spring, 60, 63, 83
maps, homestead. *See* surveys, homesteads
maps, military, **76**, **121**, **226**
maps, mining claim, **273**
maps, trails and roads, **74**, **78**, **91**, **95**, **302**, **303**
maps, USGS topo index, **18**
Marlow, George, 32
Marlow Ranch, 31, 32, 304
Martin, Arch, 56
Martin, George, 32, 264
Martin, Helen "Teta", 32, 264, 283
Martin, Lum, 225
Martin, William "Billy," Jr. 32, 83, 168, 241, 242, 264, 279, 283
Martin, William "Bill," Sr. 32, 56–58, 264
Martin Ranch, 58, 264, 279, 280
Mason, Robert, 110
Massacre Grounds Trail, 317
Massacre Grounds Trailhead, 44, 317
Masten, C. S. Col., 235
Masten's Peak, 235, 304
Maybell Mine, 274
Mazatzal Mountains (Sierra Mazitzal), **121**, 176
McCombe, Kevin, 142, 150
McIntosh, Archie, 32, 93, 94, **95**, 116, 225
McIntosh, Domingo, 94
McIntosh, Donald, 94
Mesa Ranger District, 23
Mesa Road Runner Prospecting Club, 178
Miami, Arizona, 21, 178, 208
Miami Market, 33
Middleton (Frank Hammon's prospecting partner), 176
Miles, J. Ney, 33, 208, 221, 224, 225, 241, 282
Miles, Rita, 221
Miles Mortuary, 33, 208
Miles Ranch, 30, 33, 202–208, 225
Miles Trailhead, 42, 202–208, 323
military, 29, 32, **78**, 79, 93, 110, 111, 117-121, 127, 168, 176, 206, 225, **226**, 234, 235
Miller Mines, 35
Millsite allotment, 264
Millsite Claim, 279
Mineral Hill District, 56
mines and claims,
  Banker's Arastra, 176
  Bedrock 1 and 2, 178
  Carney, 35

mines and claims (continued),
  Columbia, **273**, 274
  Diamond 1 through 4, 178
  Goldfield, 35
  Good Enough, **273**, 274
  Hal and Al, 176
  K & S Asbestos Group, 216
  Kane Spring, 279
  Kennedy, 216
  Last Time Group, 216
  Lost Peralta Mine of Death, 249
  Mammoth, 35
  Manhatten, **273**, 274
  Maybell, **273**, 274
  Miller, 35
  Millsite, 279
  Mucho Oro, 178
  Mystery of Mountain Group, 216
  Randolph, 249
  Rogers Mill, 248
  Silver Chief, 272, **273**, 274
  Silver King, 56
  Tunnel Site, 279
  Woodbury, 248, 249
  World Beater, **273**, 274, 276
  Yellow Bird, 274
mining, 176, 216, 248, 249, 273–276
Mitchell, John D., 176
Modock, Joe, 186
Mono County, California, 192
Montana Mountain, **290**
Montana Mountain Trailhead, 43, 289–293
Moraga, Frank, 186
Moraga, Pedro, 186
Moran, Susan, 172
Mormon Corral, 142, **144**, 146
Mounce, Henry, 56
Mound Mountain, 50, 54, **153**, 270
Mountain Spring, 136, 142–146, 229
Mount Cachimba, 248, 295

N
Narron, Alice. *See* Narron, Martha Alice
Narron, Angeline "Adis," 129
Narron, Annie (See), 129, 132
Narron, John, 34, 129, 162
Narron, Lillian (Chilson), 129
Narron, Martha Alice (Gann), 129, 133
Narron, Willie, 129
Narron Spring, 136
National Forest Scenic Byway, 315
N brand, 129
Nelssen, Kenneth, 68, 141, 142
Never Fail Spring, 146

New Spring, 240
New Spring Wash, 240, 286

O
Oak Flat, 148, 209–212, 225, **226**, **234**, 286
Oak Spring, 244, 246
Ochoa, Pilar Maldonado, 146
Old Coffee Flat Trail, 304
Oldham, John T. (Charley Hart), 198
Old Reevis Trail, 224, 292, 295
Olson, John "Jack," 264
Olson, Lenora, 264
Olson, Rollie, 264
orchards, 35, 49, **50**, 54, 57, 58, 137, 158, 159, 162, **189**, 197, 249, 270

P
Paradise Spring, 200, 216, 237
Paradise Trail, 194, 199, 200, 236, 237
Parker Pass, 31
Pateman-Akin-Kachina Foundation, 134
Peak 5057 (Rogers Ridge), 274
Pemberton, George, 106
Pemberton, Sallie, 106
Pemberton, Stella (Frazier), 106
Pemberton Ranch, 127
Peralta Canyon, 310
Peralta Road, 310–312
Peralta Trail, 310
Peralta Trailhead, 43, 310, 323–325
Perez, Jose. *See* Periz, Jose Ausere
Periz, Aurolia, 186
Periz, Fidel, 186
Periz, Jose Ausere, 30, 33, 184–186, **187**, 208
Periz, Josefha, 186
Periz, Maria, 186
Periz, Pellarr, 186
Periz Ranch, 30, 33, 184–186, **187**, 208
permits,
  treasure trove, 37, 279
  Wilderness, 22
Peters Canyon, 321
Peters Mesa, 322
Peterson, Tom, 276
Peters Trail, 322
Petrasch, Herman, 57
Picket Post Mountain, 295, 298
Pima, 120
Pinal. *See* Pinal City
Pinal City, 262, 276, 295, 298
Pinal County Hospital, 248
Pineair, 56, **74**, **303**
Pine Creek, Lower, 69–83
Pine Creek, Middle, 84–89

Pine Creek, Upper, 152, 153, 156, 162, 164–168
Pine Creek Bridge, 69, 75
Pine Creek Trail, 78, 79, 85, 88, 89
Pine Creek Trailhead, 40, 69
Pinto Butte, 206, **226**, 234
Pinto Creek, 121, 286
Pinto Creek Trailhead, 42, 175–180
Pinto Divide, 140, 148, 150, 234, **235**
Pinto Peak, 234, 304
Pinto Peak Trail, 136, 142, 144, 212, 286, **288**
Pinto Spring, 240, 286
Pinto Valley Mine Road, 175, 188, 202
Pinyon Mountain, 173
Plank House, 32
Plow Saddle, 49, 269
Plow Saddle Canyon, 66
Plow Saddle Spring, 269
Plow Saddle Trail, 49, 269
Pointer Spring, 240, 286
Pointer Spring Wash, 240
Policky, Linda, 208
Pope Spring, 224
Porter, Betty (Gilbert), **189**
Porter, Gladys V., **189**
Potter, Samuel, 110
Power Canal, **97**, 116
Powers, Freeman, **95**
Powers Gulch, 184
prehistoric Indian ruins. See ruins
Price, W. T., 178
Prieto, Manuel, 185
Pringle, Bob, 127
Punkin Center, 146

Q

Quarter Circle U Ranch, 29, 30, 32, 68, 255, 262, 304
Quarter Circle V brand, 132, 133
Queen Creek Ranch, 58
Queen Valley Road, 247, 289

R

Rafter Cross brand, 134
Rafter Cross Ranch, 134
ranches. See also brands
   3R, 29
   Anderson, 146, 180
   Armer, 93, 94, **95**, 127
   Backus, 32, 68
   Bark, 32, 255
   Barkley, 32
   Bixby, 180
   Black Brush, 113, 116

ranches (continued),
   Black Bush, 116
   Bohme, 198
   Cavaness, 32
   Charlebois, 32
   Criswell, 32, 255
   Cross P, 35, 97, 129, 134
   EK, 198
   First Water, 29, 31, 32
   Fraser, 255, **302**, 304
   Gann, 132-134, 304
   Half Diamond Cross, 134
   Hammon, 127
   Hay Hook, 96, **111**, 113
   Henderson, 134
   Herron, 33, 220, 221, 225
   Horrell, 129, 132-134, **148**, **303**
   IV, 58, 264
   J Bar B, 35, 97, 134
   JF, 30, 32, 56-58, 264, **302**
   JH6, 144, 146, 178, **179**, 180, 186, 229, **245**, 246, **303**
   JK, 33, 178
   Kennedy, 33, 208, 221, 283
   Koons, 30, 33, 178
   Layton, 144
   LeBarge, 31
   Marlow, 30, 31, 304
   Martin, 58, 264, 279, 280
   Miles, 30, 33, 202-208, 225
   Narron, 129, 132-134, 162, 304
   Pemberton, 127
   Periz, 30, 33, 184–186, **187**, 208
   Pringle, 127
   Quarter Circle U, 29, 30, 32, 68, 255, 262, 304
   Queen Creek, 58
   Rafter Cross, 134
   Reavis, 30, 32, 48, **49**, **50**, 52, **54**, 56, **57**, **58**, 64, **157**, 158, 159 162, 198, **260**, 264, 270, **302**
   Schulze, 116
   Spring Creek, 30, 118, 127, 129, 132, 134, 304
   Toney, See Tony
   Tony, 30, 32, 33, 181, 184, **185**, 193, 194, **195**, **196**, 197, 198, 220
   Tortilla, 30, 32, 58, 264
   TU, 198, 225
   Two Bar, 32, 113, 116, 173
   Upper Horrell, 32, 129, 134, **148**
   Weekes, 29
Randolph Basin, 249
Ratcliff, Richard, 262
rattlesnakes, 27

Ray, Arizona, 208
Reavis, Edward, 262
Reavis, Elisha, 31, 32, 54, 56, 134, 162, **260**, 262–264, 270, 271, 298
Reavis, James Addison, 262
Reavis, Louisa Maria, 262
Reavis, Maria (Sexton), 262
Reavis Canyon Trail, 293–298
Reavis Creek, 49, 61, 66, **68**, 83, **157**, 158, 162, 270
Reavis Falls, 59-68, 82, 83
Reavis Falls Trail, 59, **60**, 61, 63, 83
Reavis Gap, 159, **161**, **163**, **173**
Reavis Gap Butte, **161**, **173**
Reavis Gap Trail, 160–162, **163**, 166, 167, 172
Reavis Grave, 258, **263**, 271
Reavis Ranch, 30, 32, 48, **49**, **50**, 52, **54**, 56, 57, **58**, 64, **157**, 158, 159, 160, 162, 198, **260**, 264, 270, **302**
Reavis Ranch House, **49**, **58**, 260
Reavis Ranch Road, 58, 126
Reavis Ranch Trail, 46-50, 162, 250, 257–264, 269
Reavis Saddle, 258, 270, 271
Reavis Trail Canyon, 294, 295, 298
Reavis Trail Canyon Trailhead, 42, 294
Reavis Trailhead, 40, 46, 323, 324
RE brand, 241, 282
Red Mountain (Pinto Peak), 222, 235
Red Tanks Trail, 322
Reeder, Doris, 208
Reeder, Vernon "Jack," 208
Reed Spring, 88, 167
Reeds Water, 30, 304
Reevis. *See* Reavis entries
Reevis Mountain School, **20**, 35, 128, 129, 132, **133**, 134, 136, **137**, 162, 304
Reymert, James DeNoon, 248, 262, 276, 295, **298**
Reymert, Rosalie (Beyer), 248
Rice, Glen, 279
Ride Through Time, 323
Riggs, Eunice, 57
roads,
 Mesa to Globe, 301, 304
 See also FR77, FR449, FR650, etc.
road surveys. *See* surveys, road
Robertson, Peter, 94, **95**
Rock Creek, **23**, **30**, **34**, 305, 306
Rock Creek Trail, 23, 212, 217–222, 288, 305, 306
Rock Spring Corral (Haunted Canyon), 198
Rogers, James, 35, 248, 272, 274, 276
Rogers, Maria Selma (Beyer), 248
Rogers Camp District, **273**, 274, 276

Rogers Canyon, 248–256, 265-269, 273, 274
Rogers Canyon cliff dwellings, 56, 250–256
Rogers Canyon Spring, 251
Rogers Canyon Trail, 250–256
Rogers Mill, 248
Rogers Ridge, 272, **273**, 274, **275**, 276
Rogers Spring, **36**, 37, 38, 241, 249, 273, 277–280
Rogers Trough Trailhead, 42, 247, 248, **249**, 324, 325
Roosevelt, Arizona, 90, 94, **106**
Roosevelt Cemetery, 98, 100, 101, 110
Roosevelt Cemetery Trail, 98, 100, 101
Roosevelt Cemetery Trailhead, 40, 98, 110
Roosevelt Dam, Theodore, 92-94, 97, **101**, 106, 116
Roosevelt Estates, 90, 96
Roosevelt Post Office, 90
Roosevelt Lake, 89, 90-97, **101**, **103**, **111**
Roosevelt Lake Bridge, 92, **103**, 107, 110
Roosevelt Lake Marina, 92
Roosevelt Lake Resort, 90, 96
Roosevelt Lake Visitors Center, 92, 106, **111**
Rough Canyon, 269
Rowley, Clint, **275**
ruins,
 historic, 83, 184–186, **196**, 197, 198, 211, 212, 214, 216, 219, 229, **234**, **237**, 240, 242, 246, 248, 254, 256, **263**, 269, 282, **283**, **298**, 303
 prehistoric, 50, 52, 54, 60, 63, 65, 92, 93, 104, **152**, **153**, 156, 161, **212**, 214, 225, 228, 234, 250-254, **255**, 256, 269
Russell, Paul, 68

S

Saddle Horn Peak, 136
safety, 6, 26, 27, 29
Salado, 54, 93, 251, 254
Salt River Community, 94, 162
Sanchez, Josefha, 186
San Felice, Jack, **275**, **306**
Sanford, Lt. Co. G. B., 111
San Gabriel, California, 262
San Joaquin Valley, California, 132
San Pedro River, 117
Sawtooth Ridge, 214, 222, 308
Schell, Robert, **95**
Schoolhouse Recreation Area, 90
Schroeder, K. J., **36**
Schulze, Helen, 116
Schulze, John, 116
Schulze Ranch, 116
Scotts Valley, California, 196

Second Water Spring, 318
Second Water Trail, 31, 318, 320
See, Annie (Narron), 129, 132
See, John, 129, 132
Sexton, Maria (Reavis), 262
Shanley, E. P., 176
sheep herder camp, 211
Sherry Spring, 214
Shoebridge, Earl "Lane," 178
Short, Duane, **36**
Shute, George (Sheriff), 35, 176
Shute, Harry, 134
shuttle trips (Trans-Wilderness Trips), 323–325
Sieber, Al, 35, 93, 176
Silver Chief Canyon, 274
Silver Chief Mine, 272, **273**
Silver Chief Trail, 272, **275**
Silver City, New Mexico, 196, **197**, 198
Silver King, 56, 146, 262, 295
silver ore, 35, 81, 176, 274, 276
Silver Spur Cabin, 240, 241, 280–282, **283**, 304
Siphon Draw Trail, 315, 316
Siphon Draw Trailhead, 315
Skeleton Canyon, Cochise County, Arizona, 196
Skeleton Cave, 79, 118, 120, 127
Skeleton Cave Massacre, 79, 120
Skeleton Peak, 136
Skull Cave. *See* Skeleton Cave
Sloan, Ross, 196
smelter, 248, 295
Smith, Bill, **66**, **68**
Smith, Stan, 63
Spencer Canyon Road, 292, 301, 302
Spencer Spring, 224, 225, 299, **300**, 302
Spencer Spring Creek, **226**, 286, 302
Spencer Spring Trail, 223–225, 299, 300, 302
Spring Creek, 118, **121**
Spring Creek Ranch, 30, 118, 127, 129, 132, 134, 304
Spring Creek Store, 90, 97, 128
springs, water tanks, and water troughs
　Angel, 256
　Bear, 146
　Black Jack, 140, 142, 148, 152, 156, 234
　Black Mesquite, 94, 116
　Bluff, 38, 310, 318
　Brushy, 137, 140, 156, 234
　Can, 248. *See also* springs, Rogers
　Cane, 248. *See also* springs, Rogers
　Cement, **222**, 224, 300
　Charlebois, 38, 310, 318
　Coon, 33, 178

springs, water tanks (continued)
　Cottonwood (Marlow Ranch), 31
　Cottonwood (Trail 120), 113, 116, 174
　Crocket, 240, 286
　Cuff Button, 228, **229**, 245
　Deer, 242, 283
　Frog, 269
　Gans Hole, 127
　Grapevine (at Roosevelt Lake), 32, 93, 94, 116, 327n28
　Grapevine (on Trail 203), 194, 200
　Hackberry, 38
　Hill, 197
　Hole, 268, 269
　Honeycutt, 258, 270
　Iron Mountain, 241, 282
　Iron Trough, 228
　Javelina, 215
　Jerky, 210, 211, 228
　Kane, 249, 279. *See also* springs, Rogers
　Klondike, 88, 167, 172
　La Barge, 38
　Lost Dutchman, 123, 126
　Maple, 60, 63, 83
　Morman Corral, 142, **144**
　Mountain, 136, 142–146, 229
　Narron, 136
　Never Fail, 146
　New, 240
　Oak, 244, 246
　Paradise, 200, 216, 237
　Pinto, 240, 286
　Plow Saddle, 49, 269
　Pointer, 240, 286
　Pope, 224
　Reed, 88, 167
　Rogers, **36**, 37, 38, 241, 249, 273, 277, 279, 280
　Rogers Canyon, 251
　Second Water, 318
　Sherry, 214
　Spencer, 224, 225, 299, **300**, 302, 303
　Sycamore, 146, 228, 229
　Thicket, 228, 245
　Thompson, 104, 110
　Tony Ranch, 184, 194, 196
　Trail 203 dirt tank, 194, 200, 215, 237
　Tub, 228
　Tule, 118, 126, 127
　Upper Campaign, 148
　Viejo Potrero, 246
　Walnut, 38, 88, 126, 159, 161, 166–168, 172, 303
　Whiskey (on Fire Line Trail), 52, 158
　Wildcat, 246

springs, water tanks (continued)
    Winger, 75, 79
    Yellow Jacket, 79, 80, **81**
Steinbach, Erik, 279
Stewart, Elizabeth, **185**, **235**, **242**, **263**, 351
Stone, Floyd "Stoney," 32, 58, 264
Stone, Lucille "Alice" (Bacon), 58
Storm, Barry (Clymenson, John), 89
Superior, Arizona, 33, **189**, 247, 289
Superstition Area Land Trust, 33, **196**, 198
Superstition Mountain, 21, 22
Superstition Mountain Historical Society, 20, 22, 163
Superstition Mountain Museum, 54, 142, 150, 235
Superstition Mountain Peak 5057, 21, 274
Superstition Mountain Ridge Line Trail, 312
Superstition Wilderness, 22–26, 58
surveys, homestead,
    HES 71 (Marion Horrell), **179**
    HES 164 (Jose Periz), **187**
    HES 412 (William Knight), **57**
    HES 435 (William Toney), **195**
    HES 441 (Ed Horrell), **179**
    HES 448 (Ed Horrell), **133**
    HES 554 (Rae Clark), **28**, **207**, 209
surveys, road, 30, 225, 229, 235, 242, 301, **302**, **303**, 304
Swanson, James, 54
Sycamore Spring, 146, 228, 229

T

Tarr, Henry R., 97
Taylor, Ann, 32, 198
Taylor, Ben, 198
Taylor, George, 32, 197, 198
Taylor, Henry (Forest Ranger), 197
Taylor, Milford, 198,
Tebbs, Charles, **95**
Tebbs, Quintus, **95**
Tempe Normal School, 56
Theodore Roosevelt, **101**
Theodore Roosevelt Dam. *See* Roosevelt Dam
Thicket Spring, 228, 245
Thicket Spring Wash, 228
Thomas, Frank, 97
Thompson, Henry (Sheriff), 129, 132
Thompson Spring, 104, 110
Thompson Trail, 102, **103**, 110
Thomson, Louis, **95**
Three R Ranch, 29
Tidwell, Earline (Horrell), 34, 35, 97, 134, **148**, **180**
Tidwell, James, 34, 35, 97, 134

Tighe, Kelly, 172
Toney, Boyd, **45**, 198
Toney, Delbert, **45**
Toney, Ella Mary (Wilson), **45**, **189**, 196, **197**, 198
Toney, Ellis, **45**, **58**, 198
Toney, Gladys (Porter), **45**
Toney, Leona, **45**
Toney, Ophie (Hunter), **45**, 198
Toney, Seth, 196
Toney, Wilda, **45**
Toney, William T., 32, **45**, **58**, 194, **195**, **196**, **197**, 208
Toney Ranch. *See* Tony Ranch
Tonto Basin Ranger District, 23, 68, 142, 150
Tonto National Forest, 22, 23, 32, **49**, 56, 58, 92, 97, 150, 163. *See also* Forest Service
Tonto National Monument, 92, 93
Tony (horse), 220
Tony Ranch, 30, 32, 33, 181, 184, **185**, 193, 194, **195**, 196, 197, 198, 220
Tony Ranch Spring, 184, 194, 196
Tordillo Peak, 295
Tortilla Campground, 321
Tortilla Creek, 321
Tortilla Flat, Arizona, 321
Tortilla Flat Restaurant, 321
Tortilla Flat Trailhead, 45, 321
Tortilla Pass, 323
Tortilla Ranch, 30, 32, 58, 264
Tortilla Trailhead, 45, 322
Tortilla Well, 322
"Trail 193," 244, 246
trails. *See* individual trail names
trailheads. *See* Table of Contents or individual trailhead name
Trailheads and Trails map, 352
Trainor, Mark, 298
Trans-Wilderness Trips, 323-325
traps. *See* corrals
treasure hunting, 35, **36**, 37, 279
Treasure Loop Trail, 316
Treasure Loop Trailhead, 315
treasure trove permit, 37, 279
TU brand, 225
Tub Spring, 228
Tule Canyon, 172
Tule Creek, **78**
Tule Spring, 118, 126, 127
Tule Trail, 117–127, 167, 168, 172
Tule Trailhead, 40, 117, **118**, 324
Tunnel Site Claim, 279
TU Ranch, 198, 225
Two Bar brand, 116
Two Bar Mountain, **118**, 161

Two Bar Ranch, 32, 113, 116, 173
Two Bar Ridge, **120**, 122, 126, **127**, 168, 172
Two Bar Ridge Trail, 126, **127**, 161, **163**, 166, 167, 169, 172, 173, **174**
Two E brand, 264
Two Lazy H brand, 97

U

Upper Campaign Spring, 148
Upper Cottonwood Trail, 110
Upper Horrell Place, 32, 129, 134, **148**
Upper Horrell Trailhead. *See* Campaign Trailhead
Upper Pine Creek Trail, 167, 168
Upper Trailhead (Trail 203), 188
Upton, Charles "Tubby," 32, 58, **256**, 264, 269
U.S. Army. *See* military
U.S. Forest Service. *See* Forest Service
U.S. Infantry. *See* military
U.S. Military. *See* military

V

V brand, 96
Viejo Potrero Spring, 246
Vineyard Trail, 92, **103**
Vinyard, John, 94, **95**
Visitors Center, Roosevelt Lake, 92, 106, 111

W

Wagstaff, Michael, 113
Wallauer, Bob, 83
Walnut Spring, 38, 88, 126, 159, 161, 166–168, 172, 303
Walp, Richard "Dick," **275**, **306**
Walton, Jerry, **66**, 68
Waltz, Jacob, 89, 176
water, 37, 38. *See also* springs
waterfalls, **23**, 59–61, **62**, 63-67, **68**, 200, 216, 219, **221**, 224, 236, 237, **306**, 308
Weavers Needle, **76**, **121**, 310
Webb, Milo, 129
Weekes Ranch, 29
West Boulder Trail, 311, 312
West Fork Pinto Creek, 147, 148, 206, **210**, 211, 225, **234**, 240, 282, 286
West Pinto Trail, 209–212, 238–242, 284, 286
Whalley, Robert J., 96
Whalley, William, 96
Whalley Lumber Company, 96
Wheatfields, 178, 180
Whiskey Spring (on Fire Line Trail), 52, 158
Whitford Canyon, 294, 295, 298
Wilburn, John, 35, 178

Wildcat Canyon, 228, **242**, 243, 244, **245**, 246
Wildcat Spring, 246
Wilderness, 10, 22–26, 58
Wilderness Act, 35
Wilderness ethics. *See* ethics, Wilderness
Willey, Julius, **95**
Wilmott, Mr. (friend of Elisha Reavis), 262
Wilson, Alice (Horrell), 180
windmills, **144**, 309, 322
Windy Hill, 93
Windy Hill Campground, 89, 92, 97
Windy Pass, 49
Winger Spring, 75, 79
Winger Wash, 75, **76**, **77**, 79, 80, 118
Woodbury family, 35, 248, 249
Woodbury Mill, 248
Woodbury Mines, 35, 248
Woodbury Trail, 309
Woodbury Trailhead, 43, 309, 325
Wood Camp Canyon, 294, 295
Wood Creek, 184
woodcutters, 248, 294
wood station, 295, **298**
Woolsey, King S., 35, 93
World Beater Claim, **273**, 274, 276
Wright, Grover, 134

X

X Bar P brand, 241

Y

Yavapai, 54, 79, 93, 118, 120
Y Bar B brand, **30**, 31, 219, 221
Y Bar brand, 225
Yeager, Merlin, 68
Yellow Bird Mine, 274
Yellow Jacket Butte, 74, 76
Yellow Jacket Spring, 79, 80, **81**
Yellow Jacket Spring Wash, 81
YJ brand, 129
Y Lazy Y brand, 224, 225, 241, 282, **300**
YY brand, 224, 225, **300**, 303

About the Authors

Jack Carlson and Elizabeth Stewart are also the authors of *Superstition Wilderness Trails West* (a companion volume to this book) and *Hiker's Guide to the Superstition Wilderness*.

Jack has been hiking and exploring the Superstition Mountains since 1974. He is a native of Harrisburg, Pennsylvania, and graduated from Pennsylvania State University with a B.S.E.E. degree in 1965. He received an M.B.A. degree in 1974 from Northern Arizona University.

In Chicago, Jack was employed with the steel industry and worked on computer automated industrial equipment. In Arizona, he has worked as an electrical engineer in semiconductor manufacturing.

He is a member of the Arizona Book Publishing Association and the Superstition Mountain Historical Society. He resides in Tempe, Arizona.

Elizabeth has always loved the outdoors. As a child she traveled with her parents on many family vacations to the National Parks where she experienced the freedom of hiking and camping.

Elizabeth was born in San Francisco, California, and spent two of her high school years in London, England. She graduated from the University of California, Berkeley, in 1966 with an A.B. degree and from the University of Arizona in 1969 with a J.D. degree. She worked for the Maricopa County Attorney in the Juvenile, Criminal, and Civil Divisions and as an Assistant Attorney General for the State of Arizona in the Civil Division.

Elizabeth served a six-year term on the Arizona State Parks Board, including a year as chairman. She is a member of the Arizona History Convention Board, the McFarland State Park Advisory Committee, and the Anza Trail Coalition of Arizona. She resides in Tempe, Arizona.

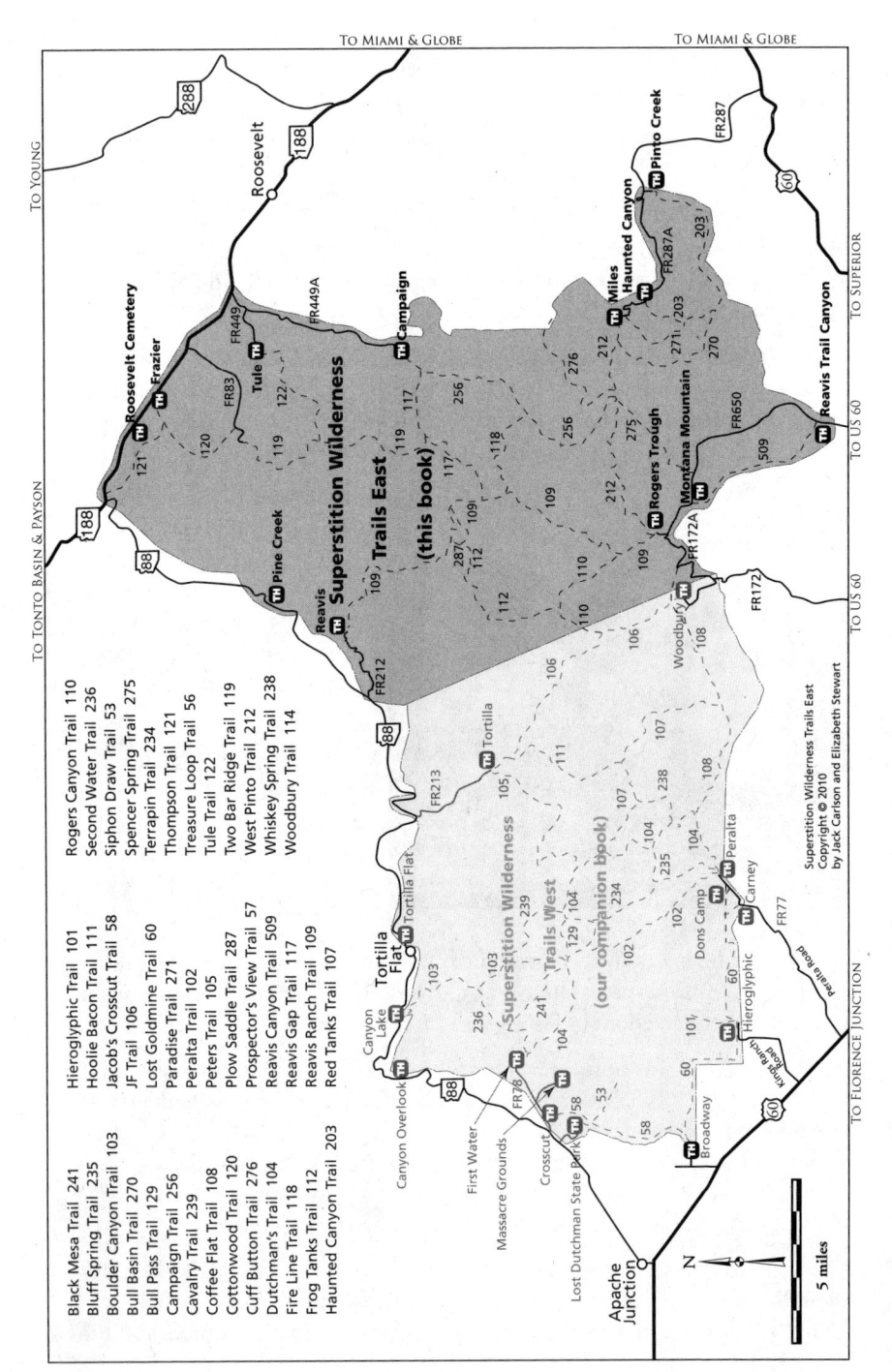

Trailheads and Trails in and near the Superstition Wilderness

Black Mesa Trail 241
Bluff Spring Trail 235
Boulder Canyon Trail 103
Bull Basin Trail 270
Bull Pass Trail 129
Campaign Trail 256
Cavalry Trail 239
Coffee Flat Trail 108
Cottonwood Trail 120
Cuff Button Trail 276
Dutchman's Trail 104
Fire Line Trail 118
Frog Tanks Trail 112
Haunted Canyon Trail 203

Hieroglyphic Trail 101
Hoolie Bacon Trail 111
Jacob's Crosscut Trail 58
JF Trail 106
Lost Goldmine Trail 60
Paradise Trail 271
Peralta Trail 102
Peters Trail 105
Plow Saddle Trail 287
Prospector's View Trail 57
Reavis Canyon Trail 509
Reavis Gap Trail 117
Reavis Ranch Trail 109
Red Tanks Trail 107

Rogers Canyon Trail 110
Second Water Trail 236
Siphon Draw Trail 53
Spencer Spring Trail 275
Terrapin Trail 234
Thompson Trail 121
Treasure Loop Trail 56
Tule Trail 122
Two Bar Ridge Trail 119
West Pinto Trail 212
Whiskey Spring Trail 238
Woodbury Trail 114